Software Reusability

Volume II
Applications and Experience

ACM PRESS

Editor-in-Chief:

Peter Wegner, *Brown University*

ACM Press books represent a collaboration between the Association for Computing Machinery (ACM) and Addison-Wesley Publishing Company to develop and publish a broad range of new works. These works generally fall into one of four series.

Frontier Series. Books focused on novel and exploratory material at the leading edge of computer science and practice.

Anthology Series. Collected works of general interest to computer professionals and/or society at large.

Tutorial Series. Introductory books to help nonspecialists quickly grasp either the general concepts or the needed details of some specific topic.

History Series. Books documenting past developments in the field and linking them to the present.

In addition, ACM Press books include selected conference and workshop proceedings.

Software Reusability

Volume II

Applications and Experience

Edited by

Ted J. Biggerstaff

Microelectronics and Computer Technology Corporation (MCC)

Alan J. Perlis

Yale University

ACM Press
New York, New York

Addison-Wesley Publishing Company

Reading, Massachusetts • Menlo Park, California • New York
Don Mills, Ontario • Wokingham, England • Amsterdam • Bonn
Sydney • Singapore • Tokyo • Madrid • San Juan

ACM Press Frontier Series

Library of Congress Cataloging-in-Publication Data

Biggerstaff, Ted J.
    Software reusability / Ted J. Biggerstaff, Alan J. Perlis.
       p.   cm.
    Contents: V. 1. Concepts and models — v. 2. Applications and
experience.
    Bibliography: v. 1, p.
    Includes index.
    ISBN 0-201-08017-6 (v. 1). — ISBN 0-201-50018-3 (v. 2)
    1. Computer software—Reusability.   I. Perlis, Alan J.
II. Title.
QA76.76.R47B543   1989
005—dc19   88-34280
                                                          CIP

    ABCDEFGHIJ-AL-89

CONTENTS

FOREWORD

This is a handbook of modern software reusability. I find it hard to imagine any aspect missing—whether viewed by a computer scientist or the software practitioner. This is no surprise: Rarely does one see a book on a single subject by authors with such a variety of backgrounds.

Whence is this breadth? For a moment I thought that the usual had happened again: As a new buzzword emerges, much ongoing work is re-presented in a new light in order to attract attention. But this is not the case here. Each chapter is relevant and the volume spans the entire spectrum of reusability well. The real reason for the breadth is that reusability is the best manifestation of software engineering industrialized, and that the software engineer is becoming less the programmer and more the system designer.

Ultimately, a program is a fiction, not made of matter that wears and tears; it is closer to encapsulated human thought than to physical artifact. Yet software in the form of physical pattern, captured for instance by magnetics, becomes an increasingly important part of an increasingly large number of products and processes, from washing machines to space ships to computer-ized enterprises. As a result of this trend, software people become exposed to the traditional engineering culture. At the same time, engineers in industry recognize software as the glue that tightens hardware components into system products and information-based processes.

Only the recent edition of an unabridged dictionary contains the word *reuse* and its derivatives, yet traditional engineering survived centuries without explicitly "reusing." Accumulation of experience (reuse of design?), reduction of variety by standardization (reuse of parameterized programs?), and well-defined interfaces for interchangeability and reduced complexity (information hiding?) have always been considered fundamental to engineering and in no need of an explicit term: They are the lifeblood of good design practice.

Introducing all these time-proven concepts to software in a single volume and by such distinguished authors is a huge and welcome step toward further maturing the engineering of software. We need these books now as we must solve problems of increasing complexity. Islands of computer applications gradually become integrated into networks of programs; the hardware vehicle carrying these applications becomes less of a monolith and more of a network of microprocessor-based workstations; and after decades of serving individuals—scientists, accountants, teachers, secretaries—the computer in the network will soon coordinate human cooperative efforts.[1] This requires the design of large, distributed, asynchronous systems of great complexity. We have no choice but to base the design on cumulative wisdom through reuse.

Given this tall order, we cannot focus only on programming in the small, but must pay increasing attention to the upstream (i.e., system design) portion of the software development process. We have been passing on ever more tasks to the machine, the first step being the delegation of code generation and optimization to the compiler. Now we must learn how to step on fellow software engineers' shoulders and not only on their toes, by absorbing and putting to practical use as much of these books' wisdom as our engineering instinct suggests.

L. A. BELADY

Vice President and Program Director
Software Technology Program
MCC

---

[1] *Proceedings: CSCW '86: Conference on Computer-Supported Cooperative Work*, December 3–5, 1986, Austin, Texas. Sponsored by Microelectronics & Computer Technology Corporation, in cooperation with the Association for Computing Machinery *et al.*

PREFACE

Software Reusability: Applications and Experience, with its accompanying volume, *Software Reusability: Concepts and Models*, is aimed at describing an emerging technical area. In the books, we have tried

- [ ] to present a technological framework or context for understanding software reuse,
- [ ] to present a representative spectrum of the technologies that may be applied to the reuse problem so that the reader who wants to exploit software reuse may start by standing on the shoulders of others,
- [ ] to present a spectrum of viewpoints so that the book will be of value to both the researcher and the working software engineer, and finally,
- [ ] to provide a sense of what works in reuse and what does not.

This book will be of value to a variety of readers:

- [ ] the graduate student grappling with the issues of software development and how to improve it through technology,
- [ ] the industrial manager or senior scientist of a software research, advanced planning, or advanced development organization who is looking for ways to guide his company to improvements in productivity and quality, and
- [ ] the industrial application manager or senior scientist who is tracking advanced technology to keep his department on the leading edge of software development.

Graduate students may be especially interested in papers on component classification and search, on the theory of specification, on knowledge bases and reuse, and on the role of languages and environments in reuse. Each of these papers presents a context of completed work but opens up a number of areas for further research. These papers will provide ample material for a one term discussion seminar and will suggest a rich list of topics for master's projects and Ph.D. dissertations.

Managers or senior scientists from advanced development or planning departments will find some early data on quantitative results of reuse, case studies of reuse in both academic and company environments, and some descriptions of various technical approaches to reuse. These papers should provide a rich set of material to aid in the planning and establishment of reuse projects within industrial settings.

Of particular interest to the applications manager or senior scientist are several overview papers that provide both a technical and political context for reuse. These papers serve to inform the reader not only about the technology that can be applied to realize reuse, but also about the forces that foster or impede the application of reuse in software development.

The Introduction is for all readers, in that it attempts to place each paper in a context and to explain the contributions of that paper in the overall framework of reuse research and application. The Introduction goes a bit farther by providing some editorial comment on the adoption of reuse, the risks of ignoring it, and its successes and failures, where we feel that such comment may help the reader to better appreciate a given paper or better understand and foster reuse in his or her environment.

We have resisted the temptation to cast reuse into a strictly language paradigm. That is, we have not taken the position that some language, say Ada, is the answer to all or most reuse issues. Such a position implies that there are no further problems to be solved, or if there are, they are trivially simple. Some people do take a position that is almost as radical as this, but we believe that such an approach misses all of the deep issues and hard problems in reuse and in the end will exploit very little of the significant productivity and quality opportunities that reuse can provide. Yes, the reuse problem does indeed have representational aspects (read that "language aspects," if you like), but these are only part of the problem. Choosing a target programming language is barely a start because programming languages provide so little of the structure necessary for powerful reuse—Ada packages, generics, and parameterization notwithstanding.

There is no consensus about what technical approaches are best for various kinds of reuse problems and little understanding of the nature of reuse opportunities, let alone the constraints, difficulties and shortcomings of reuse. In this book, we have tried to present a balanced picture of reuse, dispensing with hype and being conservative in promises. We have tried to focus upon the most promising, robust, and well-tested results—those theories that have been well worked out, those technologies that have been tested over some period of time or have been used in a real world environment, and those concepts that grapple with important issues in reuse. We have tried to avoid the "yet another" syndrome of presenting a credible result, but one that is not really distinguished along any of the lines mentioned above. In summary, we have tried to present results that are unique, that stand out and that will endure.

ACKNOWLEDGMENTS

We would like to thank a number of people who have helped to bring this book into existence. First, the authors. They have been cooperative, understanding, and helpful in a project whose scale necessitated such cooperation. Second, the reviewers. We would like to acknowledge the valuable suggestions of the referees who reviewed the manuscript for this book, Dr. John Knight, Professor Marvin Zelkowitz, and Professor C. V. Ramamoorthy. Their comments changed the shape of the book and improved it significantly. Thirdly, the Addison-Wesley editors and representatives, including Peter Gordon and Helen Goldstein, who all labored to help solve problems when they arose, took on tasks the editors could not find the time to do, and generally worked to eliminate road blocks that would have slowed us down. Fourth, Jane Carlton of the ACM, who helped with reprint permissions. Fifth, Gloria Gutierrez, who helped with the early administration, correspondence, and organization of the materials in the book. And finally, Jeanne Kintner has been responsible more recently for administration, organization, correspondence, some text entry, and editing of a few papers, and a myriad of other tasks. Without Jeanne's hard work, commitment, and organizational ability in the face of chaos, the book would have taken far longer.

Ted J. Biggerstaff
Alan Perlis

CONTRIBUTORS

Robert Balzer
USC/Information Sciences Institute

Michael J. Cavaliere
The Hartford Insurance Group

Bill Curtis
Microelectronics and Computer
Technology Corporation (MCC)

L. Peter Deutsch
ParcPlace Systems

Kate Ehrlich
Honeywell Information Systems, Inc.

David Garlan
Tektronix, Inc.

Mike Goodell
Cullinet Software, Inc.

Charles A. Grasso
Raytheon Company

Mehdi T. Harandi
University of Illinois at
Urbana-Champaign

Christina Jette
Schlumberger Austin Systems Center

Gail E. Kaiser
Columbia University

Robert G. Lanergan
Raytheon Company

Evan D. Lock
Computer Command and Control Co.

Mitchell D. Lubars
Microelectronics and Computer
Technology Corporation (MCC)

Yoshihiro Matsumoto
Kyoto University

Bertrand Meyer
Interactive Software Engineering

Östen Oskarsson
LM Ericsson

Noah S. Prywes
University of Pennsylvania

Charles Rich
Massachusetts Institute of Technology

Richard W. Selby
University of California, Irvine

Reid Smith
Schlumberger Laboratory for
Computer Science

Elliot Soloway
University of Michigan

Richard C. Waters
Massachusetts Institute of Technology

INTRODUCTION

VOLUME I

The first volume of this set provides a view of the concepts and models of software reuse. It provides an overview of software reuse, defines what reuse is, points out what the key problems and dilemmas are, suggests what characteristics foster reuse, and suggests what characteristics impede it.

The volume also examines the composition-based and the generation-based models of reuse. The composition-based model of reuse is based on the notion of plugging components together, with little or no modification to those components, in order to create target software systems. The composition-based model is the software analog to the hardware notion of plugging together integrated circuit chips to develop hardware systems.

The generation-based system, on the other hand, is aimed at reusing patterns that drive the creation of specific or customized versions of themselves. That is, the patterns are the "seeds" from which new, specialized components are grown. The volume includes papers that exemplify these approaches to the reuse of software knowledge.

VOLUME II

This volume is divided into three sections.

PRACTICE AND EXPERIENCE

This section reviews experience with the various approaches to reuse.

A. The Role of Languages and Environments

It is often true that having the right representation of information or having the right tools fosters the solving of a problem. The calculus is a prime example of a representation that made solving certain extremely hard problems in mathematics and physics very much easier. The same is true for reuse, and in these chapters, we consider some of those representations and tools.

The paper by Meyer makes a strong case for object-oriented programming as a way to enhance reusability. He has developed an object-oriented language called Eiffel and developed an environment for it that runs on high-performance workstations. His paper demonstrates the difference between conventional top-down functional designs and object-oriented designs and makes the case that the object-oriented designs are conceptually cleaner, easier to understand, and ultimately more reusable.

Meyer's new language and new environment raise interesting issues about technology transfer and introduction. While new language and development environments may offer significant improvements over existing languages and environments, they point up the difficulties in technology transfer. Languages and development environments are generally highly integrated into their organizational environments and thereby possess a large amount of momentum. This momentum arises out of "infrastructure"—that is, all of the interdependencies with other software, products, supporting hardware and facilities, organizations, training, documentation, and people. Therefore, adoption of new development environments and technologies becomes a significant commitment, and change seems to happen incredibly slowly. In order to embrace new technologies, all of that infrastructure must be recreated in the context of the new language and environment. This is an intensive and lengthy process, and in the end it is one of the most difficult problems in establishing new technologies for reuse. The reality is that introduction of new technology is costly, is perceived as disruptive, and is often difficult to retrofit to existing systems. Even though new technologies are significantly better, the difficulties of technology transfer sometimes make it easier to look elsewhere for magic solutions, and that "elsewhere" is often the panacea of better management.

Current management often has the attitude that the software problem can simply be solved by improved management techniques and tools. It is probably true that management techniques and tools could be vastly improved, but as Meyer points out, "the overemphasis on management issues is premature." Some very simple technical improvements can be made that not only would improve the reusability of software, but more generally, would vastly improve the productivity and quality of software development in general. Ironically, it is often true that the organizations that feel most strongly about the need for improvement in management techniques are the same ones that provide the worst environments for their programmers and designers—shared glass tty-style terminals (often several programmers to one glass tty-style terminal) that are hosted on an overloaded minicomputer, with inadequate memory, inadequate tools, and little investment in the integration of these tools and facilities. If our agricultural system were capitalized at an analogous level, we would still be an agrarian society struggling to feed our population.

Recent studies have shown that the two easiest ways to improve software development productivity and quality (in general) are to (1) capitalize the programmers/designers with fully loaded workstations and environments (one per programmer/designer) and (2) put programmer/designers in soundproof offices so that they can close out the interference and concentrate on the work at hand. In other words, capitalize them to do their job. The steps that enhance the productivity and quality of programming in general also enhance the reusability of the resulting software. Thus the proper management strategy is to give the programmer/designer better tools and environments. Both productivity and quality will improve, and by the way, the reuse of software will be fostered.

The next paper examines reuse through a language that describes how to assemble programs from components. Kaiser and Garlan describe a specification language called Meld that uses the concept of *feature* as the unit of modularity, rather than module. The objective is to be able to construct a module within a language-specific environment by composing features. The idea of Meld is to make the specification of the features language independent, but at the same time provide sufficient information so that a desired module (e.g., a memory management system) can be generated for some language-specific environment, and thereby to provide reusability across language-specific environments.

The next two papers discuss rich object-oriented environments that have a track record of use, and consider the contribution of the object-oriented paradigm to reuse. The paper by Deutsch is based on the work of the Smalltalk project. The pioneering ideas of the Smalltalk environment—objects, methods, inheritance, windows, pop-up menus, and so forth—have had sweeping effects on today's development environments. These ideas have also had a significant effect on reuse, and this paper offers an additional related idea that fosters reuse.

This paper begins to address the problem of large-scale reuse. That is, how does one get the benefits of large-scale components, while avoiding their drawbacks (i.e., reduced reusability). Earlier we stated that it would be desirable to find representations for large grain components that would allow one to describe precisely the broad, important architectural structures of those components while leaving many of the small unimportant details uncommitted. Deutsch's paper introduces the concept of a framework, a reusable component that is larger than an object. Frameworks provide some of the properties that we are seeking. They allow many of the broad architectural features to be specified while deferring commitment on many of the detailed features. The detailed features can be specified at the time of the component's reuse. While this does not totally solve the Very Large Scale Reuse problem, it is an important contribution.

In the paper by Jette and Smith, we see a situation where the object-oriented technology pioneered by the Smalltalk research has been modified and adapted to an existing, powerful development environment, the Lisp development environment. The overriding objective of this work has been to provide an environment in which sophisticated oil well analysis tools can be applied to raw data derived from analysis of drill holes. On the surface, the problem may seem like one of numerical analysis, but the need to integrate the functionality of a suite of analysis tools and to share the raw data over many tools and users turns it into a more challenging problem. Instead of viewing this as a simple data management problem, the Schlumberger team has recognized that the data must carry along enough definition of itself to be easily adapted to new tools and new situations. Further, they recognized that the processing of the data is itself an adaptive process in which the designers must frequently alter the course of data analysis based on the discoveries that they make from preceding analyses. Such requirements are not easily satisfied by simple databases and rigid data interfaces. They require the flexibility and adaptability of an object-oriented system with powerful data management facilities, general development tools, and a variety of existing component tools that can be applied dynamically to the varying demands of new situations. That is, the workstation users are reusing on the fly by dynamically assembling multiple analysis tools to achieve a single computational goal. Thus they are building a series of small analysis systems from available components.

The HyperClass system is interesting for several reasons. First, it has been in use solving real-world problems for as long or longer than almost any other object-oriented system, save Smalltalk. Second, it has had to face many unpleasant real-world requirements, such as the integration of a variety of existing non-object-oriented tools. Third, it has had to extend the object-oriented model to allow for persistent objects—that is, objects that live longer than the execution of a single application program and are therefore sharable among applications. (The concept of persistent objects combines the notion of objects with the notion of databases and is currently an area of active research.)   Fourth, the HyperClass system has focused on the notion of model reuse, or to put it into Neighbors's terminology, domain reuse. Finally, HyperClass provides a baseline of experience with such systems and can provide informed comments as to their effect on reusability. For all of these reasons, this is a valuable paper for those who are headed in similar directions.

B. Case Studies

The case study papers are valuable to read for those trying to decide what they can and should do about reuse. The Prywes and Lock paper and the Cavaliere paper discuss reuse in the domain of business applications. Over the last several years Prywes has been developing an environment that is tailored specifically to support business applications. If we had to classify it, we would probably put it in the class of program generators, although one could make a case for it to be classed as a problem-oriented language system. Prywes and Lock report on an experiment in creating target systems using the Model specification language. They have discovered that it is about three times faster for developing similar applications than conventional programming languages.

By contrast, the ITT Hartford Insurance experience, as reported by Cavaliere, took a more ad-hoc approach to the problem but with good results. In this case, I believe that the success of the project was largely a result of the fact that the Hartford management supported, capitalized, and actively moved to assure the success of the project. I think this experience, along with the Toshiba and Raytheon experiences, reflects what can be accomplished with enlightened and committed management coupled with existing technology. A manager who is considering embarking upon a reuse project would do well to read about the experiences of these organizations.

The other two papers in this section describe reuse in an entirely different kind of environment. Oskarsson describes reuse in the development of telephony software, and Matsumoto describes reuse in process control software. The importance of these experiences lies in the fact that the nature of both target environments makes development difficult and costly, and critics of reuse are often skeptical about the possibilities of reuse within such target environments. These environments impose unusually strict memory and performance constraints on the target systems. Both environments require real-time software that must respond quickly in many situations. Such software systems are often among the most complex software systems in existence. It is valuable to realize that reuse can be effective in such environments.

The Toshiba organization, for example, is not applying any elaborate secret technology to their developments. They have settled on a reasonable set of well-known software engineering representation and design disciplines (e.g., object-oriented design) and are religiously adhering to them. They have developed tools and environments to support these disciplines, and they enforce these design, environment, and tool standards. The method works. They have continued over the years to increase the output of their software factory by a few percentage points every year while keeping the staffing level nearly level. The results speak for themselves.

I would summarize the experience of the various experiments in reuse *Chapter 6* (from throughout the whole book) as follows:

1. Capitalize your developmental programmers with the fullest and best resources (workstations, tools, environments, and offices).
2. Establish organizational standards for design, reuse, and programming. Once those standards are validated on a reasonably large scale,
3. Enforce them over the whole development organization.
4. Get management's commitment to make the whole thing work by fostering a climate where good practices and reuse are rewarded, and the alternatives are not.
5. Concurrently, establish R and D organizations whose missions are to explore new technologies that extend your existing development stan-

dards, tools, environments, and technologies to improve the payoff and answer similar moves by the competition.

The first four steps prepare your development organizations to compete in the existing market. The last step prepares them to compete in the future markets. You will need both kinds of actions to compete over the long haul. Just setting and using standards on the one hand, or just doing research into advanced reuse techniques on the other, is insufficient. A competitive organization must have a balance of both over the long run.

II   QUANTITATIVE RESULTS

This section provides some quantitative results on the potential of reuse as well as actual reuse. Lanergan and Grasso report that potentially 40 to 60 percent of the Cobol source code that they examined was redundant and showed high potential of being replaced by reused code. In practice they have reported that about 60 percent of the programs that they developed were made up of reused code. Goodell's analysis of code redundancy in a variety of business programs revealed similar figures.

In a careful analysis of 25 NASA systems developed in an environment where reuse was encouraged, Selby found that the average reuse on each system was 32 percent. He goes on to perform a statistical analysis of these systems in order to characterize the nature of reuse at several levels.

III   COGNITIVE RESULTS

This section addresses the problem of reuse by examining cognitive models, that is, the models of how the human programmer's and designer's minds are "wired." Since the human designer is especially good at reusing components, we will look at what we can learn about the representations and operations of the human mind, with the hope that these insights will provide guidance to designers of reuse systems. In addition, we will look at some computer-based representations that may provide some insight into the cognitive issues. These representations may also help in automating the reuse of abstract components.

A. Empirical Research

Soloway and Ehrlich have conducted some studies on programmers in order to understand what they know and how they apply that knowledge to the task of programming. While their results focus largely upon programming knowledge rather than domain knowledge, they are informative. In short, it is clear that expert programmers operate differently from novices. The experts clearly do not start from scratch in the development of a program; rather they appear to operate with program "plans," that is, skeletal programs that incorporate some preorganized portion of the program or function that the programmer intends to produce. That is to say, experts have reusable components stored somewhere in their "wetware," and these components are the starting point for developing programs.

This should not be too surprising, given the difference in performance of the two groups. Experts produce better programs faster than novices (and faster than they themselves did when they were novices). Some new mental structures must be available to these experts after they have practiced developing programs. There is a further clue. These structures (plans) must have certain canonical or preferred forms, because if one shows the experts programs that deviate from the canonical forms, the performance of the experts is degraded.

Curtis takes a global perspective in reviewing the results of cognitive research as it applies to the task of programming, and in the course of this review he makes a strong case for reuse of preorganized structures stored in the programmer/designer's head. He argues that in addition to schemas (i.e., the analogs of Soloway's plans), the programmer/designer reuses domain knowledge in the development of a design. This is the same theme that Neighbors discusses, this time from the cognitive point of view. It is the domain knowledge, Curtis believes, that provides the connective tissue integrating the variety of schemas that an expert programmer/designer has at his or her beck and call.

Finally, Curtis argues for the development of certain classes of tools for the designer who wants to reuse software, and these tools are based on the structures that are suggested by the cognitive research.

B. Knowledge-Based Representations

The first paper of this section presents a historical perspective on automatic programming that may contain lessons for reuse researchers. Based on the seminal work of Cordell Green and Richard Waldinger demonstrating the existence of general algorithms for translating formal program specifications into working programs, there was a flush of optimism in the early 70s about the possibility of fully automating program development. Many researchers took up the cause and began to build automatic programming systems. Most dropped out as the difficulty of the task began to be realized, but a few continued to work. The resulting systems are quite different from the expectations that we had in the early 70s. The notions of full automation died years ago and were replaced by more realistic notions of automated systems that aid the intelligent programmer. Balzer's paper provides a guided tour of the 15-year struggle with a really hard problem. The lessons learned about what realistically can be automated and what probably cannot are highly informative and may represent guideposts that will help software reuse researchers.

The following two papers examine representations for reusable design components and their application within specific programming support systems.

Cognitive research can never really pry open the head of a designer/programmer and examine in great detail the representations that he or she uses. So, the next best thing may be to hypothesize a structure for those representations and build systems that use the hypothetical representations. If the hypotheses are correct, these systems should behave much like a human programmer/designer, and if they are not correct, the systems will have significantly different behavior. While not specifically motivated by this rationale, the following two systems can be viewed as experiments of this nature.

The Programmer's Apprentice (PA) project has been an ongoing project at MIT for a number of years. In the PA system, the programmer/designer is solidly in the developmental loop and provides most of the creative insight, with the machine relegated to the more mundane tasks of symbol pushing, consistency checking, code generation, and so forth. The PA system provides the designer with a knowledge-based editor that allows him or her to edit program plans, that is, abstractions of the target program. These plans are built from components that are stored in a plan library. In some sense, these plans are an attempt to cast into a formal, machine-processible representation the plans and schemas that Soloway and Curtis have postulated.

The PA system also provides a coder subsystem that translates the plan into program code. Since the programmer may directly edit the resulting program code, the PA system also provides an analyzer, whose job is to analyze programs and keep the target program and its plan synchronized.

In another system, Lubars and Harandi chose a somewhat different representation to capture such plans, or as they call them, schemas. In this system, called IDeA, the computer plays a larger role in the generation of the target system. The designer specifies the target system by specifying the input and output data types. IDeA then searches its reuse base for schemas that loosely match that specification and presents to the user any schemas that are found (in the form of data flow diagrams). The user then adds constraints to the inputs and outputs. At this point, IDeA may fire a design rule demon that informs the user that the existing data flow diagram may be further refined based on another schema that it has in its database. This continues until all transformations are translated into "primitive" transformations, that is, transformations that the system knows how to compile. At this point, the system will generate code for the target system.

In summary, we have shown reuse is possible and profitable, although not a free lunch. Today, some in the software community are actively involved in doing reuse while others are performing research aimed at trying to improve the existing results. There are a number of options and approaches open to those who want to reap the benefits of reuse. No one approach will work for all technological or organizational cultures, but there is probably at least one approach among the many that will work for any given culture. The objective of this book is to provide the reader with an understanding of reusability so that he or she can make good judgments, and to provide the reader with the motivation to act, to try, and to experiment.

PART **I**

PRACTICE AND EXPERIENCE

CHAPTER 1

REUSABILITY: THE CASE FOR OBJECT-ORIENTED DESIGN

BERTRAND MEYER
Interactive Software Engineering

"Why isn't software more like hardware? Why must every new development start from scratch? There should be catalogs of software modules, as there are catalogs of VLSI devices: When we build a new system, we should be ordering components from these catalogs and combining them, rather than reinventing the wheel every time. We would write less software, and perhaps do a better job at that which we do develop. Then wouldn't the problems everyone laments—the high costs, the overruns, the lack of reliability—just go away? Why isn't it so?"

If you are a software developer or manager, you have probably heard such remarks before. Perhaps you have uttered them yourself.

The repetitive nature of computer programming is indeed striking. Over and over again, programmers weave a number of basic patterns: sorting, searching, reading, writing, comparing, traversing, allocating, synchronizing—experienced programmers know well the feeling of *déja vu* that is so characteristic of their trade.

Attempts have been made to measure this phenomenon; one estimate is that less than 15 percent of new code serves an original purpose [Jones, 1984].

A way to assess this situation less quantitatively but perhaps closer to home is to answer the following question honestly, again assuming you develop software or direct people who do. Consider the problem of table searching: an element of some kind, say x, is given with a set of similar elements, t; the program is to determine if x appears in t. The question is: How many times in the last six months did you or people working for you write some program fragment for table searching?

Chances are the answer will be one or more. But what is really remarkable is that, most likely, the fragment or fragments will have been written at the lowest reasonable level of abstraction—as code instead of by calling existing routines.

Yet table searching is one of the best-researched areas of computer science. Excellent books describe the fundamental algorithms—it would seem nobody should need to code a searching algorithm in standard cases anymore. After all, electronic engineers don't design standard inverters, they buy them.

This article addresses this fundamental goal of software engineering, reusability, and a companion requirement, extendibility (the ease with which software can be modified to reflect changes in specification). Progress in one of these areas usually advances the aims of the other as well, so when we discuss reusability, we will be adding, *in petto*, " . . . and extendibility."

Our main thesis is that object-oriented design is the most promising technique now known for attaining the goals of extendibility and reusability.

1.1 NI TOUT A FAIT LA MEME . . .

Why isn't reuse more common? Some of the reasons are nontechnical:

- [ ] Economic incentives tend to work against reusability. If you, as a contractor, deliver software that is too general and too reusable, you won't get the next job—your client won't need a next job!
- [ ] The famous not-invented-here complex also works against reusability.
- [ ] Reusable software must be retrievable, which means we need libraries of reusable modules and good database-searching tools so client programmers can find appropriate modules easily. (Some terminology: A *client* of a module M is any module relying on M; a *client programmer* is a person who writes a client module; an *implementer* of M is the programmer who writes M.)

In the U.S., the STARS project is an effort that aims, among other things, to overcome such obstacles.

Tip of the Iceberg

In my opinion, these issues are only the tip of the iceberg; the main roadblocks are technical. Reuse is limited because designing reusable software is hard. This article elaborates on what makes it so hard and should dispel any naive hope that software problems would just go away if we were more organized in filing program units.

Let's take a closer look at the repetitive nature of software development. Programmers do tend to do the same kinds of things time and time again, but they are not *exactly* the same things. If they were, the solution would be easy, at least on paper; but in practice, so many details may change as to render moot any simple-minded attempt at capturing commonality.

Such is the software engineer's plight: time and time again composing a new variation that elaborates on the same basic theme: "Neither ever quite the same, nor ever quite another."[1]

This paradigm applies to all standard cases of data representation (unsorted or sorted array, unsorted or sorted linked list, sequential file, binary tree, B-tree, hash table, etc.). It may be expressed more precisely as a program schema:

```
Search (x : ELEMENT, t:
TABLE_OF_ELEMENT)
return boolean is
    --Look for element x in table t
    pos: POSITION
begin
    pos:= INITIAL_POSITION (x,t);
    while not EXHAUSTED (pos,t)
    and then not FOUND (pos,x,t) do
    pos:= NEXT (pos,x,t);
end;
    return not EXHAUSTED (pos,t)
end -- Search
```

Too Many Variants

The difficulty in coming up with a general software element for searching is apparent: Even though the pattern is fixed, the amount of variable information is considerable. Details that may change include the type of table elements (ELEMENT), how the initial position is selected (INITIAL_POSITION), how the algorithm proceeds from one position to the next (NEXT), and all the types and routines in upper case, which will admit a different refinement for each variant of the algorithm.

Not only is it hard to implement a general-purpose searching module, it is almost as hard to *specify* such a module so that client modules could rely on it without knowing the implementation.

Beyond the basic problem of factoring out the parts that are common to all implementations of table searching, an even tougher challenge is to

---

[1]*Et quin n'est chaque fois ni tout á fait la même. Ni tout á fait une autre:* And [she] who from one [dream] to the next is neither ever quite the same, nor ever quite another. —Gerard de Nerval.

TABLE 1.1
IMPLEMENTATION VARIANTS FOR SEQUENTIAL SEARCH

	Sequential array	Linked list	Sequential file
Start search at first position	$i: = 1$	$l: = \textit{first}$	rewind
Move to next position	$i: = l + 1$	$l: = \textit{l.next}$	read
Test for table exhausted	$i > \text{size}$	$l = \text{null}$	end_of_file

capture the commonality within some conceptual subset. For example, an implementation using sequential search in arrays is very similar to one based on sequential linked lists; the code will differ only by small (yet crucial) details, shown in Table 1.1.

Within each group of implementations (all sequential tables, for example), there are similarities. If we really want to write carefully organized libraries of reusable software elements, we must be able to use commonalities at all levels of abstraction.

All these issues are purely technical; solving all the managerial and economical obstacles to reusability that one hears about in executives' meetings will not help a bit here.

1.2 ROUTINES

Work on reusability has followed several approaches (see Appendix). The classical technique is to build libraries of routines (we use the word *routine* to cover what is variously called *procedure, function, subroutine,* or *subprogram*). Each routine in the library implements a well-defined operation. This approach has been quite successful in scientific computation—excellent libraries exist for numerical applications.

Indeed, the routine-library approach seems to work well in areas where a set of individual problems can be identified, provided the following limitations hold:

☐ Every instance of each problem should be identifiable with a small set of parameters.

☐ The individual problems should be clearly distinct. Any significant commonality that might exist cannot be put to good use, except by reusing some of the design.

☐ No complex data structures should be involved, because they would have
to be distributed among the routines and the conceptual autonomy of
modules would be lost.

The table-searching example may be used to show the limitations of
this approach. We can either write a single routine or set of routines, each
corresponding to a specific case.

A single routine will have many parameters and will probably be structured like a gigantic set of case instructions. Its complexity and inefficiency
will make it unusable. Worse, the addition of any new case will mean modification and recompilation of the whole routine. A set of routines will be large
and contain many routines that look very similar (like the searching routines
for sequential arrays and sequential linked lists). But there is no simple way
for the implementers to use this similarity. Client programmers will have to
find their way through a maze of routines.

1.3 MODULAR LANGUAGES

Languages like Modula-2 and Ada offer a first step toward a solution. These
languages use the notion of module (the Ada term is *package*), providing a
higher-level structuring facility than the routine. A module may contain more
than one routine, together with declarations of types, constants, and variables.
A module may thus be devoted to an entire data structure and its associated
operations.

This approach is rooted in the theory of data abstraction, but its basic
concepts may be illustrated simply with our table-searching example.

A table-searching routine isn't worth very much by itself; it must be
complemented by routines that create and delete tables and insert and delete
elements, all governed by a certain representation of the table, given by a type
declaration. These routines and the type declaration are closely connected
logically, so they might as well be part of the same syntactic unit. Such units
are basically what modular languages offer.

This is a significant improvement: We can now keep under one roof a
set of related routines that pertain to a specific implementation of a data
abstraction. For example, the module for a binary search tree of integers
(INT_BINARY_TREE) will contain the declaration of a type intbintree and
routines Create, Search, Insert, and so on. The client code might look like
this:

```
x : integer; b : boolean; p :
INT_BINARY_TREE.intbintree;
INT_BINARY_TREE.Create(t);
INT_BINARY_TREE.Insert(x,b);
b:= INT_BINARY_TREE.Search(x,p)
```

(Here I use the Ada dot notation: *A.f* means "feature" *f*, such as a type or routine, from module *A*. In Ada and other languages, simpler notations are available when a client repeatedly uses features from a given module.)

For reusability, these techniques are useful but limited. They are useful because encapsulating groups of related features helps implementers (in gathering features) as well as clients (in retrieving features), and all of this favors reusability. But they are limited because they do not reduce significantly the amount of software that needs to be written. Specifically, they don't offer any new clue as to how to capture common features.

1.4 OVERLOADING AND GENERICITY

A futher improvement is *overloading,* as provided in Algol 68 and Ada. Overloading means attaching more than one meaning to a name, such as the name of an operation.

For example, when different representations of tables are each defined by a separate type declaration, you would use overloading to give the same name, say Search, to all associated search procedures. In this way, a search operation will always be invoked as b := Search (x,t), regardless of the implementation chosen for t and the type of table elements.

Overloading works well in a strictly typed language where the compiler has enough type information about *x* and *t* to choose the right version of search.

A companion technique is genericity, provided in Ada and Clu. Genericity allows a module to be defined with generic parameters that represent types. Instances of the module are then produced by supplying different types as actual parameters. This is a definite aid to reusability because just one generic module is defined, instead of a group of modules that differ only in the types of objects they manipulate.

For example, instead of having an INT_BINARY_TREE module, a REAL_BINARY_TREE module, and so on, you could define a single generic BINARY_TREE[T]module. Any actual type (INTEGER, REAL, etc.) could correspond to the formal generic parameter T. The search routine can be defined in the generic module to act on an argument *x* of type T. Then every instance of the module automatically has its own version of search.

In summary, overloading and genericity each offer something toward reuse:

☐ With overloading, the client programmer may write the same code when using different implementations of the same data abstraction, as provided by different modules.

☐ With genericity, the implementer may write a single module for all instances of the same implementation of a data abstraction, applied to various types of objects.

These techniques are interesting advancements in reusability. But they do not go far enough. Roughly speaking, they do not provide enough flexibility, and they force programmers to decide too much too soon.

Not Enough Flexibility

The techniques that have been described are not flexible enough because they cannot capture fine grains of commonality between groups of implementations of the same general data abstraction. This is because there are only two levels of modules: generic modules, which are parameterized and thus open to variation, but not directly usable; and fully instantiated modules, which are directly usable but not open to refinement. Thus we cannot describe a complex hierarchy of representations that have different levels of parameterizations.

Too Much Too Soon

Neither genericity nor overloading allows a client to use various implementations of a data abstraction (say the table) without knowing which implementation is used in each instance.

On one hand, each generic module refers to a single, explicitly specified instance of that module. Overloading, on the other hand, is essentially a syntactic facility that relieves the programmer of having to invent names for different implementations; the burden is placed on the compiler instead. Nevertheless, each invocation of an overloaded operation name, say Search (x, t), refers to a specific version of the operation—and both the client programmer and compiler know which version that is.

Client programmers do not actually need to know how each version is implemented, since Ada and Modula-2 modules are used by clients through an interface that lists the available routines, independent of their implementation. But they do need to decide explicitly which version is used. For example, if your modules use various kinds of tables, you don't have to know how to implement hash tables, indexed sequential files, and the like—but you must say which representation you want each time you use a table operation.

True representation independence only happens when a client can write the invocation Search (x, t) and mean, "look for x in t using the appropriate algorithm for whatever kind of table and element x and t happen to be at the time the invocation is executed."

This degree of flexibility, essential for the construction of reusable software elements, can only be achieved with object-oriented design.

1.5 OBJECT-ORIENTED DESIGN

This fashionable term has been somewhat overused in recent years. The definition used here is fairly dogmatic. Object-oriented design is viewed as a *software decomposition technique*. An overview of some object-oriented languages is given in the Appendix.

Object-oriented design may be defined as a technique that, unlike classical (functional) design, bases the modular decomposition of a software system on the classes of objects the system manipulates, not on the functions the system performs. Classical approaches like functional top-down design (even, to a large extent, data flow analysis methods) require designers to first ask what the system does. Object-oriented design avoids such questions as long as possible, in fact until the system actually is run. Why?

The top-down functional approach is probably adequate if the program you are writing solves a fixed problem once and for all. But the picture changes when you take a long-term view, for what the system will do in its first release is probably going to be a little different from what you think it will do at requirements time, and *very* different from what it will do five years later, if it survives that long.

However, the categories of objects on which the system acts will probably be more or less the same. An operating system will always work on devices, memories, processing units, communication channels, and so on; a document-processing system will always work on documents, chapters, sections, paragraphs, and so on.

Thus it is wiser in the long term to rely on categories of objects as a basis for decomposition, but (and this is an important *but*) only if these categories are viewed at a sufficiently high level of abstraction. This is where abstract data types come in.[2]

1.6 ABSTRACT DATA TYPES

If we use the physical structure of objects as the basis for decomposition, we won't go very far toward protecting our software's structure against requirement changes. In fact, we will probably be worse off than we would be with functional design. A study by Lientz and Swanson [1979], quoted by Boehm [1979], shows that 17.5 percent of the cost of software maintenance stems from changes in programs that reflect changes in data formats. This empha-

---

[2]One other design method that does emphasize the motto "Look at the data before you look at the functions" is Jackson's method [Jackson, 1983]. However, a comparative analysis of Jackson's method and object-oriented design falls beyond the scope of this article.

sizes the need to separate the programs from the physical structure of the objects they handle.

Abstract data types provide a remarkable solution to this problem. An abstract data type describes a class of objects through the external properties of these objects instead of their computer representation. More precisely, an abstract data type is a class of objects characterized by the operations available on them and the abstract properties of these operations.

It turns out that abstract data types, which provide an excellent basis for software specification, are also useful at the design and implementation stage. In fact, they are essential to the object-oriented approach and enable us to refine the definition of object-oriented design: Object-oriented design is the construction of software systems as structured collections of abstract data type implementations.

An important aspect of the object-oriented method is that it actually identifies modules with implementations of abstract data types. It is not only that modules *comprise* these implementations (as in Ada and Modula-2, and in Fortran-77, thanks to multiple-entry subroutines); a single program structure *is* both a module and a type. Such a dual-purpose structure was dubbed a "class" by the creators of the pioneer object-oriented language, Simula 67.

Two words should be emphasized in the above definition. The first is *implementation*: A module of an object-oriented program is not an abstract data type, but one implementation of an abstract data type. However, the details of the implementation are not normally available to the rest of the world, which only sees the official specification of the abstract data type.

The second word to be emphasized is *structured*. Collections of classes may indeed be structured using two different relations: *client* and *inheritance*. Figure 1.1 illustrates these two relations. The client relation is represented by a horizontal double arrow; inheritance by a single, vertical arrow.

FIGURE 1.1
THE CLIENT AND INHERITANCE RELATIONS IN ABSTRACT DATA TYPES. THE CLIENT IS REPRESENTED BY A HORIZONTAL DOUBLE ARROW; INHERITANCE BY A SINGLE, VERTICAL ARROW.

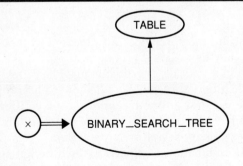

Class *A* is said to be a client of B if A contains a declaration of the form bb: B. (In this and all other object-oriented examples, I use the notations and terminology of the object-oriented language Eiffel. See the Appendix for more about Eiffel.) In this case, A may manipulate bb only through the features defined in the specification of B. Features comprise both attributes (data items associated with objects of type B) and routines (operations for accessing or changing these objects). In Eiffel, features are applied through dot notation, as in bb.x, and bb.f(u,w,x).

As an example, consider a client class X of class BINARY_SEARCH_TREE that implements a specific form of tables. Client X may contain elements of the form

```
bb: BINARY_SEARCH_TREE
--declare bb as binary search tree
bb.Create;
--allocate table (routine call)
bb.insert (x);
--insert x into bb (routine call)
y := bb.size;
--(attribute access)
```

The second relation between classes, inheritance, is fundamental to true object-oriented languages. For example, our BINARY_SEARCH_TREE class may be defined as an *heir* (possibly indirect) to a class TABLE that describes the general properties of tables, independent of the representation.

A class C defined as an heir to a class A has all the features of A, to which it may add its own. The *descendants* of a class include its heirs, the heirs of its heirs, and so on. The relationship between C and A may be defined from the viewpoints of both the module and the type.

From the module perspective, inheritance allows the programmer to take an existing world (class A) and plunge it as a whole into a new world, C, which will inherit all its properties and add its own. In *multiple* inheritance, as present in Eiffel, more than one world may be used to define a new one.

From the type perspective, C is considered a special case of A: Any object of type C may also be interpreted as an object of type A. In particular, a variable of type A may be assigned an object of type C, although the reverse is not true, at least in a statically typed language like Eiffel. This also holds in the case of multiple inheritance, as Fig. 1.2 shows. This property is extremely important because it allows program entities to take different forms at run time. The relation between C and A is an instance of the "is-a" relation (every lily *is a* flower; every binary search tree *is a* table).

The powerful combination of object-oriented design and these two relations—client and inheritance—is a key element in achieving extendibility and reusability.

FIGURE 1.2
MULTIPLE INHERITANCE. IN EIFFEL, MORE THAN ONE WORLD CAN BE USED
TO DEFINE A NEW WORLD, WHICH WILL INHERIT ALL THE PROPERTIES AND
ADD ITS OWN.

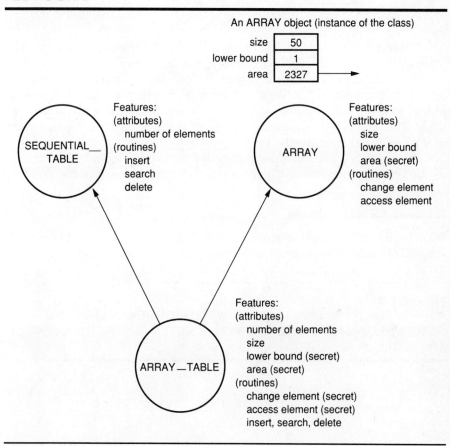

1.7   AN ILLUSTRATIVE EXAMPLE

A new example, a full-screen entry system, will help contrast the object-oriented approach with classical functional decomposition. The example, a common data processing problem, should be interesting on its own: The problem is to write an interactive application that guides the user with full-screen panels at each stage.

The Problem

Interactive sessions for such systems go through a series of states, each with a well-defined general pattern: A panel is displayed with questions for the user;

the user supplies the required answer; the answer is checked for consistency (questions are asked until an acceptable answer is supplied); and the answer is processed somehow (a database is updated, for example). Part of the user's answer is a choice of the next steps; the system translates the user's choice into a transition to another state, and the same process is applied in the new state.

Figure 1.3 shows a panel for an imaginary airline reservation system. The screen shown is toward the end of a step; the user's answers are in italics.

The process begins in some initial state and ends whenever any among a set of final states is reached. A transition graph, like that in Fig. 1.4, shows the overall structure of a session—the possible states and the transitions between them. The edges of the graph are labeled by numbers that correspond to the user's possible choices for the next step.

Our mission is to come up with a design and an implementation for such applications that have as much generality and flexibility as possible.

A Simple-Minded Solution

We'll begin with a straightforward, unsophisticated program scheme. This version is made of a number of blocks, one for each state of the system: $B_{Enquiry}$, $B_{Reservation}$, $B_{Cancellation}$, and so on. A typical block looks like:

FIGURE 1.3
A PANEL FOR AN INTERACTIVE AIRLINE RESERVATION SYSTEM. THE SCREEN SHOWN IS TOWARD THE END OF A STEP; THE USER'S ANSWERS ARE IN ITALICS.

Enquiry on Flights

Flight sought from: *Santa Barbara*　　　　to: *Paris*
Departure on or after: *Nov 21*　　on or before: *Nov 21*

Preferred airline(s):
Special requirements:

AVAILABLE FLIGHTS: 1
Flt# AA 42　　Dep 8:25　　Arr 7:45　　Thru Chicago

Choose next action:

　　0 – Exit
　　1 – Help
　　2 – Further enquiry
　　3 – Reserve a seat

FIGURE 1.4
A STATE TRANSITION GRAPH FOR AN INTERACTIVE APPLICATION. THE
EDGES OF THE GRAPH ARE LABELED BY NUMBERS THAT CORRESPOND
TO THE USER'S POSSIBLE CHOICES FOR THE NEXT STEP.

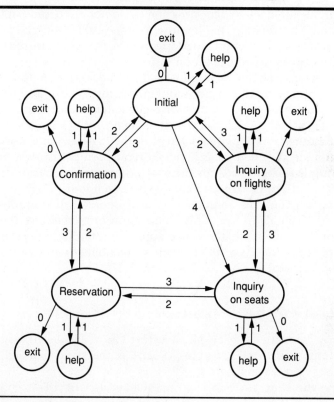

```
B_Enquiry
   output "enquiry on flight" panel;
   repeat
      read user's answers and choice C for
      next step;
      if error in answer then
      output appropriate message
   end until not error in answer end;
   process answer;
   case C in
      C_0 : goto Exit,
      C_1 : goto B_help,
      C_2 : goto B_Reservation,
      ...
   end
```

(And similarly for each state.)

This structure will do the job, but of course there is much to criticize. The numerous *goto* instructions give it that famous spaghetti bowl look. This may be viewed as a cosmetic issue, solved by restructuring the program to eliminate jumps. But that would miss the point.

The problem is deeper. This program is bad not just because it has a lot of explicit branch instructions, but because the physical form of the problem has been wired into it. The branching structure of the program reflects exactly the transition structure of the graph in Fig. 1.4.

This is terrible from a reusability and extendability standpoint. In real-world data entry systems, the graph of Fig. 1.4 might be quite complex—one study mentions examples with 300 different states [Dwyer, 1981].

It is highly unlikely that the transition structure of such a system will be right the first time it is designed. Even after the first version is working, users will inevitably request new transitions, shortcuts, or help states. The prospect of modifying the whole program structure (not just program elements—the overall organization) for any one change is horrendous.

To improve on this solution we must separate the graph structure from the traversal algorithm. This seems appropriate because the structure depends on the particular interactive application (airline reservation), while its traversal is generic. As a side benefit, a functional decomposition will also remove the heretical *goto*s.

A Procedural, "Top-Down" Solution

We may encapsulate the graph structure in a two-argument function, Transition, such that Transition(s,c) is the state obtained when the user chooses c on leaving state s.

We use the word *function* in a mathematical sense: Transition may be represented either by a function in the programming sense (a routine that returns a value) or by a data structure, such as an array. The first solution may be preferable for readability because the transitions will appear in the program code itself. The second is better for flexibility because it is easier to change a data structure than a program. We can afford to postpone this decision.

The function Transition is not sufficient to describe the transition graph. We must also define the state, initial, that begins the traversal and a Boolean-valued function is-final(s) that determines when a state is final. Initial and final states are treated dissymmetrically; while it is reasonable to expect the dialog to always begin in the same state, we cannot expect it to always end in the same state.

Figure 1.5 shows the orthodox, functional architecture derived from this solution. As the top-down method teaches, this system has a "top," or main program. What else could it be but the routine that describes how to execute a complete interactive session?

FIGURE 1.5

AN ORTHODOX, FUNCTIONAL ARCHITECTURE FOR AN INTERACTIVE
APPLICATION. THE "TOP," OR MAIN PROGRAM, IS THE ROUTINE SESSION.

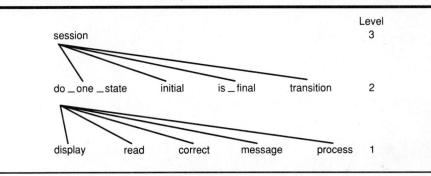

This routine may be written to emphasize application independence.
Assume that a suitable representation is found for states (type STATE) and
for the user's choice after each state (CHOICE):

```
session is
  --execute a complete session of
  --the interactive system
  current: STATE; next: CHOICE
begin
  current := initial;
  repeat
      do_one_state(current,next);
    --the value of next is returned by routine
    --do_one_state
      current := transition(current,next)
  until is_final(current) end
end -- session
```

This procedure does not show direct dependency upon any interactive
application. To describe such an application, we must provide three of the
elements on level 2 in Fig. 1.5: a transition function (routine or data structure), an initial state, and an is_final predicate.

To complete the design, we refine the do_one_state routine, which
describes the actions to be performed in each state. The body of this routine
is essentially an abstracted form of the blocks in our spaghetti version:

```
do_one_state(in s: STATE; out c: CHOICE) is
    --execute the actions associated with
    --state s,
    --returning into c the user's choice
    --for the next state
  a: ANSWER; ok: BOOLEAN;
```

```
begin
  repeat
    display (s); read (s,a) end
    ok := correct(s,a);
    if not ok then message(s,a) end
  until ok end;
  process (s, a); c := next_choice (a)
end -- do_one_state
```

For remaining routines, we can only give a specification, because the implementations depend on the details of the application and its various states: display(s) outputs the panel associated with state s; read(s,a) reads the user's answer to state s into a; correct(s,a) returns true if and only if a is an acceptable answer; if it is, process(s,a) processes answer a; if it isn't, messages(s,a) outputs the relevant error message.

Type ANSWER is left unspecified. A value of this type, say a, globally represents the input entered by the user in a given state, including the user's choice of the next step, next_choice(a).

Data Transmission

Is this solution satisfactory? Not from the standpoint of reusability.

True, we did separate what is generic and what is specific to a particular application, but this does not buy much flexibility. The main problem is the system's data transmission structure. Consider the functionalities (types of arguments and results) of the routines:

> do_one_state: (in s: STATE; out c: CHOICE)
> display: (in s: STATE)
> read: (in s: STATE; out a: ANSWER)
> correct: (in s: STATE; a: ANSWER): BOOLEAN
> message: (in s: STATE; a: ANSWER)
> process: (in s: STATE; a: ANSWER)

All these routines share the state s as a parameter, coming from the top module Session (where it is known as Current). The flow of data, illustrated in Fig. 1.6, shows that (as a conservative economist might say) there's far too much state intervention. As a result, all the above routines must perform some form of case discrimination on s:

```
case s of
  State₁: . . . ,
      . . . ,
  Stateₙ: . . . ,
end
```

FIGURE 1.6
DATA TRANSMISSION IN THE ARCHITECTURE DERIVED FROM WITH WITH
TOP-DOWN APPROACH.

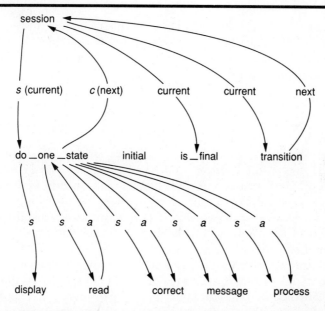

This implies long, complex code (a problem that could be solved with further decomposition) and (more annoying) it means that every routine must deal with, and thus know about, all possible states of the application. This makes it very difficult to implement extensions. Adding a new state, for example, entails modifications throughout. Such a situation is all too common in software development. System evolution becomes a nightmare as simple changes touch off a complex chain reaction in the system.

The situation is even worse than it appears. It would seem desirable to profit from the similar aspects of these types of interactive applications by storing the common parts in library routines. But this is unrealistic in the solution above: On top of the explicit parameters, all routines have an implicit one—the application itself, airline reservations.

A general-purpose version of display, for example, should know about all states of all possible applications in a given environment! The function Transition should contain the transition graph for all applications. This is clearly impossible.

The Law of Inversion

What is wrong? Figure 1.6 exposes the flaw: There is too much data transmission in the software architecture. The remedy, which leads directly to object-oriented design, may be expressed by the following law: If there is too much data transmission in your routines, then put your routines into your data.

Instead of building modules around operations (session, do_one_state) and distributing data structures among the resulting routines, object-oriented design does the reverse. It uses the most important data structures as the basis for modularization and attaches each routine to the data structure to which it applies most closely.

This law of inversion is the key to turning a functional decomposition into an object-oriented design: Reverse the viewpoint and attach the routines to the data structures. To programmers trained in functional approaches, this is as revolutionary as making the Sun orbit Earth.

Of course, it's best to design in an object-oriented fashion from the beginning. However, the process of moving from a functional decomposition to an object-oriented structure is itself interesting. How do we find the most important data structures, around which modules are to be built?

Data transmission provides a clue. The data structures that are constantly transmitted between routines must be important, mustn't they?

Here the first candidate is obvious, the state (current, s). So our object-oriented solution will include a class STATE to implement the corresponding abstract data type. Among the features of a state are the five routines of level 1 in Fig. 1.5 which describe the operations performed in a state (display, read, message, correct, and process), and the routine do_one_state without the state parameter.

In Eiffel notation, the class STATE may be written

```
class STATE export
  next_choice, display, read, correct,
  message, process, do_one_state
feature
  user_answer: ANSWER;
  next_choice: INTEGER;
  do_one_state is
    do
    ... body of the routine ...
    end;
  display is ...;
  read is ...;
  correct: BOOLEAN is ...;
  message is ...;
  process is ...;
end -- class STATE
```

The features of the class include two attributes, next_choice and user_answer, and six routines. Routines are divided into functions, which return a result (like correct, which returns a Boolean value) and procedures, which don't.

The export clause is used for information hiding: In a client class containing a declaration s: STATE, a feature application s f is only correct if f is one of the features listed in the clause. Here all features are exported except for user_answer, which is accessible by STATE routines but not by the outside world. A nonexported feature is said to be *secret*. As before, we assume that type ANSWER is declared elsewhere, now as a class. Values that represent exit choices are coded as integers.

Unlike its counterpart in a functional decomposition, each routine has no explicit STATE parameter. The state to which routines apply reappears in calls made by clients:

```
s: STATE; b: BOOLEAN;
choicecode: INTEGER;
s.do_one_state; s.read;
b := s.correct;
choicecode, := s.next_choice;
etc.
```

We have also replaced the answer parameter in level-1 routines with the secret attribute user_answer. Information hiding is the motive—client code doesn't need to look at answers except through the interface provided by the exported features.

Inheritance and Deferred Features

There's a problem, however. How can we write the class STATE without knowing the properties of a specific state?. Routine do_one_state and attribute next_choice are the same for all states, but display is not.

Inheritance is the key to this problem. At the STATE level we know (1) all details of routine do_one_state, (2) the attribute next_choice; (3) the fact that routines like display must exist and (4) what their functionalities are.

So we write the class and define these partially known routines as *deferred*. This means that, while any actual state must have them, their details are postponed to descendant classes that describe specific states. (The notion of deferred routines come from Simula 67, where they are called *virtual*.) Thus the class is written

```
class STATE export
    next_choice, display, read, correct,
    message, process, do_one_state

feature
    user_answer: ANSWER;
      --secret attribute
    next_choice: INTEGER;
```

```
do_one_state is
    --execute the actions associated
    --with the current state
    --and assign to next_choice the
    --user's choice for the next state
  local
    ok: BOOLEAN
  do
    from
      ok := false
    until
      ok
    loop
      display; read; ok := correct;
      if not ok then
        message
      end
    end; -- loop
    process
  ensure
    correct
  end; -- do_one_state

display is
  --display the panel associated
  --with current state
  deferred
  end; -- display
  read is
    --return the user's answer
    --into user_answer
    --and the user's next choice
    --into next_choice
  deferred
  end; -- read

  correct: BOOLEAN is
    --return true if and only if
    --user_answer is
    --a correct answer
  deferred
  end; -- correct

  message is
    -- output the error message
    -- associated with user_answer
    require
      not correct
  deferred
  end; -- message
```

```
   process is
     --process user_answer
     require
       correct
     deferred
     end -- process
 end -- class STATE
```

Note the syntax of the Eiffel loop, with initialization in the from clause and the exit test in the until clause. This is equivalent to a while loop, with an exit test rather than a continuation test.

Also note the require clauses that appear at the beginning of routine message and process. These clauses introduce preconditions that must be obeyed whenever a routine is called. Similarly, a postcondition, introduced by the keyword ensure, may be associated with a routine. Preconditions and postconditions express the precise effect of a routine. They can also be monitored at run time for debugging and control.

The class just described does not by itself describe any actual states—it expresses the pattern common to all states. Specific states are defined by descendants of STATE. It is incumbent on these descendants to provide actual implementations of the deferred routines, such as:

```
class ENQUIRY_ON_FLIGHTS export . . .
inherit
  STATE
feature
  display is
    do
    . . . specific display procedure . . .
    end;
      . . . and similarly for read, correct,
      message, and process . . .
end -- class ENQUIRY_ON_FLIGHTS
```

Several important comments are in order:

We have succeeded in separating—at the exact grain of detail required—the elements common to all states from those specific to individual states. Common elements are concentrated in STATE and need not be redeclared in descendants of STATE like ENQUIRY_ON_FLIGHTS.

If s is an object of type STATE and d an object of type DS, where DS is a descendant of STATE, the assignment s := d is permitted and d is acceptable whenever an element of type STATE is required. For example, the array Transition introduced later to represent the transition graph of an application may be declared of type STATE and filled with elements of descendant types.

This goes beyond Ada-style separation of interface and implementation. First, an Ada interface may contain only bodiless routines; it corresponds to a class where all routines are deferred. In Eiffel, however, you may freely combine nondeferred and deferred routines in the same class. Even more important, Eiffel allows any number of descendant types of STATE to coexist in the same application, whereas Ada allows at most one implementation per interface. This openness of classes (a class may always be extended by new descendants) is a fundamental advantage of object-oriented languages over the closed modules of such languages as Ada and Modula-2.

The presence of preconditions and postconditions in Eiffel maintains the conceptual integrity of a system. A precondition and postcondition may be associated with a routine even in a deferred declaration. These conditions are then binding on any actual definition of the routine in a descendant of the original class. The technique is paramount in using Eiffel as design language: A design module will be written as a class with deferred routines, whose effects are characterized by pre- and postconditions.

A Complete System

The final step in our example is to adapt the routine that was at the top of the functional decomposition: session. But we should be a little wiser by now.

The top of the top-down method is mythical. Most real systems have no such thing, especially if the top is meant to be a routine—*the* function of the system. Large software systems perform many functions, all equally important. Again, the abstract data type approach is more appropriate because it considers the system as an abstract entity capable of rendering many services.

In this case the obvious candidate is the notion of application: a specific interactive system like the airline reservation system. It makes sense to associate with this concept a full-fledged abstract data type that will yield a class, say INTERACTIVE_APPLICATION, at the design and implementation stages. For, although INTERACTIVE_APPLICATION will include as one of its features the routine session describing the execution of an application, there are other things we may want to do with an application, all of which may be added incrementally to class APPLICATION.

By renouncing the notion of "main program" and seeing session as just one feature of the class INTERACTIVE_APPLICATION, we have added considerable flexibility.

The class is given in Fig. 1.7. Its principal features include the remaining elements at levels 2 and 3 in Fig. 1.5. The following implementations decisions have been made:

☐ The transition function is represented by a two-dimensional array, transition, of size $n \times m$, where n is the number of states and m the number of possible exit choices.

FIGURE 1.7
THE CLASS INTERACTIVE_APPLICATION

```
classINTERACTIVE_APPLICATION export
  session, first_number, enter_state,
  choose_initial, enter_transition, n...
feature
  transition: ARRAY2[STATE]; associated_state: ARRAY[STATE];
  --secret attributes
  first_number: INTEGER
  Create (n.m.:INTEGER) is
  -- allocated application with n states and m possible choices
    do
      transition.Create(1,n,1,m);
      associated_state.Create(1,n)
    end; -- Create

session is -- execute application
  local
    st: STATE; st_number:INTEGER;
  do
    from
      st_number;=first_number;
    invariant
      0 < next; next < n
    until st_number = 0 loop
      st:=associated_state.entry(st_number);
      st.do_one_state;                        `
      st_number:=transition.entry(st_number, st.next_choice)
    end -- loop
  end; -- session
enter_state(s: STATE ; number: INTEGER) is
-- enter state s with index number
    require
      1 <= number;
      number <= associated_state.upper
    do
      associated_state.enter(number,s)
    end; -- enter_state

choose_initial(number: INTEGER) is
-- define state number number as the initial state
    require
      1 <= number;
      number <= associated_state.upper
    do
      first_number:=number
    end; -- choose_initial
```

FIGURE 1.7 *(Cont.)*

```
enter_transition (source: INTEGER ; target:INTEGER ; label: INTEGER) is
-- enter transition labeled "label" from state number source
-- to state number target
   require
     1 <= source; source <= associated_state.upper ;
     0 <= target; target <= associated_state.upper ;
     1 <= label; label <= transition.upper2 ;
   do
     transition.enter (source,label,target)
   end -- enter_transmission

...other features

invariant
  0 <= st_number ; st_number <= n ;
  transition.upper1 = associated_state.upper ;
end -- class INTERACTIVE_APPLICATION
```

☐ States are numbered 1 to n. An auxiliary, one-dimensional array, associated_state, yields the state corresponding to any integer.

☐ The number of the initial state is set by the routine choose_initial and kept in the attribute first_number. The convention for final states is a transition to pseudostate 0; normal states have positive numbers.

The class includes a Create procedure that will be executed on object initialization. As in most object-oriented languages, objects are created dynamically. If a is declared of type C, the instruction a.Create creates an object of type C and associates it with a.

The Create procedure and its parameters makes it possible to execute specific initialization actions on creation, instead of initializing the new object with standard default values.

The procedure Create of class INTERACTIVE_ APPLICATION itself uses the Create procedures of library classes ARRAY and ARRAY2, which allocate arrays dynamically within the bounds given as parameters. For example, a two-dimensional array may be created by a.Create(1,25,1,10).

Classes ARRAY and ARRAY2 also include features Entry and Enter for array access and modification. Other features of an array are its bounds, upper and lower for a one-dimensional array, and so on.

These classes are declared as ARRAY[T] and ARRAY2[T], an example of Eiffel classes with generic parameters, in this case the type of array elements. Many fundamental classes in the Eiffel library (lists, trees, stacks) are generic. With Eiffel a programmer can combine genericity with inheritance in a type-safe manner [Meyer].

Class INTERACTIVE_ APPLICATION uses Eiffel assertions, an aspect of the language designed to emphasize correctness and reliability. Assertions express formal properties of program elements. They may appear in preconditions and postconditions, in the loop invariants, and in the class invariants.

Such constructs are used primarily to ensure correct program designs and to document the correctness of arguments, but they may also be used as checks at run time. More profoundly, assertions (especially pre- and postconditions and class invariants) bring the formal properties of abstract data types back into classes.

An interactive application will be represented by an entity, air_reservation, declared of type INTERACTIVE_APPLICATION and initialized by

```
air_reservation.Create(number_of_states,
        number_of_possible_choices)
```

The states of the application must be defined separately as entities, declared of descendants STATE, and created. Each state s is assigned a number i:

```
air_reservation.enter_state(s,i)
```

One state, i_0, is chosen as the initial:

```
air_reservation.choose_initial(i_0)
```

Each succesive transition (from state number sn to state tn, with label l) is entered by

```
air_reservation.enter_transition (sn,tn,l)
```

This includes exits, for which tn is 0. The application may now be executed by air_reservation.session.

The same routines can be used during system evolution to add a new state, a new transition, and so on. The class may be extended, of course (either by itself or through descendants).

Multiple Inheritance

This example exposes many of the principles in Eiffel but not the concept of multiple inheritance (a previous article on the same example [Meyer, 1982 1983] relied on Simula 67, which supports only single inheritance). Multiple inheritance is another concept that is essential to a practical use of object-oriented design and programming.

Multiple inheritance makes it possible to define a class as heir to more than one other class, thus combining the features of several previously defined environments. Multiple inheritance would be essential, for example, to implement a satisfactory solution to the table management problem, detailed in Appendix A.

Even in the previous example, multiple inheritance is not far away— if we had defined a data abstraction WINDOW to describe screen panels, some descendants of STATE might inherit from this class, too.

1.8 IN LIEU OF CONCLUSION

This article has promoted the view that, if one accepts that reusability is essential to better software quality, the object-oriented approach—defined as the construction of software systems as structured collections of abstract data type implementations—provides a promising set of solutions.

One epithet this approach certainly does not deserve is "top-down." It is puzzling to see this adjective used almost universally as a synonym for "good." Top-down design may be an effective method for developing individual algorithms and routines, but applying it at the system level is inappropriate unless the system can be characterized by a single, frozen, top-level function, a case that is rare in practice.

More importantly, top-down design goes against the key factor of software reusability because it promotes one-of-a-kind developments, rather than general-purpose, combinable software elements.

It is surprising to see top-down design built in as an essential requirement in the U.S. Department of Defense directive MIL-STD-2167, which by the sheer power of its sponsor is bound to have a serious (and, we fear, negative) influence for years to come.

Of course, the bottom-up method promoted here does not mean that system design should start at the lowest possible level. What it implies is construction of systems by reusing and combining existing software. This is a bootstrapping approach in which software elements are progressively combined into more and more ambitious systems.

As a consequence of this approach, there is no notion of main program in Eiffel. Classes are meant to be developed separately. Integrating those classes into an Eiffel system is the last, and least binding, decision.

A system is a set of classes with one distinguishing element, the root. The only role of the root is to initiate the execution of the system (by creating an object of the root type and executing its create procedure). A system has no existence as an Eiffel construct; it is simply a particular assembly of classes.

Such an approach is viable only if there are adequate facilities to produce flexible software elements and combine them effectively. The concepts of object-oriented design with multiple inheritance and genericity provide such facilities.

Object-oriented design means more than just putting data types into modules; the inheritance concept is essential. This requires an object-oriented language. As structured programming showed a few years ago, you can attempt to implement new methodologies without a language that directly supports them—but it will never be quite as good as the real thing: using the right language to implement the right concepts.

Another aspect of the approach promoted here is that it tends to blur the distinction between design and implementation. While this distinction may be unavoidable today, it is undesirable because it tends to introduce an artificial discontinuity in software construction.

Design and implementation are essentially the same activity: constructing software to satisfy a certain specification. The only difference is the level of abstraction—during design certain details may be left unspecified, but in an implementation everything should be expressed in full. However, the process of filling in the details should be continuous, from system architecture to working program. Language constructs such as deferred features are particularly helpful in this process. Software development is made much smoother when you use a language that encompasses the traditional area of design and implementation, but that is no more difficult to master than conventional programming languages. Such is the aim of Eiffel.

We do not propose, however, to remove the boundary between design and implementation, on the one hand, and system specification on the other. These activities are of different natures: Specification states problems, design and implementation solve them. (A companion effort, the specification method M [Meyer, 1985], applies similar concepts to formal, nonexecutable specifications.)

One more fundamental theme has been guiding this discussion: the idea that today the essential problems of software engineering are *technical* problems.

Not everybody agrees. There is a large and influential school of thought that sees management, organization, and economic issues as the biggest obstacles to progress in software development. In this view, technical issues, such as the choice of programming language, are less important for reusability than such things as an easily accessible database of components.

As evidence of the limitations of the managerial approach to reusability, consider the relations that might exist between software components, such as specialization (a hash table is a specialized table, a B-tree is a specialized tree). If an object-oriented language is used, specializations can be expressed directly by inheritance and recorded within the components themselves. But if the language does not provide direct support for expressing this relation, the information must be entered explicitly into the database, separate from the components.

This immediately raises some difficult issues, namely, how to provide an adequate user interface, check the consistency of the relation information, and maintain the integrity of this information as components are updated.

Advanced project management techniques are required to solve these issues. This is a typical example of an organizational solution to a technical problem, with the resulting complexity and loss of effectiveness.

Overemphasis on management issues is premature. While it is indeed true that many software projects are plagued with management problems, focusing on these problems first confuses the symptom with cause. It's like expecting better hospital management to solve the public hygiene problem 10 years before Pasteur came along!

Give your poor, your huddled projects a decent technical environment in the first place. *Then* worry about whether you are managing them properly.

Acknowledgments

The comments and suggestions made by the referees, those who agreed with the article's thesis and those who didn't, were much appreciated. The influence of Simula 67, the first object-oriented language and still one of the best, is gratefully acknowledged.

Appendix

Reuse in Practice

It would be unfair to suggest that reuse never occurs in software. Much research has been published on the issue and various approaches to reusability have gained some acceptance.

Source code reusability is common in academic environments. Unix, for example, has spread through universities and research laboratories thanks to the on-line availability of the source code that allowed users to study, imitate, and extend the system. This is also true of many Lisp environments. It is unlikely that this form of reusability is going to happen in traditional industrial environments however. Beyond the obvious economical and psychological obstacles to source code dissemination, this technique does not support information hiding, an essential requirement for large-scale reuse.

Another form of reusability that is widely practiced in industry (some say the only one) is reusing personnel. By transferring software engineers from project to project, companies maintain know-how and ensure that previous experience is applied to new developments. This nontechnical approach to reusability is obviously limited in scope, if only because of the high turnover in the data processing professions.

Japanese software factories rely on the approach that designs, not implementations, should be reused. This technique may be viewed as an extension of the personnel approach, if you consider designs as formalized pieces of know-how.

But reuse of *design* does not appear to go much further than this idea. The very notion of designs as independent software products, having lives separate from those of the corresponding implementations, seems dubious. Perpetual consistency between design and code, which software engineering textbooks (rightly) promote as a desirable goal, is notoriously hard to maintain throughout the evolution of a software system. Thus, if only the design is reused, there is a strong risk of reusing incorrect or obsolete elements.

Background Reading

The first published discussion of reusability was most likely the contribution of M. D. McIlroy, "Mass-Produced Software Components," to the 1968 NATO conference on software engineering.

A particularly good source is the September 1984 issue of the *IEEE Transactions on Software Engineering*, especially the articles of Horowitz and Munson, Standish, Goguen, and Curry and Ayers. An important work not described in that issue is the MIT Programmer's Apprentice project, which relies on the notion of reusable plans and clichés (*IEEE Trans. Software Eng.*, Jan. 1987).

The proceedings of the First DoD-Industry Symposium on the STARS program (Nat'l Security Industry Assoc., 1985) contains several discussions of reusability from an industrial, Ada-oriented perspective.

Object-Oriented Languages

Other languages implement the concept of object-oriented programming with inheritance and would allow solutions to our airline reservation system example, in a manner similar to the one given here in Eiffel.

These include Simula, the father of all object-oriented languages, object-oriented expressions of C such as Objective C and C++; and an extension of Pascal, Object Pascal. These four languages, however, support only single inheritance. Other object-oriented languages include Smalltalk and extensions of Lisp such as Loops, Flavors, and Ceyx. The Clu language shares some of the properties of these languages, but does not offer inheritance.

In recent years, many languages have been added to the above list, mostly for exploratory programming and artificial intelligence purposes.

Bibliography

Birstwistle, G., *et al.* *Simula Begin.* Berlin: Studentliteratur and Auerbach Publishers, 1973.

Bobrow, D. G. , and M. J. Sefik. Loops: An object-oriented programming system for Interlisp. Xerox PARC, Palo Alto, Calif., 1982.

Booch, G. Object-oriented software development. *IEEE Trans. Software Eng.*, pp. 211–221, Feb. 1986.

Cannon, J. I. Flavors. MIT Artificial Intelligence Lab, Cambridge, Mass., 1980.

Cox, B. *Object-Oriented Programming: An Evolutionary Approach.* Reading, Mass.: Addison-Wesley, 1986.

Goldberg, A., and D. Robson. *Smalltalk-80: The Language and Its Implementation.* Reading, Mass.: Addison-Wesley, 1983.

Hulot, J.-H. Ceyx, version 15: 1—une initiation, Tech. report 44, INRIA, Paris, 1984.

Liskov, *et al.* *Clu Reference Manual.* Berlin and New York: Springer-Verlag, 1981.

Stroustrup, B. *The C++ Programming Language.* Menlo Park, Calif.: Addison-Wesley, 1986.

Tesler, L. Object Pascal report. *Structured Language World*, 1985.

More on Eiffel

The Eiffel language is part of an environment developed by the author and his colleagues at Interactive Software Engineering. It is accompanied by a design method, a library, and a set of supporting tools. It promotes reusability, extendibility, and software construction by a combination of flexible modules.

The Eiffel library provides the basic building blocks: a set of classes implementing some of the most important data structures and associated operations.

Inheritance plays a central role in this approach. The language supports multiple inheritance, used heavily in the basic library; we have found single inheritance to be insufficient. (Repeated inheritance, not described here, is also supported.) The use of inheritance is made safe and practical with renaming and redefinition techniques. Type parameterization (genericity) is also available.

Inheritance and genericity are powerful techniques for building reusable, extendible software. Their very power entails a risk of misuse. To enhance correctness and reliability, Eiffel includes primitives for systematic software construction: class and loop invariants, and routine preconditions and postconditions, all of which describe semantic constraints imposed on classes and their features.

These constraints (which may be monitored at run time to help in debugging) must be obeyed by any redefinition of the features in descendant classes, thus preserving the semantic consistency of descendants and helping to control the scope of the inheritance mechanism.

Eiffel is a typed language, where all type checking may be done statically. The language and method are intended for the development of sizable software systems; thus the implementation, which uses C as an intermediate language, emphasizes efficiency. Access to any feature of an object (as in a . f) always takes constant time, despite the possibilities for overloading provided by multiple inheritance, renaming, redefinition, and genericity (which imply that the version of f to be applied depends on the run time form of a). Also, the code for a routine is not duplicated in classes that inherit the routine, even in the presence of multiple inheritance and genericity.

Because the emphasis is on the incremental development of large systems, the Eiffel translator supports separate compilation, class by class. Automatic configuration management is provided, so that each needed module is always used in an up-to-date version (necessary recompilations, and these only, being automatically triggered by the system). The implementation includes a set of supporting tools, in particular for automatic memory management, execution tracing, symbolic debugging, and documentation. The implementation is currently available on Unix systems.

The language and method are described in "Eiffel: A Language and Environment for Software Engineering," to appear in the *Journal of Systems and Software*, and "Eiffel: Programming for Reusability and Extendibility," *SIGPlan Notices*, 1987.

A Table-Searching Module

It is impossible to give, in one article, a satisfactory solution to the problem of designing a general-purpose table-searching module. But we can outline how Eiffel would be applied to that case.

First, it is obvious that we are talking not just about a table-searching module, but about a module for table management. In fact, we are talking just about the table as an abstract data type with operations such as search, insert, delete, and so on.

As with STATE, the most general notion of table will be represented by a class with deferred routines. The various kinds of tables are descendants of this class. To obtain them, an in-depth analysis of the notion of table and its possible implementations is required. Such an analysis and the associated design and implementation effort are a considerable endeavor, especially as you realize that there is not a single notion of table, but a network of related notions.

The inheritance mechanism can help express the structure of this network and capture differences and similarities at the exact grain of detail required. For example, we may have a descendant of TABLE, SEQUENTIAL_TABLE, that covers tables stored sequentially in arrays, linked lists, or files, with a version of the function *search (x)*:

```
from
   restart
until
   off_limits or else current_value = x
invariant
   --x does not appear in the table before
         current position
loop
   move_forth
end;
if off_limits . . . (etc.)
```

The structure is similar to that of STATE, where the essential routine *do_one_state* was not deferred, but was expressed in terms of other deferred routines. In this case, *search* is not deferred but uses deferred routines for which the descendants of TABLE must provide implementations.

What's remarkable is that an entity *t* declared of type TABLE may dynamically refer to an object of any descendant type of TABLE; however, the call *t.search(x)* may be written without any knowledge of what kind of table implementation *t* will actually be at run time.

This approach captures—at the exact grain of detail required—the commonality within a family of implementations for the same data abstractions. A family will consist of a header class (SEQUENTIAL_TABLE) and specific descendants (ARRAY_TABLE). The inheritance graph may span more than one level. Features common to all members of the family (like Search for sequential tables) are concentrated at the header level and shared; features unique to various members are deferred in the header and expanded on in the individual members. The diagram that follows illustrates this inheritance structure.

Both genericity and multiple inheritance are essential to this problem's solution: All table classes take the type of table elements as a generic parameter, and several will combine two or more parent classes (BINARY_SEARCH_TREE from both BINARY_TREE and TABLE).

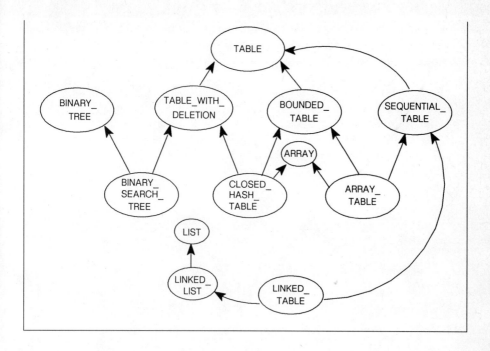

REFERENCES

Boehm, B. W. Software engineering—as it is. *Proc. Fourth Int'l Conf. Software Eng.*, pp. 11–21. Los Alamitos, Calif.: CS Press, 1979.

Dwyer, B. A user-friendly algorithm. *Comm. ACM*, pp. 556–561, Sept. 1981.

Jackson, M. A. *System Development.* Englewood Cliffs, N.J.: Prentice-Hall, 1983.

Jones, T. C. Reusability in programming: A survey of the state of the art. *IEEE Trans. Software Eng.*, pp. 488–494, Sept. 1984.

Lientz, P. P., and E. B. Swanson. Software maintenance: A user/management tug of war. *Data Management*, pp.26–30, April 1979.

Meyer, B. Vers un environnement conversationnel à deux dimensions. *Journées BIGRE*, Grenoble, France, pp. 27–39, Jan. 1982.

———. Towards a two-dimensional programming environment. *Proc. 1982 European Conf. Integrated Computer Syst.*, P. Degano and R. Sandewall, eds., pp. 167–179, Amsterdam: North-Holland, 1983.

———. M: A system description method. Tech. report TRCS 85-15, Computer Science Dept., University of California, Santa Barbara, May 1985.

———. Genericity versus inheritance. *Proc. ACM Conf. Object-oriented Programming Systems, Languages, and Applications*, pp. 391–405. New York: ACM. (Revised version to appear in *J. Pascal, Ada, and Modula-2.*)

CHAPTER 2

Synthesizing Programming Environments from Reusable Features

GAIL E. KAISER
Columbia University

DAVID GARLAN
Tektronix, Inc.

2.1 INTRODUCTION

The generation of programming environments is one of the more promising areas of software reusability research. The predominant method calls for the implementor to write a description of the desired programming language. The generator system then combines this with a language-independent kernel to produce a language-specific programming environment. The kernel provides the common facilities that are reused across all environments, including the user interface, the file system interface, invocation of programming tools, and manipulation of the internal representation of programs and auxiliary structures. The implementor provides the details of the programming language and any specialized programming tools. Representative examples of programming environment generators include the Synthesizer Generator [Reps and Teitelbaum, 1984], Gandalf [Habermann and Notkin, 1986],

Mentor [Donzeau-Gouge *et al.*, 1984], Pecan [Reiss, 1984] and PoeGen [Johnson and Fischer, 1982].

Unfortunately, such reusability is severely limited because only the language-independent kernel can be reused. The language-specific descriptions are invariably bound to linguistic and functional context—it is rare that parts of the descriptions can be reused to define different tools or environments for different programming languages. This is a serious problem, since language descriptions can be quite large. For example, the Gandalf Prototype—a C environment that supports module interface checking, version control, and system generation—was generated from a 17,000-line language description [Notkin, 1985]. (The kernel of the generation system is 33,000 lines.) In response to this problem, more and more functionality has been pushed into the kernel itself by adding support for symbol tables, memory management, debugging, and so forth. But this does not really solve the problem: It is unrealistic to expect any set of basic facilities to satisfy all needs for reusability. Further, the facilities incorporated in the kernel usually cannot be tailored to specific needs.

In this paper we show how the generation of programming environments can be extended to support much wider reusability. In particular, we present a notation, called MELD, that allows an implementor to compose an environment from a collection of descriptions, called features, each of which implements a basic unit of functionality. Implementors can encapsulate a set of facilities as a feature, reuse features across multiple environments, integrate features with other features, and tailor features to specific environments. The benefits of this approach are:

☐ An environment can be built from manageable, interacting, functional units;
☐ These units can be collected in libraries of reusable building blocks;
☐ These units provide appropriate boundaries of abstraction without limiting sharing of data among units.

Section 2.2 describes MELD as an extension of current notations for defining programming environments. An example of a small environment for programming-in-the-large [DeRemer and Kron, 1976] illustrates the use of reusable features in the synthesis of programming environments. Section 2.3 describes how MELD is used to write the tools provided by these features. An example then shows how tools (defined as features) can be integrated with the facilities defined by other features to produce a working programming environment. Section 2.4 describes the implementation of MELD, and Section 2.5 discusses related work. Although motivated by programming environments, our results extend well beyond these bounds. Indeed, as we argue in our concluding section, MELD supports an appropriate paradigm for constructing reusable building blocks for any software system.

2.2 FEATURES: AN EXAMPLE

We take as our starting point the automatic generation of programming environments from language descriptions. A typical environment generation system consists of two parts: a kernel and a translator. The kernel provides a collection of facilities that can be used across different environments: user interface, file system interface, help facilities, and so on. The translator transforms an environment description for a specific programming language into an internal representation that can be linked with the kernel to provide a programming environment for that language. The environment description also consists of two parts, describing the syntax and semantics, respectively, of the desired programming language. The first, an extended form of BNF [Backus, 1959], formally specifies the objects to be manipulated by the environment (procedures, statements, expressions, etc.). The second defines the tools provided by the environment (symbol resolution, type checking, code generation, and so on). The tools may be described declaratively using a notation such as attribute grammars [Reps, 1984; Johnson and Fischer, 1985] or procedurally using some programming language [Medina-Mora, 1982; Ambriola *et al.*, 1984].

If, for example, we want to generate an environment for Pascal [Jensen and Wirth, 1974] we would first produce a BNFlike description of Pascal syntax. We would then augment the syntax definition with a description of the tools needed in the environment. Typically these tools would perform static semantic checking, code generation, and so on. The combined environment description would then be given to the translator, which would turn these notations into a form that can be combined with the common kernel facilities to support an interactive programming environment for Pascal (Fig. 2.1).

A programming environment generator consists of a (reusable) translator and environment kernel. The translator transforms a programming environment description into a form that can be linked with the kernel to produce an executable environment.

FIGURE 2.1
AUTOMATIC GENERATION OF PROGRAMMING ENVIRONMENTS

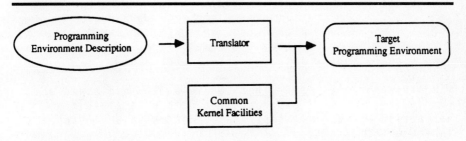

We diverge from existing approaches to environment generation in that we specify a programming environment not by one, but by a collection of descriptions called features. Each feature defines both syntax and semantics of a unit of functionality that can be incorporated into a variety of environments. Features are described using a new object-oriented notation called MELD. (The dictionary definition of *meld* is *melt + weld* or *to merge*. MELD also stands for Multiple Elucidations of Language Descriptions, suggested by David Barstow.) MELD extends existing notations for describing environments. In particular, it supports modularity and integration of separately defined facilities through multiple inheritance, and it provides a formal notation for describing tools. As we will now illustrate, together these extensions support reusability of functional units.

2.2.1 A Module Interconnection Language

Figure 2.2 shows a feature that defines a simple module interconnection language. The purpose of this description is to define the types of objects that might be manipulated in a small environment for programming in the large. In this case, the primary objects of interest are those of type (or class) MODULE.

Like all features, the Module Interconnection Language feature consists of an interface part and an implementation part. The interface lists a set of exports; these are the facilities defined by the feature and made available to other features. In this case the shorthand *all* is used, meaning all the facilities defined in the implementation part are exported. The interface also lists a

FIGURE 2.2
SIMPLE EXAMPLE FEATURE

```
Feature Module Interconnection Language
Interface:
    Exports all
    Imports Programming Language
Implementation:
    Class MODULE ::= name: identifier
                     imports: seq of identifier
                     exports: seq of SIGNATURE
                     body: IMPLEMENTATION
    End Feature Module Interconnection Language
```

MELD keywords are underlined, while built-in classes are in *italics*. ''::='' separates the name of a class from its definition while ''':'' separates the name of an instance variable from its type.

possibly empty set of imports; these are the other features whose exported facilities can be used within the implementation part. Here, the Programming Language feature (not shown) is imported.

The implementation part consists of one or more classes that define the abstract data types manipulated by the feature. In this case, the feature's implementation consists of one class: MODULE. A class is defined by a set of instance variables and set of methods. (Only the instance variables for MODULE are shown in the figure—methods are described later in Section 2.3.) Instance variables constitute the local data of objects defined by the class, while methods describe the behavior of tools that operate on the objects. (A MELD class corresponds to a *production* or *operator* in other environment description notations. Instance variables correspond to *components* or *children*, while methods correspond to *semantic equations* or *semantic routines*.) Each instance variable is typed. The type is either a primitive type (*identifier*, *integer*, *text*, and so on), another class, or else a collection such as *sequence* (an ordered list) or *set*.

In this example, the MODULE class defines four instance variables. The first, **name**, gives the name of the module. The next two are sequences. **Imports** lists the names of imported modules and **exports** lists the signatures of exported facilities. SIGNATURE is imported from the Programming Language feature, to define the type information for the various kinds of facilities (such as procedure, global variable, type, etc.). The fourth instance variable, **body**, gives the source code for the module; like SIGNATURE, IMPLEMENTATION is imported from Programming Language. (In general, the free variables in the implementation of a feature are assumed to be defined by its imported features.) In addition to what is shown here, the Module Interconnection Language might also contain methods that describe the operation of several tools, for example, to check interfaces between modules.

Comparing MELD, as described so far, with traditional programming environment descriptions, the most significant differences are that (a) MELD groups classes together into modular units (i.e., features) and (b) an interface defines the abstraction implemented by those classes. As we will now illustrate, these improvements make it possible to mix and match the Module Interconnection Language feature with other features to generate specific environments.

2.2.2 Make

Suppose we would like our example environment for programming in the large to consist of a programming language, a module interconnection language, and a system generation tool. We have already described the module interconnection language, and we will assume that the programming language is similarly described elsewhere. The system generation tool is based on the Unix Make utility [Feldman, 1979] for automatically compiling and linking as necessary to regenerate an executable system after source code changes. In a traditional environment generation system we would combine the programming language, the module interconnection language, and the system generation tool into a single language description (as in the Gandalf Prototype). This has the disadvantage that we could not then reuse parts of the description separately. Alternatively, we might include Make in the common kernel, allowing it to be reused across all environments. But then, as implementors of a particular environment, we could not tailor or extend the facility for that environment. Using MELD, however, we take a modular approach: We define an independent feature that can be incorporated into and tailored for any environment requiring Makelike facilities.

The Make feature (Fig. 2.3) describes the world from Make's point of view. Its world consists of a collection of manufacturing steps [Borison, 1986], each represented by a dependency unit (DEPUNIT class). A dependency unit consists of a list of the output entities whose manufacture depends on the listed input entities; in particular, applying the given command to the input entities produces the output entities. Each entity (ENTITY class) consists of a time at which it was produced and an origin (Fig. 2.4).

The type of ENTITY's origin is ORIGIN, which is defined as a MELD union type. A union type consists of a set of alternative types and represents a standard disjoint type union. (A MELD union corresponds to a *class* or *phyla* in other environment description notations.) It may be used as the type of an instance variable and may be exported from a feature. In this example,

FIGURE 2.3
MAKE FEATURE, WITH METHODS OMITTED

```
Feature Make
Interface:
     Exports  all
     Imports Time
Implementation:
     Class DEPUNIT ::= inputs:   seq  of ENTITY
                       outputs:  seq  of ENTITY
                       command: string
     Class ENTITY ::= time: TIMESTAMP
                      origin: ORIGIN
                      content:  any
     Union ORIGIN ::= DEPUNIT | PRIMITIVE
     Class PRIMITIVE ::=
End Feature Make
```

``|`` separates the alternative classes of a union. The PRIMITIVE class has no instance variables because it is an atomic value.

FIGURE 2.4
THE MAKE TOOL

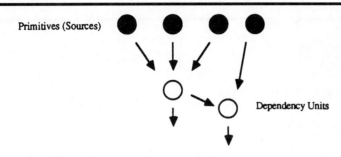

it indicates that an ORIGIN is either a dependency unit (if the entity was produced by applying a command to other entities) or else a primitive.

The system generation tool works as follows. When the Make command is issued by some external agent, such as the human user of the programming environment, Make checks each dependency unit to determine whether every output entity is up to date with respect to its input entity. If any input entity has a more recent timestamp than any one of its output entities, then the command string is applied to the inputs to rederive the outputs. This checking and command string application is done in such a way as to minimize computation. We present the methods that implement this behavior in Section 2.3, but first we explain how to integrate the Make feature with the Module Interconnection Language feature described earlier.

2.2.3 A System Modeler

Using MELD we generate specific programming environments by combining collections of reusable features in two ways. The first combination mechanism has already been illustrated; the Imports clause of a feature's interface part permits the feature's implementation part to refer to the types exported by the imported features. These types can be used to define the types of instance variables in classes and the alternative members of unions. The second combination mechanism is merging. Merging permits types of one feature to inherit instance variables and methods defined by the types of other imported features.

To illustrate merging, the System Modeler feature (Fig. 2.5) merges (1) the DEPUNIT and MODULE classes, (2) the ENTITY and IMPLEMENTA-TION classes, and (3) the ENTITY and OBJECTCODE classes (OBJECT-CODE as well as SYMBOLTABLE are imported from the Compiler feature, not shown). MODULE inherits from DEPUNIT, IMPLEMENTATION from ENTITY, and OBJECTCODE also from ENTITY. This means, for example,

FIGURE 2.5

SYSTEM MODELLER FEATURE MERGES MAKE AND MODULE
INTERCONNECTION LANGUAGE FEATURES

```
Feature System Modeler
Interface:
    Exports ...
    Imports Module Interconnection Language,
            Make, Compiler
Implementation:
    Merges
        Feature Module Interconnection Language
        Feature Make
            With DEPUNIT  As MODULE
                 ENTITY   As IMPLEMENTATION
                 ENTITY   As OBJECTCODE
        Class MODULE ::= objcode: OBJECTCODE
                         symtab: SYMBOLTABLE
End Feature System Modeler
```

that the MODULE class consists of all the instance variables and methods defined by the DEPUNIT class (imported from Make) as well as by the MODULE class (imported from Module Interconnection Language). Further, the MODULE class also consists of all the additional facilities, in this case the **objcode** and **symtab** instance variables, added by the Merges clause of the System Modeler feature. No additional facilities are defined here for IMPLE-MENTATION or OBJECTCODE.

Together, the Imports clause and the Merges Clause support synthesis of programming environments from reusable features. The Imports clause permits independently developed types (classes and unions) to contribute to the definitions of new types by implementing the types of instance variables (including their internal representations and operations). Thus Imports supports reuse through data abstraction in the same fashion as Ada packages [US Defense Dept., 1983], Modula-2 modules [Wirth, 1985], Clu clusters [Liskov *et al.*, 1978], and so on. The Merges clause permits independently developed classes and unions to be extended with new instance variables and methods. Thus Merges supports reuse through multiple inheritance in the same fashion as Flavors [Moon, 1986], Loops [Stefik and Bobrow, 1986], Trellis/Owl [Schaffert *et al.*, 1986] and other object-oriented languages.

Neither modularization nor inheritance is, of course, novel in itself. However, no other environment description notation supports both importing and merging. Many existing programming languages support either strict modular interfaces or inheritance, but none combines them. The Flavors language is closest to our approach; it supports multiple inheritance through mixins and separate development-through packages. However, Flavors package interfaces are not strict; facilities internal to one package can in fact be used in any other package if the reference to the facility is qualified by the name of its home package. Further, inherited mixins cannot be fully encapsulated because of potential interactions among multiple methods with the same name or among multiple methods that access and/or modify the same instance variables. The first problem is solved by MELD's features, and the second by MELD's notation for writing methods.

2.3 METHODS

Figures 2.6 and 2.7 contain methods that implement Makelike facilities. The details of these methods are not essential for an initial understanding of MELD. It suffices to appreciate that they define the operation of system generation, that they are automatically evaluated as needed, and that other features merged with the Make feature do not have to be concerned with these methods or their operation.

FIGURE 2.6
METHODS FOR DEPENDENCY UNIT

```
Class DEPUNIT ::= ...
    Methods:
    MAKE -->
        Send MAKE To inputs[all]
        If Min(outputs[all].time) < Max(inputs[all].time)
        Then Send APPLY To self
    APPLY -->
        outputs[all].origin := self
        default outputs := Apply(command, inputs)

"-->" attaches the name of a method to the equations that
define its implementation.
```

FIGURE 2.7
METHODS FOR ENTITIES

```
Class ENTITY ::= ...
    Methods:
    MAKE --> If TypeOf(origin) <> ''PRIMITIVE''
             Then Send MAKE To origin
    time := content Return Now()
```

As we will show, these properties are made possible because MELD methods are written as systems of equations rather than as routines consisting of sequences of statements. If routines were used, it would be necessary for the implementor to understand the details of the routines provided by all the merged features in order to correctly order their invocations. In contrast, equations are evaluated in nondeterministic order, or in parallel, except in the case where there are dependencies among the equations. In particular, each equation that computes a value used in the evaluation of another equation is automatically evaluated before the other equation.

In this section, we first present the MELD methods that implement the behavior of the Make feature, defined above, and then show how tools written as equations can be tailored to the particular environment by augmenting the set of methods and by overriding default methods. The following section briefly explains the algorithms required for MELD's implementation. These two sections require more technical sophistication than the rest of the paper, and the reader may want to skip to Section 2.5 on first reading.

2.3.1 Methods for Make

Our notation for methods is called action equations [Kaiser, 1986]. Action equations are an extension of attribute grammars [Knuth, 1968], which have been applied successfully to compiler-compilers [Farrow, 1984; Ganzinger *et al.*, 1977] and to generation of programming environments [Reps and Teitelbaum, 1984; Johnson and Fischer, 1982]. While attribute grammars support type checking, code generation, and other programming tools that inspect the source code, action equations can also define dynamic, interactive tools such as interpreters, debuggers, and run-time support.

Figure 2.6 associates two methods with the DEPUNIT class, MAKE and APPLY. Each of these methods consists of two equations. The first equation for MAKE is a send equation; it sends a message to one or more destination objects. This equation sends the MAKE message to every member of the sequence of inputs, where it is propagated to every input that transitively contributes to the desired output. The second equation is a conditional. A conditional checks whether a certain condition is true or false; depending on the result, an equation may be activated to display an error, correct a problem, and so on. This conditional detects when an input entity of a dependency unit is more recent than an output entity, and it sends the APPLY message to rederive the output entities.

The two equations for the APPLY method are assignments. The left-hand side addresses an object, while the right-hand side is an arbitrary expression. The first equation sets the origin of each of the resulting outputs to the corresponding DEPUNIT object. The second sets the value of the outputs to the result of calling the *Apply* function (which should not be confused with the APPLY method) with the command string and its input arguments. The equations in a method are evaluated only once when the corresponding message is received. However, the inputs to each equation must be calculated before the equation can be evaluated. In this case, the first equation depends on the second because the origin of an output entity cannot be set until the output itself is available; thus the kernel automatically evaluates the second equation before the first when the APPLY message is received by a DEPUNIT object.

Notice that the second assignment is qualified with the keyword *default*. This means that it can be overridden by another assignment with the same left-hand side; we will explain this in the next section.

The ENTITY class has two methods, shown in Fig. 2.7. The conditional is activated by the MAKE message. It checks whether the entity is primitive. If not, it propagates MAKE to the originating dependency unit to rederive the entity. The second method is a special kind of method that is not attached to a message name. This method is called a constraint. It constrains its left-hand side to always denote the value represented by its right-hand side; the kernel automatically reevaluates the constraint whenever an argument to the right-hand side changes, in order to update the left-hand side. In this case, **time** is updated to the current time whenever **content** changes in value. **Content** is a pseudo-input to **time** that is not actually used in the computation, except to enforce that the Now function returns the current time exactly when **content** changes in value.

When the user gives the Make command, the System Modeler feature works as follows: The kernel sends the MAKE message to each module, activating the corresponding methods. In this example, the only MAKE method is defined by the DEPUNIT class, which is merged with the MODULE class in the System Modeler feature. This method propagates MAKE through the chain of outputs and inputs until arriving at primitive source objects (i.e., the implementation of each module). In each case where the module's implementation is more recent than the module's object code, the object code is rederived.

Note that the Make feature is completely generic and thus reusable; in particular, it does not know anything about modules, implementations, or object code. The Make feature could be merged with other features that define completely different input and output entities. For example, we could merge input entities with some internal representation of arbitrary data structures and output entities with the windows that display these data structures. Then the same methods provided by the Make feature would respond to the Make command by updating the windows for exactly those data structures that changed.

2.3.2 Tool Tailoring

The System Modeler feature (see Fig. 2.5) adds the **objcode** and **symtab** instance variables to the MODULE class, as places to save the corresponding object code and symbol table, respectively. It is also necessary to add methods

FIGURE 2.8
METHODS THAT AUGMENT MODULE'S BEHAVIOR

```
Class MODULE ::= ...
   Methods:
   inputs[1] := body
   inputs[2,..] := imports[all]
   command := ''Compile''
   objcode := outputs[1]
   symtab := outputs[2]
```

The instance variables for MODULE are omitted here. Let
i,.. indicate the *i*th and all following members of the
sequence. Literal strings are between double quotes.

that specify how the facilities inherited from the Make feature are used in this context—in particular, source code is compiled to produce object code. The System Modeler feature associates five new methods with the MODULE class (Fig. 2.8). The first and second methods are constraints that maintain the **inputs** instance variable to consist of the module's implementation and imports, respectively. The third method sets the **command** to Compile; the Compile command is implemented by equations (not shown) defined in the Compiler feature. The fourth method constrains the new **objcode** instance variable to be the same as the first element of **outputs**; that is, the object code for the module is the first of the output entities produced by applying the Make command to the module. Similarly, the fifth method sets the new **symtab** instance variable to be the second output.

Suppose we would like to override, rather than augment, part of the Make tool. Our goal is to modify Make's processing to implement smart recompilation [Tichy, 1986]. Smart recompilation refines the granularity of dependency. In the original Make (on Unix), all the outputs of dependency units depend on all the inputs; we would now like to consider the language-specific dependencies among the source code symbols (e.g., procedure, type, and variable names) defined within the input modules. Consider the case where a module M imports a module N. Using the Make feature as originally defined, M is a dependency unit that depends on N; this means that whenever N's interface changes, M's object code must be rederived. A smart recompilation strategy would keep track of the particular facilities exported by N that are actually used by M. Say N exports procedures p and q, and M uses only p. Then if N changes only to the extent that procedure q is modified, it is not necessary to recompile M.

We would like to incorporate this new notion of Make, but only with respect to the System Modeler feature, and thus to any programming environ-

FIGURE 2.9
METHODS THAT OVERRIDE MODULE'S BEHAVIOR

```
Class MODULE ::= ...
     Methods:
     APPLY -->
          outputs := Smart(command, inputs)
```

ments that incorporate the System Modeler. We do not want to change the Make feature itself, because that would affect all current and potential applications of Make facilities. Instead, the System Modeler feature implements this change by overriding the default part of the Make feature's APPLY method (see Fig. 2.6). This is done by adding a new equation to the System Modeler feature (Fig. 2.9); notice it has the same left-hand side **outputs** as the default equation. Since MODULE has been merged with DEPUNIT, it inherits all the equations defined for DEPUNIT in the Make feature, including the default assignment. However, this new equation overrides the default equation, removing it from consideration during the kernel's ordering of equation evaluation. The difference is that the new equation calls the Smart function, whereas the default equation calls Apply. Smart is defined by a set of equations (not shown) that apply the compilation command only if the symbol tables for the input entities actually reference those source code symbols that have changed since the previous compilation.

2.4 IMPLEMENTATION

An early version of MELD has been implemented for MacGnome [Chandhok, et al., 1985], a Macintosh Pascal environment to be marketed commercially. Routines rather than equations describe behavior, and merging of data structures is not supported. This implementation demonstrates the practicality of merging alternative display descriptions [Garlan, 1985]. The Gandalf project designed a variant of MELD called Janus [Habermann, et al., 1988] that supports multiple views of shared data structures. Parallel evaluation of attribute equations has been implemented as part of Mercury [Kaiser, Kaplan, and Micallef, 1987], a system for generating multiple-user distributed programming environments. The MELD data modeling sublanguage has been implemented as part of the Marvel Strategy Language [Kaiser, 1988a], a process modeling language for realizing intelligent assistance within programming environments. While work on Janus, Mercury, and Marvel progressed, MELD itself evolved into a general purpose programming language [Kaiser and Garlan, 1987a, 1987b, 1987c, 1987d]. The most complete implementation of MELD is as a concurrent language, with small-granularity pseudoparallelism provided by the dataflow within methods and large-granularity parallelism provided by message passing among distributed objects.

Full implementation of MELD involves translation of structural descriptions and action equations, plus run-time support. Each synthesized data structure consists of one or more facets, one for each of the classes from different features that have been merged together into one class. In general, only facets defined in the same feature are visible to methods, and facets of the same object from different features might even reside on different machines. Structural descriptions translate easily into corresponding data types. For instance, each object could be represented by a record, where each field is an instance variable or a pointer to an instance variable (depending on its type). The difficulty arises in maintaining connections and consistency among the various facets of an object; auxiliary equations are generated to update certain facets in response to changes in other facets.

The equations for a synthesized data structure are grouped together and a local dependency graph is produced to represent all the equations that are associated with the same message. The vertices represent equations and the edges represent dependencies among the inputs and outputs of equations. Another graph represents all constraints (for the same synthesized type) that are not attached to any message. The kernel orders the evaluation of equations according to these graphs. Each individual equation is translated into an evaluation procedure that takes advantage of the implementation-language facilities as well as the kernel primitives.

The kernel provides the primitives used by tools for creating, destroying, and moving among objects. It also sends the messages defined in the features by selecting the corresponding local dependency graphs. The kernel's most important job is ordering evaluation of equations. It uses an adaptation of Reps's incremental attribute evaluation algorithm [Reps, 1984], which generates language-based editors from attribute grammars. The local dependency graphs are combined into a composite dependency graph at run time to reflect the actual connections among objects and facets of objects. The composition considers only the graphs for the current message(s) and those not specific to any message. The graph is sorted topologically to order the evaluation of equations. This algorithm is asymptotically optimal—linear in the number of affected objects. Algorithm details and further complexity results are given in Garlan's and Kaiser's dissertations [Garlan, 1987a; Kaiser, 1985].

2.5 RELATED WORK

Our approach both extends and unifies work from five major areas: structure-oriented environments, interface-description languages, object-oriented programming, abstract data types, and specification languages.

Structure-Oriented Environments. We use the term *structure-oriented envi-ronment* synonymously with *language-based editor, structure editor-based environ-ment, syntax-directed editor,* and so forth. Our work extends current research in this area by synthesizing the language description used to generate an environment from reusable building blocks. In our examples, MELD extends the notation used for the Display Oriented Structure Editor (DOSE) system [Kaiser, 1988b]. Generation of structure-oriented environments in turn builds on compiler-compilers such as Yacc [Johnson and Lesk, 1978]. Our results apply directly to these areas, since features are not specific to any particular formal notation for syntax description. However, in order for independently developed tools to merge automatically, they must be described using equa-tions or some similar declarative notation rather than routines; otherwise, the implementor of the structure-oriented environment is forced to combine the routines by hand.

Interface Description Language. *Interface description language* (IDL) [Lamb, 1987] is a formal notation for defining the data structures passed among tools; it grew out of research on the PQCC compiler-compiler [Leverett *et al.*, 1979]. IDL has been extended to support tight integration among tools while still supporting reuse of tools [Snodgrass and Shannon, 1986]. Tool behavior is implemented by separately defined routines, permitting only sequential processing of data by tools. In contrast, MELD supports inter-leaved operation by defining tools by equations, where the processing of different tools is automatically interleaved—for example, if an equation for one tool depends on an equation for another tool, which in turn depends on another equation for the first tool. Further discussion of the relationship between MELD and IDL appears elsewhere [Garlan, 1987b; Feiler, 1987].

Object-Oriented Programming. Other than structure-oriented environ-ments and IDL, our results are closest to *object-oriented programming.* As we have discussed (see Section 2.2.3), the MELD Merges clause, the glue that binds features together, is similar to the multiple inheritance of object-oriented programming languages. The most significant difference between merging and existing forms of multiple inheritance is that merging in MELD does not require the implementor to deal with the interactions among sep-arately defined merged methods; this is possible because the methods are described by equations that are evaluated in the order implied by their dependencies, rather than by routines that must be invoked in some explicit order.

Abstract Data Types. Features resemble the encapsulated *abstract data types* of modern programming languages [Shaw, 1984]. Features are strongly typed, with an interface and an implementation; they are similarly motivated (decomposability, abstraction, information hiding, protection, etc.). However, abstract data types do not by themselves lead to a high degree of reusability since (a) they are language-dependent and (b) they can be tailored to a particular context in limited ways—specifically, the subtypes of generic modules in Ada can be instantiated by each client. Features, on the other hand, are language-independent. While our notation is itself a language, descriptions of features written in that notation are translated during the environment generation process into some specific executable language (e.g., Pascal). As we have seen, features also permit a high degree of specialization by their clients with respect to both the data structure and the operations.

Specification Languages. Some *specification languages*, notably Clear [Burstall and Goguen, 1977], OBJ [Goguen, 1983], and Larch [Guttag, *et al.*, 1985], support composition of distinct functionalities in the style of multiple inheritance. However, these languages are oriented toward verification and cannot yet support completely automated translation to an efficient executable form. More significantly, they frequently specify data implicitly, and thus cannot describe data sharing.

2.6   REUSABILITY REVISITED

Current approaches to software reuse have had relatively little effect on software engineering practice. Subroutine libraries have had the most success. However, subroutine libraries and most other existing approaches are strongly tied to linguistic and/or functional context. A software building block can be reused only as the original programmer envisioned. A generic stack module in Ada manipulates only Ada stacks. A window manager manages only windows.

There are three important prerequisites to achieving an order of magnitude improvement in software production through reuse: (1) language independence, (2) component reuse through composition, and (3) reuse of components in ways not anticipated by the original programmer. For example, we would like to reuse a window manager as a file system written in a different programming language. We believe this is realistic. A window manager creates and destroys windows, moves windows, defines subwindows, and reads/writes windows; a file system creates and destroys files, renames files, includes files in directories, and reads/writes files. The structures of the two programs are very likely similar, although the devices and implementation languages may be quite different.

Our goal is to support this degree of reusability without sacrificing previously written software. Our approach is broadly based on a framework (suggested to us by Nico Habermann) where software building blocks can be transformed between two forms: programs and language-independent descriptions. Old code is in a particular programming language, but new software could often be written as a language-independent description.

Unfortunately, no language-independent notation has yet achieved widespread acceptance; we cannot transform automatically from programming languages to such a notation, and we cannot transform automatically back to the desired implementation language. All three problems must be solved.

We believe that MELD represents a significant step toward solving the first and third problems. This claim derives in part from Notkin's results [Notkin, 1984]. He applied environment generation technology to generate a wide variety of integrated systems from language descriptions, including mail systems and document formatters; we are in the process of extending his results by applying reusable features to synthesis of arbitrary systems [Garlan, 1988]. More concretely, our confidence in the generality of features comes from our design of numerous reusable features for programming environments, including a memory manager [Kaiser and Garlan, 1987c], a configuration manager, and a module interconnection language with intermodule consistency checking [Garlan, 1986] and incremental recompilation, interpretation, and language-oriented debugging facilities [Kaiser, 1986].

This research contributes directly to synthesis of programming environments from reusable building blocks. We can now describe abstract units of functionality as features, define features in terms of other features, and combine features with other features that specify both separate and shared subparts and distinct tools that operate on the same objects. We can further compose synthesized features to generage arbitrarily complex programming environments incorporating specially tailored programming tools.

ACKNOWLEDGMENTS

Yael Cycowicz, Dannie Durand, Charlie Krueger, David Miller, and Benjamin Pierce read drafts of this paper and made useful criticisms and suggestions. We would also like to thank Nico Habermann and Mark Tucker for motivating our interest in reusable software.

Kaiser is supported by National Science Foundation grants CCR-8858029 and CCR-8802741, by grants from AT&T, DEC, IBM, Siemens, Sun and Xerox, by the Center for Advanced Technology and by the Center for Telecommunications Research. When this research was conducted, Garlan was a member of the Gandalf project at Carnegie Mellon University and supported in part by the United States Army, Software Technology Development Division of CECOM COMM/ADP, Fort Monmouth, N. J., and in part by ZTI-SOF of Siemens Corporation, Munich, Germany.

The authors' full addresses are as follows: Prof. Gail E. Kaiser, Columbia University, Department of Computer Science, 450 Computer Science Building, New York, NY 10027, ArpaNet: Kaiser @columbia.edu. Dr. David Garlan, Computer Research Lab, Tektronix, Inc., P. O. Box 500, MS 50-662, Beaverton, OR 97077, CSNet: Garlan @crl. tek. com.

REFERENCES

Ambriola, V.; Kaiser, G. E.; and Ellison, R. J. An action routine model for ALOE. Technical Report CMU-CS-84-156, Carnegie Mellon University Department of Computer Science, Pittsburgh, Pa. August 1984.

Backus, J. W. The syntax and semantics of the proposed international algebraic language of the Zurich ACM-GAMM conference. In *International Conference on Information Processing*, 1959.

Borison, E. A model of software manufacture. In Lecture Notes in Computer Science. Volume 244: *Advanced Programming Environments*. Conradi, R., Didriksen, T. M., and Wanvik, D. H. (eds.) Springer-Verlag, Berlin, 1986.

Burstall, R. M., and Goguen, J. A. Putting theories together to make specifications. In *Fifth International Joint Conference on Artificial Intelligence*, p. 1045. Cambridge, Mass., 1977.

Chandhok, R.; Garlan, D. B.; Goldenson, D.; Miller, P. L.; and Tucker, M. Programming environments based on structure editing: the Gnome approach. In Wojcik, A. S. (ed.), *1985 National Computer Conference*, p. 359. AFIPS, Chicago, Ill., July 1985.

DeRemer, F., and Kron, H. H. Programming-in-the-large versus programming-in-the-small. *IEEE Transactions on Software Engineering* SE-2(2), June 1976.

Donzeau-Gouge, V.; Huet, G.; Kahn, G.; and Lang, B. Programming environments based on structured editors: the Mentor experience. In *Interactive Programming Environments*. McGraw-Hill Book Co., New York, N. Y., 1984.

Farrow, R. Generating a production compiler from an attribute grammar. *IEEE Software* 1(4), October 1984.

Feiler, P. H. Relationship between IDL and structure editor technology. *SIGPLAN Notices* 22(11):87, November 1987.

Feldman, S. I. Make a program for maintaining computer programs. *Software–Practice & Experience* 9(4), April 1979.

Ganzinger, H.; Ripken, K.; and Wilhelm, R. Automatic generation of optimizing multipass compilers. In *Information Processing 77*, p. 535. North-Holland Pub. Co., New York, N. Y., 1977.

Garlan, D. Flexible unparsing in a structure editing environment. Technical Report CMU-CS-85-129, Carnegie Mellon University Department of Computer Science, Pittsburgh, Pa. , April 1985.

———. Views for tools in integrated environments. In Lecture Notes in Computer Science. Volume 244: *Advanced Programming Environments*. Conradi, R., Didriksen, T. M., and Wanvik, D. H. (ed.) Springer-Verlag, Berlin, 1986.

————. Views for tools in integrated environments. Ph.D. thesis, Technical Report CMU-CS-87-147. Carnegie Mellon University Department of Computer Science, May 1987a.

————. Extending IDL to support concurrent views. *SIGPLAN Notices* 22(11):95, November 1987b.

Garlan, D.; Kaiser, G. E.; and Notkin, D. *On the Criteria To Be Used In Composing Tools Into Systems.* Technical Report TR 88-08-09, University of Washington Department of Computer Science, August, 1988.

Goguen, J. Parameterized programming. In *Workship on Reusability in Programming*, p. 138. Newport, R. I., September 1983.

Guttag, J. V.; Horning, J. J.; and Wing, J. M. The Larch family of specification languages. *IEEE Software* 2(5):24, September 1985.

Habermann, A. N., and Notkin, D. Gandalf: software development environments. *IEEE Transactions on Software Engineering* SE-12(12), December 1986.

Habermann, A. N.; Krueger, C.; Pierce, B.; Staudt, B.; and Wenn, J. Programming with views. Technical Report CMU-CS-87-177, Carnegie Mellon University Department of Computer Science, Pittsburgh, Pa., January 1988.

Jensen, K., and Wirth, N. *Pascal User Manual and Report.* Springer-Verlag, New York, N. Y. 1974.

Johnson, G. F., and Fischer, C. N. Non-syntactic attribute flow in language based editors. In *Ninth Annual ACM Symposium on Principles of Programming Languages.* January 1982.

Johnson, G. F., and Fischer, C. N. A meta-language and system for nonlocal incremental attribute evaluation in language-based editors. In *Twelfth Annual ACM Symposium on Principles of Programming Languages.* New Orleans, La., January 1985.

Johnson, S. C., and Lesk, M. E. Language development tools. *The Bell System Technical Journal* 57(6):2155, July-August 1978.

Kaiser, G. E. Semantics of structure editing environments. Ph.D. thesis, Technical Report CMU–CS–85–131. Carnegie Mellon University Department of Computer Science, May 1985.

————. Generation of run-time environments. Presented at SIGPlan '86 Symposium on Compiler Construction, Palo Alto, Calif., June 1986. Proceedings published as *SIGPLAN Notices*, 21(7), July 1986.

Kaiser, G. E.; Barghouti, N. S.; Feiler, P. H.; and Schwanke, R. W. Database support for knowledge-based engineering environments. *IEEE Expert* 3(2):18–32, Summer, 1988.

Kaiser, G. E.; Feiler, P. H.; Jalili, F.; and Schlichter, J. H. A Retrospective on DOSE: an interpretive approach to structure editor generation. *Software—Practice & Experience* 18(8):733-748, August, 1988.

Kaiser, G. E., and Garlan, D. Composing software systems from reusable building blocks. In *Twentieth Annual Hawaii International Conference on System Sciences*, p. 536. Kona, Hawaii, January 1987a.

————. Meld: a declarative notation for writing methods. In *Sixth Annual International Phoenix Conference on Computers and Communications*, p. 280. Scottsdale, Ariz., February 1987b.

————. Melding software systems from reusable building blocks. *IEEE Software*:17, July 1987c.

————. Melding data flow and object-oriented programming. Presented at Object-Oriented Programming Systems, Languages, and Applications Conference, Kissimmee, Fla., October 1987d. Proceedings published as *SIGPLAN Notices*, 22(12), December 1987.

Kaiser, G. E.; Kaplan, S. M.; and Micallef, J. Multiuser, distributed language-based environments. *IEEE Software*:58, November 1987.

Knuth, D. E. Semantics of context-free languages. *Mathematical Systems Theory* 2(2), June 1968.

Lamb, D. A. IDL: sharing intermediate representations. *ACM Transactions on Programming Languages and Systems* 9(3):297, July 1987.

Leverett, B. W.; Cattell, R. G. G.; Hobbs, S. O.; Newcomer, J. M.; Reiner, A. H.; Schatz, B. R.; and Wulf, W. A. *An overview of the production quality compiler-compiler project.* Technical Report CMU-CS-79-105, Carnegie Mellon University, Department of Computer Science, Pittsburgh Pa., 1979.

Liskov, B.; Moss, E.; Schaffert, C.; Scheifler, B.; and Snyder, A. *Clu Reference Manual.* Technical Report Memo 161, MIT Laboratory for Computer Science, Computations Structures Group, Cambridge, Mass., July 1978. Draft.

Medina-Mora, R. Syntax-Directed Editing: Towards Integrated Programming Environments. Ph.D. thesis, Carnegie Mellon University Department of Computer Science, March 1982.

Moon, D. A. Object-oriented programming with Flavors. Presented at Object-Oriented Systems, Languages, and Applications Conference, Portland, Oregon, September, 1986. Proceedings published as *SIGPLAN Notices*, 21(11), November 1986.

Notkin, D. S. Interactive structure-oriented computing. Ph.D. thesis, Technical Report CMU-CS-84-103. Carnegie Mellon University Department of Computer Science, February 1984.

Notkin, D. The Gandalf project. *The Journal of Systems and Software* 5(2), May 1985.

Reiss, S. P. Graphical program development with Pecan program development systems. Presented at SIGSoft/SIGPlan Software Engineering Symposium on Practical Software Development Environments, Pittsburgh, Pa., April 1984. Proceedings published as *SIGPLAN Notices*, 19(5), May 1984.

Reps, T., and Teitelbaum, T. The Synthesizer Generator. Presented at SIGSoft/SIGPlan Software Engineering Symposium on Practical Software Development Environments, Pittsburgh, Pa., April 1984. Proceedings published as *SIGPLAN Notices*, 19(5), May 1984.

Reps, T. *Generating Language-Based Environments.* The M.I.T. Press, Cambridge, Mass., 1984.

Schaffert, C.; Cooper, T.; Bullis, B.; Kilian, M.; and Wilpolt, C. An introduction to Trellis Owl. In *Object-Oriented Systems, Languages, and Applications Conference*, pp. 9–16. Portland, Oreg., September 1986. Proceedings published as *SIGPLAN Notices*, 21(11), November 1986.

Shaw, M. Abstraction techniques in modern programming languages. *IEEE Software* 1(4):10, October 1984.

Snodgrass, R., and Shannon, K. Supporting flexible and efficient tool integration. In Lecture Notes in Computer Science. Volume 244: *Advanced Programming Environments*, Conradi, R., Didriksen, T. M., and Wanvik, D. H. (eds.) p. 290. Springer-Verlag, Berlin, 1986.

Stefik, M., and Bobrow, D. G. Object-oriented programming: themes and variations. *AI Magazine* 6(4):40, Winter 1986.

Tichy, W. F. Smart recompilation. *ACM Transactions on Programming Languages and Systems* 8(3):273, July 1986.

United States Department of Defense. *Reference Manual for the Ada Programming Language*. ANSI/Military standard MIL-STD-1815A, 1983.

Wirth, N. *Programming in Modula-2*. Springer-Verlag, New York, N. Y., 1985.

CHAPTER 3

DESIGN REUSE AND FRAMEWORKS IN THE SMALLTALK-80 SYSTEM

L. PETER DEUTSCH
ParcPlace Systems

The Smalltalk-80 (TM) interactive programming system supports a type of reuse that is unique to the object-oriented approach: reuse of design through frameworks of partially completed code. A framework binds certain choices about state partitioning and control flow; the (re)user completes or extends the framework to produce an actual application. This paper compares the framework approach to the code-based and documentation-based reuse available in traditional languages.

3.1 INTRODUCTION

The Smalltalk-80 (TM) interactive programming system supports four different kinds of reuse:

1. The Smalltalk-80 language (henceforth abbreviated *ST80*) includes a powerful form of data abstraction allowing reuse of algorithms across a variety of data structures.
2. Built-in facilities of the Smalltalk-80 system include many building blocks and conventions for implementing interactive applications (reuse of a framework across applications).

57

3. The Smalltalk-80 programming tools can be reapplied to programming in other languages, within the context of the Smalltalk-80 system.

4. Finally, the Smalltalk-80 system is designed to be entirely portable to a variety of machines with modest effort, allowing reuse of the complete system across hardware environments.

In a previous paper [Deutsch, 1987], we characterized each of these kinds of reuse in more detail. In this paper, we focus specifically on framework reuse, which distinguishes object-oriented systems in general and the Smalltalk-80 system in particular from procedural, module-oriented languages such as Ada (TM).

For those unfamiliar with the Smalltalk-80 language, the Appendix contains a synopsis; Goldberg and Robson [1983] provide a description. The Appendix should be sufficient for readers acquainted with the basic concepts of object-oriented programming (classes, instances, messages, and inheritance) to follow the discussion and examples.

The class hierarchies, message protocols, and code examples (including comments and other documentation) in this paper are drawn from the Smalltalk-80 Virtual Image versions 2.2 and 2.4, copyright 1987 and 1988 respectively by ParcPlace Systems, Inc., and reprinted here by permission.

3.2 SOFTWARE REUSE

What does it mean to reuse something? Fundamentally, it means that another act of using occurs in which something is the same as in a prior act (specifically, some part of what is being used) but in which something is also different than in the prior act. Confining our attention to the software world and (for the most part) to artifacts rather than human processes, we observe that two fundamental things get reused: code and specification (or interface). Reusing code means that the code stays the same and only the client changes. Reusing an interface, however, allows the client code, the implementation code, or both to change. We believe that interface design and functional factoring constitute the key intellectual content of software and that they are far more difficult to create or re-create than code. For these reasons, we see the reuse of interfaces and factoring as the critical problem in software reuse.

In conventional languages, the modality of reuse is the procedural interface. A procedural interface typically consists of a set of procedure names, together with their argument and result types, and some documentation. It permits the same (or equivalent) code to be reused by many clients. Note that some of the reused interface has direct operational meaning to the computer (the names, for a linker, and the types, for a compiler); some of the interface (the documentation) has meaning only for human readers.

In a conventional language, there is a strong linkage between the client/service relationship, encapsulation, and the caller/callee relationship. In particular, the following are essentially equivalent:

☐ *X* is a client of *Y*;

☐ *X* has no access to the implementation of *Y*;

☐ *X* calls routines in *Y*.

The interface that is reused is fully opaque and is essentially a caller/callee interface. In these respects, Ada is no different from its predecessors that included data abstraction: even though a reused interface contains types and parametric values as well as procedures, the three relationships still coincide.

In object-oriented design, the relationship between system components is potentially richer than the simple caller/callee relationship of procedure libraries. In particular, clients may build on existing designs in the following ways:

☐ A client may instantiate an existing class *YC* to produce a new object *Y*, and interact with *Y* by sending messages to it. This is similar to using a library package in a procedural language.

☐ A client may supply an instance *X* of one of its own classes as a parameter to an existing object *Y*, in the expectation that *Y* will send agreed-upon messages to *X*. In this case, we call *Y* the framework and the client an internal client, to distinguish it from external clients that instantiate and interact with the combination. In procedural languages, this is similar to procedure parameters or some cases of call-by-name. While these techniques are available in many procedural languages, they are often awkward (e.g., C and Pascal provide no mechanism for writing anonymous procedures in-line) and are usually regarded as specialized and exceptional.

☐ A client may define a subclass *XC* of an existing class *YC*, supplying additional or specialized functionality. Again, we call the existing class the framework and the client an internal client. From a design perspective, this is probably the most important type of reuse, since it allows for selective reuse of design with corresponding reuse of implementation. The only analogue in the procedural world is the use of cascaded libraries at link time. For example, consider a client *X* that uses a procedure *P* in library *L*, and another library *M* that wants to supply a new definition for *P* that supercedes (but may use) the one in *L*. Some linkers, given these modules in the order *X*, *M*, *L*, will link *X*'s references to *P* to the definition in *M*, and *M*'s references to *P* to the definition in *L*. However, the semantics of linkers are notoriously variable and fall outside the definition of the programming language.

It is the latter two types of reuse that are of interest in the remainder of this paper, since the first is the same as the kind of library reuse found in conventional languages.

As a preface to examining object-oriented design reuse, we observe that there are three interesting interfaces involved in a framework structure:

1. The interface that the reused framework supplies to its external clients (instantiators). The framework defines this interface, which is constant across all reuses of the framework. We call this the *framework external interface* (FEI).
2. The interface between the framework and its internal clients (subclasses or parametrizers.) We often speak of this interface as a set of constraints on the subclass code or parameter object's protocol. Again, the framework defines this interface, which stays the same across reuse. We call this the *framework internal interface* (FII).
3. The interface that the combination of the framework and the internal client supplies to external clients of the result. This consists of the FEI plus any additional external messages implemented by the internal client, and it is different for each such client. We call this the *resulting interface* (RI).

Ensuing examples follow the principle [Liskov, 1987] that subclasses should only extend, not invalidate, the specification (interface) of their superclass; that is, the RI should be strictly a superset of the FEI. We agree with Liskov that this is the most appropriate use of subclassing in object-oriented design and that it tends to produce more maintainable and reusable code. Much of the actual Smalltalk-80 system predates this insight, so in some cases subclassing is used only to inherit implementation, not specification. Liskov, Snyder, and others have proposed an even stronger form of isolation between subclasses and superclasses, namely, that subclasses should not be allowed to reference the instance variables or perhaps even the private messages of the superclass. While strict isolation clearly enhances potential reusability of subclasses in the event of changes in the superclass, it may not be worth the cost of the necessary additional code.

3.3 SINGLE-CLASS FRAMEWORKS

The simplest example of a framework is a class that is partially abstract; that is, a class that supplies a partial specification and implementation but expects subclasses or parameters to complete the implementation. In the Smalltalk-80 system, the division of function between the framework class and the client subclass or parameter object varies widely. At one extreme, the framework places very few constraints on the subclass or parameter, and/or it implements very little functionality. At the other extreme, the framework supplies nearly the entire functionality and relies on the client to supply only a few algorithms. We refer to these as the *open* and *closed* extremes of the spectrum.

EXAMPLE 1: MAGNITUDE

One of the most open single-class frameworks in the Smalltalk-80 system is class Magnitude. This class provides a framework for quantities that have a linear ordering relationship, as shown by its inheritance hierarchy:

```
Magnitude
         Character
         Date
         Number
                  Float
                  Fraction
                  Integer
                           LargeNegativeInteger
                           LargePositiveInteger
                           SmallInteger
         Time
```

Since Magnitude supplies so little and since many of its features will reappear in later examples, we reproduce its entire code here. The punctuation is slightly different from what a user normally writes (for details, see chapter 3 of Krasner, [1983]).

```
Magnitude comment: 'The abstract class Magnitude provides common protocol for
objects that have the ability to be compared along a linear dimension like dates
or times. Subclasses of Magnitude include Date, Number, and Time, as well as
Character, LookupKey, and MessageTally.

Subclasses must implement methods for comparison messages
      <
      =
      hash'!

!Magnitude methodsFor: 'comparing'!

<   aMagnitude
         "Answer whether the receiver is less than the argument."

         ^self subclassResponsibility!

<=  aMagnitude
         "Answer whether the receiver is less than or equal to the argument."

         ^(self > aMagnitude) not!

=   aMagnitude
         "Answer whether the receiver is equal to the argument."

         ^self subclassResponsibility!

>   aMagnitude
         "Answer whether the receiver is greater than the argument."

         ^aMagnitude < self!

>=  aMagnitude
         "Answer whether the receiver is greater than or equal to the argument."

         ^(self < aMagnitude) not!
```

```
between: min and: max
        "Answer whether the receiver is less than or equal to the
        argument, max, and greater than or equal to the argument, min."

        ^self >= min and: [self <= max]!

hash
        "Answer a SmallInteger unique to the receiver."

        ^self subclassResponsibility!
max: aMagnitude
        "Answer the receiver or the argument, whichever has the
        greater magnitude."

        self > aMagnitude
                ifTrue: [^self]
                ifFalse: [^aMagnitude]!

min: aMagnitude
        "Answer the receiver or the argument, whichever has the
        lesser magnitude."

        self < aMagnitude
                ifTrue: [^self]
                ifFalse: [^aMagnitude]! !
```

From this code we can see that the FEI for Magnitude consists of a complete set of comparison operations that follow the familiar mathematical rules, some associated utility functions (**between:and:**, **max:**, and **min:**), and the **hash** function. The FII consists of the requirement that subclasses implement certain messages (with semantics that, in this case, are understood from the usual mathematical meanings of < and =, and the comment in **hash**). The RI is different for the various subclasses: for example, Numbers implement messages like + and *, whereas Characters implement messages like **isDigit** and Dates implement messages like **monthName**.

From even this simple example, we can see three benefits from this kind of reuse of a partial design.

1. The message protocol of a new subclass is automatically completed to contain a useful set of composite functions.
2. New classes that are similar to old classes can be built with an effort that is proportional to the degree of dissimilarity.
3. Default implementations of common operations are available with no effort and can be tuned later without changing any client programs (since the implementation in the subclass will take precedence over the implementation in the superclass).

A fourth property, which also distinguishes object-oriented design with inheritance from conventional subroutine libraries, is that this kind of framework can be nested with no cost in execution time. In modern implementations of languages with inheritance, the time conceptually required to search up the subclass hierarchy at execution time is reduced to a (near-)constant by compilation techniques or caches. In the example just presented, Number and Integer are also frameworks, supplying progressively greater structure and a richer FEI, with only slightly larger FII (for example, Number adds the requirement that the subclass implement the four basic mathematical operations).

As we can see, the class hierarchy tends to soften the distinction between design and implementation at the algorithm level. Algorithms that depend on very few properties of their operands can be written as executable code in highly abstract classes. However, a strong separate design element remains in the assignment of functional roles to classes, the definition of the protocols (operations and their meanings) for different classes, and the construction of the class hierarchy itself.

EXAMPLE 2: COLLECTIONS

In the previous example, the FII just consisted of a set of requirements that the internal client must follow. However, framework classes can also supply private utility operations for use by subclasses. An example of this is in class SequenceableCollection, which represents a powerful abstraction for aggregates, as shown by its documentation:

```
SequenceableCollection comment: 'Abstract superclass for collections that
have a well-defined order associated with their elements.  All
SequenceableCollections are accessible through keys that are integer indices.
Subclasses are distinguished by how the ordering is created and whether or
not the elements are restricted kinds of objects.  Subclasses are

   ordered determined externally
        OrderedCollection    elements ordered by user adding and removing
        LinkedList           uses a chain of elements that must be links
        ArrayedCollection    elements accessible by integers as external keys.

   ordered determined internally
        Interval             elements must be numbers

Concrete subclasses must implement methods for
        adding
                add:
        accessing
                size

Subclasses should not implement methods for
        removing
                remove: ifAbsent:'!
```

One of the messages implemented in class SequenceableCollection is a utility message for interchanging two elements of the collection. This is a private message, not intended for use by external clients, defined as follows:

```
!SequenceableCollection methodsFor: 'private'!

swap: oneIndex with: anotherIndex
        "Move the element at oneIndex to anotherIndex, and vice-versa."

        | element |
        element _ self at: oneIndex.
        self at: oneIndex put: (self at: anotherIndex).
        self at: anotherIndex put: element! !
```

The implementation uses the messages **at:** and **at:put:**, which in turn are meant to be defined by subclasses; that is, they are part of the requirements defined by the FII. (In the actual Smalltalk-80 system, as a result of historical accident, these messages have a default implementation in class Object. We consider this a design flaw to be corrected in future releases of the system.) This message is actually used by SortedCollection to interchange elements when resorting, and by IdentityDictionary when moving elements after a deletion. (It could probably also be used for the latter purpose by Set and Dictionary.)

The use of the term *private* needs a little explanation. By convention, any message not meant for use by external clients is categorized as *private*: there is no distinction between messages available to subclasses and messages that are entirely private to the class. In fact, the Smalltalk-80 language and (current) programming tools do not actually support the concept of public and private messages.

The **swap:with:** message is defined in SequenceableCollection because this is the most general framework class whose FEI + FII include the necessary semantic raw material—namely, the ability to access elements by key or index. The principle here is that one should define utility messages in the most general class whose specification includes the needed base semantics. We have found this to be a valuable guideline in assigning functionality to classes.

EXAMPLE 3: PROGRAMMING TOOLS

We have just seen two examples where the FEI was sparse, and most of the RI was supplied by the subclass. We now turn to an example where the RI is the same as the FEI and where the key element supplied by the subclass is the implementation of a complex function that appears in the FEI.

As described by Goldberg [1984], the major tool for writing and reading code in the Smalltalk-80 programming environment is the Browser, a complex visual interface that provides a large number of mutually supporting facilities. We can divide these functions into those that do and those that do not depend on the detailed semantics of the Smalltalk-80 programming language. In the relatively language-independent category we have

☐ A 4-level tree structure for organizing classes and methods,
☐ The ability to search any subtree for all occurrences of a name or a string,
☐ The ability to find all the references to a name anywhere in the system (all system code, as well as user-written code, is available for browsing and retrieval in source form), and
☐ The ability to find all the implementations of a given message.

In the language-dependent category, the Browser provides

☐ Interactive compilation and formatting (prettyprinting) of individual methods, and
☐ The ability to explain any name or syntactic construct by giving its definition.

The Browser implements these facilities by sending appropriate messages to the objects that actually represent classes, source code, compiled code, and other internal structures. For example, the Browser executes the following code when asked to compile a method:

```
acceptMethod: aText from: aController
        ...
        newSelector _ self selectedClass
                        compile: aText
                        classified: protocol
                        notifying: aController.
        ...
```

For those unfamiliar with Smalltalk syntax, an English translation of this expression might be:

Send myself (the Browser) the message 'selectedClass' with no arguments.

To the object returned by this, send the message **compile:classified:notifying:** with three arguments: aText (the first argument of **acceptMethod:from:**), protocol (an instance variable of myself), and aController (the second argument of **acceptMethod:from:**).

Assign the resulting object to the variable newSelector.

In turn, class Behavior (the superclass of all classes) implements the message **compile:classified:notifying:** in the following way:

```
compile: code classified: heading notifying: requestor
    ...
    methodNode _ self compilerClass new
                    compile: code
                    in: self
                    notifying: requestor
                    ifFail: [^nil].
    selector _ methodNode selector.
    self
            addSelector: selector
            withMethod: methodNode.
    ...
```

The message **self compilerClass** constitutes an element of the FII for Behavior. Each class is expected to provide, in response to this message, a compiler object that responds properly to the message **compile:in:notifying:ifFail:**, by returning an object that in its turn responds properly to the messages **selector** and **generate**. (The latter must generate compiled code that is compatible with the output of the standard compiler, of course.) In this way, any class that wishes to provide an alternative compiler need only redefine (override the default implementation of) the message **compilerClass**, which is defined in Behavior in the obvious way:

```
compilerClass
        ^SmalltalkCompiler
```

Similar messages provide the prettyprinter and the explainer objects.

In this example, we see not only a very different balance between the framework and the subclass, but also the idea that the framework may provide default implementations of some of the elements of the FII. Indeed, there are examples of this in the Number and Collection classes as well. For example, Collection provides a default implementation of the **size** message that iterates through the collection counting the number of repetitions. Collections implemented with linear storage structures (Array, OrderedCollection) redefine this message to return the size of the structure efficiently.

3.4 MULTIPLE-CLASS FRAMEWORKS

When the framework consists of a single class, the FEI is simply the message protocol of that class, and the FII is a set of expectations about the behavior of the subclass and a set of utility messages that the framework provides for the subclass. However, as we expand the idea of framework to encompass the design of a family of related classes, the FII in particular becomes more complex: instead of just defining a subclass of a single framework class, the client may define subclasses or insert parameter objects that have to fulfill constraints spanning many objects. We will look at just one example from the Smalltalk-80 system—the framework for interactive applications. Other examples include the code generation framework of the compiler (actually two interacting frameworks, one relatively language-independent, the other relatively independent of the instruction set), and the interface to the file system (File, FileStream, and FileDirectory).

EXAMPLE 4: USER INTERFACE FRAMEWORK

The Smalltalk-80 user interface is based on three closely coupled hierarchies of framework classes. The user interface architecture uses a uniform metaphor of "viewing" objects. To interact with an object (called a *model*), three components are required:

1. A *view* object must exist that knows how to convert some interesting aspect(s) of the model to visible form.
2. A *controller* object must exist that knows how to interpret user-initiated events (button clicks, keystrokes, movement of the pointing device) as selection and editing commands in the functional space provided by the view.
3. The model itself must provide interfaces that allow the view to access and update the aspects being viewed. Since ST80 does not allow the internal structure of an object to be accessed directly from the outside, these "aspects" may be as simple as individual state variables, or they may be arbitrarily complex characteristics mediated by accessing and updating procedures.

There is an abstract class View that provides much of the mechanism for handling screen clipping, coordinate conversion, automatic updating of the screen when the model's state changes, and so on. Concrete subclasses are expected to provide an implementation for the operation **displayView**, which redisplays the representation of the selected information from the model within the appropriate area on the display screen. Simple concrete views need only implement this single operation to take advantage of the framework. In other words, the FII for View consists only of the **displayView** message. The two relevant messages from View are as follows:

```
!View methodsFor: 'displaying'!

display
        "Display the receiver's border, the model of the receiver, and then
        the subviews of the receiver."

        self displayBorder.
        self displayView.
        self displaySubViews!

displayView
        "Subclasses should redefine displayView in order to display particular
        objects associated with the View such as labels, lines, boxes, etc."

        ^self! !
```

As in the programming tools example, the framework here provides a default implementation of the FII—in this case, one that does nothing. This is useful for Views that have subviews but no content of their own (for example, menus or palettes).

The same view object, if properly designed, can be used with many different kinds of model objects, and the same model can be viewed in many different ways. ST80 provides several kinds of views and associated controllers that have been successfully reused across many different applications. These, in fact, form a kind of standard user interface builder's kit that writers of new applications naturally employ rather than building their own from scratch. Here are some examples of such view/controller structures:

☐ List view: a list that remains on the screen, can be scrolled within a clipping region, and whose selected element is displayed in some other view on the screen.

☐ Text view: a region that contains editable text, with a standard command repertoire (copy, cut, paste, find, undo) that can be extended by an individual application (e.g., **accept** for compiling code, **put** for storing a document).

☐ Switch/button: a region that initiates some action when a button is depressed while the cursor is within it, or that simply retains its on/off state.

☐ Inspector: a combination of a list view and a text view that views a list of state variables of a model. The variables can be viewed one at a time in the text view and can be altered by typing in a new value. (This violates the normal protection of an object's internal state, and is intended for debugging.)

The subclassing mechanism described earlier plays a crucial role in making views reusable. For example, the code view used by the source code browser is a subclass of the standard system text view, adding only procedures for three commands: **accept**, which invokes the compiler, **explain**, which provides an explanation of source code constructs or names, and **format**, which reformats the source code with standard indentation and spacing.

3.5 CONCLUSIONS

The structure of the Smalltalk-80 language and system makes it possible to design reusable structures of a greater variety than in most other languages. This results primarily from the use of inheritance as an inexpensive, nestable, organizing mechanism and from a conscious effort to identify the FEI and FII when building new system components.

Observations

Many systems based on abstract data types or interface abstraction have the property that interfaces can be reused. Examples of such systems include CLU, Alphard, Cedar Mesa, Modula–2, and Ada. However, all of these systems make a strong distinction between abstractions and procedures, and they require considerable advance planning in the form of type declarations and choices of which elements of an implementation are themselves treated abstractly. In contrast, in ST80, the only concrete elements that code can access directly are the instance variables of the class in which the code is defined. (There is a style of programming in ST80 in which even these are accessed indirectly through messages, which enhances abstraction still further. As noted earlier, it is not entirely clear that the increased abstraction is worth the increased inconvenience.) As a result, it is actually easier to write code that does not depend on the concrete implementation of the objects it operates on. In turn, this means that opportunities for reuse are often discovered long after the code was originally written, and taking advantage of them often requires little or no change in the code being redeployed. The third example, programming tools, is a striking instance of this. In the original code, literal class names were used (e.g., Compiler instead of self **compilerClass**); **compilerClass** and others were added to the FII many years later, and fully implementing this change only required minor changes to about 15 system procedures.

Problems

While the Smalltalk-80 system employs framework reuse to good effect, it does so entirely by convention. There is no support in the language, and little support in the programming tools, for identifying either the reusable interfaces or the constraints (specifications) that client-supplied objects or subclasses must obey.

Designing good frameworks is an especially hard instance of the general hard problem of designing good procedural interfaces. Several heavily used frameworks in ST80 lack generality. For example, View is designed for static layouts with dynamically changing contents and does not readily support dynamic changes in the layout of the screen. List views only handle lists of single-line strings, not arbitrary views, as their elements.

Acknowledgments

Adele Goldberg provided stimulating discussions regarding design reuse in the context of the Smalltalk-80 system. I am indebted to Barbara Liskov's presentation at OOPSLA '87 for the distinction between inheriting specification and inheriting implementation.

APPENDIX: THE SMALLTALK-80 LANGUAGE

ST80 is fully object-oriented. Every object in the system is described by (is an instance of) some class. This includes primitive objects such as integers and strings, and internal objects such as compiled procedures, processes, and classes themselves. The only compositional construct in ST80 is the message sending operation, which takes a receiver object, a literal message name (called a *selector*), and possibly some arguments, and looks up the selector in the message dictionary for the class of the receiver to determine what method to run.

Classes are arranged in an inheritance tree with the property that if class *A* is a subclass of class *B*, then all operations implemented in *B* are recognized by instances of *A* and have the same meaning (unless reimplemented in *A*, or in some class between *B* and *A* in the hierarchy). Subclasses have free access to instance variables declared in a superclass. Some Smalltalk-80 implementations include a multiple inheritance capability, but it is not part of the standard language.

ST80 is a dynamically typed language (no type declarations). The type (class) of an object is fixed when the object is created.

At the level of individual procedures, ST80 has a fairly conventional statement and expression syntax, with a few twists:

- [ ] The character for assignment is _ (underscore).
- [ ] Returning a value from a procedure (*method* in Smalltalk terminology) is indicated by a prefix ∧ (caret).
- [ ] Applications (i.e., the combination of a message receiver, a literal message name, and possibly arguments) have three different syntaxes: a postfix identifier (e.g., **3 factorial**), an infix special character(s) (e.g., **x > y**), or an alternating sequence of keywords and expressions (e.g., **x between: y and: z**). The postfix unary syntax binds most tightly, the keyword syntax least tightly.
- [ ] There is a convenient syntax for writing closures (called *blocks* in Smalltalk terminology) using square brackets, which we will illustrate with an example:

```
1 to: 10 do: [:i | s _ s + i].
```

- [ ] All control structures are ordinary applications, generally involving a block as an argument or receiver. For example, here is the definition of absolute value:

```
∧ self > = 0 ifTrue: [self] ifFalse: [self negated].
```

For further details, the reader should consult Goldberg and Robson [1983].

TRADEMARK NOTICES

Smalltalk-80 is a trademark of ParcPlace Systems, Inc.

Unix is a trademark of AT&T Technologies.

Ada is a registered trademark of the U. S. government Ada Joint Program Office.

REFERENCES

Deutsch, L. P. Levels of reuse in the Smalltalk-80 programming system. In *Tutorial: Software Reusability*, Freeman, P. (ed.). Washington, D.C.: IEEE Computer Society Press, 1987.

Goldberg, A. *Smalltalk-80: The Interactive Programming Environment*. Reading, Mass.: Addison-Wesley, 1984.

Goldberg, A.; Robson, D.; Tesler, L.; Reenskaug, T.; Ingalls, D.; Althoff, J.; Krasner, G.; Deutsch, P.; Ross, J.; Bowman, W.; Flegal, R.; and Kaehler, T. 12 articles on the Smalltalk-80 language and system. *Byte* magazine, August 1981.

Goldberg, A., and Robson, D. *Smalltalk-80: The Language and Its Implementation*. Reading, Mass.: Addison-Wesley, 1983.

Krasner, G. (ed.). *Smalltalk-80: Bits of History, Words of Advice*. Reading, Mass.: Addison-Wesley, 1983.

Liskov, B. Oral presentation at OOPSLA 87. Orlando, Fla.: October 1987.

Meyrowitz, N. (ed.). Proceedings of the 1986 Conference on Object-Oriented Programming Systems, Languages, and Applications. Special issue of *ACM SIGPLAN Notices*, November 1986.

Meyrowitz, N. (ed.). Proceedings of the 1987 Conference on Object-Oriented Programming Systems, Languages, and Applications. Special issue of *ACM SIGPLAN Notices*, November 1987.

Pope, S. T.; Goldberg, A.; and Deutsch, L. P. Object-oriented approaches to the software lifecycle using the Smalltalk-80 system as a CASE toolkit. *Proceedings of the 1987 Fall Joint Computer Conference*. Washington, D.C.: IEEE Computer Society Press, 1987.

Shriver, B., and Wegner, P. (eds.). *Research Directions in Object-Oriented Programming*. Cambridge, Mass.: MIT Press, 1987.

Snyder, A. Encapsulation and Inheritance in Object-Oriented Programming Languages. In Proceedings of OOPSLA 86. Special issue of *ACM SIGPLAN Notices*, November 1987.

CHAPTER 4

EXAMPLES OF REUSABILITY IN AN OBJECT-ORIENTED PROGRAMMING ENVIRONMENT

CHRISTINA JETTE
Schlumberger Austin Systems Center

REID SMITH
Schlumberger Laboratory for Computer Science

4.1 INTRODUCTION

Reusability is widely believed to be an important methodology for improving the software development process, and for increasing software productivity. Multiple approaches to reuse have been noted and investigated, including subroutine libraries, piping in Unix, code skeletons, and application program generators [Biggerstaff and Richter, 1987].

A common theme for many of these approaches is to construct new systems by selecting and combining reusable components from a components library; deriving a new program is a matter of building-block composition, applying a few well-defined composition principles to the components. This approach requires that the components be *atomic*, or treated as such even if they are not atomic, so that composition is easily accomplished without much (if any) change during their reuse. It also requires that components be stored in a coherent fashion for easy cataloging and that powerful browsing tools be available to assist in retrieval.

Our experience with object-oriented programming is in support of the construction of interactive interfaces to knowledge-based systems [Barth, 1986; Smith, 1984]. One such system is a user interface toolkit called HyperClass™, which encapsulates knowledge about user interfaces in terms of "editors" and editor parts [Schoen and Smith, 1983; Smith *et al.*, 1987]. In our work, we have made extensive use of object-oriented programming techniques to *reuse* portions of the knowledge encapsulated in HyperClass both for extending the "kernel" (i.e., providing additional user interface abstractions) and for implementing application-specific extensions.[1]

This paper looks at the usage of object-oriented programming for software reusability in the context of specific examples. We first identify issues specific to software reuse and then address those issues with key features provided by object-oriented programming. Using HyperClass as an example, we illustrate in detail our use of object-oriented programming for reuse.

4.1.1 Software Reuse and the Software Life-Cycle Process

The best way to enhance software productivity is to avoid writing software. Part of the time spent to write software is then replaced by time spent to *find, understand, modify,* and *compose* reusable software parts. Meyer [1987] points out that object-oriented design may be defined as a technique for decomposing systems into a structured collection of objects the system manipulates, rather than decomposing the system into a collection of functions that the system performs. By defining this collection of objects, one defines a *model* of the system behavior, parts of which may be reused as the system is extended and maintained.

Biggerstaff and Richter [1987] identify a number of fundamental problems that any reusability system must address, including:

knowing the existence of a part

knowing how to access the part

knowing when to use the part

knowing what the part does

knowing how to modify and compose parts.

While the solutions to these problems are not supported directly by an object-oriented programming environment, we will show ways in which the problems may be addressed.

---

[1]HyperClass, MetaClass, and Class are trademarks of Schlumberger Technologies, Inc. HyperClass is a collection of knowledge based tools; MetaClass is a knowledge-based editor, and Class is an object-oriented extension to Lisp. MetaClass was originally called Impulse-86, and Class was originally called Strobe.

4.2 KEY FEATURES OF OBJECT-ORIENTED LANGUAGES

There are several important requirements for a system to be reused. For example, the system must provide enough useful functionality to encourage others to reuse it, or parts of it, "as-is"—without modification. For this to be the case, the system design must define components that provide the functionality in terms of abstractions at appropriate levels of granularity. In addition, the system must be flexible enough to allow for evolutionary design, in which abstractions are adjusted or decomposed into finer grain abstractions over time as the system is generalized and extended.

This section identifies the common features of object-oriented languages that address these requirements.

4.2.1 Encapsulation

An object description encapsulates information about an entity in a problem domain of interest. It completely describes the behavior of the entity in terms of both *variables* (i.e., state) and *methods* (i.e., state–changing functions).

For example, the class[2] definition for **Window** below has local variables **Size** and **Position**, and methods **Open** and **Close**. **Open** and **Close** both contain actual functions (denoted by *‹code›*), while values for **Size** and **Position** will be defined in instances of **Window**.

```
Class:  Window
   Size:
   Position:
   Open:  <code>
   Close: <code>
```

An instance of **Window** (i.e., an instantiation of the class **Window**) follows:

```
Instance:  Window-10
   Size:  200 X 300
   Position: (10,30)
```

The instance has values for both **Size** and **Position** that are set by the **Open** method of the **Window** class.

A programmer using object-oriented programming techniques focuses on the real world atomic entities: what they are and how they may be composed. In the operating systems domain, for example, atomic entities include device, queue, and scheduler. In the word processing domain they include document, chapter, and paragraph. The structure of the resulting software system is determined by the structure of the physical world being modeled, not by the

---

[2]In object-oriented systems, classes represent sets of entities in a domain. Instances represent particular, unique individual entities in a domain.

specific task at hand. In principle, we may be able to reuse the model in several different applications.

4.2.2 Hierarchies and Property Inheritance

Collections of objects (classes and instances) form a taxonomic hierarchy in which objects may *inherit* properties of their parents. Inheritance allows objects that are specializations of other objects to reuse (inherit) both variable and method definitions of parent objects unless overridden. A subclass of **Window**, **WindowWithTitle** is defined as follows:

```
Class:  WindowWithTitle
SuperClass:  Window
   Title:
   TitleFont:
   Open:  <code>
   WriteTitle:  <code>
```

In the class definition above, **WindowWithTitle** is a descendant, or specialization, of **Window**. Likewise, **Window** is said to be a superclass, or generalization of **WindowWithTitle**. The links between ancestors and subclasses are read as "is-a" links; for example, **WindowWithTitle** is-a **Window**. The **Close** method of **Window** is implicitly available for this class, whereas the **Open** method is overridden or reimplemented with a new method. Two additional variables (**Title** and **TitleFont**) and one additional method (**WriteTitle**) are defined in this class. The new class, **WindowWithTitle**, is defined by differentiation with its superclass, **Window**, and reuses all other inherited behaviors.

4.2.3 Messages

Methods in class definitions are invoked by sending messages. In Class™, an object-oriented extension to Common Lisp, the syntax

```
(send a selector b c)
```

translates to

```
(funcall
        (method-specified-by selector (type-of a))
        a b c).
```

For example,

```
(send 'Window-10 'Open)
```

translates to

```
(funcall
        (method-specified-by 'Open 'Window)
        Window-10 ).
```

In some languages (e.g., CLOS [Keene, 1989]) the syntax is

```
(selector a b c)
```

or

```
(Open 'Window-10)
```

A selector is said to be *overloaded* if several different implementations of the selector method exist, each associated with a different class. This is a form of *polymorphism* [Stefik and Bobrow, 1986]. The **Open** method for **WindowWithTitle** is an example of this. It overrides the **Open** method defined in the **Window** class.

Polymorphism allows different objects to respond to the same protocol with varying behavior. In Hyperclass for example, there are several dozen kinds of Menu, but each responds to the same protocol for creating and displaying itself to the user. This is important for reusability. Defining a protocol lends structure to the interaction between various parts of the system. One can alter the parts of the system, yet reuse the protocol itself.

4.2.4 Method Combination

Methods can be combined in a number of ways. One way is through *top-down additive combination*, where *sequencing* is the composition operator—like Unix pipes. Each object in the hierarchy, starting from the top (i.e., the most general class), is scanned for a method with the name specified by the selector. Each method found is invoked in sequence.

For example, the following class object is a specialization of **WindowWith-Title**:

```
Class:  WindowWithBorder
SuperClass:  WindowWithTitle
   BorderWidth:
   Open:  <code>
```

To open a **WindowWithBorder**, **Open** is applied in sequence for each object in the hierarchy from **Window** to **WindowWithBorder**. Each individual method has the following *additive* effect on the resulting window:

```
(send 'Window 'Open)     => Creates a window and displays
                            it on the screen

+  (send 'WindowWithTitle 'Open)   => Adds the title to
                                      the window

+  (send 'WindowWithBorder 'Open)  => Adds the border
                                      to the window
```

We could also have *bottom-up additive method combination*, which causes each method to be invoked, starting at the most specific class, and ending with the most general class. In other object-oriented languages, this is equivalent to the method including a "send super" message to its superclass. In Flavors [Moon, 1986], top-down additive combination is equivalent to using ":after" combination; bottom-up additive combination is equivalent to using ":before" combination. Other forms of method combination allow conditionals [Stefik and Bobrow, 1986]. The possibilities, and the way they are invoked, are language-dependent. This is useful for reusability because it allows code fragments to be composed without having to decide a priori on the composition; code fragments can be composed in ways not necessarily as anticipated by the original designers. Clearly this will not work for arbitrary fragments. It suggests relatively fine-grain modular methods.

Continuing with the **WindowWithBorder** example defined above, there is a problem with the structure as defined so far. Suppose we wanted to build another "titled" structure, perhaps a menu, which is not necessarily a subclass of **Window**. We would have to write duplicate code for the **WriteTitle** method of the new titled structure. While this is not unreasonable, it isn't convenient or necessary.

The notion of a *mixin*, a class that will not be instantiated [Stefik and Bobrow, 1986], is used to address this problem. Mixins are used to define a set of operations that may be used in a variety of contexts via inheritance. Using mixins, we could restructure the object hierarchy as follows:

```
Class:  Window
SuperClass:  Object
   Size:
   Position:
   Open:  <code>


Class:  BorderMixin
SuperClass:  Object
   Border:  <code>


Class:  TitleMixin
SuperClass:  Object
   Title:
   TitleFont:
   WriteTitle:  <code>


Class:  WindowWithTitleandBorder
SuperClass:  (Window, BorderMixin, TitleMixin)
```

WindowWithTitleandBorder inherits behavior from more than one superclass. This is called *multiple inheritance*, and leads to inheritance graphs rather than trees. This is useful because it further assists reuse of code and simplifies defining models and composing fragments.

4.2.5 Declarative Programming Style

Object-oriented programming encourages a declarative programming style, in which much of the state or control information is stored and recorded as a part of a class or instance definition. This allows for "generic" algorithms (in methods) to be defined that are specialized at run time with the data bindings found in instance (or class) variables. The alternative implementation is to have CASE statements and code about the datatypes spread throughout an application. When datatype information is spread throughout the code, the result is a system that is difficult to modify and extend. To add a new datatype, a user must search the existing code to find all datatype dependencies and add clauses to CASE statements. This process is often tedious and error-prone, and it assumes the user has access to source code to make the necessary modifications. In the object-oriented formulation, the analog to adding a new datatype is adding a new class. Because of the modularity of classes, there is not the same need to search existing code to find dependencies.

4.3 HYPERCLASS, A USER INTERFACE TOOLKIT

As with many other software systems, our experience with knowledge-based systems has shown the vital importance of the user interface. We designed HyperClass to experiment with interfaces to knowledge-based systems. HyperClass is based on Class [Smith, 1983; Smith and Carando, 1986], an object-oriented extension to Lisp. Class is implemented in Common Lisp, Interlisp, and C. It runs on workstations offered by Sun MicroSystems, Digital, Xerox, Symbolics, and TI.

4.3.1 HyperClass Overview

HyperClass provides a general and extensible substrate upon which to construct a wide variety of interactive user interfaces for developing, maintaining, and using knowledge-based systems. HyperClass takes the perspective that the process of editing may be defined as any series of interactions between a user and a system in which the user both *views* and *controls* the state of the system. As such, a knowledge-based editor should support different perspectives corresponding to three types of users: 1) developer/maintainer, 2) domain specialist, and 3) end user. An editor must provide a reactive environment for developers, enable domain specialists to focus on encoded domain knowledge, and provide transparent and easy-to-use interfaces for end users.

To enable easy construction of a wide variety of editing tools and interface styles, HyperClass was conceived as a modular, extensible interface construction kit. A user may customize and extend the behavior of an interface by overriding default values and methods, and by specializing objects.

Figure 4.1 is an example of an object editor in HyperClass. The object being edited encodes geologic knowledge taken from the *Dipmeter Advisor*

FIGURE 4.1
OBJECT EDITOR FOR NORMAL-FAULT

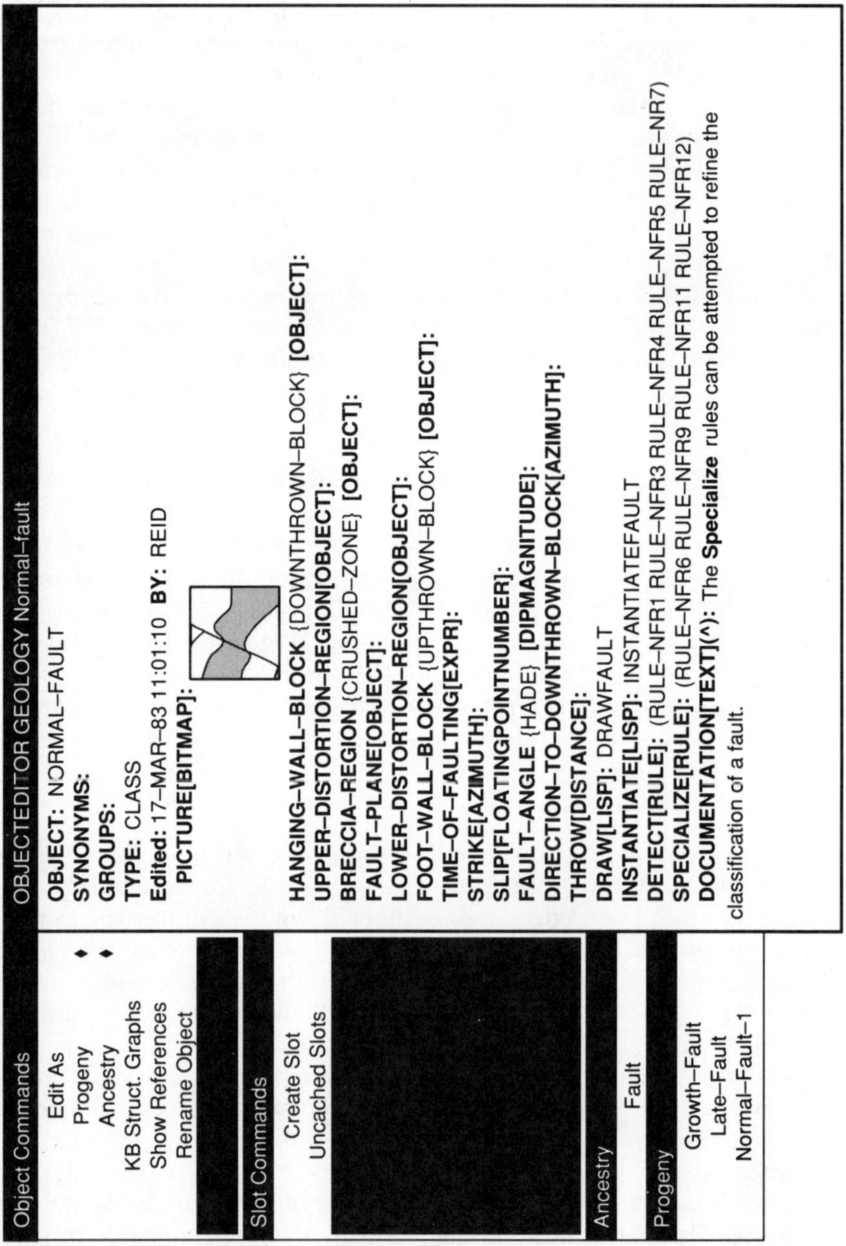

OBJECTEDITOR GEOLOGY Normal-fault

OBJECT: NORMAL-FAULT
SYNONYMS:
GROUPS:
TYPE: CLASS
Edited: 17-MAR-83 11:01:10 **BY:** REID
PICTURE[BITMAP]:

HANGING-WALL-BLOCK {DOWNTHROWN-BLOCK} **[OBJECT]:**
UPPER-DISTORTION-REGION[OBJECT]:
BRECCIA-REGION {CRUSHED-ZONE} **[OBJECT]:**
FAULT-PLANE[OBJECT]:
LOWER-DISTORTION-REGION[OBJECT]:
FOOT-WALL-BLOCK {UPTHROWN-BLOCK} **[OBJECT]:**
TIME-OF-FAULTING[EXPR]:
STRIKE[AZIMUTH]:
SLIP[FLOATINGPOINTNUMBER]:
FAULT-ANGLE {HADE} **[DIPMAGNITUDE]:**
DIRECTION-TO-DOWNTHROWN-BLOCK[AZIMUTH]:
THROW[DISTANCE]:
DRAW[LISP]: DRAWFAULT
INSTANTIATE[LISP]: INSTANTIATEFAULT
DETECT[RULE]: (RULE-NFR1 RULE-NFR3 RULE-NFR4 RULE-NFR5 RULE-NR7)
SPECIALIZE[RULE]: (RULE-NFR6 RULE-NFR9 RULE-NFR11 RULE-NFR12)
DOCUMENTATION[TEXT](^): The **Specialize** rules can be attempted to refine the
classification of a fault.

Object Commands
    Edit As
    Progeny
    Ancestry
    KB Struct. Graphs
    Show References
    Rename Object

Slot Commands
    Create Slot
    Uncached Slots

Ancestry   Fault

Progeny
    Growth-Fault
    Late-Fault
    Normal-Fault-1

system[3] [Smith, 1984]. In the figure, the object editor for **Normal-Fault** consists of a description of the object (e.g., name of the object, synonyms, groups, type, and editing information), and a collection of *slots* or attributes of the object (e.g., **Hanging-Wall-Block**, or **Upper-Distortion-Region**). In Class terminology, slots are used to collectively describe variables and methods in an object. For example, **Instantiate** is a method for instantiating a specific instance of a **Normal-Fault**, while **Detect** is a rule for detecting such faults. (The datatype of each slot is shown in brackets in the object.)

Figure 4.2 is an example of a graph editor that shows the taxonomic hierarchy associated with tectonic features in a geological modeling system. **Normal-Fault** is-a **Fault**, which in turn is-a **Tectonic-Feature**.

Figure 4.3 shows an editor which displays the picture of a geological fault. In this editor, the fault blocks can be moved forward and backward in geological time by selecting commands in the command menu. The commands invoke a simulator (implemented as a geometric model in a separate knowledge base) and then display the results as changes in the picture.

Each of the interfaces in Figs. 4.1–4.3 describes some aspects of the entities of interest, namely geological faults, but each gives the user a different perspective and a different set of operations for that entity. HyperClass makes this customization relatively easy.

The HyperClass kernel consists of a library of building blocks (200–300). Applications extend the number of building blocks for application-specific interfaces. The building blocks have evolved over time, after many reuse attempts. The main design problem to be solved is finding the right set of intermediate abstractions, because with object-oriented programming, *the abstractions are being reused* — not just the code or the leaf nodes in a hierarchy.

4.3.2 HyperClass Building Block Components

The HyperClass building blocks are organized around the following five abstractions: **Editor**, **EditorWindow**, **PropertyDisplay**, **Menu**, and **Operations**. Each building block is a Class object in the HyperClass knowledge base. The user of HyperClass can customize or extend the behavior of an existing interface by modifying or specializing the structure of some of its building blocks. Figure 4.4 illustrates how these building blocks are related to each other.

The **Editor** is the central object. It mediates interactions between the user and the current domain focus, or **editee**. Editor instances are created from an editor class by template instantiation. Editors have components drawn from any of the five classes of editor parts listed above. Editors are explicitly able to have other editors as components, allowing recursion in the part-whole hierarchy. This component structuring and composition increases the possibilities for reuse of existing structures.

Figure 4.5 shows the editor structure for the class of object editors. Each

---

[3]Mark of Schlumberger.

FIGURE 4.2
GRAPH EDITOR FOR TECTONIC-FEATURE TAXONOMIC HIERARCHY

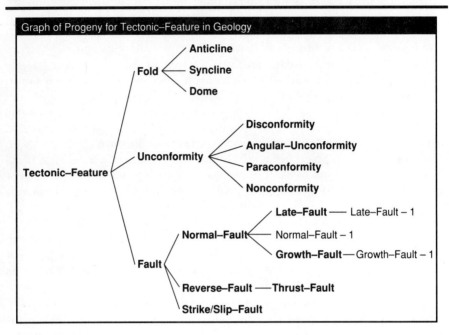

FIGURE 4.3
GEOLOGIC FAULT EDITOR

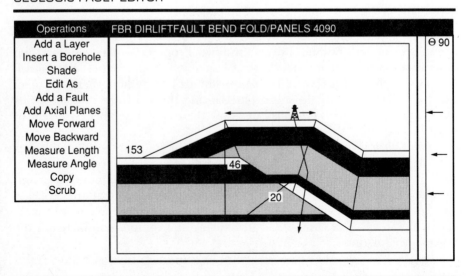

FIGURE 4.4
HYPERCLASS BUILDING BLOCKS

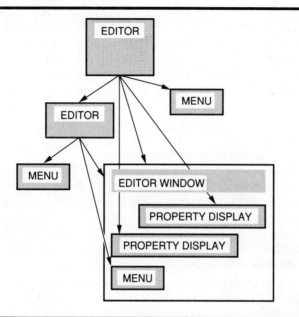

FIGURE 4.5
COMPONENTS STRUCTURE OF THE HYPERCLASS OBJECT EDITOR

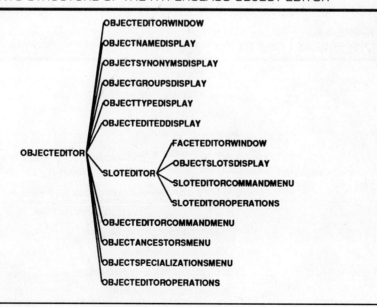

editor instance is generated from this template. Figure 4.6 shows the instance corresponding to the object editor shown in Fig. 4.1. In both graphs, an arc indicates that the object on the right is a *component* of the object on the left. Instantiated components are shown in lightface; noninstantiated components are in boldface. (Figs. 4.5 and 4.6 were generated from HyperClass specialized graph editors.)

In this example, the **ObjectEditor** and **SlotEditor** classes are both subclasses of the **Editor** class. ObjectEditor mediates interactions with the object-specific properties (e.g., the object's name and synonyms), while SlotEditor mediates interaction with the slot-specific properties (e.g., the slot's name and value).

The **EditorWindow** manages the screen context of a collection of editors. It is responsible for performing usual window operations (e.g., scrolling, repainting). It also maintains a correspondence between editees and the window regions in which the editees are displayed. Each editor may have at most one window among its components. When an editor has subeditors, some or all may share the same window, or utilize separate windows. Figure 4.6 shows that **ObjectEditor** and **SlotEditor** instances both share the same instance of **ObjectEditorWindow**.

The **PropertyDisplay** presents a *view* of an editee in a window. A number of different kinds of displays are defined, and the user can define new types of displays. There are six displays in the object editor example. The first five are components of the **ObjectEditor** (**ObjectNameDisplay**, **ObjectSynonyms-Display**, **ObjectGroupsDisplay**, **ObjectTypeDisplay**, **ObjectEditedDisplay**); each displays one of the five properties associated with the object itself. The sixth (**ObjectSlotsDisplay**) is a component of **SlotEditor**; it iterates over all

FIGURE 4.6
A HYPERCLASS OBJECT EDITOR INSTANCE

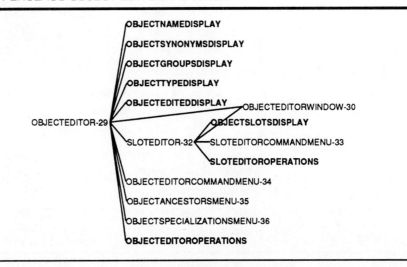

the slots. Each of these displays is responsible for printing some datum in the **ObjectEditorWindow**.

HyperClass provides a large number of **Menu** styles ranging from static to pop-up and push-button menus. Menus are used to display choices to be made or operations to be invoked. Menus may be unique to a particular editor or shared among a collection of editors. The separation of **ObjectEditor** and **SlotEditor** is used to advantage in indicating which commands are appropriate to a user-selected item in the editor window. This is shown in Figure 4.1 where the slot commands are grayed over; selecting a slot name in the editor causes these menu items to be visible and active for the selected slot.

Methods that perform commands defined for an editor are grouped into an **Operations** object. The methods are invoked by a message from the editor. For example, **ObjectEditorOperations** knows how to execute the operations listed in the **ObjectEditorCommandMenu**. Separating operations from menus permits the same editing operations to be invoked in a variety of ways, including menu selection, type-in, function invocation, or message from a remote processor.

The number of building blocks is less important than the organizing principle: *Partition responsibility*. We distinguish between *view* and *control* activities. View activities include display and locus, which correspond to the roles of property display and windows. Control activities include selection and execution, which correspond to the roles of menus and operations.

4.4 EXAMPLES OF REUSE IN HYPERCLASS

This section contains a number of examples showing how the HyperClass building blocks are reused.

4.4.1 FastObjectEditor vs. ObjectEditor Example

The object editor for Fig. 4.1 contains several attached menus. This style of object editing depicts menus that are always visible to the user. Looking at Fig. 4.6, we see that there are four menu instances, corresponding to the four attached menus, including

```
ObjectEditorCommandMenu-34
SlotEditorCommandMenu-33
ObjectAncestorsMenu-35
ObjectSpecializationsMenu-36.
```

Another object editor style would not use attached menus at all, but rather have these menus appear as pop-up menus upon demand, when a mouse button is pressed in the title bar area of the window. More specifically, one could define the object commands menu to appear as a result of selections in the title bar area, and the slot commands menu to appear as a result of selecting a slot name.

This change is fairly simple in the HyperClass framework, and most of the **ObjectEditor** structure, including the menus, can be reused. The following example illustrates this technique in the ensuing **FastObjectEditor** definition.

Figure 4.7 shows the editor components for the **FastObjectEditor**. There are several differences: (1) a new window class that allows for menu access in the title bar area, (2) a new slot editor for slots that likewise will pop up a menu of slot editor commands, and (3) no explicit menu parts in the editor components list.

The way that these editors differ in their use of pop-up menus vs. attached menus is captured in the **FastObjectEditorWindow** class and the slot that defines an associated menu. **FastObjectEditorWindow** is a specialization of **ObjectEditorWindow**.

EditorWindow, which is a component of **ObjectEditor**, contains the following definition:

```
Class:   ObjectEditorWindow
SuperClass:  EditorWindow
   TitleBarMenu:  EditorWindowTitleBarMenu
   Title:  <code>
   TitleBarFn:  <code>
```

The menu, denoted by the object **EditorWindowTitleBarMenu** is defined as

```
Class:  EditorWindowTitleBarMenu
SuperClass:  SubCommandMenu
   Help:
      Role:  MenuItem
   Refetch:
      Role:  MenuItem
```

FIGURE 4.7
COMPONENTS STRUCTURE OF THE HYPERCLASS FAST OBJECT EDITOR

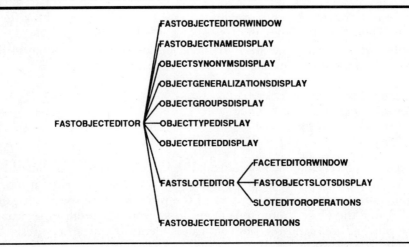

The default action for **ObjectEditor** when the mouse is buttoned in the title bar area is controlled by **TitleBarFn**. The default method displays the menu specified by the **TitleBarMenu** slot. In this case the menu is defined in the **EditorWindowTitleBarMenu** class, which has two menu items, **Help** and **Refetch**. These are denoted by the "Role: MenuItem" attribute on the **Help** slot of the class definition. (This exposes further object structure in Class. Slots have more structure than just an attribute and a value. In this example, menu items have an attribute, called a *facet*, named Role.)

In **FastObjectEditorWindow**, **TitleBarMenu** is redefined as follows:

```
Class:   FastObjectEditorWindow
SuperClass:   ObjectEditorWindow
    TitleBarMenu:   FastObjectEditorWindowTitleBarMenu
```

where **TitleBarFn** is the same as in **EditorWindow** above (that is, reused as is). **FastObjectEditorWindowTitleBarMenu** has the following definition:

```
Class:   FastObjectEditorWindowTitleBarMenu
SuperClass:   EditorWindowTitleBarMenu
    EditObject:
        Role:   MenuItem
    PrintObject:
        Role:   MenuItem
    CreateSlot:
        Role:   MenuItem
    UncachedSlots:
        Role:   MenuItem
```

Now when the user presses the mouse button in the title bar area of the window, the menu specified by **FastObjectEditorWindowTitleBar-Menu** is invoked. But notice also that this menu class is a specialization of **EditorWindowTitleBarMenu**. The method that collects the list of menu items to be displayed will search up the hierarchy for slots that have "Role: Menu-Item" attributes; in this case, it will also find the **Help** and **Refetch** items of the **EditorWindowTitleBarMenu**. This results in a menu containing the composition of menu items found in both the menu class specialization and its parent object.

If we were to examine the subeditor, **FastSlotEditor**, we would find that the slot command menu is now a menu-class object associated with the **Fast-ObjectSlotsDisplay** object, which is defined in such a way that when the slot name is selected (with the mouse), the associated selection method for the slot name access pops up the slot command menu. In fact, **FastObjectSlots-Display** inherits its mouse button behavior from the class **PropertyDisplay-WithMenu**, and its caption and value behavior from **ObjectSlotsDisplay**. This is an example of method combination via mixins, which is more fully explored in the next example.

In summary, the **FastObjectEditor** reuses many of the abstractions defined for **ObjectEditor** and, for example, only redefines the title bar menu contents in the window specialization, **FastObjectEditorWindow**, although it still reuses existing menu item contents.

4.4.2 HyperClass Menu Hierarchy Example

The design of the menu hierarchy in HyperClass takes advantage of mixins, described earlier, to maximize the reuse of various menu-specific behaviors. This design is superior to one without mixins in that it reduces the total number of specialized objects while increasing the reuse of shared behaviors. Figure 4.8 shows a partial menu hierarchy of HyperClass. (The numbers indicate how many direct subclasses of a class have been elided from the graph.)

At the top of the hierarchy, **Menu** is defined with the following generic menu behaviors. (**Menu** is a type of **Window** in the HyperClass framework.)

```
Class:  Menu
SuperClass:  Window
    Items:  <code>
    Repaint:  <code>
```

Generic menu behaviors include an **Items** method for generating a list of items for the menu, and a **Repaint** method for redisplaying the menu. (This is only a partial definition of **Menu** in HyperClass.)

Other menu behaviors that are of possible interest to any specific menu instance include:

Whether the menu is statically displayed on the screen (e.g., attached to an editor window), or whether the menu is dynamically created each time (e.g., popped up on demand)—static vs. dynamic.

Whether the menu items represent choices (i.e., items to be returned to a calling function) or whether the items represent commands to be executed—choice vs. command.

Whether the menu allows a user to select and return a single item, or allows the user to select and return multiple items—single choice vs. multiple choice.

Whether the menu items remain highlighted after they have been selected—sticky vs. nonsticky.

Whether the menu is implemented by one vendor's menu package versus another vendor's menu package.

From this list, one can see that any specific menu may be a combination of one or more of these behaviors (plus possibly additional application-specific behaviors). To maximize the reuse of these specific characteristics, the best way we have found is to structure them as mixins, as shown in the graph of Fig. 4.8.

To better understand this, we will look at how we build a pop-up menu that allows for multiple choices to be returned to the caller. As an example, we will construct the following menu:

My Fruit Menu
<abort>
<done>
apples
oranges
bananas

Examining the menu hierarchy in Fig. 4.8, so far we know that our Fruit Menu will use the **DynamicMenu**, **ChoiceMenu**, and **MultipleChoiceMenu** mixins due to the characteristics required (i.e., pop-up menu, choices, and one or more of them). We will also mix in the **MenuToolsMenu** as a particular implementation of a Lisp package menu.[4] We will also mix in the **StickyMenu** class so that the items remain highlighted after selection.

We create a new class, **MyFruitMenu**, as a combination of menu mixins as defined below:

```
Class:  MyFruitMenu
SuperClass:  (DynamicMenu, ChoiceMenu, StickyMenu
             MultipleChoiceMenu, MenuToolsMenu)
    Title:  ''My Fruit Menu''
    Apples:
       Order:  1
       Role:  MenuItem
    Oranges:
       Order:  2
       Role:  MenuItem
```

[4]The Lisp Package mixin allows us to encapsulate and reuse vendor-supplied menu implementations. The associated menu functions—for example, to create a Lisp window for the menu—are specified for each menu package. Menu Tools is one such package in HyperClass.

FIGURE 4.8
(PARTIAL) MENU HIERARCHY IN HYPERCLASS

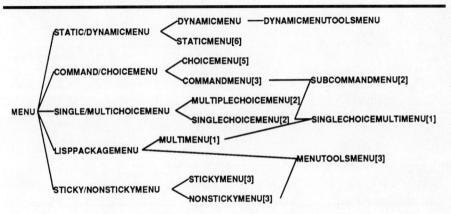

In this example, menu items have *facets* with names Order and Role. These facets are used by the default **Items** method in the **Menu** class to collect the list of items to be displayed in the menu in the order specified (determined by the Order facet).

The protocol for pop-up menus is to (1) instantiate the menu object, (2) display the menu on the screen, (3) initiate an interaction, (4) respond to the selection, and (5) clean up. This protocol accesses methods from the menu hierarchy in combination as defined by the mixins. The hierarchy for our example is shown in Fig. 4.9.

The new class, **MyFruitMenu** (shown in italics), uses five mixins. The **StickyMenu** mixin will cause the selected menu item to be highlighted. The **DynamicMenu** mixin will instantiate and pop up a menu and return a selected value. The **MultipleChoiceMenu** mixin will allow for multiple choices. The **ChoiceMenu** mixin specifies a **Choice** type menu, and the **MenuToolsMenu** specifies a specific style of menu package.

First we look at the process of instantiating the menu and displaying it. The process starts when the **Select** message is sent to the menu class, **MyFruitMenu**. The **Select** method messaged is the one found in the **DynamicMenu** class. The **Select** method follows the following protocol:

```
A c t i o n                                                          R e c e i v e r
(1) (send 'MyFruitMenu 'select) -->                                 DynamicMenu
     ;; instantiate the menu and display it
(2)    <menuinstance> = (send 'MyFruitMenu 'Code)-->                 Menu
(3)         FruitMenu-01 = (send 'MyFruitMenu 'Create)               Root
```

FIGURE 4.9
PORTIONS OF THE MENU HIERARCHY FOR MYFRUITMENU EXAMPLE MENU

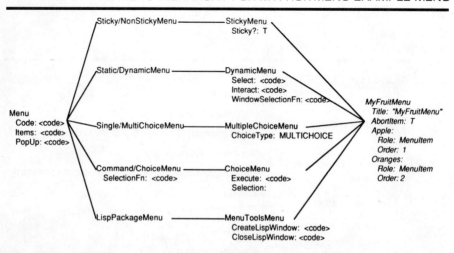

```
Action                                                            Receiver
(4)              (send 'MyFruitMenu-01 'CreateLispWindow)-->      MenuToolsMenu
(5)                      <items> = (send 'MyFruitMenu-01 'Items)  Menu
(6)      (send 'FruitMenu-01 'PopUp)                              Menu
         ;; menu interaction, response, and cleanup
              ...
```

DynamicMenu is the receiver of the **Select** message (1) and tries to create a (dynamic) menu by sending the **Code** message (2) to the class **MyFruitMenu**. The **Code** method associated with **Menu** creates an instance of the menu (via the **Create** method in **Root**) (3) and then creates a window for the new menu by sending the **CreateLispWindow** message (4). **CreateLispWindow** is defined in **MenuToolsMenu** and builds an instance of a **MenuTools** style menu creating a list of the items as specified by the **Items** method also defined in **Menu** (5). The menu is displayed when it receives the **PopUp** message (6).

Because of the disjoint behaviors each mixin represents, a standard protocol for menu creation and display is defined, and the binding of actual methods occurs as a result of messaging this mixin structure.

The second part of the menu protocol is to initiate an interaction, respond to it, and clean up. The protocol for making a selection from a menu continues as a result of the **Select** method:

```
Action                                                            Receiver
(1) (send 'MyFruitMenu 'Select) -->                              DynamicMenu
     ;; menu instantiation and display
          .
          .
          .
     ;; menu interaction, response and cleanup
(7)      <result> = (send 'MyFruitMenu-01 'Interact) -->          DynamicMenu
(8)      <result> =
         (send 'MyFruitMenu-01 'WindowSelectionFn ) -->           DynamicMenu
(9)      if (send 'MyFruitMenu-01' Sticky?) then Highlight        StickyMenu
(10)     (send 'MyFruitMenu-01' SelectionFn <result>)            Command/ChoiceMenu
(11)     <choicetype> =
         (send 'MyFruitMenu-01 'ChoiceType 'Get)                  MultipleChoiceMenu
(12)     <result> = if (<choicetype> = singlechoice) then
                       (first <result>) else...
(13)     (send 'MyFruitMenu-01' Execute <result>) -->             ChoiceMenu
(13.1)   (send 'MyFruitMenu-01' Selection 'Put <result>)         FruitMenu-01
(14)     (send 'MyFruitMenu-01 'CloseLispWindow)                  MenuToolsMenu
```

Once the menu has been created and displayed (see above), the **Select** method (1) of the menu eventually returns the value(s) selected to the caller by putting the selection in the **Selection** slot of the menu (13.1). To accomplish this, the **Interact** method is invoked (7) to get the selection from the user. **WindowSelectionFn** highlights and returns the selected item(s) (8, 9). **SelectionFn** (10) responds to the selection. It determines the choice type (11) and modifies the result accordingly (12). (For multiple choice, a list of items is returned.) The result is saved in the menu instance when the **Execute** message is sent (13). The process is terminated by closing the menu (removing the menu from the display) (14).

The object-oriented nature of HyperClass simplifies another kind of reuse—namely, reuse of runtime data structures. For example, HyperClass also reuses menu structures by caching menu instances. Menus that are shared by multiple editor complexes can be reused as is, adding the name of the editor that is using it to a list of editors in the menu instance. This way, new menus need not always be created at runtime, saving the cost of instantiating and creating new menus. This strategy also works for reusing whole editor complexes; the editor component instances serve as templates for the editor class. When no longer needed, the particular bindings for the editee are broken, but the interconnected editor complex is retained for future use. When the editor complex is reused, new bindings are created for the new editee. This saves initial start-up time for the editor complex. Caching is particularly useful in server-based window systems, for example, the X Window System [Scheifler, 1987], where it dramatically improves performance.

To complete the menu example, we observe that the same protocol can be used for a different type of menu, changing only the bindings of methods. To illustrate this, suppose we have a command menu instead of a choice menu, resulting in a command execution when an item is selected. Figure 4.10 shows the menu hierarchy for another menu, with items **Edit** and **Refetch**, which when selected will result in an operation being executed. The items and arcs in boldface are those added for the new command menu.

FIGURE 4.10
MENU HIERARCHY FOR AN EXAMPLE COMMAND MENU

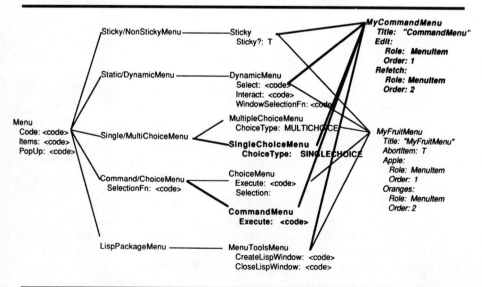

In this hierarchy, another class, **MyCommandMenu** is created. It is a new menu with two menu items, Edit and Refetch. It inherits from two different existing mixins, **SingleChoiceMenu**, which will allow for a single item to be selected, and **CommandMenu**, which will invoke a command upon item selection. We will see that the main difference is that the **SelectionFn** method of **Command/ChoiceMenu** passes the selected item as an operation to the Editor of which the menu is a part, resulting in a command execution.

The protocol for menu instantiation and display is the same as previously shown. The protocol for selecting the item is defined as follows:

```
Action                                                          Receiver
(1) (send 'MyCommandMenu 'Select) -->                           DynamicMenu
      ;; menu instantiation and display
           .
           .
           .
      ;; menu interaction, response and cleanup
(7)    <result> = (send 'MyCommandMenu-01 'Interact) -->        DynamicMenu
(8)    <result> =
       (send 'MyCommandMenu-01 'WindowSelectionFn ) -->         DynamicMenu
(9)    if (send 'MyCommandMenu-01' Sticky?) then Highlight      StickyMenu
(10)   (send 'MyCommandMenu-01' SelectionFn <result>)           Command/ChoiceMenu
(11)   <choicetype> =
       (send 'MyCommandMenu-01 'ChoiceType 'Get)                SingleChoiceMenu
(12)   <result> = if (<choicetype> = singlechoice) then
                     (first <result>) else...
(13)   (send 'MyCommandMenu-01' Execute <result>) -->           CommandMenu
(13.1)     (send '<editor-instance> 'Execute <result>)          Editor-Class
(14)   (send 'MyCommandMenu-01 'CloseLispWindow)                MenuToolsMenu
```

The differences are shown in italics. The **Execute** message (13) is the main difference between this example and the previous one. The **Execute** method in a **CommandMenu** causes the item selected to be invoked as an operation of the associated editor (13.1).

4.4.3 PropertyDisplay Example

Another example of reuse may be found in the PropertyDisplay components of HyperClass. This is an example showing the evolutionary design of the HyperClass kernel, where design-driven extensions often involve moving to a finer-grain level of detail in the sequence of methods that make up a particular protocol.

In this example, the problem is to display a caption and value pair in an object editor. The caption and value are displayed as follows:

Object: Foo

The caption, **Object**, is shown in boldface and is an active region (i.e., sen-

FIGURE 4.11

HYPERCLASS CAPTION&VALUE PROPERTY DISPLAY HIERARCHY

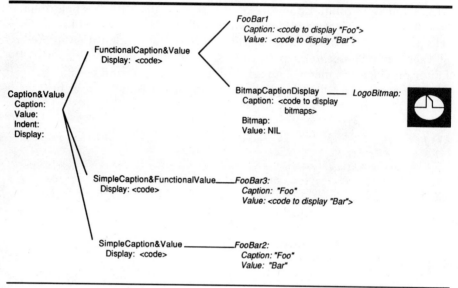

sitive to mouse clicks). The value, **Foo**, is shown in lightface and is not active. Another variant on this is to print the caption and value pair as follows:

Here the value is a bitmap and requires a different printing method than does the textual value in the previous example.

These display behaviors may be characterized by whether the caption and/or value are printed in a simple format (supplied by the system kernel), or whether the caption and/or value are printed according to a user-defined printing method.

In an earlier version of HyperClass, the class hierarchy for **Caption&-Value** property displays was as shown in Figure 4.11.

Caption&Value is a specialization of **PropertyDisplay** in HyperClass. When a caption and value pair is displayed in an object editor window, the **Display** method is invoked. Note that each of the direct descendants of **Caption&Value** have distinct (and different) **Display** methods. There is no reuse of any portion of the **Display** method. **Display** basically takes the following actions:

1. Set the initial *x* and *y* position
2. Display the caption

3. Display the value
4. Set the final *x* and *y* position
5. Return an instance of a window region structure for the display.

For the **FunctionalCaption&Value** class, the **Display** method assumes that the **Caption** and **Value** slots contain printing functions. For FooBar1, the **Caption** method is a printing function for the string "Foo." Likewise, the **Value** method is a printing function for the string "Bar." **BitmapCaptionDisplay** is also a specialization of **FunctionalCaption&Display**. It uses the same **Display** method as FooBar1, and the **Caption** method is a printing function for bitmaps. **LogoDisplay** is a bitmap caption, with a **Bitmap** whose value is the bitmap shown.

SimpleCaption&FunctionalValue has a **Display** method that assumes the caption is a simple text string and will format the text in the **Caption** slot in boldface. It assumes the **Value** slot contains a printing function for the value. FooBar3 is a class description whose **Caption** slot contains the string "Foo", which will be printed by the **Display** method, and the **Value** slot contains a printing function for the string "Bar".

Finally, **SimpleCaption&Value** contains a **Display** method that assumes both the **Caption** and **Value** slots contain simple strings and therefore provides printing methods for both.

One way to enhance reusability in this structure is to break the **Display** method into five finer-grain methods. They are:

1. **SetInitialPosition**, for setting the initial *x* and *y* position,
2. **Display-Caption**, for displaying the caption,
3. **Display-Value**, for displaying the value,
4. **SetFinalPosition**, for setting the final *x* and *y* position, and
5. **Create-Region** for creating and returning a window region structure for the display.

With this new formulation, a single **Display** method can be defined that sends a message to each of the new methods above, reusing **SetInitialPosition**, **SetFinalPosition**, and **Create-Region**. The **Display-Caption** and **Display-Value** methods can be specialized for each of the combined **Caption** and **Value** printing behaviors. The revised hierarchy is shown in Figure 4.12.

The new, finer-grain methods are associated with the **Caption&Value** class. These will be used by all of its specializations. There are now two descendants of **Caption&Value**. Each has distinct methods for displaying the caption and value pairs. For FooBar1, a descendant of **FunctionalCaption&Value**, the **Display-Caption** method assumes that the **Caption** slot of the class contains a printing function for the caption and messages the **Caption** slot. Likewise, the **Display-Value** method assumes that the **Value** slot also contains a printing function for the value.

For the class FooBar2, a descendant of **SimpleCaption&Value**, the **Display-Caption** method assumes the **Caption** slot contains a simple text string, and so it contains a printing function for the string. The **Display-Value**

FIGURE 4.12

REVISED HYPERCLASS CAPTION&VALUE PROPERTY DISPLAY HIERARCHY

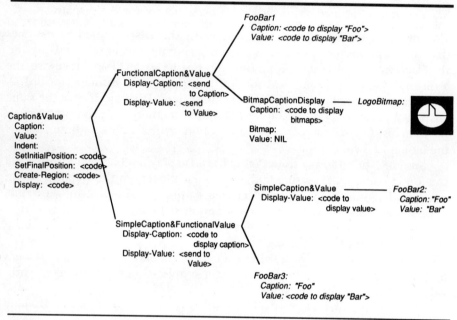

method (which overrides the method in **SimpleCaption&FunctionalValue**) also assumes that the **Value** slot contains a simple string, and it also contains a printing function for the value.

Actually, since we are combining several distinct and disjoint behaviors, one other alternative design structure would be to organize it as a collection of mixins. Figure 4.13 shows this alternative class hierarchy.

FIGURE 4.13

HYPERCLASS CAPTION&VALUE PROPERTY DISPLAY HIERARCHY USING MIXINS

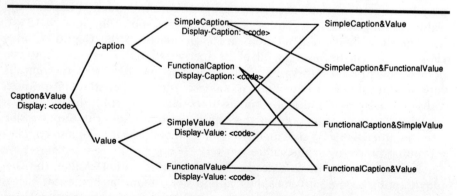

We see that there are alternative designs, both for class hierarchy organization and for method decomposition. The difficulty in building these systems comes in deciding what collection of abstractions and methods to use.
Halbert and O'Brien [1987] discuss guidelines for making these types of
design decisions. To decide whether to use subclasses (as in Fig. 4.12), or
comixins (as in Fig. 4.13), the programmer should consider several factors, including reusability. If the behavior can be shared and reused by several
subclasses, then Halbert suggests that a new class be defined. Other factors
may influence the decision, such as how complex the behavior is to implement or how applicable the behavior is to the class where it is defined. Often
the decision is one of style. In Fig. 4.12, each of the classes in the hierarchy
is a complete implementation of the conceptual type. Each will respond correctly to the protocol for printing a caption and a value. In Fig. 4.13, only
the leaf nodes define complete implementations. The mixins are incomplete
implementations that must be combined into new classes to be complete.

4.4.4 Examples Summary

What has been reused and how? In the **Menu** hierarchy example, not only are
individual functions reused, but more importantly, entire classes are reused.
This increases the amount of code reused since each class contains a number
of methods. The conceptual structure for **Menus** is reused essentially as is.
We saw this with the reuse of **Menu**, **Window**, and other class structures. It
goes without saying that all of this is possible only because of the inheritance
and message-passing capabilities of an object-oriented framework.

Mixins play a large role in reuse. Through proper partitioning of functionality across menus, new menus may be created by combining different
desired behaviors, but without inheriting more than was bargained for since
the mixins are designed in such a way as to have disjoint behaviors. In this
case, adding or changing a single type of behavior (e.g., single choice versus multiple choice) means changing from one superclass (**SingleChoice**) to
another (**MultipleChoice**). We change the superclass link but nothing in the
class definition itself. This was also demonstrated by showing how a command
menu was built. Simply replacing the **ChoiceMenu** with the **CommandMenu**
in the superclass for the new menu class changes the particular behavior
from choice to command without any other changes—most important, without code changes.

One factor that enhances reuse using object-oriented programming is
declarative programming. Representing multiple possible states by a variable (as
with the **ChoiceType**: MULTICHOICE vs. **ChoiceType**: SINGLECHOICE),
we can write a single **SelectionFn** method that gets the value of this variable and takes the appropriate action. An alternative would be to have two
separate **SelectionFn** functions, each one specialized for **SingleChoice** vs.
MultipleChoice.

In the **PropertyDisplay** example, the leverage of using finer-grain methods was illustrated. Reuse is enhanced when smaller, shared behaviors can

be defined and placed higher in the hierarchy, making the common parts of processing available to descendants.

Reuse of the conceptual structure (in HyperClass) becomes easier with more familiarity with the structure. Creating the example **MyFruitMenu** is relatively easy if one knows the menu hierarchy and its decomposition. The general development paradigm in HyperClass is to find an example of an editor, or editor component, that is something like what is desired and then to *copy and specialize* that structure. That is essentially what was done for the examples.

This points to a problem: When the system gets large, how does one find the right jumping-off place? HyperClass provides some help here in that a user can bring up an example editor, and then access the HyperClass structure behind it. Specialized editors are also provided to assist in the process, but it remains a challenge and a very real problem for software reuse.

4.5 RELATED WORK

Object-oriented programming has been noted by many others for its ability to enhance reusability. Biggerstaff and Richter [1987] place object-oriented programming high on a continuum of reusability techniques that maximize generality and flexibility. Cox [1986] defines the notion of "software IC's," making an analogy to hardware reusability, by construction of well-defined libraries of classes with well-defined purposes. To maximize reuse, these classes must be structured very carefully. Our experience with HyperClass also supports this conclusion.

Smalltalk [Goldberg, 1983] was a pioneer system in the use and reuse of objects for building user interfaces. Smalltalk introduced many important ideas about object classes and taxonomic inheritance. Taxonomies of objects for graphics and interfaces have since appeared in specific user interfaces [Cox, 1986; Curry and Ayers, 1984].

Meyer [1987] also makes a strong argument for the use of object-oriented programming techniques for reuse. He argues that many of the features of object-oriented programming, such as inheritance and message passing, enhance its ability to reuse code by direct language support far beyond standard languages without such facilities.

4.6 ASSESSMENT AND PERSPECTIVE

The strength that object-oriented programming brings to bear on the problem of software reuse stems from a number of factors—most notably, the ability to define structured libraries of classes and the ability to use inheritance to navigate the resulting hierarchy to access reusable components (via messages). A well-structured library also helps the developer manage the complexity of the problem. Reuse of the class definitions is reuse at a higher level of abstraction than simple code reuse, which is an important option: Even if a particular leaf node cannot be reused, one may be able to back off to an abstraction and reuse it.

An obvious advantage to systems designed and built with reuse in mind is that they will have a common look and feel—certainly with respect to a user interface, but also with respect to other internal system interfaces—since so many components and protocols are common. Maintaining such systems is potentially simpler because the maintainer need look in only one place for a common component to change. However, using mixins, messages, and inheritance tends to spread responsibility throughout the class hierarchy so that without powerful browsing tools, it may be more difficult to isolate what class or what method is responsible for a problem.

As an object-oriented system matures, there is less and less code required to add new extensions. With HyperClass, an application-specific extension (which closely fits existing functionality) will need several class definitions but very little new code (if any). For new areas of functionality, however, such as adding a "box-and-arrows" graphics interface [Barth, 1986; Smith *et al.*, 1987], the extensions are more substantive: Reusing general capabilities such as the window, menu and interaction behaviors is possible, but new classes and methods must be defined and integrated into the framework.

However, there are weaknesses of the approach. Since both classes and methods are reused, the problem the programmer is faced with is (1) determining whether there is a class or set of classes which may be reused, (2) determining which methods may be reused and which must be overridden, and (3) understanding the higher-level protocols used by the classes. This process often requires an additional step in which parts of the kernel hierarchy must first be modified (redesigned), methods decomposed into finer-grain detail, and then a new class defined with accompanying methods. These changes mostly consist of design enhancements that make explicit what was previously implicit in the design of the kernel hierarchy. This is the way it usually goes: To maximize reuse one must often go back and rethink the design and the code to be reused. It is experience that makes this work, but additional future work on tools to support this process (e.g., making protocols explicit) would help tremendously.

Object-oriented systems are not extended only at the leaf nodes. Rather, a portion of the kernel is often modified and then an extension is applied. Hopefully, as the system design matures, the necessity for redesign will be reduced; that is, some parts of the system will stabilize. But software is such a malleable medium that we continually mold it to everchanging applications, new requirements, and so on. This evolutionary design process raises important questions about object-oriented programming system implementations in terms of what is required to facilitate the process over the lifetime of the application system as it is applied to various problems. One question, for example, is whether the original source code is required to extend the framework. Others include whether methods can be added incrementally or how to deal with multiple incompatible versions of the software.

Solving the problems of understanding the framework and finding components to be reused will require specialized tools. HyperClass provides basic browsing support for this activity, but we are only beginning to augment it with inferencing capabilities that provide active assistance [Schoen *et al.*, 1988]. The paradigm of *copy and specialize* for object-oriented programming systems is still the most powerful one for the "modify" part of the reuse process, but it assumes there is something obvious or visible to help the user in the "understanding" part of the process. With a user interface toolkit, the understanding process is simplified by the fact that the user can actually see examples on a screen. With an operating system, the analogy is more difficult to make. It all boils down to the fact that designing good models is art!

One final comment pertains to performance. There is certainly a trade-off between a highly modular design that maximizes reuse and one that maximizes runtime performance. The cost of that modularity is found in the extra message passing needed to invoke (fine-grain) methods, the need to search for shared methods in a hierarchy, and class instantiation. Some of this may be avoided as object-oriented compilation techniques develop, but today there is not a clear-cut solution. Caching and reusing existing structures is one way to reduce the amount of time required. In HyperClass, instantiated editor complexes are saved for later reuse by another editee. When an editor is deactivated (e.g., its window is closed), the binding to the editee is broken; to reuse this structure, new bindings are made, which is much cheaper than recreating the instances but costs the space required to save these instances.

Despite these problems, it is noteworthy that most of the customized HyperClass interfaces built for applications require only a few days or weeks to build. This short development time can be attributed mostly to the particular set of behaviors encapsulated in HyperClass, with a uniform, relatively fine-grain protocol used throughout. These characteristics ease the problem of determining what is in the system and what mixins to use as starting points for customizing interfaces. One indicator of the ease with which interfaces can be implemented in HyperClass is the growing collection of special-purpose editors and tools. To date, more than 50 specialized editors have been built by HyperClass users. The toolkit is now mature enough to support interfaces as complex as that in the *Dipmeter Advisor* system, as well as the control-panel interface to the *Crystal* well-logging environment [Smith *et al.*, 1984].

ACKNOWLEDGMENTS

HyperClass is a direct descendant of the first two versions of Impulse, both of which were designed and implemented by Eric Schoen. Mike Kleyn designed the structural geology editor. Eric Schoen and Bob Young provided significant comments on the content and organization of this paper.

References

Barth, Paul B. An object-oriented approach to graphical interfaces. *ACM Transactions on Graphics Special Issue on User Interface Software*, 5(2):142–172, April 1986.

Biggerstaff, T., and Richter, C. Reusability framework, assessment, and directions. *IEEE Software*, 4(2): 41–49, March 1987.

Cox, B. J. *Object-Oriented Programming, An Evolutionary Approach*. Reading, Mass.: Addison-Wesley, 1986.

Curry, G. A., and Ayers, R. M. Experience with traits in the Xerox Star workstation. *IEEE Software*, 10(5): 519–527, September 1984.

Goldberg, A. *Smalltalk-80: The Language and Its Implementation*. Reading, Mass.: Addison-Wesley, 1983.

Halbert, D. C., and O'Brien, P. D. Using types and inheritance in object-oriented programming. *IEEE Software*, 4(5):71–79, September 1987.

Keene, S. *Object Oriented Programming in Common Lisp: A Programmer's Guide to CLOS*. Reading, Mass.: Addison-Wesley, 1989.

Meyer, B. Reusability: the case for object-oriented programming. *IEEE Software*, 4(2): 50–63, March 1987.

Moon, D. A. Object-oriented programming with flavors. *Proceedings of the First ACM Conference on Object-Oriented Systems, Languages, and Applications*, pp. 1–8. New York: ACM, 1986.

Scheifler, R. W. *X Window System Protocol*. Cambridge, Mass.: MIT, 1987.

Schoen, E., and Smith, R. G. Impulse: A display-oriented editor for Strobe. *Proceedings of the National Conference on Artificial Intelligence*, 356–358, August 1983.

Schoen, E.; Smith, R. G.; and Buchanan, B. Design of knowledge-based systems with a knowledge-based assistant. *IEEE Transactions on Software Engineering*, (14)12: 1771–1791, December 1988.

Smith, R. G. Strobe: Support for structured object knowledge representation. *Proceedings of the Eighth International Joint Conference on Artificial Intelligence*, IJCAI, pp. 855–858, August 1983.

Smith, R. G.; Lafue, G. M. E.; Schoen, E.; and Vestal, S. C. Declarative task description as a user interface structuring mechanism. *Computer*, 17(9): 29–38, September 1984.

Smith, R. G. On the development of commercial expert systems. *AI Magazine*, 5(3): 61–73, Fall 1984.

Smith, R. G., and Carando, P. Structured object programming in Strobe (Interlisp D Version). SDR Research Note, SYS-86-23, December 1986.

Smith, R. G.; Barth, P. S.; and Young, R. L. A substrate for object-oriented user interface design. In *Research Directions in Object-Oriented Programming*. B. Shriver and P. Wegner (eds.). Cambridge, Mass.: MIT Press, pp. 253–315, 1987.

Stefik, M. J., and Bobrow, D. G. Object oriented programming: Themes and variations. *AI Magazine*, 6(4): 40–62, 1986.

CHAPTER 5

USE OF THE MODEL
EQUATIONAL LANGUAGE
AND PROGRAM GENERATOR
BY MANAGEMENT
PROFESSIONALS

NOAH S. PRYWES
University of Pennsylvania

EVAN D. LOCK
Computer Command and Control Co.

5.1 INTRODUCTION

The introduction of nonprocedural equational-type languages and respective compilers rather than procedural languages significantly improves the productivity of composing, testing, and maintaining computer software. Nonprocedural equational languages state rules as formal equations without regard to the order of the computations. An important characteristic of these languages is that variables may assume only a single value [Ashcroft and Wadge, 1977; Backus, 1978; Ackerman, 1982; Agerwala and Arvind,

Prepared with support from the Office of Naval Research, Contract No.N00014-76-C-0416.

1982; Prywes and Pnueli, 1983]. The description of a computational task is an abstract definition that does the same job as the series of commands that comprise a procedural program; therefore we refer to it as a specification. Such a specification is much shorter and more concise than a corresponding conventional program. It consists primarily of equations that specify transformations between variable structures, without regard to controlling, timing, or sequencing of program events. It is concerned with the rules of the problem and not with how to perform the computation efficiently. This reduces the level of computer programming skills required of the developers. Furthermore, documentation and a prototype are produced automatically, allowing the user to verify how closely the specification reflects the true intentions. Due to the nonprocedural semantics, the equational language compiler contains much more comprehensive checking than conventional compilers, which contributes to reduction in debugging time. The compiler also optimizes the produced programs.

This paper addresses the question of whether it is feasible and advantageous for the nonprogrammer professional to express a problem precisely in a language that will be both implemented by the automated environment and understood by the nonprogrammer community. The objective is to reduce dependence on the data processing department, which is typically strained to assign staff for changes that involve searching through complicated documentation and making tedious, error-prone modifications. It will shorten the current long development times and strengthen the professional's independence. The professional can then directly reuse the specification in future applications.

The approach to the above question has been to use a language that is comfortable for the nonprogrammer professional to use, yet is directly accepted by an automatic program generator that implements the specified system. In this study we used a mathematically oriented specification language and an automatic program generator, called MODEL [Davis, 1981; Prywes, Pnueli, and Shastry, 1979; Prywes and Pnueli, 1983]. It has been used for stating rules (described in accounting publications), extending and modifying them, and implementing an accounting system. The MODEL language describes the data and its interrelationships without referencing any computer operations. The result is a language that is free of the conventional programming control and flow concepts. The language and program generator have been designed to offer greater productivity in development and greater ease in maintenance. The MODEL language and program generator permit a person with limited computer background to specify computation rules, databases, displays, and reports. A program corresponding to this specification is automatically generated along with documentation. The program generator also assists in the development of a specification by conducting extensive checking of completeness and consistency and by issuing warning and error messages. These messages guide the user in producing a specification that is complete, consistent, and unambiguous.

Conducting experiments to obtain software development statistics is expensive and difficult to manage. The scope of this experiment was limited to one developer but emphasized the realism and extensive features of the accounting system that was developed and the careful recording of development time statistics. It should be emphasized that MODEL is a general-purpose language. Thus it is applicable to both business and scientific computations in batch or interactive modes. The choice of an accounting example does not imply a limitation in applicability. The developed accounting system compared favorably with commercially offered accounting systems and incorporated state-of-the-art features, including current prices and valuation of assets [Ernst and Whinney, 1979; FASB, 1979, 1981]. It was developed progressively in three stages, with interruptions of three to six months between stages, to investigate reusability, system extension, and maintenance aspects. Statistics were collected by module (7 modules), by stage of development, by development steps (described further) and by types of errors detected and corrected. The developer (the second author) was an accounting student who was not familiar with the PL/1 language in which object programs were generated by the MODEL program generator. The time taken to learn MODEL is included in the reported development times.

The first two stages of the development consisted of the general ledger and inventory systems. A pertinent case of dynamically introducing a new accounting standard has been studied in the third stage of the development. It consisted of introducing Financial Accounting Standard 33 (FAS 33) [Alexander, Oct. 1981]. FAS 33 requires financial statements with supplementary information to reflect changing prices. As FAS 33 affects large corporations, one can reasonably assume that changes to the accounting system are to be made in a complex computerized environment. FAS 33 is both highly controversial and complex [Cougar, 1975]. It is controversial in that the current set of regulations are subject to change. The Financial Accounting Standards Board has a policy of researching and assessing the probable effects of the standard on those who must incur costs in providing the information [Endress, 1979; Ernst and Whinney, 1979]. Financial reporting of changing prices is complex mainly because of measurement problems. There has been considerable research performed on the choice of accounting and reporting methods, the selection of indexes, and the construction of those indexes [Bell, 1982; Benston and Krasney, 1978; Vasarhelyi and Pearson, 1979]. Characteristics of special industries impose further difficulties (e.g., financial services, real estate, and oil and gas [FASB, May 1981].) Significant difficulties surround the choice of an index (consumer prices, general prices, or specific prices) and which prices (expert assessments, internal pricing systems, buying, selling, or yet others) to use for calculating the appropriate adjustment for changing prices. To incorporate these choices into an accounting system in a large corporation would require extensive funds and time [Martinelli, 1982]. Accounting systems in large companies include an enormous amount of software that has limited freedom. Expansion, let alone change, is limited because of the complexity of the programs and the inadequacy of documentation. To update the programs, new code must be inserted and thoroughly tested. This is an expensive process.

Numerous companies have installed software packages to handle the accounting system (for a survey, see [FASB, July 1982]). Modifications to such a system may require a significant additional investment to purchase another portion of the software package or expensive customization. Alternatively, companies may purchase database management systems (e.g., IDMS, ADABAS, IMS), report writers and/or application generators (e.g., Natural, Generation Five) [Snyders, 1981] to reduce programming costs. These systems require special skills to use [Lientz and Swanson, 1978]. MODEL is a general-purpose language that is not limited in capabilities by a special application or database environment. Also, while application generators sacrifice efficiency and some have even been developed as interpreters, the MODEL program generator is a compiler, translating the specification into highly efficient conventional programs that can be used repeatedly in production runs.

5.2 THE ACCOUNTING SYSTEM AND THE MODIFICATIONS

The initial stage in the experimental study consisted of developing a general ledger. This was followed in the second stage by adding an inventory accounting system. The modification for valuing assets at current prices was introduced in the third stage. Figure 5.1 shows the program modules and files for each stage. The first two stages were relatively independent. Establishing their requirements involved reviewing state-of-the-art accounting systems. The system in Fig. 5.1 takes transactions as input, updates accounts, and generates reports. There are two levels of detail for a given type of account. The summary account database, SUMADB, contains summary information for producing up-to-date financial reports. For example, ACCTDB contains numerous separate accounts for accounts receivable from different customers, whereas the accounts receivable account in SUMADB contains the sum of all receivables in ACCTDB. Information on accounts are separated into current year accounts (SUMADB, ACCTDB, INVADB) and historical accounts (SUMAHIST, ACCTHIST, CCHIST). SUMADB and ACCTDB contain all accounts except for the inventory account, which is detailed in INVADB and CCHIST. Reports are produced either to describe transactions that took place or to detail the contents of a particular account.

The third stage investigated how an accountant would go about incorporating accounting for changing prices. The declarations in the specification were revised to replace the previous year's results with the current cost column in the financial statements (STMTREP), as shown in Figs. 5.2–5.4.

FIGURE 5.1
ACCOUNTING SYSTEM CONSTRUCTED

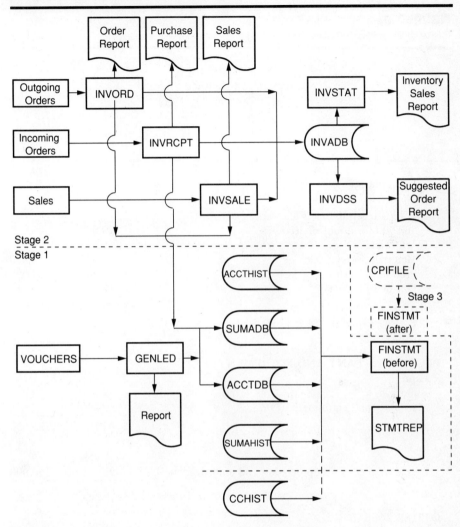

Legend:

File	Description
ACCTDB	Sub-ledger Account Data Base
ACCTHIST	History data base for ACCTDB
CCHIST	History data base for current cost numbers
CPIFILE	Monthly Consumer Price Index
INVADB	Inventory Account Data Base
STMTREP	Financial Statements (Balance Sheet, Income Statement, Statement of Changes in Financial Position)
SUMADB	Summary Account Data Base
SUMAHIST	History data base for SUMADB
VOUCHERS	Transaction vouchers input to GENLED

Module	Description
GENLED	Updates general ledger with daily transactions
INVORD	Updates inventory account for goods on order
INVRCPT	Updates inventory account for receipt of goods
INVSALE	Updates inventory account for sale of goods
INVSTAT	Produces inventory status report
INVDSS	Produces suggested order report
FINSTMT	Produces financial statements (STMTREP), closes income and expense accounts, updates history accounts

FIGURE 5.2a
BALANCE SHEET (ASSETS)

XYZ Company
Consolidated Balance Sheet
as at December 31, 1982
(in $thousands)

	Historical Cost	Current Cost
ASSETS		
CURRENT ASSETS		
Cash	$ 7,500	$ 7,500
Accounts receivable, less allowances		
300,000 for doubtful accounts	29,000	29,500
Inventories:		
Materials and Supplies	7,000	8,900
Products in Process	35,000	44,600
Finished Products	17,000	21,710
	$ 59,000	$ 75,210
Prepaid expenses	500	500
	$ 96,000	$112,710
PROPERTY, PLANT AND EQUIPMENT		
Land	$ 6,000	$ 7,750
Buildings	39,000	50,000
Machinery and equipment	59,900	77,800
	$104,900	$135,550
Less allowances for depreciation and amortization	36,400	40,000
	$ 68,500	$ 95,500
OTHER ASSETS		
Miscellaneous investments and deposits	$ 2,800	$ 2,800
Notes receivable arising from sale		
of real estate	1,000	1,000
Notes receivable from directors,		
officers and employees	150	150
Deferred charges	1,000	1,000
	$ 4,950	$ 4,950
TOTAL ASSETS	$169,450	$213,210

FIGURE 5.2b
BALANCE SHEET (LIABILITIES AND EQUITIES)

XYZ Company
Consolidated Balance Sheet
as at December 31, 1982
(in $thousands)

	Historical Cost	Current Cost
LIABILITIES AND EQUITIES		
CURRENT LIABILITIES		
Notes payable	$ 3,000	$ 3,000
Commercial paper	3,000	3,000
Trade accounts payable	15,000	15,000
Accrued expenses	9,500	9,500
Federal and state income taxes	5,000	5,000
Current portion of long-term debt	1,000	1,000
Current portion of capital lease obligations	500	500
	$ 37,000	$ 37,000
LONG-TERM DEBT (less current portion)		
7% convertible sinking fund debentures due 1998	$ 20,000	$ 20,000
10% debentures due 1992	15,000	15,000
	$ 35,000	$ 35,000
CAPITAL LEASE OBLIGATIONS, less current portion	16,500	16,500
DEFERRED INCOME TAXES	3,000	3,000
	$ 54,500	$ 54,500
SHAREHOLDERS' EQUITY		
Common stock, $1 par value:		
Authorized shares—5,000,000		
Issued and outstanding shares—3,000,000	$ 3,000	$ 3,000
Additional paid-in capital	15,000	15,000
Retained earnings	59,950	103,710
	$ 77,950	$141,710
TOTAL LIABILITIES AND EQUITIES	$169,450	$213,210

The format for these statements and the definition of historical numbers were adapted from the report on inflation accounting by Ernst and Whinney [1979]. The Statement of Changes in Financial Position (Fig. 5.4) is based on information derived from the Balance Sheet (Fig. 5.2) and the Income Statement (Fig. 5.3). Existing equations were modified and new equations were added to define the effects of changes in prices. Direct pricing was used to relate the inventory and property, plant and equipment in terms of current cost. Using these indexes, current cost amounts in normal dollars are adjusted to average-year dollars via the Consumer Price Index. The current cost numbers in average-year dollars appear in the second column in Figs. 5.2–5.4. The retained earnings are adjusted by the residual from an increase or decrease in value due to changing prices. Although FAS 33 only requires financial reporting for changing prices as supplementary information and does not require the entire set of financial statements to be adjusted, the Balance Sheet, Income Statement, and Statement of Changes in Financial Position have to be restated and reported as supplementary information.

FIGURE 5.3
INCOME STATEMENT

XYZ Company
Consolidated Income Statement
as at December 31, 1982
(in $thousands)

	Historical Cost	Current Cost
Sales (Net)	$370,000	$370,000
Costs and expenses:		
Cost of goods sold	$275,000	$275,000
Selling and administrative	71,450	71,450
Depreciation	4,000	5,900
Interest	5,550	5,550
	$356,000	$357,900
INCOME BEFORE INCOME TAXES	$ 14,000	$ 12,100
Federal and state income taxes	6,000	6,000
NET INCOME	$ 8,000	$ 6,100

FIGURE 5.4
STATEMENT OF CHANGES IN FINANCIAL POSITION

XYZ Company
Consolidated Statement of Changes in Financial Position
for the year ending December 31, 1982

	Historical Cost	Current Cost
Working Capital provided by:		
From Operations	$ 8,000	$ 6,100
Depreciation	3,500	5,400
Working Capital provided by continuing operations	$ 11,500	$ 11,500
Other sources		
10% debentures due 1992	$ 15,000	$ 15,000
Deferred income taxes	1,000	1,000
Notes Receivable	500	500
Miscellaneous investments and deposits	60	60
	$ 16,650	$ 16,650
	$ 28,060	$ 28,060
Working Capital used for:		
Retirement 7% debt	1,000	1,000
Lease Payments	500	500
Purchase of Machinery	11,500	11,700
Note Receivable from directors	10	10
Payment of dividend	3,000	3,000
	$ 16,010	$ 16,210
NET INCREASE IN WORKING CAPITAL	$ 12,050	$ 11,850

ANALYSIS OF CHANGES IN WORKING CAPITAL

	Historical Cost	Current Cost
Increase (Decrease) in Working Capital:		
Cash	$ 1,500	$ 1,500
Accounts Receivable	1,000	1,000
Inventories	8,000	7,800
Notes Payable	6,000	6,000
Commercial paper	1,000	1,000
Trade accounts payable	(1,000)	(1,000)
Accrued expenses	(1,400)	(1,400)
Federal and state income taxes	(3,000)	(3,000)
Current portion of capital lease obligations	(50)	(50)
NET INCREASE IN WORKING CAPITAL	$ 12,050	$ 11,850

5.3 USE OF MODEL IN ACCOUNTING SYSTEM DEVELOPMENT

MODEL specification development process is superficially similar to that of conventional development. There is a compiling phase in both cases that produces a series of reports summarizing the compiler's understanding of the user's input, including error messages and warnings. If the analysis determines that a certain threshold of acceptability has been reached, the compiler produces also the corresponding object program. A first feedback cycle is formed by the user consulting the compiler reports and diagnostic messages and modifying the input to the compiler. This stage of checking is called static, since it does not involve program execution. If the specification is satisfactory, the user may proceed to the next stage, called dynamic, of running the program with appropriate test data. As a result of the test run, the user may notice new errors and discrepancies in the outputs, and a second feedback cycle is formed by making modifications in the compiler input and repeating the whole process. However, the similarity is only superficial. The MODEL specification is typically one seventh the length of the produced program. Also, much more analysis and checking is done by the MODEL compiler, and many more errors are found in the static state than are found by conventional compilers.

These aspects are illustrated in the seven-step procedure for using the MODEL language and compiler, shown in Fig. 5.5. The outlined steps and the types of errors detected served as a basis for categorizing the times expended in the development. In step 1, the user conceptualizes the function of modules. In step 2, the user declares each module's name, source and target files, and the data organization, and then undertakes formulation of equations that define the rules of the problem leading to the output variables. In step 3, the MODEL compiler checks the specification and determines efficient sequencing of corresponding program events, including scope and nesting of loops, variable definitions, and input/output. Finally, it generates a program. This eliminates the need, present in conventional programming, to conceptualize the control flow of a program. It also avoids the main source of errors connected with iterations, other controls, and sequencing of program events [Endress, 1979; Green *et al.*, 1976; Schneiderwind and Hoffman, 1979].

Briefly, the operation of the MODEL compiler in step 3 is as follows: The compiler first constructs a directed graph that represents the specification and is used for checking and optimization. It is tolerant of many omissions and inconsistencies made inadvertently. This also saves tedious work. Subscripts, sizes of dimensions of arrays, interim data declarations, and certain equations may be omitted in certain situations. Error messages soliciting corrections are sent when other types of errors are detected. The messages explain the errors in terms of the specification and not in terms of any scheme of execution of the computation, which is invisible to the user.

FIGURE 5.5
OVERALL USE OF MODEL PROCESSOR

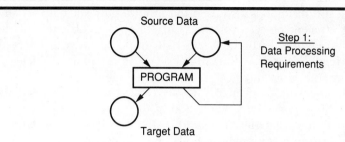

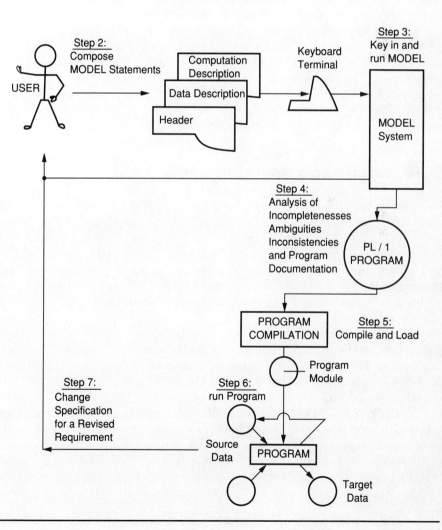

The compiler produces documentation including formatted listings and cross-reference tables of various attributes of entities in the specification. The graph of the specification is also used to optimize the execution scheme and generate an efficient object program [Lu, 1981]. The objective of the static checking is to identify early the errors that would be costly if deferred. The static inner feedback cycle is thus intended to be the major vehicle for obtaining an error-free program.

The dynamic checking is primarily to alert the user to the need for improvements in the requirements. Validation of the program based on execution with test data (i.e., dynamic checking) is still necessary, but to a lesser degree than when using traditional methods. This is performed in steps 5 and 6, where the produced program is compiled and run in a computer with test data. In step 7, the user examines whether the results conform with the intended requirements. Changes and corrections resulting from the test run are expressed by MODEL repeating the static and dynamic cycles in steps 2 through 7. The corrections are simpler than with a procedural language because the order of specification statements is arbitrary and corrections are made in statements that define the affected variables or by adding new statements at the end of the specification.

5.4   SPECIFYING A MODULE IN MODEL

The modules are too numerous to discuss in this paper. Therefore a reduced specification of the module FINSTMT (Fig. 5.1) is presented in Fig. 5.6 in order to provide a sample of the MODEL language. The function of this specification is to produce an Income Statement similar to the one in Fig. 5.3 and to close the accounts for year-end. To further simplify the example, the Income Statement is reduced to contain only one column of this year's results rather than maintaining the two column format, which includes the previous year's results.

The specification in Fig. 5.6 is in four parts: header, data description, data parameters, and equations. The user typically starts by composing the data description, followed by the equations that specify transformations. These parts are briefly explained in relation to Fig. 5.6.

The header (lines 1–3) consists of the name of the module (REDUCED_FINSTMT) the source file (SUMADB) and the target files (SUMADB and INCOME_STATEMENT). The user may consider both source and target as if they were available a priori and his task is mainly to formulate equations that define relations among data. MODEL's concise SOURCE and TARGET statements allow the user to forgo the complex READ, WRITE, OPEN, and CLOSE statements in conventional programming.

The data description section gives the organization of the above files. A data structure is described in MODEL hierarchically as a tree. This is

FIGURE 5.6
EXAMPLE OF SPECIFICATION

```
/* HEADER */
 1 MODULE: REDUCED_FINSTMT;
 2 SOURCE: SUMADB;
 3 TARGET: SUMADB, INCOME_STATEMENT;

/* DATA DESCRIPTION */
 4 1 SUMADB IS FILE, /* SUMMARY ACCOUNT DATA BASE FOR INCOME STMT */
 5   2 SUMACCT (*) IS RECORD, /* ACCOUNT RECORD */
 6     3 SUM_DESC IS FIELD (CHAR 20), /* DESCRIPTION OF ACCOUNT */
 7     3 SUM_TYPE IS FIELD (CHAR 3),   /* TYPE OF ACCOUNT */
 8     3 BEG_BALANCE IS FIELD (PIC'(9)ZVZZ'), /* BEGINNING BALANCE */
 9     3 DB_BALANCE IS FIELD (PIC'(9)ZVZZ'), /* DEBIT BALANCE OVER PERIOD */
10     3 CR_BALANCE IS FIELD (PIC'(9)ZVZZ'); /* CREDIT BALANCE OVER PERIOD */

11 1 INCOME_STATMENT IS FILE, /* INCOME STATEMENT */
12   2 HEADING (5) IS RECORD,
13     3 TITLE IS FIELD (CHAR 80), /* HEADER FOR INCOME STATEMENT */
14   2 BODY_REC (*) IS GROUP,
15     3 STMT_REC IS RECORD,
16       4 STMT_DESC IS FIELD(CHAR 50), /* ACCT. DESCRIPTION ON INCOME STMT*/
17       4 STMT_BALANCE IS FIELD (PIC'(9)ZVZZBB'), /* SINGLE COLUMN ON STMT */
18     3 BAR_REC (0: 1) IS RECORD,
19       4 BAR IS FIELD (CHAR 50); /* BAR SEPARATING SUM FROM ADDENDS */

20 1 INTVAR IS FILE, /* INVERIM VARIABLES */
21   2 SCALARS IS GROUP,
22     3 STMTDATE IS FIELD (CHAR 8); /* STATEMENT DATE FOR HEADER */

/* DATA PARAMETERS */
23 (I, J) ARE SUBSCRIPTS; /* I LINES IN HEADING; J OCCURENCES OF BAR; */
24 /* 'ST' REPRESENTS SECTION TOTAL */
25 SIZE.BAR_REC = IF SUBSTR (OLD.SUM_TYPE, 1,2) = 'ST' THEN 1 ELSE 0;

/* ASSERTIONS FOR NEW.SUMADB FILE */
26 NEW.BEG_BALANCE = OLD.BEG_BALANCE + OLD.DB_BALANCE + OLD.CR_BALANCE;
27 NEW.DB_BALANCE = 0;
28 NEW.CR_BALANCE = 0;
```

FIGURE 5.6 *(Cont.)*

```
/* ASSERTIONS FOR INCOME_STATEMENT */
29 TITLE(I) = IF I=1 THEN COPY(' ',34)||'XYZ COMPANY'
30        ELSE IF I=2 THEN COPY(' ',25)||'CONSOLIDATED INCOME STATEMENT'
31        ELSE IF I=3 THEN COPY(' ',26)||'FOR THE YEAR ENDING'|| STMTDATE
32        ELSE ' ';
33 STMT_DESC = OLD.SUM_DESC;
34 STMT_BALANCE = NEW.BEG_BALANCE;
35 /* 'STE' REPRESENTS THE ENDING SECTION TOTAL */
36 BAR(J) = IF OLD.SUM_TYPE = 'STE' THEN COPY(' ',50)||'----------'
37                                  ELSE COPY(' ',50)||'----------'
38 /* (DATE IS A MODEL FUNCTION THAT RETURNS YYMMDD) */
39 STMTDATE = SUBSTR(DATE,3,2)||'/'||SUBSTR(DATE,5,2)||'/'||SUBSTR(DATE,1,2);
```

similar to COBOL and PL/1. The apex node is called a FILE, an intermediate node is either a GROUP or a RECORD. A RECORD is the smallest data structure exchanged between the external environment and the module. A terminal node is denoted a FIELD. Each of the nodes is named and may repeat—denoted by the number of repetitions in parentheses following the name (* indicates a variable number of repetitions). MODEL uses the primitive data types of PL/1: picture, decimal (fixed or float), binary, bit, and character. An array may be a repeating node or a descendent (in the tree) of a repeating node. For example, the SUMADB file (lines 4–10) contains a vector of account descriptions, SUM_DESC. Likewise, in the target file, INCOME_STATEMENT, the field STMT_DESC is viewed as a vector of account descriptions. These entire two vectors are assumed by the specifier as available simultaneously, and the specifier need not consider their order of definition or timing. The program generator has the task of attaining computation and memory efficiently without the user's involvement.

Lines 4–10 of Fig. 5.6 describe SUMADB, which contains an unspecified number of accounts. Each account is detailed with a description, an account type, a beginning balance, and the debit and credit balances since the beginning of the period. The sequence of accounts corresponds to the sequence of accounts in the Income Statement in Fig. 5.3.

Reports can be described either directly, through data declarations and equations, or indirectly, through declaring a layout of the report from which the data declarations and equations are generated automatically. For brevity, the use of layouts of reports or screens is omitted here.

INCOME_STATEMENT, viewed in Fig. 5.3, has three types of lines, or records: headings, accounts, and bars. The data description for this file (lines 11–19 of Fig. 5.6) reflects this by having a record that repeats five times for the heading followed by a group of repeating account and bar records. The heading records contain character strings whereas an account record contains account descriptions followed by account balances. Intermixed between some of the account records are bars to separate sums, with a double bar denoting the final sum. Declaration of interim variables is optional in MODEL.

Interim data declarations may be omitted and they are being produced automatically by the compiler. The description of the interim file INTVAR (lines 20–22) is shown in Fig. 5.6 to improve clarity. It describes a variable that is neither source nor target, but is used in defining some other variable. The interim variable STMDATE is defined in line 22 using the built-in DATE function to depict the date in the form mm/dd/yy. The date could have been directly defined in the TITLE equation (line 31), but was defined separately for clarity.

The arrays in the data structures have variable size dimensions. Individual elements of these arrays are referenced by using subscript expressions. Line 23 declares two free variables, I and J, that are used as subscripts. They assume all the integer values in their respective ranges. These may be ranges of dimensions of the variables that they are used to index. Note that this differs from ordinary variables, which can assume only a single value. I represents the index of a heading element in INCOME_STATEMENT and J represents the index of a BAR_REC element.

Attributes of the data such as size of dimensions are called data parameters. The size of I is explicitly defined to be 5 in line 12. The range of J is defined by the equation in line 25. This equation uses the MODEL prefix SIZE to denote the number of elements in the variable named in the suffix. The size, however, may only vary in this case from 0 to 1; that is, if the size is 0, the data structure and equations that reference it are omitted entirely; if the size is 1, there is a single occurrence. This determines whether bars appear in the income statement (SIZE.BAR_REC = 1) or not (SIZE.BAR_REC = 0). The bar appears if the account just above it was a section total as described in the field SUM_TYPE. The size of the vector of accounts (line 5 in SUMADB and line 14 in INCOME_STATEMENT) has been represented by an asterisk, implying an unspecified number of elements. MODEL automatically defines this size to be determined by the end of the SUMADB file.

An equation, though similar in syntax to an assignment statement in procedural languages should be regarded quite differently by the user of MODEL. The meaning is identical to the mathematical notion of equivalence between the two sides of the equal sign. This aspect is basic to the difference between procedural and nonprocedural languages. Each variable name in a nonprocedural language may denote only one value. Also the historical values of data, namely those that would not be needed further in a computation, must be explicitly represented by symbolic names. In contrast, procedural languages allow assigning different values to the same variable and historical values are overwritten if not needed further.

For the variables in the SUMADB file, which are updated (listed as both source and target in lines 2 and 3), MODEL offers two versions of a file, prefixed by OLD and NEW. The equation for the beginning balance is shown in line 26. This type of equation is common to specifications involving transactions on accounts. The debit and credit balances are in lines 27 and 28.

If an OLD or NEW prefix is accidentally omitted, an error message will be issued citing the ambiguity. Equations are automatically generated for samenamed fields that remain unchanged. For example, the field SUM_DESC in SUMADB (the account description) is not altered and the "OLD...= NEW..." equation is automatically generated with a message of this action issued in the error and warning report.

The equations that define the Income Statement are found in lines 29–37. The heading is described (lines 29–32) as having the title "XYZ COMPANY" on the first line, "CONSOLIDATED INCOME STATEMENT" on the second line, and the date on the third line. The fourth and fifth lines are blank (' '). The body of the report, as detailed in the data description section, contains columns of account names and the debit or credit balances. The equations that define these target variables are in lines 33–34. Dashed lines are used in lines 36–37 via the field BAR to separate the addends from the sum.

5.5 INCORPORATING FAS 33 INTO THE ACCOUNTING SYSTEM

The purpose of incorporating FAS 33 into the accounting system (in the third stage), was to show how an accountant can reuse and modify old specifications and to demonstrate how to express complex accounting rules in a precise manner acceptable to the program generator. The sample reduced specification, REDUCED_FINSTMT, from Fig. 5.6 is used.

To incorporate FAS 33 into the accounting system, it is necessary to differentiate between monetary and nonmonetary accounts. FAS_TYPE, denoting the type of the account, was therefore added to the summary account file, SUMADB (see Fig. 5.6). The expanded portion of SUMADB is

```
1 SUMADB is FILE
   2 SUMACCT (*) IS RECORD
      3 SUM_DESC IS FIELD (CHAR 45)
      3 SUM_TYPE IS FIELD (CHAR 3)
      3 FAS-TYPE IS FIELD (CHAR 1), /* ADDED VARIABLE */
```

The remainder of the file description is omitted for simplicity.

Next the report INCOME_STATEMENT must be modified to include an additional column for current cost numbers CC_COLUMN, which is added to the INCOME_STATEMENT as follows:

```
2 BODY_REC (*) IS GROUP
   3 STMT_REC IS RECORD,
      4 STMT_DESC IS FIELD(CHAR 50)
      4 HC_COLUMN IS FIELD (PIC '(9)ZVZZBB'),
      /* HISTORICAL COST COLUMN */
      4 CC_COLUMN IS FIELD (PIC '(9)ZVZZBB'),
      /* CURRENT COST COLUMN */
```

The rest of the data description is unchanged from Fig. 5.6.

The added column must have a respective heading in the report. This requires no change in data description and solely affects the equation for the TITLE field.

```
TITLE(I) = IF I=1 THEN COPY(' ',34)||'XYZ COMPANY'
       ELSE IF I=2 THEN COPY(' ',25)||'CONSOLIDATED INCOME STATEMENT'
       ELSE IF I=3 THEN COPY(' ',26)||'FOR THE YEAR ENDING'||STMTDATE
       ELSE IF I=4 THEN COPY(' ',50)||'HISTORICAL '||'   CURRENT   '
     ELSE COPY(' ',50)||'    COST   '||'    COST    ';
```

COPY is a built-in function that repeats the first argument the number of times specified in the second argument. In the given code, 34 spaces are copied before 'XYZ COMPANY'. The concatenation operator, '||', is used to glue the string of 34 spaces to the string of 'XYZ COMPANY'.

CC_COLUMN must be defined by an equation:

```
CC_COLUMN = IF OLD.FAS_TYPE='M' THEN HC_COLUMN
     ELSE HC_COLUMN + CC_ADJUSTMENT;
```

This equation states that the numbers in the current cost column (CC_COLUMN) are the same as the numbers in the historical cost column (HC_COLUMN) except when the account is nonmonetary, in which case the current cost column includes an adjustment (CC_ADJUSTMENT). The equation for the current cost adjustment CC_ADJUSTMENT, is not shown here for the sake of brevity, but it is described later in the more general discussion of modifications to FINSTMT. The equation OLD.FAS_TYPE = NEW.FAS_TYPE is generated by the system.

More generally, modifications made to the full specification of FINSTMT (see Fig. 5.1) include changes similar to those made to REDUCED_FINSTMT, as well as some additional and more complex modifications. As the dotted lines in the area of stage 3 in Fig. 5.1 indicate, additional files are required in FINSTMT for current cost history (CCHIST) and monthly current price indexes (CPIFILE). The current cost history file (CCHIST) serves both as source and target, since it must be updated with the current period's results. The modified header section of the FINSTMT specification follows, updated with the names of the additional files (CCHIST and CPIFILE).

```
SOURCE: SUMADB, SUMAHIST,ACCTDB,ACCTHIST,INVADB,
CCHIST, CPIFILE;
TARGET: STMTREP,SUMADB,ACCTDB,SUMAHIST,ACCTHIST,
INVADB,CCHIST;
```

In order to produce current cost-adjusted numbers, for instance, ending inventory balances must be restated from nominal dollars to average-year dollars. The following equations involve adjusting for average-year dollars, and summing all items to get the current cost total value.

```
CC_AVG(ITEM) = CC_ENDBAL(ITEM)*CPI(1,AVG_MONTH)
/CPI(1,THIS_MONTH);
CC_TOT = SUM(DCC_AVG(ITEM),ITEM);
```

CC_AVG is the current cost valuation of ending inventory for a particular item in average-year dollars and CC_TOT is the sum over the current cost valuation for all items. ITEM is the index of an inventory item. It is used here as a free subscript variable. In a conventional programming language, the user would be concerned with placing this statement in the proper loop for all inventory items. There are no loops in MODEL and the ranges of the generated loops are determined by the program generator from information in the specification. Inconsistencies or omissions of range information are detected by the program generator. CPI is given by year (in reverse order, starting with present year) and by month. The subscript value (1) in the first dimension of CPI corresponds to the present year. The second dimension of CPI denotes a monthly value. AVG_MONTH is the midpoint (D) between the first month of the corporation's year and the present month, here named THIS_MONTH. Thus both AVG_MONTH and THIS_MONTH are scalar variables. Their definition is not shown here.

The equation for the current cost adjustment CC_ADJUSTMENT depends on CC_TOT (on the right hand side). In general, the difference between the current cost valuation of an account and the historical cost valuation of an account is placed in CC_ADJUSTMENT. The equations that define the current cost pertain to the inventory account, but would be similar for other accounts, such as fixed assets.

5.6 THE OPERATION OF THE MODEL COMPILER

A brief description is given here of the key methods used in the MODEL compiler. It performs the following major tasks in translation of a specification into the procedural program. After syntax analysis, the compiler constructs a dataflowlike graph to represent the specification in a convenient form. Based on the graph, implicit information is derived and entered, checks are conducted, and an optimally efficient schedule of program execution is derived. The optimized schedule is finally transformed into a procedural program (in PL/1 or C). The program includes analysis of various conditions of program failure, such as data-type errors or absence of expected records, and recovery from such failures.

The specification is represented by an array graph, where a node represents the accessing, storing, or evaluation of an entire array. A data node in the array graph has as attributes the subscripts and ranges for its dimensions. An equation node has as attributes the subscripts and ranges corresponding to the union of subscripts of the variables appearing in the equation. Thus an m-dimensional node A represents the elements from $A(1,1,\ldots,1)$ to $A(N_1, N_2, \ldots, N_m)$, where $N_1, \ldots, N_m$ are the sizes of dimensions 1 to m respectively. Similarly, a directed edge between two nodes represents all the instances of dependencies among the array elements of the nodes. The edge has as attributes the subscript expressions for each dimension. The underlying graph, where each element and equation instance is a separate node, may be derived from the array graph based on the attributes of dimensionality, range, and forms of subscript expressions that are associated with each node and edge in an array graph. The dependencies between nodes imply precedence relationships in the execution of the respective implied actions. There are several types of them. For example, a hierarchical precedence refers to the need to access a source structure before its components can be accessed, or conversely, the need to evaluate the components before a structure is stored away. Data dependency precedence refers to the need to evaluate the independent variables of an equation before the dependent variable can be evaluated. Similarly, data parameters of a structure (such as SIZE) must be evaluated before evaluating the respective structure. It is inevitable that the user will make mistakes in specifying a computation, and it is necessary to have a dialog that helps the user formulate a specification and make corrections. The automatic program design cannot be completed when a specification is inconsistent or incomplete. Therefore checking of structural consistency on a global basis has been emphasized, with special focus on iterative and recursive relations that usually encompass many entities in a specification. The specification-wide checks are categorized into checks of completeness, nonambiguity, and consistency. Incompleteness and ambiguity are detected in constructing the array graph while special procedures were designed for consistency checks. The checking of the entire specification may be essentially regarded as propagation from node to node of attributes, such as data-type dimensionality and ranges, based on the relations of one node to another and on the expressions in respective equations. The problems discovered are described to the user in terms of the specification language without referring to programming details. The following general types of analysis take place.

1. Consistency of dimensionality, subscripting, sizes of dimensions, and data types of variables are checked through propagating them from node to node.

2. Data description statements are generated for variables referenced in the equations but not described by the user.

3. Equations are generated to relate same-named input and output variables.

4. Circular logic is recognized as cycles in the array graph and analyzed in depth.

In composing a specification of a computational task, the user chooses a natural and convenient representation without concern for efficiency of computations and memory. It is up to the MODEL compiler to map the user's representation into an efficient procedural computer program. An overall flow of program events is then produced in a skeletal form (independent of object language) called a schedule. The final program generation phase translates individual entries in the schedule into statements in the object language.

The MODEL compiler determines the optimal schedule based on the array graph as follows. The general approach to scheduling consists of first creating a component graph made up of all the maximally strongly connected components (MSCC) in the array graph and the edges connecting the MSCCs. The component graph is therefore an acyclic directed graph. This graph can be topologically sorted. There is a large number of possible linear arrangements of the schedule that have varying efficiency. The objective is to find a nearly optimal schedule.

This is done as follows. The subscripts for each component are determined. Iterations for these subscripts must bracket the respective components to define all the values of the variables in the component. Each component is enclosed within loops, which might be nested if the respective equations or data arrays are of multiple dimensions. Next, attempts are made to enlarge the scope of iterations. Iterations of components with the same range are merged. Merging scope of iterations may enable elements of the same or related array variables to share memory locations. If it is possible to retain in memory only a window of the entire dimension of a variable, then the respective dimension is called virtual, otherwise it is called physical. When there are a number of ways that the scope of iterations of components can be merged (for different dimensions or ranges) then the memory requirements of different candidate scopes of iterations serves as the criterion for selecting the optimal scope. Virtual dimensions are found by the present MODEL compiler only where the subscript expressions used to reference a variable are of certain forms, such as I, $I-k$ (I is any subscript, k is 0 or a positive integer), and others [Lu, 1981].

It is then necessary to schedule the nodes in each MSCC. This consists first of an attempt to decompose the MSCC by deleting edges that represent dependencies already ensured by the order of iterations. If the MSCC is not decomposable, the user is advised and given the nodes and edges of the MSCC. It is up to the user to verify that they do not represent an inconsistency, such as circular logic. The other possibility is that they constitute a set of simultaneous equations. In the latter case a solution method is automatically incorporated into the produced program.

Additional optimization is performed to reduce computation time. By further merging variables that have the same values into common memory space, it is possible to eliminate statements that copy values from one variable to another. Transformation of remaining statements sometimes allows the elimination of entire iteration loops.

5.7 EVALUATION

Using MODEL, an accounting system was developed to evaluate the distribution of times required for respective development steps. The overall development of the accounting system was carried out in three stages, with interruptions of three to six months between stages. The three stages were selected to determine the variability in software development times required for (a) initial development, (b) extension and (c) modification, respectively. The system eventually consisted of eight modules: two in the first stage for general ledger, five in the second stage for inventory, and one module modified (general ledger module) in the third stage for incorporating valuation of assets at current prices. Development times included the research necessary prior to each stage to determine the requirements of the accounting system to be competitive with existing or proposed state-of-the-art accounting systems. Development times were recorded for each of the steps enumerated in Fig. 5.5 and for each type of error encountered.

Figs. 5.7, 5.8, and 5.9 show overall statistics of program module sizes and development times. The rows in Fig. 5.7 are for respective steps in the procedure illustrated in Fig. 5.5. Step 1 in Fig. 5.7 includes the time for learning MODEL and the research for determining state-of-the-art capabilities of accounting systems. The general ledger and inventory management systems primarily involved reviewing commercial systems to select competitive capabilities. The last stage involved reviewing FASB 33 [FASB, 1979]

FIGURE 5.7
TIME BREAKDOWN FOR 3-STAGE DEVELOPMENT OF ACCOUNTING SYSTEM

| | \multicolumn{6}{c}{Stages in Development} | |
Steps in Fig. 1	\multicolumn{2}{c}{1 General Ledger}	\multicolumn{2}{c}{2 Inventory}	\multicolumn{2}{c}{3 Valuation at Current Price Modification}	\multicolumn{2}{c}{Total}
1	40	28	30	12	8	11	78	17
2	23	16	49	20	13	17	85	19
Cycle 2-4	44	31	93	38	31	41	168	36
Cycle 2-7	36	25	72	30	23	31	131	28
System Total	143	100	244	100	75	100	462	100

Symbol	Units
xx	yy
xx	Hours
yy	Column (stage) Percentage

FIGURE 5.8
PROGRAM MODULES, STAGES DEVELOPED/MODIFIED AND SIZES

Specification	Stage	MODEL lines	PL/I lines	PL/1 to MODEL lines Ratio	MODEL Stmts.	PL/I Stmts.	PL/1 to MODEL Stmts. Ratio
Financial Stmt	1/3	335	1340	4.00	88	932	10.6
Gen. Ledger	1	280	575	2.05	65	457	7.03
Inv. Order	2	161	396	2.46	33	258	7.82
Inv. Receipt	2	195	792	4.06	45	512	11.38
Inv. Sale	2	264	888	3.36	60	651	10.85
Inv. Status	2	177	698	3.94	41	385	9.30
Inv. On-Order	2	119	426	3.58	31	275	8.87
Total		1531	5115	3.34	363	3470	8.40

MODEL Lines Produced per Hour	3.31
PL/I Lines Produced per Hour	11.07
MODEL Statements Produced per Hour	.785
PL/I Statements Produced per Hour	7.5

and other publications on financial reporting. The differences in the percentages for step 1 in the three stages are due to the learning of MODEL, and also due to the different number and sizes of the respective modules. In developing a larger system, a smaller percentage of time is used in step 1 and larger percentages in the debugging. In Figure 5.7 the row for step 2 includes the time for composition of the specification and correction of syntax errors. Time statistics on syntax errors, which are simple and easy to correct, were retained separately from other types of errors. They are not

FIGURE 5.9
NUMBER OF STATEMENTS AND DEVELOPMENT TIMES BY STAGE

Stage	MODEL Stmts.	PL/1 Stmts.	Ratio	Hours	MODEL Stmts/hr	PL/1 Stmts/hr
1	125	990	7.92	143	.87	6.9
2	210	2081	9.9	244	.86	8.5
3	60 (before)	533	8.9	75	NA	NA
	88 (after)	932	10.7			
	28 (modified)					

NA - Not Applicable

considered indicative of the software development methodology. Errors discovered in the static debugging (inner loop) were considered separately from errors discovered in dynamic debugging.

Stages 1 and 2, initial general ledger development and the extension for inventory, had very similar relative development times. This is because the extension of inventory in stage 2 was relatively independent of stage 1. The communications between the general ledger and inventory was only by sharing the general ledger files (see Fig. 5.1). (MODEL also has capabilities for direct program to program communications, not illustrated here.) Stage 3 involved a complex modification of a program module which produced the financial statements. It involved addition of input files, changes in reports and a new computational methodology. It is not justified to compute development times and corrected errors per statement on the basis of numbers of statements added or modified. This is discussed further in connection with Fig. 5.11.

Figures 5.7, 5.8, and 5.9 show that the MODEL specification is consistently shorter in number of statements than the produced PL/1 program by a range of ratios between 1 to 7 and 1 to 11 and that 0.7 to 1.0 hours of development were required per MODEL statement, or 7 to 12 PL/1 statements per hour. Figure 5.8 shows the statistics for the number of lines for MODEL specifications and respective PL/1 program. Note that the MODEL specification includes comments while the generated PL/1 program does not. Static debugging time (excluding syntax) exceeds the dynamic debugging time. There is considerable improvement in that a much larger portion of errors are detected in the static cycle. As will be shown later, the development incurred 100 errors (including syntax), of which 88 were detected and corrected in the static cycle and 12 in the dynamic cycle. Note that the error count includes changes motivated by a desire to improve the system (e.g., better report layout) and not only errors made inadvertently.

The dynamic cycle required preparation of test data, which served also for quality assurance testing of the entire system. The compiler can be used to generate a program that generates test data.

The focus in Fig. 5.10 is on the debugging process. It shows average times per module to correct each type of error (except syntax errors). Also shown are average numbers of errors per MODEL and PL/1 statements (including stage 3). There were minor differences between the three stages in the error correction times or in the percentages of time expended for correcting various types of errors.

Figure 5.11 shows the extent of the third-stage modification by giving the sizes of the affected specification and program before and after the modification as well as the number of statements modified. Figure 5.11 also shows how the produced program has become more complex through statistics on the numbers of loops and variables used in the produced program. Note the effect of the optimization which changed MODEL array variables into scalar variables in the produced PL/1 program.

FIGURE 5.10

FREQUENCY OF ERRORS AND CORRECTION TIMES, PER MODULE

Fig. 1 Steps	Error Type	Average Occurence/ Module	Average Cycles/ to correct	Average Cycles/ Module	Average Hours/ Cycle	Total Hours/%
1	NA	NA	NA	NA	NA	11/17%
2,3	Syntax	5.5	1.1	6.0	NA	12/19%
Compiler	Ambiguity	3.2	1.4	4.5		
Cycle	Incompleteness	1.8	2.5	4.5	1.5	24/36%
2,3,4	Inconsistency	2.1	3.3	6.9		
Run Cycle 2-7	Test with Data	1.6	2.6	4.2	4.5	19/28%
Total Errors (excl. syntax)		8.7		20.1		
Errors per MODEL stmt		.167		.39		
per PL/1 stmt		.017		.04		

Legend:

Error Type	Description
Syntax	Within single statement.
Ambiguity	Use of same name for different purposes
Incompleteness	Omission of entire statement
Inconsistency	Found between statements (ambiguity, datatype, dimensionality, range, circular logic)
Test With Data	Based on examining output reports or data.

FIGURE 5.11

PROGRAM MODIFICATION COMPARISONS

Complexity Measure	MODEL Before	PL/1 Before	MODEL After	PL/1 After
Lines of code	198	760	335	1340
Statements	60	533	88	932
Loop Structures	0	21	0	33
# of Variables	50	169	99	262
# of Arrays	46	19	94	41

	Untouched	Added	Modified	Total
Data Statements:	9	3	1	13
Assertion Statements:	47	25	3	75
				88

5.8 CONCLUSION

The study and statistics reported above provide insight into the development steps and their relative development times using an equational-type language. Due to the high cost of such experiments only one developer was employed but the development was extensive, thus giving significance to relative rather than absolute values of expenditures of times. The central question of how much more effective are nonprocedural equational languages than procedural languages is difficult to answer with precision. For example, it was not practical to develop the same accounting system using a procedural language and compare software productivity for two reasons. First, we assumed that the developer need not have the computer programming skills. Second, determining the requirements of the accounting system has been an integral part of the development process and it is unlikely that two developers, one using a MODEL and the other PL/1 would select the same requirements, which is necessary to make a comparison meaningful.

However, ample statistics have been published on productivity in statements or lines per hour and errors per statement or line using conventional methods [Endress, 1979; Green *et al.*, 1976; Horowitz, 1975; Perlis *et al.*, 1981; Schneiderwind and Hoffman, 1979; Walston and Felix, 1977; Wolverton, 1974]. These statistics have been collected under a variety of conditions and sometimes include correction of syntax errors. They may be used as a basis for rough comparison of the MODEL and procedural language methodologies. Our extensive experience in use of MODEL for both business and scientific computations, not documented here, generally confirms the overall productivity rates reported here for the use of MODEL. Published rates of statements per hour and errors per statement for using procedural languages can be compared with similar rates for statements generated by the MODEL compiler. On this basis the MODEL methodology productivity reported in Figs. 5.8 and 5.9 is in a region exceeding a three-fold improvement in statements per hour. It was expected that the number of errors in using MODEL would be much less than in using procedural languages. This expectation was based on elimination in MODEL of control, program flow, and sequencing, which are acknowledged as the areas that contribute the most to making errors. However, the error rate reported in using MODEL is only 15 percent lower than that incurred using a procedural language (not counting syntax errors). On the other hand, the error count using MODEL included modifications made to improve the system. These improvements may be viewed as part of establishing the requirements for the system. It was very difficult to distinguish such changes from true inadvertent errors as long as determining the requirements is an integral part of software development. A much greater portion of the errors were detected and corrected in the static cycle. The time to correct an error in the MODEL static cycle is much shorter, which explains the faster debugging.

The ease of specification and the extensive help from the error checking facilities enabled the accountant to independently develop his system. Again, because there was only one developer, it is difficult to conclude that any accountant would be able to generate his own systems, but under these experimental conditions, it was possible for the accountant to solve his system problems without the help of a professional programming staff.

REFERENCES

Ackerman, W. B. Data flow languages. *Computer* 15:15–25, February 1982.

Agerwala, T., and Arvind. Data flow systems. *Computer* 15:10–13, February 1982.

Alexander, M. O. Statement 33 and the future: Research and decision. *FASB Viewpoints* 3; 10 October 1981.

Ashcroft, E. A., and Wadge, W. W. LUCID, a nonprocedural language with iteration. *Commun. ACM* 20:519–526, July 1977.

Backus, J. Can programming be liberated from the von Neumann style; a functional style and its algebra of programs. *Commun. ACM* 21:613–641, August 1978.

Bell, P. W. CVA, CCA, and CoCoA: How fundamental are the differences. Aust. Accounting Res. Foundation, Melbourne, Australia, 1982.

Benston, G. J., and Krasney, M. A. DAAM: The demand for alternative accounting measurement. *Journal Accounting Res.*, Suppl:1–45, 1978.

Chace, S. Computer companies develop devices to ease programming. *Wall Street Journal* 21; 25 June 1982.

Cougar, J. D. Evaluation of business systems analysis techniques. *Comput. Surveys*, 167–236, March 1975.

Data decisions. Application software survey, 1982. *Datamation*, 94–110, May 1982.

Davis, H. Compiler or interpreter. *Interface Age*, 90–91, January 1981.

Endress, A. An analysis of errors and their causes in system pro-programs. *IEEE Trans. Software Eng.*, 140–149, June 1979.

Ernst and Whinney. Financial reporting developments: Inflation accounting. December 1979.

Financial Accounting Standards Board. Financial reporting and changing prices. *Statement of Financial Accounting Standards* 33, September 1979.

Financial Accounting Standards Board. Disclosures about oil and gas producing activities. 13 May 1981.

Financial Accounting Standards Board, Committee on Financial Reporting and Changing Prices. A discussion of the FASB's views and suggestions for research by others. 15 June 1981.

Financial Accounting Standards Board. FASB plan for technical projects, research, and other technical activities. Status report, 10 July 1981.

Green, T. F. Program structures, complexity and error characteristics. *Proc. Symp. Comput. Software Eng.*, 139–154, 1976.

Horowitz, E. (ed.). *Practical strategies for developing large software systems*. Reading, Mass.: Addison-Wesley, 1975.

Johns Hopkins University, Applied Physics Laboratory. DOD weapon systems software management study. Silver Springs, Md. 1975.

Lientz, B. P., and Swanson, E. B. Discovering issues in software maintenance. *Data Management*, 15–16, October 1978.

Lu, K. S. Program optimization based on a non-procedural specification. Ph.D. thesis, Univ. of Pennsylvania, Philadelphia, Pa., 1981.

Martinelli, W. P. Unique application needs force in-house creation of financial programs. *Software Focus*, 21–22, March 1982.

Perlis, A. J.; Sayward, F. G.; and Shaw, M. (eds.). *Software Metrics*. Cambridge, Mass.: MIT Press, 1981.

Prywes, N. S., and Pnueli, A. Compilation of nonprocedural specification into computer programs. *IEEE Trans Software Eng.*, SE-9:267–279, May 1983.

Prywes, N. S.; Pnueli, A.; and Shastry, S. Use of non-procedural specification language and associated program generator in software development. *ACM Trans, Programming Languages Syst.*, 196–217, October 1979.

Rubey, R. J.; Dana, J. A.; and Biche, P. N. Quantitative aspects of software validation. *IEEE Trans. Software Eng.* SE-1:150–155, June 1975.

Schneiderwind, N. F., and Hoffman, H. M. An experiment in software error data collection and analysis. *IEEE Trans. Software Eng.* SE-5:276–286, June 1979.

Securities and Exchange Commission. Notice of adoption of amendment to regulation S-X requiring disclosure of certain replacement cost data in notes to financial statements. Securities and Exchange Commission, Accounting Series, 190; 23 March 1976.

Snyders, J. Generators overcome programmer shortages. *Comput. Decisions*, 34, March 1981.

Thackray, J. Birth of inflation accounting. *Institutional Investor* 172, April 1980.

Vasarhelyi, M. A., and Pearson, E. F. Studies in inflation accounting: A taxonomization approach. *Quarterly Rev. Econ. Business*, 9–27, Spring 1979.

Walston, C. E., and Felix, C. P. A method of programming measurement and estimation. *IBM Syst. Journal* 16:54–73, January 1977.

Wolverton, R. W. The cost of developing large scale software. *IEEE Trans. Comput.* C–23:615–636, June 1974.

CHAPTER 6

REUSABLE CODE AT THE HARTFORD INSURANCE GROUP

MICHAEL J. CAVALIERE
The Hartford Insurance Group

6.1 BACKGROUND

Time and resources are often expended generating program code that, in many cases, already exists. Reinvention of the wheel is a common practice at altogether too many programming organizations. Consequently, *reusable code* was established as one of the key areas to be pursued by The Hartford in the effort to improve application development productivity.

Early in 1981, a project team was formed to address the issue of reusable code with the following main objectives:

☐ To develop and implement a procedure for collecting and communicating reusable code and techniques;

From *ITT Proceedings of the Workshop on Reusability in Programming, Newport, R.I., 1983.* Reprint with permission of Hartford Fire Insurance Company.

☐ To promote awareness and acceptance of reusable code as an effective productivity tool by the data processing staff;

☐ To assess and recommend long-term support requirements for reusable code, including training, tools, techniques and management support.

Before we consider the ways in which these objectives were met, let's look at exactly what we mean by the term *reusable code*.

6.2 DEFINITION AND BENEFITS

At the Hartford, *reusable code* was defined as any technique that increases productivity by eliminating redundant practices in program generation.

The net advantage here is reduced program creation time and a consequent reduction in resource consumption. The testing phase of development also benefits; since reusable code is pretested, application testing can concentrate on newly coded areas of a program/system. Additionally, errors stemming from the interdependence of code are reduced because reusable program routines, by their nature, tend to foster greater independence among logic functions.

Finally, reusable code can boost the quality of programs, meaning that less time and resources are required for maintenance. Many types of reusable code work to make the applications in which they are employed similar in design and structure. Consequently, maintenance becomes easier for the programmer new to the application but familiar with the basic design.

Various types of reusable code have been in use in program development for many years. The aim of the Reusable Code Project was to render the best of this code and/or the techniques for developing it more widely available through training, coordination, and communication.

6.3 TYPES OF REUSABLE CODE

What follows is a brief description of the various types of code that make up the reusable code inventory, and some examples of what has been implemented.

6.3.1 Program Skeletons

The majority of the reusable code effort at The Hartford has been aimed at the COBOL programmer. COBOL program skeletons eliminate the need for coding routine entries such as DIVISION and SECTION headers, AUTHOR and PROGRAM ID lines, and SOURCE and OBJECT COMPUTER entries. Commonly needed DATA and PROCEDURE DIVISION entries are also included.

Before the availability of program skeletons, such routine coding was avoided in a timesharing environment by copying (from a source library) a module similar to the one to be developed, deleting unneeded code, and adding one's new code. Common program skeletons end the need for, and the risk inherent in, seeking out and deleting unwanted code. They also ensure that each program coded using them starts from baseline code that fully conforms to company coding standards.

We have introduced two forms of program skeletons: a static skeleton available on TSO and a dynamic facility on VM/CMS. The static skeleton provides a source code dataset that the programmer may modify through full-screen editing to suit specific needs. This skeleton provides all necessary COBOL divisions and their commonly coded entries as well as comments identifying particular functional areas of the skeleton. (The TSO CLIST, which allows access to this skeleton also provides access to the logic structures discussed later.)

The dynamic skeleton is provided by a VM/CMS facility developed in-house called FASTBALL. The dynamic nature of FASTBALL stems from its user's ability to build a COBOL module by piecing together desired portions of the module (code segments) selected from menu screens. FASTBALL retrieves the selected piece of code and places it on the screen in full-screen editing mode. FILEing the segment results in its being appended to the module under construction.

The basic options available to the FASTBALL user include

1. Building a new module,
2. Continuing work on an existing module,
3. Utilizing a logic structure, and
4. Compiling a module.

Each option is explained here:

New Module Option.   Needed skeletal code segments may be selected to satisfy common needs in the four divisions of a COBOL program. Code segments may be retrieved, either for browsing or for actual editing and incorporation into the module being built.

Existing Module Option.   All code segments noted above are available within this option. The difference is that selected segments are appended to already existing code.

Logic Structure Option. FASTBALL makes these expanded skeletons available on VM/CMS. The various types of logic structures are discussed next as a separate topic in this paper. The facility also provides graphic, high-level structure charts online for each of the logic structures.

Compilation Option. This option provides for an online compile of the module and a facility for location and correction of diagnostic errors.

Thus far, FASTBALL has proven especially valuable to programmers working on large development projects. There, the requirements of our programming method (employing one function/one module whenever possible) have made it imperative that the programmers be able to develop many COBOL modules quickly. FASTBALL helps provide this capability in a format that is easy to learn and use.

6.3.2 Logic Structures

The term LOGIC STRUCTURE refers to a type of program skeleton that incorporates procedural code, as well as other routine entries, to support a particular program function. We have employed the same concept of logic structures as was developed at Raytheon in the late 1970s [Lanergan and Grasso, 1983]. Logic structures do not represent completed, usable programs but do include high-level procedural logic appropriate to their function. Application-specific low-level code must be added to develop a logic structure into a complete program.

Here is a list of the available logic structures, with descriptions of the processing that they would support as completed modules:

Table access: On the first call to this module, a file is read into working storage and a table constructed. On subsequent calls, the module receives an argument and retrieves the corresponding table entry. Error messages are returned for invalid arguments.

Audit report: This module is intended to be called once, using the balance control fields needed to produce an audit report. Balance calculations are performed, an in-out-of-balance condition is posted, and the table is dumped to print via a standard print utility program.

Controlled user abend: This module is invoked with a user-supplied abend code. An in-house dump utility is called to halt processing and print the reason for the abend on an output listing.

File strip/split: This module will identify records based on a user-specified control field and will strip those records to a separate file. This module can be used to create test files, to purify files, or merely to enumerate instances of some specific condition on a file.

Master file update: This module performs standard transaction-to-master-file update processing. Appropriate auditing and error detection is performed. The module assumes that both files have been sorted by the mutual control field.

Duplicate record search: This module reads through a file checking for duplicate records based on user-specified control field(s). The first record of a series of duplicates is written to an output file with duplicates and totals being logged on an audit report.

6.3.3 Common Processing Modules

These are standard black box modules that perform generic program functions. Common modules exhibit the desirable design characteristics of

1. High cohesion (meaning that they perform one specific function);
2. Loose coupling (meaning that they are passed no more data from the invoking program than they need to perform their function. They return only their input, an input validity code, and resulting data.

These characteristics ensure reusability in a maximum number of applications. Our current catalog of common modules provides functions including date validation, addition/subtraction of days to/from a date, month and state code conversion, automatic run-date generation, literal centering and check writing conversion (from numeric to English language representation).

Additional common modules developed in the application areas are under evaluation on an ongoing basis.

6.3.4 Code Generators

These are software products developed in house that produce code by using as input formatted layouts of either reports or screens developed in a full-screen editing environment. There are currently two basic types:

1. COBOL working storage generators—these read in a formatted report page and generates the COBOL working storage division entries which would be needed in a program producing that report.
2. MFS code generator—this reads in a formatted screen layout and generates the MFS control blocks needed to implement that screen in an IMS/VTS environment.

6.3.5 CMS Facilities

EXECS on VM/CMS are command sequences that perform often-needed functions. Among those supported as reusable code are EXECS to

☐ link a user to another CMS user's directory,

☐ obtain temporary additional work space on a directory,

☐ produce finalized versions of production JCL (job control language).

Also supported as reusable CMS facilities are

☐ a module that will print out the contents of any CMS file in hexadecimal representation;

☐ two XEDIT Macros which facilitate certain word processing operations within the CMS editor.

6.4 RESPONSE TO ORIGINAL OBJECTIVES

The approach to each of the original project objectives (noted at the beginning of this paper) is discussed here, grouped by objective.

6.4.1 Collection and Communication

Reusable Code Review Board.   This Board consists of one member from each of the application programming divisions. The Board's responsibilities include:

☐ Encouraging members of their divisions to submit suggestions for reusable code to be developed or for existing code that should be publicized,

☐ Reviewing code suggestions for usefulness and quality,

☐ Helping to refine code accepted from the divisions,

☐ Assisting in the piloting of new software facilities,

☐ Demonstrating reusable code facilities and answering questions on their use.

This review board is of great value in transferring the techniques and tools of code reuse to their actual users—the application development areas. Their review of reusable code candidates helps to ensure that we are making available code and/or tools that answer real needs out in the application areas.

Recognition Program.   This program functions to encourage department members to submit ideas/code to the review board. Incentive is provided by mementos (carrying the reusable code logo) and public recognition from upper management. As part of an overall productivity incentive program, cash awards are also made for reusable code suggestions.

Code Catalog. Currently, the communication vehicle for reusable code is the online catalog implemented on a VM/CMS-based indexing and retrieval product. All reusable code and support tools (FASTBALL, working storage generators, etc.) are documented by this product. The product operates by searching its database for documents containing user-specified words or phrases. Thus, precise phrasing used in reusable code documentation (especially in the description of code function) facilitates rapid location of desired information.

Software Inspections. As part of the software inspection process required for programs released to the production environment, developers are asked to forward to the reusable code unit information concerning the reusability potential of their code. Promising candidates are followed up on by the appropriate review board member.

6.4.2 Awareness and Acceptance

Several approaches have been taken to foster awareness and acceptance of reusable code:

☐ Articles are regularly published in the D.P. Departmental Newsletter, providing general and specific information of reusable code,

☐ A reusable code presentation is made to each basic programming training class to acquaint trainees with concepts and options available,

☐ New releases of code are publicized via bulletin boards and the online index.

6.4.3 Support Environment

Code Libraries. Approved Code is supported, in most cases, on both MVS and VM/CMS. Code libraries have been established in both mainframe environments.

MVS—A reusable code Partitioned Data Set (PDS) exists as a load library for Common Modules. The CLIST needed for access to the static COBOL skeleton resides on a CLIST library.

VM/CMS—A reusable code ID exists to which CMS users are automatically linked at LOGON. This ID contains

☐ Load modules (TEXT files) for common modules;
☐ EXECS (such as FASTBALL) and the other CMS facilities noted
   earlier.

Resource Center.   The D.P. Resource Center is staffed by personnel who
solve problems, answer questions, and offer twenty-four hour support for
common modules employed in production systems. Coordination is also
provided for the activities of the Reusable Code Review Board.

6.5 THE CHALLENGE

Implementation of reusable code has presented a number of challenges.
We have experienced some difficulty in obtaining candidates qualified for
refinement and release as common modules. Additionally, the developing
of approved modules into clean, generic, and supportable units of code has
required more time and resources than originally anticipated. It does seem
easier to obtain, and prepare for release, facilities independently developed
in-house (such as FASTBALL, working storage generators, CMS EXECS).
While these facilities are very productive in reducing redundant coding
effort, we remain convinced that reusable common modules are being written that ought to be made generally available. The modules that have
been implemented are proving valuable enough to warrant the necessary
effort.

There remains a tendency for programmers to copy known modules,
modifying them to suit new specifications, rather than to use the program
skeletons. In many cases, this is clearly justified by the known modules'
containing much application-specific code that is needed in the module to
be developed. In such cases, reuse of the old module causes reuse of more
code than would be the case if one of the skeletons were utilized. The
logic structures (see Section 6.3.2.), with their more function-specific code,
have helped reduce this reliance on older modules (there are always risks
in adapting a preowned product to one's own needs). Where appropriate,
however, the cannibalization process will never (nor should it) be eliminated.

Other problems encountered have generally centered on more technical
issues involved in rendering the various types of code and facilities available
across numerous environments, including multiple VM/CMS processors and
MVS test and production complexes. Maximizing availability of a varied collection of tools in an ever-changing operational environment requires significant ongoing time and effort.

6.6 FUTURE DIRECTION

One immediate future project for reusable code is early indexing by function of all reusable code candidates suggested to the review board. In this way, prior to their final refinement as approved common modules, these programs and the functions they provide will be available to other application areas for copying and customizing to satisfy new requirements. Modules (or parts of them) that are never approved for final reusable code implementation, generally because they support a too highly specialized function, can still be made known on an as-is basis to the staff, where reuse of them might be advantageous.

As an extension of the foregoing item, a project of broader scope has been proposed. This involves the indexing of all modules when they are released into production. This could be done by coding brief, rigorously precise, functional descriptions as comments in the actual source code of COBOL programs. These comments could then be automatically extracted and used to develop a database, eventually providing a manageable and accessible inventory of all program functions already coded in our installation. A natural expansion of this would include indexing of the production jobs and systems of which these modules are a part. These steps would make available the valuable resource of a full inventory, indexed by D.P. and business function, of existing automated systems. Additionally, such a facility would benefit future efforts involving identification of redundant program/system functionality and thus also provide opportunities for the application of reusable programming.

There is also an effort ongoing to evaluate reusability opportunities associated with our application developer workstations. Possibilities here include

- [ ] another category of reusable components specifically oriented to the minicomputer environment;
- [ ] a mini-computer–based replacement for the current mainframe index-retrieval system, to serve as the index facility for the various reusable components in the micro, mini, and mainframe environments.

The company has staffed a unit to support and maximize reusability benefits inherent in a vendor-supplied COBOL code generator that allows reuse of large percentages of code, both on a DP application divisional basis and on a cross-divisional corporate basis. This generator also enables maintenance of programs in the generator-input language, rather than in the target language, which is COBOL.

Reusability research directions being pursued at The Hartford include the reuse of design and specification information (both textual and graphic), and component assembly possibilities inherent in the object-oriented design approach.

6.7 RECOMMENDATIONS

Based upon experience gained thus far in instituting reusable code methods and practices in a large data processing organization, the following recommendations are offered:

☐ Utilize as fully as possible tendencies among staff members to develop useful code-generation tools, geared, by virtue of their in-house development, to the particular company's needs. Apart from speeding the development of the code they generate, such tools can provide the basis for a future inventory of code possessing a high degree of standardized style and structure. This, of course, translates into improved maintainability;

☐ Develop and maintain an automated index of the program functions existing at the installation. As noted above, this will be of value in (1) identifying potential existing reusable code; and (2) identifying redundant application functions that may imply a need for new reusable code.

☐ Be prepared to make full-time staff resources available, both for the start-up phase and for ongoing support of a reusability program. Considerable effort is required to sift through the many reusable component candidates that will come in, to locate those that are promising, and, especially, to prepare the best of them for true generic reuse.

☐ Resources should be made available to address productivity measurement issues associated with reusable code. Complexity, both conceptual and technical, abounds in this area. Nevertheless, there is no better way to gain an appreciation for the value of code reuse (and to justify the necessary resource commitment) than by measuring use of the new techniques against a baseline.

☐ With the growing interest in establishing systems development environments that enable reusability, much experience is being accumulated in this area. One way of reusing this experience is through workshops and conferences. Another useful approach would be the establishment of an informal "Reusability User's Group," with membership coming from organizations engaged in or interested in the establishment of reuse environments. The benefits of regularly sharing experiences and ideas in such a promising field could be considerable.

ABOUT THE AUTHOR

Michael J. Cavaliere joined The Hartford in 1979 as a member of the Company's Information Resource Management Division. Mr. Cavaliere served on the task force formed in 1981 to study the potential of Reusable Code for The Hartford's systems needs. Currently he consults with application development projects, coordinating and facilitating team-based sessions for the development and validation of user requirements.

REFERENCE

Lanergan, R. G., and Grasso, C. A. Software engineering with reusable designs and code. *Proceedings—Workshop on Reusability in Programming*, Newport, R.I., 7–9 September 1983.

CHAPTER 7

REUSABILITY OF MODULES WITH STRICTLY LOCAL DATA AND DEVICES—A CASE STUDY

ÖSTEN OSKARSSON
LM Ericsson

7.1 INTRODUCTION

Definitions

There are two ways to define the reusability of a software module:

☐ The reusability of a module is the tendency of its constituent parts to be reusable in unchanged form. This means that a module may be reusable even if it requires modification before reuse. Reusability is displayed when large parts of the module are reused without modifications.

☐ Reusability of a module is the possibility to reuse the complete module without changes. Reusability obtains when the module can be reused unchanged. Of course, if we change the concept that a certain module implements, it is unreasonable to expect that module to be reused without modifications.

From *ITT Proceedings of the Workshop on Reusability in Programming*, Newport, R.1., 1983. Reprinted with permission of the author.

In the case study to be reported here, the latter variety of reusability was studied in an investigation of the reusability of modules that are isolated from each other through inability to share data and devices.

Module Isolation

It is generally assumed that the more a software module is isolated from other software, the more reusable it is. Two modules are isolated from each other if they know little about each other's internals [Parnas, 1972].

The concepts of data abstraction [Linden, 1976] and object orientation [Cox, 1986] attempt to achieve isolation by hiding the implementation of data structures. All operations on one data structure are implemented in one module, which is either a data abstraction or an object. Other modules only know the operations; they cannot access the data structure directly.

Both data abstractions and objects may, however, allow modules to look inside each other by use of the call-by-reference parameter transfer in procedure calls. In this parameter transfer method, calling modules send pointers to their internal data structures, which then can be directly accessed by the called module.

Extreme isolation of communicating modules would be the case when modules can share no data at all, and thus not even call-by-reference is possible.

Module Reusability in New System Versions

The development of a new version of a software system is a good test of the reusability of the existing modules. Changes in functionality between system versions are similar to functional differences between different but related systems.

Of course, the software architecture rarely differs much between system versions. When building a completely new system, using existing software modules from a different system architecture, one would expect to encounter reusability problems far worse than when reusing modules between system versions.

However, attempts to make software modules reusable in radically different system architectures can rarely succeed. Software reusability is only feasible inside a specific architecture or class of architectures, so reusability in version development can tell us much about reusability in general.

7.2 BACKGROUND

The AXE System

AXE is a commercial system for public telephone exchanges, a system developed by Ericsson Telecom in Sweden. The first exchange went into operation in 1977, and in 1982, the time of the study, there were 255 installations in 25 countries. AXE had been subject to considerable modification and extension to cover new markets and new telephone functions. The system contained some millions of source code lines in a high-level programming language, and more than 1000 programmers and analysts were engaged in a continuing development of the software.

The Module Concept in AXE

Software modules in AXE have the following characteristics:

☐ No data are shared between modules. This means that transfer of data between modules can only be of the type call-by-value; that is, data are copied from one module to another.

☐ Only one software module can communicate directly with a specific hardware device. Thus, hardware is local to modules in the same way as data.

☐ A module has several entry points where it can receive messages from other modules. Several modules can have the same entry point name; message addresses consist of module identity and entry point name. Which operation is executed in a module depends on which entry point is used.

☐ The communication between software modules is asynchronous; that is, a module continues execution after it has sent a message. Called modules are not required to return control to the caller.

☐ All modules in AXE are regarded as equals in the structure. There is no hierarchy of modules. In a system in operation there is only one copy of each module.

This gives AXE software the flavor of a network of isolated, fairly autonomous modules, that exchange messages with one another. Each module offers a set of operations through its entry points. An activity in the system (e.g., setting up a call) typically jumps around among the modules, executing a small part of the program code (an operation) at a time in each module.

The modules are relatively large, more than 1000 executable high-level program statements each. There is no program code that does not belong to a module. For example, AXE has no global subroutines.

There were several reasons for the restriction to local data and message passing. It reduces the need for communication between designers of different modules, program errors in one module cannot directly damage data in the rest of the system, and the concurrency problems were simplified.

7.3 REUSABILITY OF DIFFERENT TYPES OF MODULES

For this paper we have quite subjectively grouped the software modules of AXE into three types depending on the main purpose of each module: Data modules, interface modules, and activity modules.

These module types are abstractions of data, environment, and activities respectively. For a module to be considered reusable, it should not need to be changed when the corresponding data structure, part of the environment, or activity is unchanged.

Data Modules

In AXE there are several modules handling one large data structure each. In all such modules, data can be added or changed through messages from other modules. For example, there is one table containing category information about each subscriber, indicating what services the subscriber can use. Other modules use this information through look-up operations in the table module. When a subscriber wants to use other services, the system operator changes the corresponding data in the table through a message.

The reason we call certain modules data modules is that their purpose is to supply a data structure and operations on it. Those who work with the system see such modules as entities in their own right filling well-defined purposes in the system. A data module thus implements a data abstraction.

In the development of the studied version there was no need to modify a data module just to get a new operation on the existing data structure. This indicates that the data modules were reasonably complete with respect to the types of data they contained; that is, most services these modules could offer were already implemented in them.

It is often claimed [Linden, 1976] that the possibility of changing data representations is an important advantage of data abstractions. Representation changes do not, however, seem to be a valid reason not to reuse an existing module. In fact, no such cases were found in our study.

The main reason for changing data modules was the need to extend the data structure. For example, a new column may be needed in a table. There are two ways to view these changes.

1. The data abstraction was implemented incompletely. We assume that the abstraction in itself is well founded in the area of application in question. The implementation was incomplete either on purpose or because of incomplete understanding of the abstraction.
2. The extension means that a new abstraction is implemented. Our application or our architecture has changed so that the old abstraction no longer fits.

Interface Modules

Many of the software modules in AXE are intended as interfaces with the environment of the software. They interface with subscribers, operators, hardware devices, and so forth. We can view interface modules as abstractions of parts of the environment. The rest of the system only sees a specific interface module; it never sees, for example, the actual human or hardware. The main reason for letting one software module handle all communication with a specific part of the system's environment is to make the rest of the system reusable. The same system can work with a new environment if only the interface modules are exchanged.

Further, interface modules may be reused between different systems, provided that they are well designed and the different systems use the same architecture.

In the study, 19 requirements were found not to concern environment changes. Of them, 4 still result in changes to interface modules. This means that for the remaining 15 requirements, the interface modules of AXE were reusable.

Activity Modules

An activity module acts as a main program, controlling some part of the system's behavior by sending orders to and receiving information from other modules. An activity module is an abstraction of something that the system does (e.g., setting up a call, supervision of connections). The main differences between an activity module and ordinary main programs calling subroutines are that very little data is transferred in the calls from and to activity modules and that an activity module cannot be sure to regain control from the called modules.

Changes in activity modules were caused by 19 requirements. Of these requirements, 13 concerned the activities of the changed modules. Seven activity modules were not reusable because their changes were not caused by changes in the corresponding activities.

7.4   CAUSES OF REUSABILITY

Module Identities as Data

In AXE, module identities can be sent in messages as ordinary data. In this way, a module can be informed during run time about the identity of a module with which it is expected to communicate. A module can send its own identity in messages. For example, a module may inform other modules about its existence during system start.

Using module pointers makes two contributions toward reusability:

1. When a new module is added to the system, its calling modules do not have to be modified. Instead, the identity of the new module can be entered as a parameter into the system. In the cases where the new

module is used, the calling modules will have received its identity and will use it without knowing that they are calling a new module.

2. If a module is a useful abstraction, the use of module identities as data will allow it to be used in very different environments. The module knows nothing about whom to give orders to and whom to send information to. These identities will be given to the module as data in messages before it needs them.

Example 1 illustrates the advantage of the first contribution (i.e., the reusability of calling modules when a new module is added).

EXAMPLE 1

Depending on the first digit dialed, a subscriber will get one of several services. He may get a speech connection, an alarm call, information about the price of his last call and so on. These services are produced by different activity modules. The choice of module is made by a data module through a table look-up on the first digits dialed. This look-up yields the identity of the appropriate activity module, and the data module hands control over to it through a standard message.

In this way the table module is reusable, since we can introduce any number of new services by creating new activity modules and by putting their identities in appropriate positions in the table (through a parameter). All old modules that communicate with the new one are reusable since they get the identity of the new module in messages or from data tables.

The procedure-call concept assumes a control structure in the shape of a tree. After a procedure has been called, it must sooner or later execute a return statement and give the control back to the calling program. In AXE there is no such need. A module can return control to the calling module, but only by sending a message as it would to any other module. In combination with the use of module identities as data, this property of the AXE software is a powerful tool for reusability of software modules, as illustrated in example 2.

Example 2 also illustrates how being a good abstraction makes a module reusable.

EXAMPLE 2

AJ (see Fig. 7.1) is the interface module to the calling subscriber in a call. RE is the activity module that sets up the call. When a subscriber lifts his receiver, AJ gets the identity of the module that is to control the system's behavior, normally RE, through a table look-up on the subscriber category. After that, AJ and RE keep communicating with each other. Each message they exchange informs the receiver what module to communicate with next, normally the sender.

Then there came a new requirement. A subscriber with a new category shall be able to get a tracing of his last incoming call (malicious-call tracing). In this case the procedure for activating the trace requires new, complicated behavior from

FIGURE 7.1
CHANGES IN COMMUNICATION WHEN MCT 1 IS ADDED

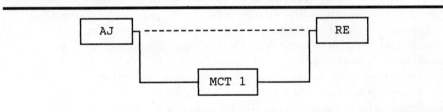

both AJ and RE. This requirement could be implemented without any changes in RE or AJ. This is how it was done:

A new module, MCT 1, was created, and its identity was inserted in the category table. When the subscriber lifts his receiver, AJ sends its usual message, but to MCT 1, instead of RE. MCT 1 then relays the message to RE together with its own identity.

Now, both AJ and RE behave in a completely new way, controlled by messages from MCT 1. AJ and RE are successful abstractions just sitting there performing their operations for anyone who asks, independently of what happens around them.

If the subscriber actually wants to make a call, MCT 1 will tell AJ and RE to communicate with each other in the normal way and will not be involved any more.

Locality of Data and Devices

The strict locality of data and devices has both advantages and disadvantages with respect to reusability. The locality of devices seems to be less specific for AXE. Regardless of modularization principles, most systems today are designed with specific interface modules to simplify modification of hardware devices.

Advantages of Locality of Data. Locality of data does not in itself force reusability into a system. However, it encourages designers to design modules with little communication with each other. Operations on a data item are best implemented in the module that already owns the data. This tends to make modules self-contained and independent of each other's implementation.

In principle, any modules can communicate with each other in AXE. In practice, however, the ways to communicate are limited by rules and common practice in order to limit the complexity of the system. Also, the fewer modules a certain module communicates with, the less risk that it cannot be reused. Two basic structures are used in AXE: the *star* shape and the sequence, or *chain*, of modules.

In the star, one central module has control. It collects information from and sends information and orders to the surrounding modules, which cannot communicate directly with one another.

In the chain of modules, the control moves between modules. Information and requests move back and forth through the chain, and the modules solve their task in cooperation.

In practice, of course, the two structures are often combined. For example, one module in the chain can be the central module in its own star-shaped structure, using a set of service modules.

The backbone of the software structure in AXE consists of a few stars and chains of modules. Although individual modules are replaced from time to time, the structures themselves proliferate as important concepts. We can see this as a reusability of the basic software architecture, which is something different from the reusability of individual modules.

Disadvantages of Locality of Data and Devices. When a module is changed and needs data from somewhere else in the system, both the owner of the data and the intermediate modules in a sequence may have to be changed. This is a problem that also occurs in structures of subroutines. AXE modules

FIGURE 7.2
THE TWO BASIC COMMUNICATION STRUCTURES FOR PROGRAM MODULES IN AXE: STAR (a) AND CHAIN (b)

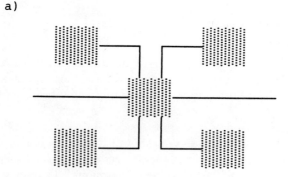

a)

b)

FIGURE 7.3

INDIRECT COMMUNICATION BETWEEN MODULES *A* AND *B* THROUGH
MODULES *X* AND *Y*

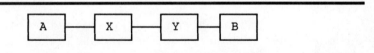

tend to be designed so that the need for transfer of data between modules is
small. It can be argued that this reduces the risk that a changed module will
need new data to which it has no access.

Here we can see an advantage of using pointers to common data (which
AXE lacks). When a module receives a pointer to an object, it gets access to all
the data in that object; so, if the module later needs more data from the object
it is already available. However, we know that unrestricted access to common
data tends to reduce reusability by making relations between modules many
and complex.

In three cases in the study, the locality of data precluded reuse of
modules. Example 3 shows one case.

EXAMPLE 3

Module *A* must be changed (see Fig. 7.3), and it needs some more data, which
belongs to module *B* and has formerly been used only inside *B*. *A* and *B* do not
communicate directly, but via modules *X* and *Y*.

This means that we must change *B* so that it sends the data to *Y*. All intermediate modules between *B* and *A* must be changed so that they can receive the new
data and forward it to the correct module.

The need to change *B* can be discussed in terms of completion or extension
of *B* as an abstraction. The reason for the the change was in *B* itself. The need
for changing *X* and *Y* came mainly from the software architecture. Actually, it is
a question of reusability of the architecture itself.

There is a chance to avoid changing intermediate modules. If module *A* needs
data from module *B*, *A* may call an operation in *B* directly and ask for that data
(see Fig. 7.4).

FIGURE 7.4

MODULE *A* DIRECTLY CALLING AN OPERATION IN MODULE *B*

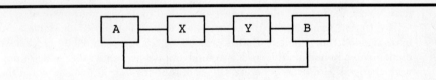

However, such a practice would lead to a system structure where modules communicate directly with many different modules and the architecture breaks down to chaos.

A different disadvantage with locality of data and devices has to do with the use of different modules abstracting varieties of the same concepts. For example, in AXE there are several modules implementing interfaces toward different types of trunk lines to other exchanges. A large amount of trunk data is common to all types of trunks.

This data could be localized in a specific data module with the common operations on it. The trunk modules could access its data and operations through messages. However, trunk modules access this data intensively, so the cost for message transfer (copying data into and out from messages) precludes this solution. Instead, all trunk modules contain operations and data are identical or almost identical.

This means that when some part of the common concept is changed, none of the trunk modules is reusable. If we had common data, only the module containing this data might have to be modified, and the actual trunk modules would be reusable.

7.5 DIFFERENT STRUCTURES — DIFFERENT REUSABILITY

The choice of system structure, and especially software architecture, strongly influences the situations in which a module will be reusable. Example 4 is an illustration of this dilemma.

EXAMPLE 4

In AXE there is a data module containing a large table. Two other modules are interfaces between the table module and the system operator. One operates when data is entered into or deleted from the table; the other operates when the table contents are printed or displayed. Thus the table module will be reusable even if the input or output formats are changed, and the input and output modules will be reusable even if the table representation is changed.

However, the only two requirements that influenced these modules led to the introduction of further types of data in the table. This meant that all three modules had to be changed. The table module must be changed to store the new column in the table, and to allow insertion and look-up. The input module must be changed to do different checks on data of the new type. The output module must be changed to include the new type of data in displays and printouts.

A different structure, with one module for each column of the table, could have avoided this problem. Both storing, look-up, input and output could be implemented in one module, which would be reusable even if other table columns were changed. However, general changes in input or output formats would then lead to changes in all modules.

7.6 SOME FIGURES

The studied version of AXE contained 183 software modules. Of these, 80 were taken over unchanged from the previous version.

Let us define module change as change in one module caused by one requirement. That is, one requirement may cause several module changes, and there may be several module changes in one module.

There were 103 module changes. Of these, 82 were caused by changes in the concept each module implemented. The remaining 21 module changes would not have been needed if the corresponding modules were reusable.

Of these 21 module changes, 10 were in activity modules and 11 were in interface modules. No data modules were changed without changes in the corresponding concept, for example, addition or removal of an operation.

The 21 "unnecessary" module changes had the following causes:

☐ In five cases, the module was an imperfect abstraction; it lacked some operation, or it had operations which did not concern the corresponding abstraction.

☐ Eight module changes were caused by new needs for transferring data. In some cases, the modules were intermediate modules that must be changed to transfer data between other modules. In other cases, the module owned the data and was changed to send it to another module.

☐ Seven module changes were caused by a change of the structure of a certain part of the system. Actually, these changes seem to stem from failures to reuse the software architecture.

☐ One module change was not accounted for.

Among the 82 module changes caused by changes in corresponding concepts, there is evidence of another obstacle for reuse of modules. Of these module changes, 32 were nonunique. That is, for each module change there was at least one other module where the same change was implemented. This comes from the use in AXE of different varieties of the same modules, with many operations identical, or almost identical.

7.7 CONCLUSIONS

We have investigated the reusability of isolated modules in a structure where data and devices are strictly local to modules and where the program code implements operations on the data or devices that belong to the same module as the code itself.

Compared with concepts that allow common data and rely on procedure calls for communication, the use of such extremely isolated modules seems to have important advantages in terms of the potential reuse of unchanged modules.

The possibility of using certain module types as plug-in units, allows the modules around these to be reused when the plug-in modules themselves change. Adaptation to new environments and introduction of certain types of subscriber services can be made through addition or replacement of specific modules. This depends on the independence of modules and how well modules implement abstractions. It also depends on the basic software architecture.

Module interfaces have to be small, because at the same time as modules can share no data, message passing is expensive both in terms of amount of program code and processor load. This encourages designers to make modules that are good abstractions. Such modules implement completely a well-defined concept and nothing else.

The combination of modules that are good abstractions with the possibility of handling module identities as data strongly contributes to both module reusability and to the reusability of the system architecture.

Regarding reusability of modules, there are two main disadvantages with a module concept that does not allow sharing of data or devices. First, locality of data and devices results in a proliferation of interface modules for similar devices, where the same operations are implemented in different modules. If a certain operation occurs in several modules, a general change of that operation may make many modules nonreusable.

The second disadvantage has to do with the transfer of data. It is necessary to restrict the number of communication paths in a large system. Thus if one module is changed and therefore needs access to more data, the intermediate modules between it and the module owning the data must sometimes be changed to transfer the data.

REFERENCES

Cohen, T. A. Data abstraction, data encapsulation, and object-oriented programming. *SIGPLAN* Notices, 19(1), 1984.

Cox, B. J. *Object Oriented Programming*. Reading, Mass: Addison-Wesley, 1986

Hemdahl, G. AXE 10—Software structure and features. *Ericsson Review* 53(2), 1976.

Heninger Britton, K. L.; Parker, R. A.; and Parnas, D. L. A procedure for designing abstract interfaces for device interface modules. *Fifth Conference on Software Engineering*, San Diego, March 1981.

Lehman, M. M., and Parr, F. N. Program evolution and its impact on software engineering. *Second Conference on Software Engineering*, San Francisco, October 1976.

Linden, T. A. The use of abstract data types to simplify program modifications. Conference on Data: Abstraction, Definition, and Structure, Special Issue, Sigplan vol 11, 1976.

Oskarsson, Ö. Mechanisms of modifiability in large software systems. Ph.D. thesis, Software Systems Research Centre, Linköping University, Linköping, Sweden, 19 May 1982.

————. Modifiability and scattering of change in AXE software. *Fifth Conference on Software Engineering for Telecommunication Switching Systems,* Lund, Sweden, June 1983.

Parnas, D. L. On the criteria to be used in decomposing systems into modules. *Communications of the ACM* 15(12), 1972.

Yau, S. S.; Collofello, J. S.; and MacGregor, T. Ripple effect analysis on software maintenance. *COMPSAC* 1978.

CHAPTER 8

SOME EXPERIENCES IN PROMOTING REUSABLE SOFTWARE: Presentation in Higher Abstract Levels

YOSHIHIRO MATSUMOTO[*]

Toshiba Corporation

8.1 INTRODUCTION

In order to increase reusability of existing program modules and code fragments, a number of experiments have been conducted. These experiments can be classified into three categories.

1) *Programs described by a very high level language:* The programmer describes, in terms of this language, the abstraction that will be realized by the execution of a target program. The target program is generated from this description by analyzing the descriptions, retrieving candidate code fragments stored in the code pool, customizing them to the problem at hand, and incorporating them into the target program [Balzer, 1981; Cheatham, 1983; Doberkat *et al.*, 1983].

[*]The author is currently a professor in the Department of Information Science, Kyoto University.

2) *Logical structures—such as program, flowchart, logical or transformational schemas—abstracted from existing code:* The designer retrieves the schema which fits his or her purpose, obtains the corresponding source code, and then customizes, incorporates, and transforms it into the target source codes. [Levitt *et al.*; Rich and Waters, 1983].

3) *Problems described using a very high level language:* From the description, the user derives target source code by applying theorem-proving and inference processes [Barstow, 1979; Green *et al.*, 1981].

In this paper, *software module* denotes a modularized set of statements including both the program source code and the requirements, design, and program specifications.

The paper first defines three levels of abstraction in which each software module is described—the requirements, design, and program levels. In the second part of the paper, software modules in the three abstract levels are presented using an Ada-like[1] language. Traceability of a module at a higher abstract level to its corresponding module at the program level is also defined and presented.

In order to promote the reuse of existing software modules, the concept of a *presentation* is proposed. A presentation is a requirements specification of a program accompanied by specifications of the ranges in which the program descriptions can be changed when it is reused in another application. Because a presentation describes an existing program at the highest level of abstraction (i.e., the requirements level), it provides two benefits:

☐ Clarity of program behavior. The requirements representation is a direct description of the program's effects.

☐ Maximization of productivity improvement. Because requirements-level abstractions generally encompass a larger number of program modules and code fragments than other levels, their use leads to higher levels of reused code, and consequently higher levels of productivity.

For example, a designer who is going to develop a new program P searches for a presentation which matches P's requirements. If presentation Q matches, program Q', which can be traced back to Q can be customized to fit P's requirements and will be reused for P. In the last part of this paper, an example of this process is presented.

8.2 REUSABILITY

To make software modules reusable, they must have the following major characteristics: (1) generality, (2) definiteness, (3) transferability, and (4) retrievability.

---

[1] Ada is a trademark of the U.S. Department of Defense (Ada Joint Program Office).

1. *Generality* is the extent to which those who do not know how a software module was developed can understand that module's objects, and the relationships between its objects and algorithms.

2. *Definiteness* represents the degree of clarity to which the module's purpose, capability, constraints, interfaces, and required resources are defined. Abstract data type packages, subroutines and functions with well-arranged parameters are good examples of clearly defined software modules. In addition to the interface definitions, each module should be accompanied by lists describing (a) other modules of code required to execute the software module, (b) the language, operating system, run-time utilities, and input/output devices, (c) automatic interrupts that affect the module, and (d) the amount of memory required by the software.

3. *Transferability* is the degree of simplicity in transporting or transferring software between different types of computers. If no modifications are necessary, the module is *transportable*; if a few minor modifications are necessary for transportation between systems, the module is considered *transferable*.

4. *Retrievability* measures the degree to which a software module can be selected, stored, maintained, and customized by users who have no prior knowledge of its existence.

8.3 LEVELS OF ABSTRACTION

Software design is an iterative refinement process in which requirements specified in a problem domain are gradually transformed into programs to be executed on a target computer. Transformation in a single step is impossible in large real-time systems. Dijkstra [1972] described the concept of an abstract machine $M(i)$ and program $P(i)$ on abstract level i such that execution of $P(i)$ on M(i) satisfies the purpose of a program P that is to be executed on a real machine M. At the next lower level, level $(i + 1)$, $P(i + 1)$ can be executed on $M(i + 1)$. If level L is the lowest level, $M(L)$ is the real machine M. A phase of the refinement process is a step that transforms $P(i)$ to $P(i + 1)$.

A software life-cycle model defines phases along a time dimension. As time progresses, the design process moves from phase to phase. Three types of life-cycle models can be defined: *waterfall*, *throwaway*, and *unified*. The waterfall life-cycle model is a strict sequence of phases, where no phase may be bypassed. This model has been widely applied in industry but is not completely successful because, in a practical industrial production environment, the development process often reuses a number of existing experiences and software modules in a nonsequential way. In contrast to the waterfall model, the throwaway model allows phases to be defined in a customized order rather than a fixed sequential order. In the throwaway model, unnecessary phases do not take place, and phases, once complete, may take place again if necessary. The process in each phase for both of these life-cycle models could be the same if the same levels of abstraction, concept for modularization, and descriptive forms in each abstract level are applied.

In a unified life-cycle model:

☐ All phases are independently defined;

☐ Each phase has well defined interfaces to other phases to allow interconnection of phases that have matching interfaces;

☐ Selected phases can be arbitrarily interconnected by the designer, either in sequential or customized order.

Given that a software design progresses through N abstract levels, a typical sequential model will be represented as follows:

$$\text{Form}(i) = \text{Trans}(i, \text{Form}(i - 1)) \text{ for } i = 1,2,\ldots,N$$

where i = number of abstract level,

$\text{Form}(i)$ = model described in ith specification language: formal representation of ith level of abstraction,

$\text{Form}(0)$ = initial needs delivered by customers,

$\text{Form}(N)$ = program codes,

$\text{Trans}(i)$ = transformation, in the ith step or the process to map every object in level $i - 1$ to the objects in level i.

Our experience has been that this process is intuitively divided in four transformations; in other words, $N = 4$. In practice, the results of these four transformations are four levels of specification: (1) the requirements level, (2) the design level, (3) the program level, and (4) the source code level. These levels are discussed in Sections 8.4 through 8.7.

The actual development processes sometimes do not follow a purely sequential model. A transformation may be made from $\text{Form}(i)$ to $\text{Form}(j)$ where j is larger than level i or level j is lower than level i. Each transformation step often overlaps part of the preceding and/or following steps. In order to enable bidirectional communication between different levels, each level's specification form should provide traceability. Consequently, if a software module in $\text{Form}(i)$ is being reused, the designer can reuse corresponding modules in $\text{Form}(j)$ through the trace.

8.4 REQUIREMENTS LEVEL

The first level of abstraction is the requirements level. Defined first are the objects that are external to the software being developed, but that have relationships to objects internal to that software. The types, attributes, and relationships associated with each external object are specified.

FIGURE 8.1
EXAMPLE SYSTEM

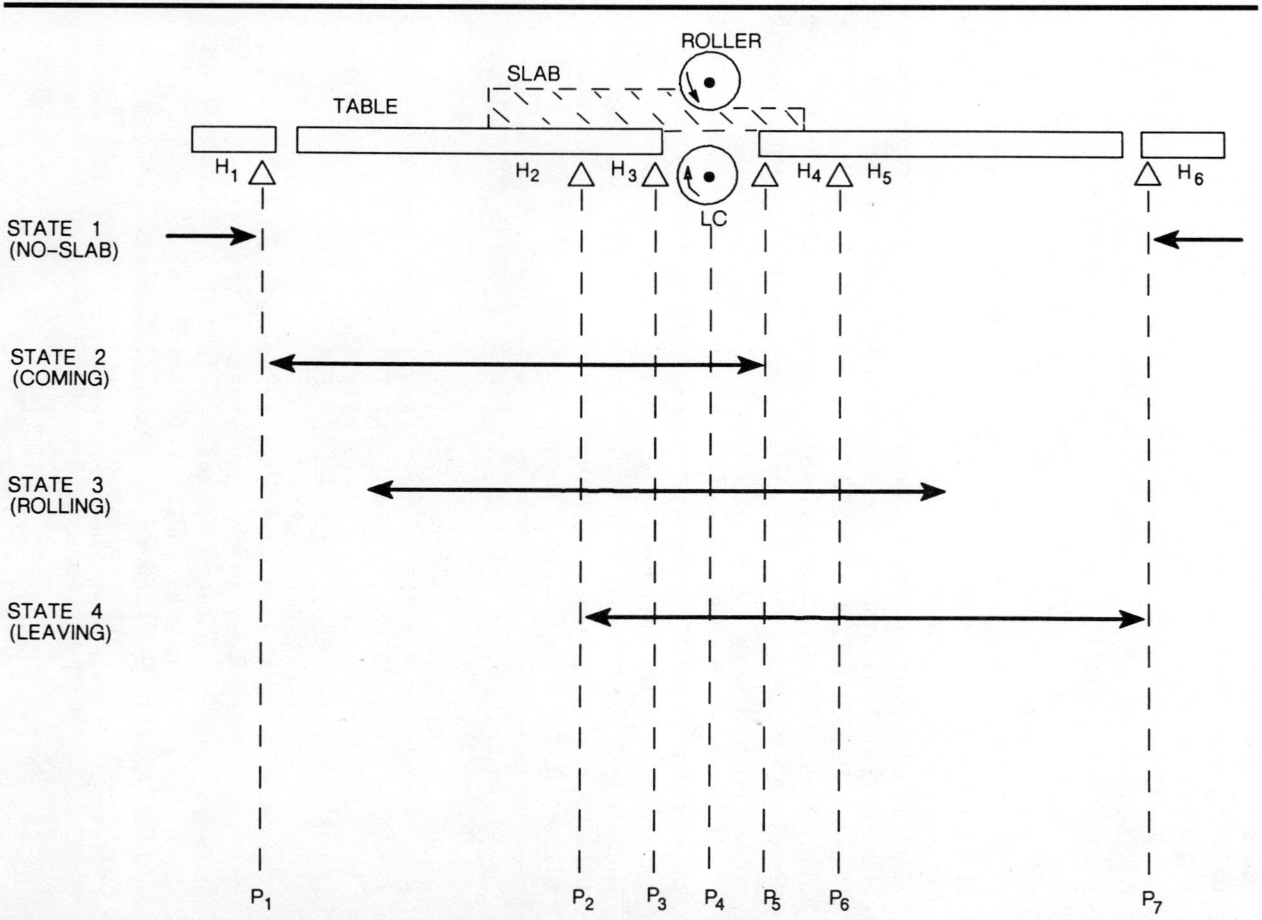

The states of the external objects are defined next. When an object in one state moves into a new state, an event occurs. Subsequently, a decision-making process may be activated in order to select the next action. That action might be a process that will transform inputs into outputs.

A requirements description, Form(1), consists of six major entities: (1) objects, (2) relationships between objects, (3) decision-making, (4) input/output transformations, (5) constraints, and (6) given facilities.

The proposed abstract levels are best illustrated with a real example—in this case, a simplified model of a rolling steel mill is used (Fig. 8.1). Design of the software to control this model will be studied in the following sections. A slab or an iron ingot moves from left to right, driven by the roller tables on which slabs are placed. The slabs are squeezed by the roller, producing sheets of steel plates. In this simplified example, four roller tables and one roller work at the same speed, which is controlled by the software. Hot metal detectors $H1$, $H2$, $H3$, $H4$, $H5$, and $H6$ close their contacts when a hot slab approaches. Load cell (LC) closes its contact when the slab is under the roller. In case of emergency, there is a manual stop switch (STP) which closes its contact when depressed by the operator.

Included here is an example of Form(1) describing the requirements of the mill control model. The description consists of a specification, or interface, and a body. The requirements are written in a capsulated style in order to simplify both the reuse of each requirement module and the mapping to modules at lower levels. Relationships to other requirement modules and to external objects are defined in the interface part.

```
01   requirements description for MILL_SPEED_CONTROL is
02   with
03   object:SLAB:EXTERNAL_ENTITY;
          - - A piece of iron to be rolled by the mill
04   object:ROLLER:EXTERNAL_ENTITY;
          - - A pair of rolls rotating uni-directionally.
05   object:TABLE1, TABLE2, TABLE3, TABLE4:
              EXTERNAL_ENTITY;
          - - Moving tables to convey slabs. Tables are
          - - located on both sides of the roller,
          - - numbered in the order of 1..4 from left to
          - - right, TABLE1 and TABLE2 exist in the left.
06   object:P1,P2,P3,P4,P5,P6,P7:EXTERNAL_ENTITY;
          - - Check points positioned along the lines.
07   object:PROCESS_INPUT_CONTROLLER:
              INPUT_INTERFACE;
08   object:MILL_SPEED_CONTROLLER:
              OUTPUT_INTERFACE;
09   object:REAL_TIME_KEEPER:INPUT_INTERFACE;
10   end with;
11   requirement MILL_SPEED_CONTROL is
12   interface relationship is
```

```
13   triggered by REAL_TIME_KEEPER
             with REAL_TIME_INTERVAL:event;
14   use PROCESS_INPUT_CONTROLLER
             to GET(SENSOR VALUE:MILL_DATA);
15              type MILL_DATA is
                  record
                  H1,H2,H3:analog;
                  LC:digital;
                  H4,H5,H6:analog;
                  STP:digital;
                  end record;
                end type;
16   acknowledge MILL_SPEED_CONTROLLER
             with READY:event;
17   used by MILL_SPEED_CONTROLLER which
             OBTAIN(MILL_SPEED:SPEED_DATA);
                type SPEED_DATA is
                (IDLE,LOW,HIGH);
                end type;
18   end interface relationship;
19   requirement body is
20   object:OBTAIN(MILL_SPEED:SPEED_DATA):
             PROCESS is
21   object:H1,H2,H3,H3,H5,H6:DATA;- -thermocouple,
        - - H1 is in P1, H2 is in P2,
        - - H3 is in P3, H4 is in P5,
        - - H5 is in P6, H6 is in P7.
22   object:LC:DATA;- -load cell
23   object:STP:DATA;- -stop switch
24   object:STATE:INTERNAL_ENTITY;
             - - In STATE1 no slab exists between P1 and P7.
             - - In STATE2 a slab exists between P1 and P5.
             - - In STATE3 a slab exists in the region which
             - - satisfies the condition that the head of the
             - - slab is beyond P5, while the tail is before P2.
             - - In STATE4 a slab exists in the region which
             - - satisfies the condition that the head of the
             - - slab is before P7, while the tail is beyond
             - - P2.
25   begin
        estimate the STATE of the SLAB using H1..H6,
        LC and STP;
        if SLAB is in STATE1 then
             MILL_SPEED:=IDLE;
        elseif SLAB is in STATE2 or STATE4 then
             MILL_SPEED:=LOW;
        elseif SLAB is in STATE3 then
             MILL_SPEED:=HIGH;
        end if;
```

```
        acknowledge MILL_SPEED_CONTROLLER
             with READY;
     end;
26   end requirement body;
27   end requirement MILL_SPEED_CONTROL;
28   end description;
```

The above description shows only part of the whole specification. The actual specifications would include the module diagrams with the preceding descriptions and would also contain:

- ☐ Traces to the objects in the next abstract levels;
- ☐ Constraints;
- ☐ Static, dynamic, and kinetic characteristics of the external objects;
- ☐ Given resources for the implementation.

8.5 DESIGN LEVEL

The second level of abstraction is called the data/function or design level. Trans(2) of the system design represents the transition from the requirements specification of Form(1) to the design specification of Form(2). Data structures, functions, data flows, and control flows are defined in this phase.

The mill speed control system example is implemented with the processing states and transitions shown in Fig. 8.2. The mill speed control software receives inputs from the sensors and converts them into the input symbols

FIGURE 8.2
STATE TRANSITION OF THE EXAMPLE

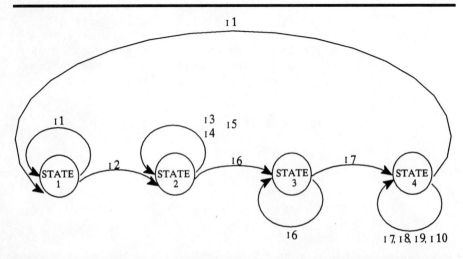

TABLE 8.1
BINARY ARRAY FOR THE INPUT OF THE EXCHANGE

	H_1	H_2	H_3	H_4	H_5	H_6	EMERG. SWITCH
I 1	0	0	0	0	0	0	0	0
I 2	1	0	0	0	0	0	0	0
I 3	0	1	0	0	0	0	0	0
I 4	0	1	1	0	0	0	0	0
I 5	0	1	1	1	0	0	0	0
I 6	0	1	1	1	1	0	0	0
I 7	0	0	1	1	1	0	0	0
I 8	0	0	0	0	1	1	0	0
I 9	0	0	0	0	0	1	0	0
I 10	0	0	0	0	0	0	1	0
I 11	DON'T CARE							1

shown on the arcs of Fig. 8.2. The relationships between the sensor inputs and the input symbols are defined in Table 8.1. For example, in row one, if the contacts of all sensors are open, the software creates input symbol *I1*.

The mill speed control software generates the mill speed in the following way (see Fig. 8.2): the program remains in *state 1* (**no_slab**) and stays there until input symbol *I2* is created. In *state 1*, the program generates IDLE speed. With the appearance of input symbol *I2*, the program transfers to *state 2* and generates LOW speed. The program continues in *state 2*, during which input symbols *I3*, *I4*, and *I5* are created. The transition to *state 3* is made when input symbol *I6* is created, and the program generates HIGH speed. The program continues in *state 3* until input symbol *I7* causes a transition to *state 4*. The program stays in *state 4* during symbols *I7*, *I8*, *I9*, and *I10* and generates LOW speed. The program returns to *state 1* when the current slab exits, generating input symbol *I1*. At this time, the mill is ready to accept a new slab. Fig. 8.2 does not show transition to *state STOP* by input symbol *I11* and the transition to *state ILL* by input symbols that are not defined. In both the STOP and ILL states, the program stops the mill and generates an alarm.

The **requirement MILL_SPEED_CONTROL** is transformed to seven modules in Form(2). These modules are PROCESS_INPUT_DRIVER, INPUT_HANDLER, SPEED_SELECTION, SPEED_CONTROL, ERROR_ HANDLER, ALARM_HANDLER, and PROCESS_OUTPUT_DRIVER.

A part of Form(2) that specifies data, functions, and control for INPUT_HANDLER is shown in the following example.

```
data/function description for INPUT_HANDLER is
  with
      object:PROCESS_INPUT_DRIVER:
              INTERFACE_FUNCTION;
      object:REAL_TIME_KEEPER:
              INPUT_INTERFACE;
      object:SPEED_SELECTION:FUNCTION;
              - - select mill speed using NEW_INPUT
              - - generated by INPUT_HANDLER.
      object:ERROR_HANDLER:FUNCTION;
      object:ALARM_HANDLER:FUNCTION;
    end with;
  data/function for INPUT_HANDLER is
    interface relationship is
      activated by REAL_TIME_KEEPER
        with REAL_TIME_INTERVAL:SIGNAL;
      converse with PROCESS_INPUT_DRIVER
        to READ(H(1), H(2), H(3), H(4), H(5), H(6):
        analog),
        to READ(LC, STP:digital);
      call ERROR_HANDLER to EHANDLE(ERROR:
      integer);
      call ALARM_HANDLER to AHANDLE(ALARM:
      integer);
      activate SPEED_SELECTION
        with READY(NEW_INPUT:FRAME):SIGNAL;
              type IN is
                      (h(1), h(2), h(3), h(4),
                        h(5), h(6), stp); end;
              type FRAME is array (IN) of boolean;
    end interface relationship;
  data/function body is
    object:CAUSE_READY(NEW_INPUT:FRAME);
    FUNCTION;
      object:SENSOR_BASE:FILE_S;
        type FILE_S is
          record
            for all process_inputs
              loop
                    PID_NO;- -identification number
                    PNAME;- -point name
                    UVL;- -upper validity limit
                    LVL;- -lower validity limit
                    EU;- -engineering units
                    SCOMM;- -scan command word
                    STYPE;- -sensor type
```

```
                    CONV;- -conversion parameters
                    UAL;- -upper alarm limit
                    LAL;- -lower alarm limit
                    NEW_VALUE;- -newest scanned values
                end loop
            end record;
        end type;
        SLAB_TEMP:const;
     begin
        loop
          wait REAL_TIME_INTERVAL;
          for I in I..6
            loop
              READ H(i) using SCOMM;
              if it is out of UVL or LVL THEN
                  call EHANDLE(ERROR:integer);
              elseif it is out of UAL or LAL then
                  call AHANDLE(ALARM:integer);
              end if;
              convert engineering unit;
              linearize;
              write into NEW_VALUE;
              if H(i) is greater than SLAB_TEMP then
                  h(i):=true;
              else h(i):=false;
            end loop;
          READ LC;
          READ STP;
          if LC=1 then lc:true;
          else lc:=false;
          if STP=1 then stp:=true;
          else stp:=false;
          generate NEW_INPUT;
          cause READY;
        end loop;
     end;
  end data/function body;
  end data/function for INPUT_HANDLER;
  end description;
```

8.6 PROGRAM LEVEL

The third level of abstraction is called the program level. Trans(3), the program design, provides a transition from the data/function domain to the programming-in-the-large domain. External structures of program modules are designed as a result of this transformation. Using data flows, data structures, functions, and control flows, programmers create a program model that defines program configurations, file structures, and package interfaces.

In designing the program model, designers try to optimize resources to satisfy given constraints and obtain the best performance. Internal design of each program module is left to the next step.

Decompositions and integrations are repeated until acceptable functional configurations and file structures are obtained. After those decompositions and integrations are completed, the following processes take place:

1. The large program structure is planned as a result of these processes:

    a. real-time tasks (i.e., concurrent processes) are determined,

    b. packages and subprograms are determined,

    c. file structures are planned.

    (*a*, *b*, and *c* proceed in parallel and, as outcome, the large program structure is planned.)

2. Package specifications are written.

3. Internal structures for packages and data structures are designed.

Of the mill speed control example's seven modules (PROCESS_INPUT_ DRIVER, INPUT_HANDLER, SPEED_SELECTION, SPEED_CONTROL, ERROR_HANDLER, ALARM_HANDLER, and PROCESS_OUTPUT_ DRIVER), the second, third, and the fourth modules are transformed into real-time tasks. The other modules are implemented by functions contained in the common utility subsystem. Ada is used to describe the program design specification. Form(3) for the mill control example is described as the MILL_SPEED_CONTROL package. The main features of this package are shown here.

```
package MILL_SPEED_CONTROL is
   type IN is (H1,H2,H3,LC,H4,H5,H6,STP);
   type FRAME is array(IN) of boolean;
   type SPEED is (IDLE, LOW, HIGH);
   task INPUT_HANDLER is
     entry REAL_TIME_INTERVAL;
   end;
   task SPEED_SELECTION is
     entry CALC_SPEED(NEW_INPUT:FRAME);
   end;
   task SPEED_CONTROL is
     entry SET_SPEED(MILL_SPEED:SPEED);
   end;
end MILL_SPEED_CONTROL:
package body MILL_SPEED_CONTROL is
   task body INPUT_HANDLER is
     NEW_INPUT:FRAME;
       . . .

   end INPUT-HANDLER;
```

```
task body SPEED_SELECTION is
   type property is
     (NO_SLAB,COMING,ROLLING,LEAVING,ILL,STP);
   subtype STATE is
     PROPERTY range(NO_SLAB..LEAVING);
   type STATUS is
     (I1,I2,I3,I4,I5,I6,I7,I8,I9,I10,I11);
       --for I1..I11 see Table 1
   type STATE_MAP is array(STATE, STATUS) of PROPERTY;
   CURR_SLAB_LOC:STATE;
   NEW_STATUS:STATUS;
   NEXT_SLAB_LOC:constant STATE_MAP:=
     ((I1=>NO_SLAB, I2=>COMING, I11=>STP,others=>ILL),
      (I3=>COMING, I4=>COMING, I5=>COMING,
          I6=>ROLLING, others=>ILL),
       (I6=>ROLLING, I7=>LEAVING,others=>ILL),
       (I1=>NO_SLAB, I7=>LEAVING,
          I8=>LEAVING,
          I9=>LEAVING, I10=>LEAVING, I11=>STP,
          others=>ILL));

   begin
     CURR_SLAB_LOC:=NO_SLAB;
     loop
       case CURR_SLAB_LOC is
         when NO_SLAB=>SET_SPEED(IDLE);
         when COMING=>SET_SPEED(LOW);
         when ROLLING=>SET_SPEED(HIGH);
         when LEAVING=>SET_SPEED(LOW);
       end case;
       accept CALC_SPEED(NEW_INPUT:FRAME)
        do
         case NEW_INPUT is
           when (others=>false)=>(NEW_STATUS:I1);
           when (H1=>true, others=>false)=>
               (NEW_STATUS:=I2);
           when (H2=>true, others=>false)=>
               (NEW_STATUS:=I3);
           when (H2=>true, H3=>true, others=>false)=>
               (NEW_STATUS:=I4);
           when (H2=>true, H3=>true, LC=>true,
               others=>false)=>
               (NEW_STATUS:I5);
           when (H2=>true, H3=>true, LC=>true,
               H4=>true, others=>false)=>
               (NEW_STATUS:=I6);
           when (LC=>true, H4=>true, H5=>true,
               others=>false)=>
               (NEW_STATUS:=I7);
```

```
        when (H4=>true, H5=>true, others=>false)=>
            (NEW_STATUS:=I8);
        when (H5=>true,others=>false)=>
            (NEW_STATUS:=I9);
        when (H6=>true,others=>false)=>
            (NEW_STATUS:=I10);
        when others=>(NEW_STATUS:=I11);
      end case;
    end do;
  CURR_SLAB_LOC:=
      NEXT_SLAB_LOC(CURR_SLAB_LOC,
      NEW_STATUS);
        if CURR_SLAB_LOC=ILL then
          raise ERROR;
        end if;
    end loop;
  end;
end SPEED_SELECTION;
task body SPEED_CONTROL is
  accept SET_SPEED(MILL_SPEED:SPEED);
      . . .
end SPEED_CONTROL;
begin
  - - initialization
      . . .
  exception
      when ERROR=>. . .
end;

end MILL_SPEED_CONTROL;
```

8.7 TRACEABILITY

Modules in Form(1), Form(2), and Form(3) described above are written in an encapsulated style primarily to allow definition of the traces between modules at different abstract levels. An example of these traces is shown in Fig. 8.3, and the mapping of the interface is shown in Fig. 8.4. In Fig. 8.3, requirement X is mapped to a set consisting of interconnected function $A1$, $A2$, $A3$, and a data structure $D1$. X is implemented by the execution of set ($A1$, $A2$, $A3$, $D1$) or a part of the set. The mapping of $A2$ to set ($P1$, $P2$, $P3$, $P4$) may be defined in the same way.

Fig. 8.4 shows the interface mapping for requirement X. X has relationship R with Y. X is mapped to set ($A1$, $A2$, $A3$), and Y is mapped to set ($B1$, $B2$, $B3$). If Bj is connected to Ai through INTERFACE i (where $i = 1$, 2, 3), then relationship R is mapped to set (INTERFACE1, INTERFACE2, INTERFACE3).

FIGURE 8.3
TRACES BETWEEN LEVELS OF ABSTRACTION

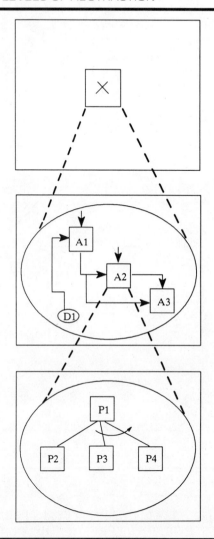

The trace is defined by the collection of those mapping descriptions and is used to compare descriptions from the early phases of software development to the final implementation. This comparison ensures the complete documentation of any code revisions.

The types of objects and relationships that are described in the preceding examples are summarized as follows:

FIGURE 8.4
MAPPING OF THE RELATIONSHIP

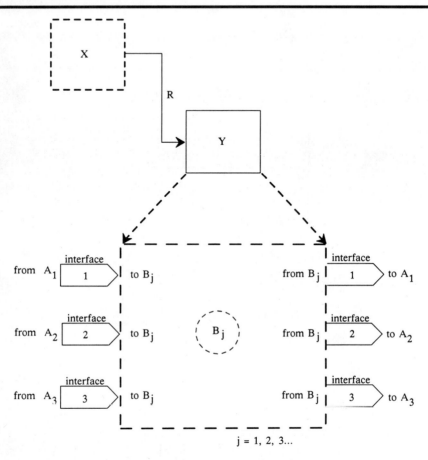

1. **Form(1)- -requirement level:**
   object type: EXTERNAL_ENTITY, INTERNAL_ENTITY, PROCESS, INPUT_INTERFACE, OUTPUT_INTERFACE, DATA, DATA-SET, EVENT;

   relationship type: with, trigger/triggered_by, use/used_by, comprise/comprised_in, acknowledge/acknowledged_by;

2. **Form(2)- -design level:**
   object type: FUNCTION, INTERFACE_FUNCTION, DATA, FILE, SIGNAL;

   relationship type: with, activate/activated_by, call/called_by, converse/conversed_by;

3. **Form(3)- -**program level:

object type: PACKAGE, SUBPROGRAM, TASK, PROCEDURE, FUNCTION, DATA;

relationship type: with, invoke/invoked_by, call/called_by, cause/accept;

8.7.1 Conversion to Reusable Program Modules

In order to increase reusability of the MILL_SPEED_CONTROL package, it is rewritten in a generalized format. The names of entities and relationships associated with the MILL_SPEED_CONTROL application are replaced by names of a more general nature. The generalized form, converted from the MILL_SPEED_CONTROL package is called "package STATE_BASED_CONTROL" and is shown below. Every variable that has been rewritten is bracketed with **&(...)&**.

```
use
   PROCESS_INPUT_DRIVER, ERROR_HANDLER,
   ALARM_HANDLER,
   PROCESS_OUTPUT_DRIVER;
package STATE_BASED_CONTROL is
   type IN is
   &(X1,X2,X3,X4,X5,X6,X7,X8)&;
   type FRAME is array(IN) of boolean;
   type OUTPUT is &(Y1,Y2,Y3)&;
   task INPUT_HANDLER is
     entry REAL_TIME_INTERVAL;
   end;
   task OUTPUT_SELECTION is
     entry CALC_OUTPUT(NEW_INPUT:FRAME);
   end;
   task OUTPUT_CONTROL is
     entry SET_OUTPUT(OUTPUT_VALUE:OUTPUT);
   end;
   private
     type PROPERTY is
       &(S1,S2,S3,S4,S5,S6)&
     subtype STATE is
       PROPERTY range &(S1,S2,S3,S4)&;
   end private;
 end STATE_BASED_CONTROL;
 package body STATE_BASED_CONTROL is
   task body INPUT_HANDLER is. . .end;
   task body OUTPUT_CONTROL is. . .end;
   task body OUTPUT_SELECTION is
```

```
type PROPERTY is
  &(S1,S2,S3,S4,S5,S6)&;
subtype STATE is
  PROPERTY range &(S1,S2,S3,S4)&;
type STATUS is
  &(I1,I2,I3,I4,I5,I6,I7,I8,I9,I10,I11)&;
type STATE_MAP is
  array (STATE, STATUS) of PROPERTY;
CURR_STATE:PROPERTY;
NEW_STATUS:STATUS;
NEXT_STATUS:constant STATE_MAP:=
  &((I1=>S1, I2=>S2, others=>S5,I11=>S6),
   (I3=>S2,I4=>S2,I5=>S2,I6=>S3,
   others=>S5),
   (I6=>S3,I7=>S4,others=>S5),
   (I1=>S2,others=>S5,I7=>S4,I8=>S4,
   I9=>S4,I10=>S4,I11=>S6))&;
begin
  CURR_STATE:=S1;
  loop
    case CURR_STATE is
      &(when S1=>SET_OUTPUT(Y1);
        when S2=>SET_OUTPUT(Y2);
        when S3=>SET_OUTPUT(Y3);
        when S4=>SET_OUTPUT(Y2);
        when S5=>raise ERROR;
        when S6=>. . .;)&- -stop
    end case;

    accept CALC_OUTPUT(NEW_INPUT:FRAME);
      do
        case NEW_INPUT is
          &(when(X1=>. . .)=>
          (NEW_STATUS:=I1);
            when(X1=>. . .)=>
            (NEW_STATUS:=I2);


            . . .

            when others=>
            (NEW_STATUS:=I11))&;
        end case;
      end do;
    CURR_STATE:=NEXT_STATE
    (CURR_STATE, NEW_STATUS);
  end loop;
end;
  end OUTPUT_SELECTION;
```

```
     begin
     - -initialization

        .   .   .
     exception
        when ERROR=.  .  .
 end STATE_BASED_CONTROL;
```

8.8 PRESENTATION

Let Form(3, $Q*$) be the abstraction of Form(3, Q) where 3 denotes the level, Q denotes the specific form (e.g., MILL_SPEED_CONTROL), and $Q*$ denotes the generalized form (e.g., STATE-BASED CONTROL). The potential for reuse of the STATE_BASED_CONTROL package, or Form (3, $Q*$), will be greater if the package can be presented at its higher level of abstraction—the requirements level.

A presentation of Form(3, $Q*$) at the requirements level is designated as 'Form(1, $Q*$), where 1 denotes the level. An example presentation (i.e., 'Form(1, STATE_BASED_CONTROL)) for the STATE_BASED_CONTROL package (i.e., Form(3, STATE_BASED_CONTROL)) is shown below.

```
Form(1, STATE_BASED_CONTROL) is
with
  object:SPACE:EXTERNAL_ENTITY;
  object:ZONE:EXTERNAL_ENTITY;
            - -SPACE is divided in ZONE1,ZONE2,
            - -ZONE3,
            - -and ZONE4.
  object:MEASURED_INPUT:EXTERNAL_ENTITY;
        - -M1,M2,M3,M5,M6,M7:analog;
        - -M4,M8:digital;
        - -(in ZONE1)=>(M1<threshold_value,
        - -M2<. . . .);
        - -(in ZONE2)=>(M1>threshold_value, . . . . . .  );
        - -(in ZONE3)=>(M1 . . .                          );
        - -(in ZONE4)=>(M1 . . .                          )·
  object:MOVING_OBJECT:EXTERNAL_ENTITY;
        - -it moves from ZONE1 to ZONE2, to ZONE3,
        - -to ZONE4
  object:PROCESS_INPUT_CONTROL:
        INPUT_INTERFACE;
        - -read M1,M2,M3,M4,M5,M6,M7,M8.
  object:REAL_TIME_KEEPER:INPUT_INTERFACE;
  object:OUTVALUE:EXTERNAL_ENTITY:
```

```
          stepped analog;
    object:OUTPUT_CONTROL:OUTPUT_INTERFACE;
          - -generate OUTPUT.
 end with;
 requirement STATE_BASED_CONTROL is
   interface relationship is
     triggered by REAL_TIME_KEEPER
       with &(REAL_TIME_INTERVAL)&:event;
     use PROCESS_INPUT_CONTROL
       to GET $(M1, M2, M3, M5, M6, M7:analog,
               M4, M8:digital)$;
     acknowledge OUTPUT_CONTROL
               with READY:event;
     used by OUTPUT_CONTROL
     to OBTAIN(OUTVALUE:STEPPED_VALUE);
     type STEPPED_VALUE is
       $(VERY_LOW_OUT, LOW_OUT,
       HIGH_OUT)$ of analog;
   end interface relationship;
 requirement body STATE_BASED_CONTROL is
   OBTAIN(OUTVALUE:STEPPED_VALUE)is
     object:$(M1, M2, M3, M5, M6, M7:analog,
         M4, M8:digital)$;
     object:SETPOINT:STEPPED_VALUE;
       type:STEPPED_VALUE is
             $(VERY_LOW_OUT,LOW_OUT,
             HIGH_OUT)$ of analog;
     object:STATE:INTERNAL.ENTITY.1;
       type INTERNAL_ENTITY.1 is
             $(STATE1,STATE2,STATE3,STATE4)$;
             - -when (MOVING_OBJECT is in ZONE1)
             - -=>STATE1.
             - -when (MOVING_OBJECT is in ZONE2)
             - -=>STATE2
             - -when (MOVING_OBJECT is in ZONE3)
             - -=>STATE3.
             - -when (MOVING_OBJECT is in ZONE4)
             - -=>STATE4.
   begin
       GET $(M1, M2, M3, M4, M5, M6, M7, M8)$;
       estimate STATE
         using $(M1, M2, M3, M4, M5, M6, M7)$;
       $(
       case INTERNAL_ENTITY.1 is
         when (STATE1=>true, others=>false)=>
                 (OUTVALUE:=
                 VERY_LOW_OUT);
         when (STATE2=>true,others=>false)=>
                 (OUTVALUE:=LOW_OUT);
```

```
            when (STATE3=>true,others=>false)=>
                    (OUTVALUE:=HIGH_OUT);
            when(STATE4=>true,others=>false)=>
                    (OUTVALUE:=LOW_OUT);
        end case;
        if M8 then
            generate output to stop
                            MOVING_OBJECT;
        end if;
          )$
    end OBTAIN;
    begin
        - - initialize;
        accept REAL_TIME_INTERVAL;
        acknowledge OUTPUT_CONTROL
          with READY;
  end requirement body STATE_BASED_CONTROL;
mapping is
      =>(package STATE_BASED_CONTROL
        which consists of INPUT_HANDLER,
        OUTPUT_SELECTION,
        OUTPUT_CONTROL
    where
      (M1, M2, M3, M4, M5, M6, M7, M8)=>
          (X1, X2, X3, X4, X5, X6, X7, X8);
          - -in OUTPUT_SELECTION
      (VERY_LOW_OUT,LOW_OUT,
      HIGH_OUT)=>
          (VERY_LOW,LOW,HIGH);- -in
          OUTPUT_SELECTION
      (STATE1,STATE2,STATE3,STATE4) is
          invariant
      (triggered by REAL_TIME_KEEPER
          with REAL_TIME_INTERVAL)=>
          (accept REAL_TIME_INTERVAL)
          - -in INPUT_HANDLER
          - -not shown in the paper
      (use PROCESS_INPUT_CONTROL
          to get (M1, M2, M3, M4, M5, M6, M7:
          analog,
              M4, M8:digital))=>
          (SCOMM:in COMMAND; X(1)..X(6):
          out ANALOG;
          X(7),X(8):out digital);
          - -in INPUT_CONTROL
          - -not shown in the paper
      (acknowledge OUTPUT_CONTROL
          with READY:event;used by
          OUTPUT_CONTROL
```

```
            to OBTAIN (OUT_VALUE:
            STEPPED_VALUE))=>
            (cause SET_OUTVALUE
            (OUT_VALUE:STEPPED_VALUE))
              - -in OUTPUT_CONTROL
              - -not shown in the paper
     end mapping;
        required facilities are
           - -operating system;
           - -utility subsystem;
           - -language processor;
           - -memory size;
        end required facilities;
     end requirement STATE_BASED_CONTROL;
```

The last section of the description above contains the mapping block. The data names, types, and operations that instantiate the requirements are listed there.

8.9 REUSE OF THE EXAMPLE

This section will demonstrate how the STATE_BASED_CONTROL package and its presentation can be reused to specify a problem called TelegramAnalysis [Jackson, 1975]. The requirements description for TelegramAnalysis is shown in the following text.

```
requirements description for TelegramAnalysis
   with
   object:MagneticTape;
        - -a FILE is stored; a FILE consists of multiple
        - -RECORDs.
        - -each RECORD has different MaxRecordSize.
   object:TELEGRAM;
        - -TELEGRAM is stored in MagneticTape.
        - -a TEXT consists of multiple RECORDs.
        - -a WORD may never be separated between different
        - -RECORDs.
     type TELEGRAM is
      record
       for all SENDERs
       loop
         record;
           Description:TEXT;
           'ZZZZ';
         end record;
```

```
                end loop;
                'EOF';
           end record;
      end TELEGRAM;
     object:TEXT;
      type TEXT is
        for all WORDs
          loop
            record
               blankspace;
               characterstring;
               end record;
          end loop;
        end TEXT;
     object:REPORT;
      type REPORT is
        - -example format:
        - -"Telegram Analysis"
        - -Telegram 1
        - -15 words of which 2 oversize
        - -Telegram 2
        - -100 words of which 10 oversize
      end REPORT;
     object LinePrinter;
        - -Lineprinter prints TEXTs.
      end with;
     requirements TelegramAnalysis is
        interface relationship is
           triggered by command "START TelegramAnalysis";
           use Magnetic Tape
             to GET(INPUT:TELEGRAM);
           acknowledge LinePrinter
             with READY:event;
           used by LinePrinter which will
             OBTAIN(DOCUMENT:REPORT);
        end interface relationship;
     requirements body TelegramAnalysis is
        relationship OBTAIN(DOCUMENT:REPORT) is
           object:WORD;
           object:InputSymbol;
             - -type of InputSymbol is (RegularWord,
             OverSizeWord).
           object:STATE;
             - -type of STATE is (STATE1,STATE2,STATE3,
                                  STATE4,STATE5,STATE6).
             - -when (initial state)              =>STATE1
             - -when (a WORD with regular size is received)
                                                  =>STATE2
```

```
        - -when (a WORD with over size is received)
                                                =>STATE3
        - -when (REPORT is to be generated)     =>STATE4
        - -when (normal end of file)            =>STATE5
        - -when (illegal end of file)           =>STATE6
      begin
        GET(INPUT);
        compute InputSymbol;
        if in STATE1 then
           initialize the system;
           elseif in STATE2 then
             count up RegularSizeWord;
           elseif in STATE3 then
             count up IrregularSizeWord;
           elseif in STATE4 then
             use LinePrinter to
             generate REPORT;
           elseif in STATE5 then
             finish;
           elseif in STATE6 then
             generate error message;
           end if;
      end relationship OBTAIN;
    begin
      initialize;
      accept "START TelegramAnalysis";
  end requirements body TelegramAnalysis;
  end requirements Telegram Analysis;
```

Assuming that TelegramAnalysis can be modeled by state transitions, the requirements description for TelegramAnalysis is compared with the presentation of STATE_BASED_CONTROL, 'Form(1, $Q*$), shown in the preceding section. In the following list, the items on the left side of the arrow ($=>$) are the entities and relationships in the STATE_BASED_CONTROL package; these can be converted to those on the right side of the arrow when the STATE_BASED_CONTROL package is to be reused for the TelegramAnalysis package.

```
(event REAL_TIME_INTERVAL)=>
   (event COMMAND("START TelegramAnalysis"),
   (event NextWordPlease);
(M1,M2,M3,M4,M5,M6,M7,M8)=>WORD;
(event CALC_SPEED(NEW_INPUT:FRAME))=>
   (event NewWordStatus(STATUS:SIZE));
(event SET_SPEED(MILL_SPEED))=>
   (print TelegramNumber, WordSize,NumOfOverWord);
(NO_SLAB, COMING, ROLLING, LEAVING, ILL,STP)=>
   (INIT, RegWord, OverWord, GenReport,EOF,IllEof);
```

```
(I1,..,I11)=>
  (RegularSize,OverSize,EndOfText,EndOfFile);
```

The text of the STATE_BASED_CONTROL package shown in the preceding section is transformed into the Telegram Analysis package using this list of conversions. The resulting program specification follows.

```
package TelegramAnalysis;
   type SIZE is
     (RegularSize,OverSize,EndOfText,EndOfFile);
   task InputHandler is
     entry COMMAND("StartTelegramAnalysis");
     entry NextWordPlease;
   end InputHandler;
   task ReportGeneration is
     entry NextWordStatus(STATUS:SIZE);
   end ReportGeneration;
end TelegramAnalysis;
package body TelegramAnalysis is
   task body InputHandler is
     accept COMMAND("StartTelegramAnalysis");
       . . .
     accept NextWordPlease;
       . . .
   end InputHandler;
   task body ReportGeneration is
     type PROPERTY is
       (INIT,RegWord,OverWord,GenReport,EOF,
        I11Eof);
     subtype STATE is
       PROPERTY range (INIT..GenReport);
     type STATEMAP is
       array (STATE,SIZE) of PROPERTY;
     CurrState:PROPERTY;
     NextState:constant STATEMAP:=
       ((RegularSize=>RegWord,OverSize=>OverWord,
         EndOfText=>GenReport,
         EndOfFile=>EOF),
        (RegularSize=>RegWord,OverSize=>OverWord,
         EndOfText=>GenReport,
         EndOfFile=>I11Eof),
        (RegularSize=>RegWord,OverSize=>OverWord,
         EndOfText=>GenReport,
         EndOfFile=>I11Eof
        (RegularSize=>RegWord,OverSize=>OverWord,
         EndOfText=>GenReport,
         EndOfFile=>EOF));
     TelegramNumber:integer;
```

```
        WordSize:integer;
        NumOfOverWord:integer;
        begin
          CurrState:=INIT;
          TelegramNumber:=0;
          loop
            case CurrState is
              when INIT=>
                do PRINT("TelegramAnalysis");
                   TelegramNumber,WordSize,
                   NumOfOverWord:=0;
                   NextWordPlease;
                end do;
              when RegWord=>
                do WordSize:=WordSize+1;
                   NextWordPlease:
                end do;
              when OverWord=>
                do WordSize:=WordSize+1;
                   NumOfOverWord:=
                   NumOfOverWord+1;
                   NextWordPlease;
                end do;
              when GenReport=>
                do TelegramNumber:=
                   TelegramNumber+1;
                   PRINT (TelegramNumber,WordSize,
                   NumOfOverWord);
                   WordSize,NumOfOverWord:=0;
                   NextWordPlease;
                end do;
              when EOF=>
                do PRINT("End Analysis");
                   exit;
                end do;
              when I11Eof=>
                do PRINT("Error-Illegal-EOF");
                   exit;
                end do;
            end case;
            accept NextWordStatus(STATUS:SIZE)
                do CurrState:=NextState(CurrState,
                   STATUS),
                end do;
          end loop;
      end ReportGeneration;
    begin
      initialization;
  end TelegramAnalysis;
```

8.10 DISCIPLINE TO INCREASE REUSABILITY

One of the software factories in which the author is located manufactures application software for real-time process control systems. The customers accept our software products after we finish test runs with our software products completely integrated into the customers' systems. The approximate amount of software products accepted by our customers in a month is an average of four million lines of equivalent assembler code (LOC). The reuse rate for our software products is about 50 percent, approximately half of our software products LOCs represent reused code. With the reuse rate kept at this value, the LOC per month at this software factory has increased more than 20 percent per year.

To increase the frequency of reuse for each program module in the software factory, we employ the following disciplines and strategies:

1. Enforce the rewriting of existing program modules for reusability.
2. Promote the writing of presentations for existing program modules.
3. Store presentations or Form(1, Q^*) and its corresponding Form(3, Q^*) in a computer-aided software design (CASD) support system.
4. When designing new software, ask each designer to follow these procedures:
   i. When the designers complete Form(1, P) for program P, they should meet to review existing code for possible reuse.
   ii. If a match is found, the designer selects Form(1, Q^*), traces back to Form(3, Q^*) and transforms it to Form(3, **P**).

8.11 PRESENTATION BY MODEL

In logic, a set of individuals is said to be a *model* of a theory if an interpretation of entities and relationships between entities describes facts observed in the set of individuals.

Similarly, a set of elements is said to be a model of reusable software if an interpretation of the reusable software describes facts observed in the model.

We could define an arbitrary number of models in which the interpretation of a given theory describes facts. Assume that the interpretation of reusable software P describes facts observed in a model $M1$. If model $M2$ exists and the interpretation of P describes facts in $M2$, then P might also be reusable for the problem modeled by $M2$.

Thus, modeling and how to present the model are the key issues in promoting reusability. Theoretic models such as *set-theoretic datatypes*, *state transition*, and *Petri-net* are widely known. We applied a state transition model in this paper.

Modeling by metaphor involves comparison with an existing system that can be easily understood. Analogies might be made to problem-solving organizations in our daily social life such as the security exchange markets or auctions.

Using a theoretic or metaphoric model to describe a software-reusability problem will clarify the problem, and presenting the model with the software intended for reuse will enhance its chances for success. For a description of creating and presenting models, see Matsumoto [1986].

8.12 CONCLUSION

Reusing modules defined in higher abstract levels increases the scope of reusable code.

Module descriptions in all abstract levels are written in an Ada-like language because:

1. We plan to use Ada in the future;
2. In our software factory (which has about 3000 employees) the cost of introducing new languages is very high; consequently, it is not to our advantage to introduce different languages for the different levels of abstraction.

Presentation of reusable modules is made in a requirements-description style because:

1. Our designers have been trained to writer-requirements specifications.
2. This style makes it easy to understand the purpose of the module.

In the presentation of a reusable module, the range of the description that might be customized for each application purpose is clearly displayed. The trace to the program modules corresponding to that presentation is also provided. Using presentations and traces stored in an archive system, the designer can find the program modules to be reused.

ACKNOWLEDGMENT

The author thanks Dr. T. J. Biggerstaff of MCC for his useful advice and kind assistance in preparing this paper.

REFERENCES

Balzer, R. Transformational implementation: an example. *IEEE Trans. Software Eng.* SE–7: 3–14, January 1981.

Barstow, D. *Knowledge Based Program Construction*. New York: Elsivier-North Holland, 1979.

Cheatham, T. E., Jr. Reusability through program transformations. In *Proc. ITT Workshop on Reusability in Programming*, pp. 122–128, September 7–9, 1983.

Dijkstra, E. W. Notes on structured programming. In *Structured Programming*. New York: Academic, 1972.

Doberkat, E.; E. Dubinsky; and J. T. Schwartz. Reusability of design for complex programs: An experiment with SETL optimizer. In *Proc. ITT Workshop on Reusability in Programming*, pp. 106–108, September 7–9, 1983.

Green, C.; J. Phillips; S. Westfield; T. Pressberger; B. Kedzierski; S. Angebranndt; B. Mont-Regnaud; and S. Tappel. Research on knowledge–based programming and algorithm design—1981. Kestrel Institute KES.U.81.2.

Levitt, K. N.; P. G. Newman; and L. Robinson. *The SRI higher-archical development methodology (HDM) and its application to the development of secure software*. SRI International. This is a report presented (from SRI International) to the U.S. Dept. of Commerce and the National Bureau of Standard. It has no publication number.

Jackson, M. A. *Principles of program design*. New York: Academic, 1975.

Matsumoto, Y. Requirements engineering and software development: A study toward another life cycle model. In *Computer Systems for Process Control*, R. Guth (ed.), pp. 241–264. New York: Plenum Press, 1986.

Prywes, N. S.; A. Pnueli; and S. Shastry. Use of non-procedural specification language and associated program generator in software development. *ACM Trans. Programming Languages and Syst.*, pp. 196–217, Oct. 1979.

Rich, C., and R. C. Waters. Formalizing reusable software components. In *Proc. ITT Workshop in Reusability in Programming*, pp. 152–159, September 7–9, 1983.

PART II

QUANTITATIVE RESULTS

CHAPTER 9

SOFTWARE ENGINEERING WITH REUSABLE DESIGNS AND CODE

ROBERT G. LANERGAN *and* **CHARLES A. GRASSO**
Missile Systems Division
Raytheon Company

Business
Routine

9.1 INTRODUCTION

It is common practice when writing scientific programs to use prewritten subroutines or functions for common mathematical operations. Examples of these are logarithmic or trigonometric subroutines. The computer manufacturer usually writes, supplies, and documents these subroutines as part of his software. For instance, they usually come with the Fortran compiler. The functions are universal. Square root is square root regardless of the computer, company, or application.

In business programming it is a common belief that each system application is unique and so must be designed and coded from the beginning.

©1984 IEEE. Reprinted with permission, from *IEEE Transactions on Software Engineering*, Vol. SE-10, #5, September, 1984

For instance, it has been assumed that the coding schemes Raytheon and its plant use for material classification code, make or buy code, vendor code, or direct labor code are unique to the company or plant. So, too, with the algorithms used for processing these data elements. Therefore, the reasoning goes, prewritten reusable modules cannot be designed, coded, and reused.

A close examination of this reasoning has led us to believe that there are two fallacies in it. The first is that, contrary to common belief, there are at least a few business functions that are sufficiently universal to be supplied by the manufacturer of a Cobol compiler. Many others could be prewritten for use in a particular company, plant, functional area, or application area.

How many manufacturers supply a Gregorian date edit routine with their compilers?

How many manufacturers supply a Gregorian to Julian date conversion routine or vice versa with their compiler?

How many manufacturers supply a date-aging routine for applications such as accounts receivable?

In each of these cases the application is probably written anew in every business shop in North America.

In addition to universal routines, there are company-wide applications. Examples in our company include

☐ part number validation routines,
☐ manufacturing day conversion routines, and
☐ edits for data fields used throughout the company, such as employee number.

Within a functional area in any company, such as manufacturing or accounting, there are routines that can be prewritten, tested, documented, and then copied into a program.

Within a system such as payroll there are often routines that also can be prewritten, such as tax routines.

Yet because we cling to the false notion of application uniqueness, prewriting is used at only about one-tenth of its potential. We will discuss later the way we have used this concept to produce programs that have an average of 60 percent reusable code.

The second fallacy, in our opinion, involves the program as a whole. It is commonly believed that each business program (as well as each data field) is so specialized that it must also be designed and developed from the start. In our opinion there are only six major functions you can perform in a business application program. You can sort data, edit or manipulate data, combine data, explode data, update data, or report on data. By identifying the common functions of these six types of programs, we have produced seven *logic structures.* These logic structures give the programmer a head start and provide a uniform approach that is of value later in testing and maintenance.

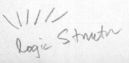

9.2 REUSABLE MODULE DESIGN APPROACH

Our reusable module design approach strategy separates reusable modules into two distinct categories—functional modules and Cobol program logic structures.

9.2.1 Functional Modules

Functional modules are designed and coded for a specific purpose. Then they are reviewed, tested, documented, and stored on a standard copy library. As mentioned earlier, some of the business routines, such as date aging, have universal application; application of tax routines and others may be more limited to a specific company, plant, functional area, or system application.

Within our company we classify these functional modules in several Cobol language categories. These categories are

- ☐ file descriptions (FDs),
- ☐ record descriptions (01 levels in an FD or in working storage),
- ☐ edit routines (the data area and procedure code to edit a specific data field),
- ☐ functional routines (the data area and procedure code to perform some function such as left justify and zero fill data elements),
- ☐ database I/O areas,
- ☐ database interface modules,
- ☐ database search arguments, and
- ☐ database procedure division calls.

As can be seen from this list, we have some modules that are solely data related, such as 01 level record descriptions. The majority of the modules involve both data areas and procedure code. For instance, a database call paragraph, designed to retrieve a specific series of segments, works in conjunction with a program control block module, a segment search argument module, and a database I/O module.

In our listed categories, there are approximately 3200 modules supporting over 50 system applications at three plants. By using these functional modules and logic structures, we have been producing programs that average 60 percent reusable code. This produces more reliable programs and requires less testing and coding. The maintainability and documentation associated with these applications has also improved substantially because the code is not physically contained in each program.

9.2.2 Cobol Program Logic Structures

A Cobol program logic structure has a prewritten identification division, environment division, data division, and procedure division. It is not a complete program because some paragraphs contain no code, and some record descriptions are also empty, consisting only of the 01 level. It does not, however, contain many complete 01 levels and procedure paragraphs.

To illustrate the concept behind logic structures we will describe three types.

The *update* is designed for the classical, sequential update. There is a version with an embedded sort and a version without it. The update is designed for situations where the transaction record contains a transaction-type field (add, change, or delete). The update logic structures are also designed to accommodate multiple transactions per master record. Error messages to a transaction register are provided for standard errors such as an attempt to add an already existing record. Final totals are also provided, as well as sequence checking.

The *report* logic structure is also written in two versions, one with and one without a sort of the input records prior to report preparation. Major, intermediate, and minor levels of totals are provided for, but more may be added if needed. If multiple sequences or reports are desired, the record can be released to the sort with multiple control prefixes. Paragraphs are also provided for editing, reformatting, and sequence checking.

The *edit* logic structure is also written in two versions, with or without a sort of the input records. This logic structure was designed for two purposes. One is the editing of input records. In effect, the input records are examined based on some criteria and written to the selected (good records) or nonselected (error) files. Another use for this logic structure is the selection, based on some criteria, of records from a file for later use in a report.

9.3 CONSTRUCTION OF LOGIC STRUCTURES

For each type of logic structure there is a central supporting paragraph.

☐ For the update program it is the high-low-equal comparison.

☐ For the report program it is the paragraph that determines which level of control break to take.

☐ For the selection program it is the select/nonselect paragraph.

Let us consider the report program as an example.

Prior to the control break paragraph we can identify support functions that must occur in order for the control break paragraph to function. Examples are: get-record, sequence-check-record, edit-record-prior-to-sort, and build-control-keys. These are supporting functions. Other functions (such as major-break, intermediate-break, minor-break, roll-counters, build-detail-line, print-detail-line, page-headers, etc.) are dependent on the control break or central paragraph.

Obviously many of these paragraphs (functions) can be either completely or partially prewritten.

Our report program logic structure procedure division contains 15 paragraphs in the version without a sort, and 20 paragraphs in the version with a sort.

To further clarify what we mean when we talk about logic structures, it might be helpful to specify some data division and procedure division areas in a report logic structure without an embedded sort.

```
Identification Division
Environment Division
Data Division
  File Section
  Working Storage Section
     01   AA1  - CARRIAGE-CONTROL-SPACING
     01   BB1  - CONSTANTS-AREA
     01   BB2  - TRANSACTIONS-STATUS
     01   BB4  - FILES-STATUS
     01   CC1  - COUNT-AREA
     01   DD1  - MESSAGE-AREA
     01   EE1  - TRANSACTION-READ-AREA
     01   FF1  - KEY-AREA
     01   GG1  - HEAD-LINE1
     01   GG2  - HEAD-LINE2
     01   GG3  - HEAD-LINE3
     01   HH1  - DETAIL-LINE
     01   LL1  - TOTALS-AREA
     01   SS1  - SUBSCRIPT-AREA
     01   TT1  - TOTAL-LINE-MINOR
     01   TT2  - TOTAL-LINE-INTER
     01   TT3  - TOTAL-LINE-MAJOR
     01   TT4  - TOTAL-LINE-FINAL

Procedure Division

     0010   - INITIALIZE
     0020   - MAIN-FLOW
     0030   - WRAP-IT-UP
     0040   - CHECK-CONTROLS
     0050   - FINAL-BREAK
     0060   - MAJOR-BREAK
     0070   - INTER-BREAK
     0080   - MINOR-BREAK
     0090   - PRINT-TOTAL
     0100   - ROLL-COUNTERS
     0110   - FILL-DETAIL-LINE
     0120   - WRITE-PRINT-LINE
     0130   - NEW-PAGE-HEADING
     0140   - GET-TRANSACTION-RECORD
     0150   - TRANSACTION-FORMAT-OR-EDIT
     0160   - SEQUENCE-CHECK
```

Combined together as a program, the above areas provide the programmer with a modular functional structure on which to build a report program very easily.

For the update logic structure, the central paragraph is the hi-low-equal control paragraph. Prior to the central control paragraph there must be supporting functions such as get-transaction, sequence-check-transaction, edit-transaction, sort-transaction, get-master, sequence-check-master, build-keys, and so forth. Adding this central paragraph will give you functions such as add-a-record, delete-a-record, change-a-record, print-activity-register, print-page-heading, print-control-totals, and others.

Our update logic structure procedure division contains 22 paragraphs in the nonsort version and 26 paragraphs in the versions with an embedded sort.

9.4 BENEFITS OF LOGIC STRUCTURES

We believe that logic structures have many benefits.

- [ ] They help clarify the programmer's thinking in terms of what he is trying to accomplish.
- [ ] They make design and program reviews easier.
- [ ] They help the analyst communicate with the programmer relative to the requirement of the system.
- [ ] They facilitate testing.
- [ ] They eliminate certain error-prone areas such as end-of-file conditions, since the logic is already built and tested.
- [ ] They reduce program preparation time, since parts of the design and coding are already done.

However, we believe that the biggest benefit comes after the program is written, when the user requests modifications or enhancements to the program. Once the learning curve is overcome and the programmers are familiar with the logic structure, the effect is similar to that of team programming with everyone on the same team. This way, when a programmer works with a program created by someone else, he finds very little that appears strange. He does not have to become familiar with another person's style because it is essentially his style.

9.5 RESEARCH STRATEGY USED TO TEST THE CONCEPT OF REUSABILITY

In August 1976 a study was performed at Raytheon Missile Systems Division to prove that the concept of logic structures was a valid one. Over 5000 production Cobol source programs were examined and classified by type, using the following procedure.

Each supervisor was given a list of the programs that he was responsible for. This list included the name and a brief description of the program along with the number of lines of code.

The supervisor then classified and tabulated each program using the following categories:

edit or validation programs,

update programs, and

report programs.

If a program did not fall into one of the above three categories, then the supervisor assigned his own category name to it.

The result of classification analysis by program type was as follows:

1089	edit programs
1099	update programs
2433	report programs
247	extract programs
245	bridge programs
161	data fix programs
5274	total programs classified

It should be noted that the bridge programs were mostly select (edit and extract) types and that the data-fix programs were all update programs. The adjusted counts were as follows:

1581	edit programs
1260	update programs
2433	report programs
5274	adjusted total programs classified.

The average lines of code by program type for the 5274 programs classified were as follows:

626	lines of code per edit program
798	lines of code per update program
507	lines of code per report program

The supervisors then selected over 50 programs that they felt would be good candidates for study. Working with the supervisors, the study team found that approximately 40 to 60 percent of the code in the programs examined was redundant and could be standardized. As a result of these promising findings, three prototype logic structures (select, update, and report) were developed and released to the programming community for selective testing and feedback. During this time a range of 15 to 85 percent reusable code was attained. As a result of this success, management decided to make logic structures a standard for all new program development in three data processing installations. To date, over 5500 logic structures have been used for new program development, averaging 60 percent reusable code when combined with reusable functional modules. The feeling is that once a programmer uses each logic structure more than three times, 60 percent reusable code can easily be attained for an average program. We believe this translates into a 50 percent increase in productivity in the development of new programs.

In addition, programmers modifying a logic structure written by someone else agree that, because of the consistent style, logic structure programs are easier to read and understand.

Greater ease of comprehension is where the real benefit lies, since most data processing installations are using 60 to 80 percent of their programming resources to support their maintenance requirements.

To summarize: the basic premise behind our reusability methodology is that a large percentage of program code for business data processing applications is redundant and can be replaced by standard program logic.

By supplying the programmer with standard logic in the form of a logic structure we can eliminate 60 percent of the design, coding, testing, and documentation in most business programs. This allows the programmer to concentrate on the unique part of the program without having to code the same logic time and time again.

The obvious benefit of this concept is that after a programmer uses a structure more than three times (learning curve time) his productivity increases 50 percent. The less obvious benefit is that programmers recognize a consistent style even when modifying a program that they themselves did not write. This eliminates 60 to 80 percent of the maintenance problems caused by each programmer using an idiosyncratic style for redundant functions in business programs—maintenance problems that require most programming shops to spend 60 to 80 percent of their time in the modification mode instead of addressing their new application development backlog.

9.6 CONCLUSION

After studying our business community for over six years, we have concluded that we do basically the same kind of programs year in and year out and that much of this work involves redundant programming functions. By standardizing those functions in the form of reusable functional modules and logic structures, a 50 percent gain in productivity is possible and programmers can concentrate on creative problems rather than on redundant ones. In addition to the one-time development benefit, data processing organizations can redeploy 60 to 80 percent of their resources to work on new systems development applications.

About the Authors

Robert G. Lanergan attended Northeastern University, Boston, Massachusetts, from 1964 to 1967.

He developed and implemented a highly successful software reusability methodology that resulted in a significant reduction in the time and effort required to develop and maintain business systems. At present he is Manager of Information Services with Raytheon Missile Systems Division, Bedford, Massachusetts. He presented papers and lectured on the subject of reusability to many national and international organizations (ACM, DPMA, NCC, ACPA, DOD, IBM Guide and Share). In 1980 he was selected as a key employee by Raytheon's Board of Directors for software productivity contributions. His research interests include software productivity, reliability, and maintenance issues. He is in the process of authoring a book entitled *How to Alleviate the Software Maintenance Dilemma: Past, Present, and Future.*

Charles A. Grasso received a B.A. degree in business from New Hampshire College, Manchester.

He is currently the Manager of the Missile System Division Systems and Programming Organization, Raytheon Company, Bedford, Massachusetts. He has been instrumental in the development of major computer applications employing a reusable code/program generator methodology created internally at Raytheon. He is affiliated with the University of Lowell, Lowell, Massachusetts, where he teaches advanced structured Cobol.

References

Armstrong, R. M. *Modular Programming in COBOL*. New York: Wiley, 1973.

Canning, R. The search for reliability. *EDP Analyzer*, vol. 12, May 1974.

Kapur, G. Toward software engineering. *Computerworld*, In-depth Section, Nov. 1979.

Lanergan, R., and Poynton, B. Reusable code—the application development technique of the future, in *Proc. IBM GUIDE/SHARE Application Symp.*, pp. 127–136, Oct. 1979.

Leavit, D. Reusable code chops 60% off creation of business programs. *Computerworld*, pp. 1–4, Oct. 1979.

Schechter, D. The skeleton program approach to standard implementation. In *Computer Programming Management*. Pennsauken, N.J.: Auerbach, 1983.

CHAPTER 10

WHAT BUSINESS PROGRAMS DO: Recurring Functions in a Sample of Commercial Applications

MIKE GOODELL
Cullinet Software, Inc.

10.1 INTRODUCTION

The reusability literature contains many proposals for tools to facilitate building software systems from component parts. Much less attention has been given to what I believe is the more basic question of what can be reused; that is, what kinds of program functions recur often enough that we would want to develop reusable versions of them? The application domain I am most familiar with—business data processing—has long been presumed to contain a large amount of functional commonality. In other words, it is believed that a great many different business programs perform similar or identical functions and that a lot of code, therefore, is rewritten needlessly. For this reason,

From *ITT Proceedings of the Workshop on Reusability in Programming*, Newport, R.I., 1983. Reprinted with permission of the author(s).

business programming is thought to be ripe for exploitation by "reusabilists" (also known as "reusers"). In fact, the extent to which it is already being exploited should be apparent from the large variety of application development systems now being used to partially automate the production of these programs. Originally done in 1977, this study was undertaken in order to provide a more precise account of the nature of this commonality of function in commercial business applications.

There are two ways to conduct a commonality study: analyze source code or analyze documentation (i.e., reference manuals or specifications). The former alternative is arduous and must be limited to relatively small samples of code. The latter alternative can cover a much broader range of programs because it is easier to do. Emery [1979] and Boehm [1981] are examples of the first approach. An example of the second approach is Lanergan and Poynton [1979]. Both approaches are needed for a complete understanding of a particular application domain—indeed, they are complementary. The present study takes the second approach.

10.2 DATA AND METHODOLOGY

The study was conducted by examining descriptions of business applications selected from the Burroughs Program Product Library (circa 1975). Burroughs application program products were classified by line of business; that is, by type of industry for which the product was intended. Lines of business include banking, manufacturing, wholesale and retail business, and medical and educational institutions. The following products were selected from this very extensive library of products:

Banking—18 Applications, 384 Programs

    Installment loan
    Savings
    General ledger
    Various demand deposit systems
    Certificates of deposit
    Proof and transit
    Various commercial loan systems
    Time deposits
    Consumer loans
    Mortgage loans
    Personal loans
    Personal trust
    Item processing
    Miscellaneous systems

Other Financial Services—2 Applications, 143 Programs

Budgetary management
Online credit union

Manufacturing—12 Applications, 98 Programs

Various requirements planning systems
Inquiry and file maintenance
Work in process
Engineering data control
Inventory
Stock status
Work center and routing
Bill of material
Costing

Wholesale—5 Applications, 266 Programs

Wholesale distribution
Accounts payable
Payroll
Invoicing, A/R, and inventory control
General ledger

Retail—5 Applications, 113 Programs

Tire, battery, and accessory systems
Hotel back office general ledger
Hotel back office accounts receivable
Hotel back office accounts payable
Hotel back office payroll

Medical and Educational—15 Applications, 283 Programs

School payroll
School scheduler systems
School financial
School student records
Hospital admissions
Hospital pharmacy
Hospital laboratory
Hospital medical records
Hospital payroll
Hospital general ledger

Hospital acounts payable

Hospital patient accounting

Multiple Lines of Business—8 Applications, 51 Programs

Various general ledger systems

Payroll

Invoicing, A/R, and inventory

Accounts payable

Miscellaneous systems

The starting point for the study was provided by program product specification sheets that described the capabilities and features of each application and included inventories of all the programs constituting each application. Programs were identified by a short, descriptive title, such as "Monetary Exceptions Report," "Customer File Maintenance Update," "Post Commitment Fee Payments," and so on. Almost without exception, these titles contained words indicative of some basic program function: "... Report," "... File Maintenance Update," "Post ...." I tabulated the frequencies of occurrence of these function words by line of business and by certain common application types to produce the statistics that were the basis of the study. I was careful to avoid inventing any categories beyond those indicated by the program titles.

Some difficulties were encountered. A few program titles contained no recognizable function words (e.g., "Related Account Service Charges"). In such cases, I got the function from the extended narrative description of the program in the appropriate reference manual for the application, when available. Sometimes two functions were indicated for a program (e.g., "Control File Update and Report"). In these cases, I arbitrarily chose one function as the primary one. A few programs performed very specialized functions that did not recur. These were put into a miscellaneous category.

After tabulating the primary functions of all 1338 programs, I was able to check the initial results by looking at the extended narrative descriptions of about seventy percent of them. I found that about ten percent of the total had been misclassified because of ambiguous program titles. These errors were then corrected in the tabulation.

10.3 RESULTS

Twenty-four primary functions were sufficient to classify ninety-seven percent of the 1338 programs. These functions are:

A. *Data entry:* original entry of user data into an application.
B. *Edit/validate:* verification that user data is legal, consistent, and complete.

C. *File maintenance:* adding, changing, or removing data on permanent storage devices.

D. *Posting/updating:* changing a single data item or group of items by adding or subtracting an amount.

E. *Inquiry:* selective retrieval and display of data.

F. *Calculate/analyze/simulate:* a catch-all for computation-intensive programs.

G. *Print report.*

H. *Print document:* I distinguish between reports and documents. A document is printed output on (typically) preprinted forms and generally has some special legal significance (e.g., checks and invoices).

I. *Work file create:* creation of intermediate, temporary files.

J. *Sort:* arranging data (in this case, file records) in some prescribed sequence.

K. *Merge:* combining the data from two or more files in a common sequence.

L. *Table file update:* changing the contents of a file containing constants or parameters.

M. *Clear/reset/roll forward:* returning cumulative totals to zero, usually at the end of an accounting period.

N. *Purge:* the selective removal of records from a file, although the term sometimes means removal of the entire file.

O. *File conversion:* reformatting the contents of a file.

P. *File initialize:* allocating disk space for a file. Sometimes includes creation of special records.

Q. *File build/load/copy:* transferring a file from one medium to another, sometimes including data reformatting, field initialization, or other processing.

R. *File reorganization:* changing the relationships among file records.

S. *Item correction:* selectively changing data (usually numeric).

T. *Extract:* selecting specific data from a file.

U. *System control:* assisting the user in the control and execution of other application functions.

V. *Device handler:* an interface between a program and a hardware device.

W. *Library create:* builds a library of (usually) common data descriptions.

X. *Message handler:* This category includes transaction routing, access control, and preliminary transaction validation.

Y. *Miscellaneous:* all nonrecurring functions.

Both relative and cumulative frequencies for these functions are shown here for the entire sample of 1338 programs. The numbers were normalized to prevent biasing of the results by unequal line-of-business sample sizes. There was little difference between the normalized and unnormalized numbers.

Function	*Relative*	*Cumulative*
Print report	.349	.349
File maintenance	.127	.476
File build/load/copy	.086	.562
Posting/updating	.063	.625
Sort	.053	.678
File initialize	.044	.722
Edit/validate	.036	.758
Print document	.029	.787
Work file create	.026	.813
Table file update	.025	.838
Data entry	.019	.857
Calculate/analyze/simulate	.019	.876
Clear/reset/roll forward	.015	.891
Inquiry	.014	.905
Purge	.009	.914
Library create	.009	.923
Merge	.008	.931
Extract	.007	.938
Message handler	.006	.944
Device handler	.005	.949
Item correction	.004	.953
File reorganize	.004	.957
File conversion	.003	.960
System control	.002	.962
Miscellaneous	.038	1.000

The applications constituting the sample can be grouped by line of business (see Section 10.2), by certain common application types such as payroll and general ledger, and by the language in which the programs were written—in this case COBOL and RPG II, the two languages most widely used for business programming when the study was done. Comparative frequencies for these groupings are shown in a graphical format in the appendix.

The study indicates that program products written for different lines of business or for specific applications do not have characteristic distributions of these function frequencies, nor was there much difference between the COBOL and RPG II applications. In fact, apart from a few (random?) deviations here and there, the similarity of the frequency profiles is quite striking.

10.4 CAVEATS AND QUALIFICATIONS

A significant limitation of this study is that only so-called primary functions were tabulated to determine frequencies of function occurrence. In fact, however, most programs performed more than just one of these functions. This fact was quite apparent from a reading of the extended narrative descriptions of the programs in the reference manuals for the applications. For example, in a much smaller sample of programs for which all documented functions were tabulated, I found that more than half of the nonreport programs (i.e., those programs whose primary function was not reporting) produced reports as a by-product of some other function. The apparently infrequent data entry function was in fact often embedded in programs of the *edit/validate* and *file maintenance* variety. My impression was that most of the listed functions could coexist in almost any program, regardless of its primary function. (It is significant that every secondary function I noticed was also the primary function of some other program.) Here are a few examples that illustrate the multiple-function nature of most of these programs:

- ☐ A *data entry* program that also performed the *edit/validate, file maintenance,* and *print report* functions.
- ☐ An *edit/validate* program that performed the *data entry, table file update, file build,* and *print report* functions.
- ☐ A *file maintenance* program that performed the *edit/validate* and *print report* functions.

Another problem is that at the time of the study, most of the program products in the catalog were batch-processing applications. These had been developed in the early seventies and have long since been replaced by online products. I am unable to say just what differences would be found in a more current sample of applications, although I would expect that *inquiry* would increase at the expense of *print report,* and that *sort* programs would be less numerous.

10.5 CONCLUSIONS

Assuming that these program products are representative commercial business applications—and I believe they are—we can conclude that such applications exhibit a high degree of consistency in the kinds of functions that they perform and even in the proportions of programs performing a given function. I attribute this consistency more to uniform business accounting practices and universal record-keeping requirements than to any other factor.

It is worth noting that many reusability advocates have suggested that program requirements, not just fragments of code, be treated as reusable units.

Finally, we are still left with the question: What can be reused? Let's take our most common function—reporting—as an example. The task of abstracting the reusable parts of a reporting program has been performed many times by the developers of report generators. Reports can be characterized by their content, structure, and format. Of these, a report's content is its most variable, least predictable, characteristic. The user of a report generator package must specify the content of a desired report completely. On the other hand, most business reports have a standard structure, consisting of repeating groups of data separated by intermediate totals at so-called control break points and ending with a set of final totals. This structure is sufficiently standardized that the user of a report generator need only specify the items of data to be used to establish this grouping structure; the package often does the rest. Many standard conventions exist for the format of business reports as well. Commercial report generator packages are often capable of arranging the data in an acceptable format with few or no directions from the user.

Similar analyses can be, and have been, applied to most of the remaining common business program functions—most notably, database updating. So far, the result has been a large variety of commercial application development systems that today are being used routinely to partially automate the construction of these kinds of programs.

Appendix: RELATIVE FREQUENCIES OF TWENTY-FOUR PRIMARY PROGRAM FUNCTIONS

Function Categories

A. Data entry
B. Edit/validate
C. File maintenance
D. Posting/updating
E. Inquiry
F. Calculate/analyze/simulate
G. Print report
H. Print document
I. Work file create
J. Sort
K. Merge
L. Table file update
M. Clear/reset/roll-forward

N. Purge
O. File conversion
P. File initalize
Q. File build/load/copy
R. File reorganization
S. Item correction
T. Extract
U. System control
V. Device handler
W. Library create
X. Message handler
Y. Miscellaneous

ALL LINES OF BUSINESS
64 APPLICATIONS—1338 PROGRAMS

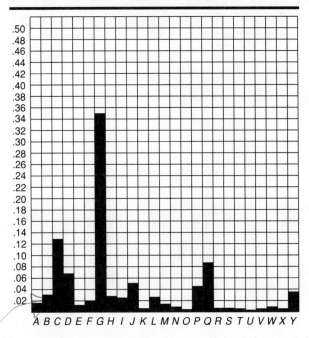

A B C D E F G H I J K L M N O P Q R S T U V W X Y

BANKING
18 APPLICATIONS—384 PROGRAMS

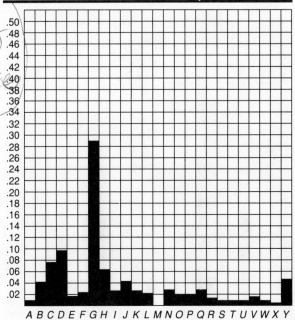

A B C D E F G H I J K L M N O P Q R S T U V W X Y

high payoff activities

OTHER FINANCIAL
2 APPLICATIONS—143 PROGRAMS

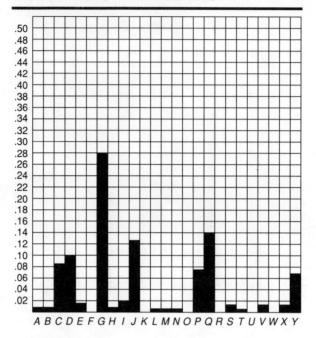

MANUFACTURING
12 APPLICATIONS—98 PROGRAMS

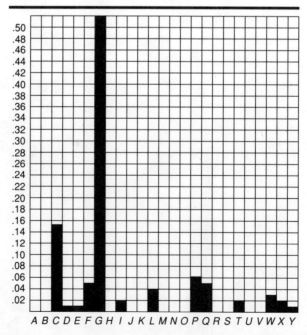

RETAIL
5 APPLICATIONS—113 PROGRAMS

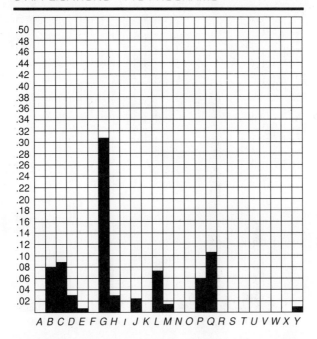

WHOLESALE
5 APPLICATIONS—266 PROGRAMS

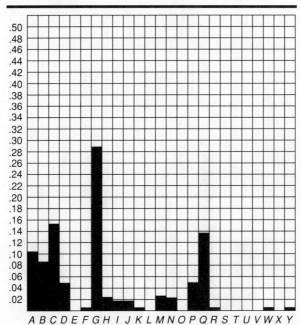

MEDICAL/EDUCATIONAL
15 APPLICATIONS—283 PROGRAMS

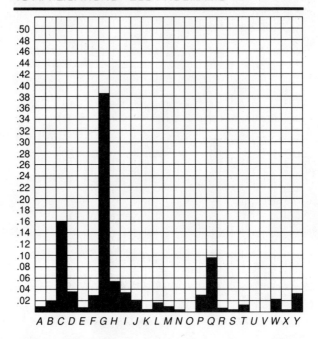

MULTIPLE LINES OF BUSINESS
8 APPLICATIONS—51 PROGRAMS

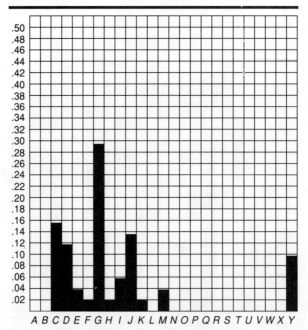

4 ACCOUNTS PAYABLE APPLICATIONS
72 APPLICATIONS

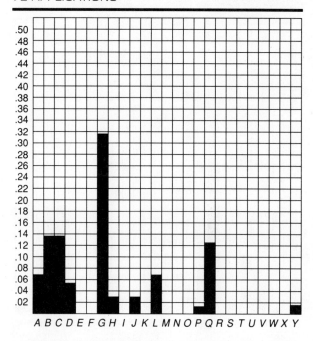

5 PAYROLL APPLICATIONS
146 APPLICATIONS

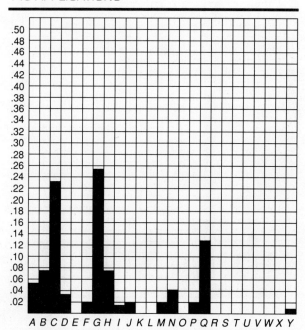

7 GENERAL LEDGER APPLICATIONS
132 PROGRAMS

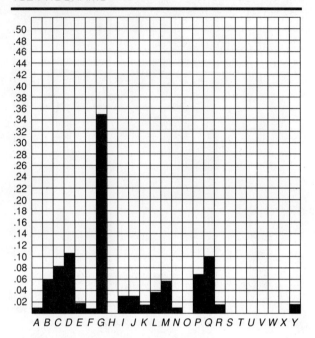

932 COBOL PROGRAMS

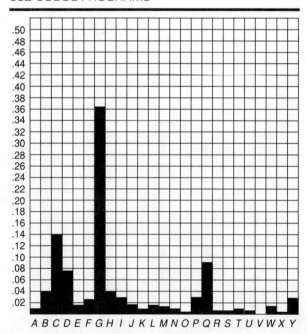

298 RPG II PROGRAMS

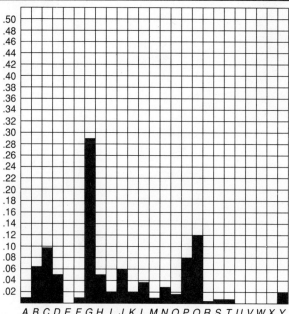

Acknowledgment

I want to thank my former colleague, John Bergfeld, for his assistance in collating the data for this study.

References

Boehm, B. An experiment in small-scale software engineering. *IEEE Transactions on Software Engineering* SE-7(5): 482, 1981.

Emery, J. E. Small-scale software components. *ACM SIGSOFT Software Engineering Notes* 4(4): 18, 1979.

Lanergan, R. G., and Poynton, B. A. Reusable code—the application development technique of the future. *Application Development Symposium*, GUIDE International and SHARE, Inc., Monterey, Calif., 1979.

CHAPTER 11

QUANTITATIVE STUDIES OF SOFTWARE REUSE

RICHARD W. SELBY
Department of Information and Computer Science
University of California at Irvine

11.1 INTRODUCTION

There is a growing recognition that reuse of software can improve quality and productivity in software development and maintenance. Several entities associated with software are candidates for reuse, including

- [ ] processes by which software is created and manipulated [Osterweil, 1987],
- [ ] technical personnel across projects [Meyer, 1987],
- [ ] design objects [Booch, 1986],
- [ ] design histories [Neighbors, 1984], and
- [ ] subroutine implementations [Conn, 1986].

This work was supported in part by the National Aeronautics and Space Administration under grant NSG−5123; the National Science Foundation under grant CCR−8704311 with cooperation from the Defense Advanced Research Projects Agency under Arpa order 6108, program code 7T10; and the National Science Foundation under grant DCR−8521398.

Proposed ideas for software reusability have been embodied in various approaches [Kaiser and Garlan, 1987]. One approach has been through software generation, such as report generators, complier-compilers, and language-based editors (e.g., [Reps, 1983; Habermann and Notkin, 1986]). Another approach has been through the use of object-oriented programming languages, such as Smalltalk-80 [Goldberg and Robson, 1983], Flavors [Cannon, 1980], Loops [Bobrow and Stefik, 1982], CommonLoops [Bobrow et al., 1986], Ceyx [Hulot, 1984], C++ [Stroustrup, 1986], Eiffel [Meyer, 1987], Object Pascal [Tesler, 1985], and Simula [Birtwistle et al., 1973]. A third approach has been through the use of subroutine libraries or catalogs (e.g., [Conn, 1986]). Some hybrid approaches have also been proposed, such as the MELD system, which is intended to combine the advantages of object-oriented programming and software generation [Kaiser and Garlan, 1987].

The purpose of this paper is to provide a basis for insights into approaches for supporting software reuse. One method for learning about how software can be reused is to study development organizations that actively reuse software. Therefore, the focus of this paper is to examine empirical data from one particular software development site that reuses software effectively. Twenty-five software projects of moderate to large size have been selected for this study from a NASA software production environment. The amount of software either reused or modified from previous systems averages 32 percent per project in this environment. (Details are given in Table 11.1.)

Given the attractive payoff of reusing software, there have been several efforts undertaken to discuss the topic of reusability (e.g., [Biggerstaff and Perlis, 1984; Biggerstaff, 1983; Tracz, 1987b]). Some recent articles in the literature have intended to capture the state of the practice in software reusability [Tracz, 1987a] and future research directions for reusability [Biggerstaff and Richter, 1987].

11.2 OVERVIEW

The objective for this study is to characterize software reuse across several projects in a large software production environment. This analysis is intended to address questions such as the following:

☐ How can reusable software be characterized?

☐ At what level (project, subsystem, module) can software be reused most effectively?

☐ How does the extent of software reuse (e.g., complete reuse, slight modification, extensive modification) affect software development effort?

TABLE 11.1
ORIGIN OF MODULES BY PROJECT DATE, PROJECT SIZE, AND
INDIVIDUAL PROJECT

Project Date	Project Size	Project ID#	Percentage (%) of Modules**				Number of Modules
			New	Major Revision	Slight Revision	Complete Reuse	
Earlier	Larger	P1	90.07	.	6.51	3.42	292
		P2	68.47	8.24	6.25	17.05	352
		P3	63.76	4.62	24.27	7.35	585
		P4	18.12	6.12	7.29	68.47	425
		P5	67.92	1.10	5.01	25.98	639
		P6	66.51	12.56	12.87	8.06	645
		P7	67.06	6.80	12.90	13.25	853
		P8	98.56	0.48	.	0.96	418
	Smaller	P9	60.87	.	13.04	26.09	23
		P10	92.86	.	2.38	4.76	42
		P11	54.46	6.93	14.85	23.76	101
		P12	91.15	2.65	.	6.19	113
		P13	79.73	5.41	12.16	2.70	74
Later	Larger	P14	48.51	8.01	16.48	27.00	437
		P15	55.41	5.18	15.09	24.32	444
		P16	75.59	0.39	.	24.02	254
		P17	76.57	3.53	15.37	4.53	397
		P18	91.37	2.40	6.24	.	417
	Smaller	P19	59.39	0.61	16.36	23.64	165
		P20	66.20	.	.	33.80	71
		P21	27.27	.	.	72.73	22
		P22	87.40	.	.	12.60	246
		P23	100.00	.	.	.	28
		P24	77.89	.	2.11	20.00	95
		P25	38.00	2.00	32.00	28.00	50
All			68.07	4.58	10.27	17.08	7188
**A period (.) means 0%.							

☐ How do the interface characteristics of a piece of software affect its frequency of reuse?

☐ How can reused software be characterized in terms of revision history, development effort, and static attributes such as size and control-flow information?

☐ How does project scale affect the amount of reused software?

☐ How can the proportion of development effort spent in design, implementation, test, and overhead be characterized when modules are newly developed, modified from previous systems, or reused without change?

The next two sections (11.3 and 11.4) describe the software development environment examined and the method of data collection and analysis. The following sections present the data analysis that characterizes software reuse at the project level, the module design level, and the module implementation level.

11.3 THE SOFTWARE ENVIRONMENT

Twenty-five moderate and large size software systems have been selected from a NASA software production environment for this study [Basili *et al.*, 1977; Card *et al.*, 1982; SEL, 1982]. The software is ground support software for unmanned spacecraft control. These systems ranged in size from 3000 to 112,000 lines of Fortran source code. They took between 5 and 140 person-months to develop over a period of 5 to 25 months. The staff size ranged from 4 to 23 persons per project. There were from 22 to 853 *modules* in each system. The term *modules* is used to refer to the subroutines, utility functions, main programs, macros, and block data in the systems. Table 11.1 characterizes the projects according to chronology, size, and distribution of module origin.

11.4 DATA COLLECTION AND ANALYSIS METHOD

A variety of information was collected about each of the software projects and their constituent modules. Modules were classified into four categories based on their degree of reuse from previous systems:

1. Complete reuse without revision.
2. Reuse with slight revision (<25 percent changes).
3. Reuse with major revision (≥25 percent changes).
4. Complete new development.

A static analysis program called SAP was employed to gather various statistics—for example, the number of module parameters and number of module versions—for the projects, module designs, and module implementations [Decker and Taylor, 1982]. A set of data collection forms was used by development personnel to record the amount of effort spent during the

various development phases [Card *et al.*, 1982]. The development effort ana-
lyzed in the study spanned design specification through acceptance testing.
The methods applied for validation of the data were described in earlier work
[Basili, Selby, and Phillips, 1983; Basili and Weiss, 1984].

The preliminary analysis and scanning of the empirical data was done
with scatter plots and histograms. The preliminary analysis showed that several of the dependent variables, such as development effort per source line,
were not normally distributed in this environment (which is consistent with
earlier studies [Card, Page, and McGarry, 1985; Card, Church, and Agresti,
1986]). Therefore the primary method for further analysis was the use of
nonparametric analysis-of-variance (ANOVA) models using ranked data
[Scheffe, 1959]. Analysis of variance models enable the assessment of the
potential contributions of a wide range of factors simultaneously. The specific
factors considered are outlined in Sections 11.4.1 and 11.4.2. Such models
also enable the interactions of the factors to be detected, not only their individual contributions. Forty-six dependent variables were analyzed by the models; the variables are described under the relevant data-interpretation sections
(Sections 11.5 through 11.8). The results are interpreted in Section 11.9.

11.4.1 Project Analysis

For the analysis of the projects, the following factors were considered in a
nonparametric analysis-of-variance model at the levels given. Note that the
classifications given below (e.g., larger vs. smaller project) are relative and
pertain to the particular environment examined. These factors were selected
because studies have indicated the importance of project size and date in the
analysis of software development data [F.P. Brooks, 1975; Walston and Felix,
1977; Boehm, 1981; W.D. Brooks, 1981; Vosburgh *et al.*, 1984].

1. Project size
    ☐ Larger (over 20,000 source lines)
    ☐ Smaller (under 20,000 source lines)
2. Project start date
    ☐ Earlier (prior to September 1979)
    ☐ Later (within or after September 1979)
3. Interaction between project size and project start date.

11.4.2 Module Design and Implementation Analysis

For the analysis of the module designs and implementations, the following
factors were considered in a nonparametric analysis of variance model at
the levels given. As above, the classifications are relative and specific to the
particular environment. These factors were selected because the focus of

this analysis is on module origin and because studies have indicated the importance of module size and individual project differences in the analysis of software development data [F.P. Brooks, 1975; Walston and Felix, 1977; Boehm, 1981; W.D. Brooks, 1981; Basili, Selby, and Phillips, 1983; Vosburgh *et al.*, 1984].

1. Module origin
   - ☐ Complete reuse without revision
   - ☐ Reuse with slight revision (less than 25 percent changes)
   - ☐ Reuse with major revision (greater than or equal to 25 percent changes)
   - ☐ Complete new development.
2. Module size
   - ☐ Larger (greater than 140 source lines)
   - ☐ Smaller (less than or equal to 140 source lines).
3. Individual Project containing the module
   - ☐ One level for each of the individual projects.
4. Interaction of module origin with module size.

The results presented in this paper focus on the statistically significant differences in the dependent variables due to the effect of module origin.

11.5 CHARACTERIZING SOFTWARE REUSE AT THE PROJECT LEVEL

Table 11.1 presents the distribution of the origin of modules according to project date, project size, and individual project. Of the 7188 total modules, 17.1 percent were reused without modification from previous systems, 10.3 percent were reused with slight modification, and 4.6 percent were reused with major modification. Hence approximately one-third (31.9 percent) of the modules in this environment were either reused or modified from previous projects. The amount of reuse varied across the projects: In project *P4* 81.9 percent of the modules were either reused or modified, while in project *P23* 0 percent of the modules were either reused or modified.

Several different perspectives were analyzed in order to characterize the type of reuse across the projects. The analysis-of-variance model described in Section 11.4.1 was applied to determine statistically significant differences in the projects according to several dependent variables. They included the following measures for each project:

1. Number of modules reused without revision.
2. Number of modules reused with slight revision.

3. Number of modules reused with major revision.
4. Number of modules newly developed.
5. Number of modules reused with either no or slight revision.
6. Number of modules reused with either slight or major revision.
7. Number of modules reused with either no, slight, or major revision.
8–14. Percentages of a project's modules in each of the preceding seven categories.

Projects of larger size had a higher number of modules in each of the first seven categories of reuse (statistically significant at $\alpha < .02$, $\alpha < .002$, $\alpha < .0002$, $\alpha < .0001$, $\alpha < .0006$, $\alpha < .0004$, $\alpha < .0003$, respectively). This result is not surprising since other studies have observed that the number of modules in a software project tends to be related to the size of the project [Walston and Felix, 1977; Boehm, 1981]. Given that there were a different number of modules in each of the projects, another interpretation examines the percentage of modules in each of the first seven categories listed above. Projects of larger size had a higher percentage of modules that were reused with major revision ($\alpha < .02$). However, project size had no statistically significant effect on any of the other percentages of module reuse ($\alpha > .05$). When the project start date was considered, it had no significant effect on any of the 14 measures listed above—either the actual numbers or the percentages of modules reused ($\alpha > .05$ for all). The data analysis at the project level does not seem to differentiate cleanly among the projects. This may be due to the variation in functionality and development factors that tends to occur across individual projects. The next step in the data analysis characterizes software reuse at finer levels of granularity: the module design level and the module implementation level.

11.6 CHARACTERIZING MODULE LEVEL DATA

11.6.1 Modules Analyzed

Of the 7188 modules appearing in Table 11.1, 2954 modules were Fortran subroutines with complete data collected on their development. The remainder of the modules were of three types: (a) not Fortran subroutines (e.g., they were assembler macros, utility functions, main programs, block data); (b) Fortran subroutines with incomplete development effort data; or (c) Fortran subroutines that have not yet been analyzed with the SAP static analysis tool mentioned in Section 11.4. The distribution of the 2954 modules according to module origin is given in Table 11.2. The overall distribution profile is similar to the one in Table 11.1. The module level analysis in this section and Sections 11.7 and 11.8 is based on applying the analysis of variance model from Section 11.4.2 to data from these 2954 modules.

TABLE 11.2
ORIGIN OF MODULES FOR FORTRAN SUBROUTINES WITH
COMPLETE DATA COLLECTED ON THEIR DEVELOPMENT

Distribution of		Module Origin			
	New	Major Revision	Slight Revision	Complete Reuse	All
Number	1629	205	300	820	2954
Percentage	55.15	6.94	10.16	27.76	100

11.6.2 Module Size and Development Effort

The size and development effort of the modules analyzed provide an initial characterization of them. Figure 11.1 displays the module averages for final implementation size in source lines. The modules reused with extensive revision were the largest, and the newly developed modules were the second largest; those reused with slight revision were the third largest, and those completely reused without revision were the smallest (simultaneous $\alpha < .05$).[1]

[1] This comparison among the module origins and all of the analogous comparisons that follow were rejected by using Tukey's multiple comparisons test [Cochran and Cox, 1950].

FIGURE 11.1
MODULE AVERAGES (AND STANDARD DEVIATIONS) FOR FINAL
IMPLEMENTATION SIZE (IN SOURCE LINES), BROKEN DOWN BY MODULE
ORIGIN. OVERALL DIFFERENCE IS STATISTICALLY SIGNIFICANT ($\alpha < .0001$).
NUMBER OF MODULES IN EACH CATEGORY IS 1629, 205, 300, 820, AND
2954, RESPECTIVELY

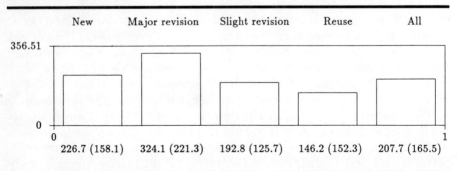

FIGURE 11.2
MODULE AVERAGES (AND STANDARD DEVIATIONS) FOR TOTAL
DEVELOPMENT EFFORT (IN TENTHS OF HOURS), BROKEN DOWN BY
MODULE ORIGIN. OVERALL DIFFERENCE IS STATISTICALLY SIGNIFICANT
($\alpha < .0001$). NUMBER OF MODULES IN EACH CATEGORY IS 1629, 205,
300, 820, AND 2954, RESPECTIVELY

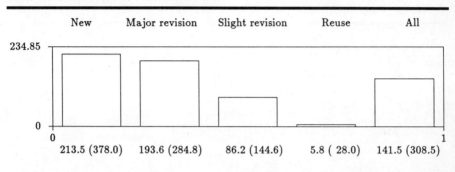

Figure 11.2 displays the module averages for total development effort. Modules that were either newly developed or extensively revised had the most development effort, while slightly revised modules had the second most, and those completely reused had the least (simultaneous $\alpha < .05$).[2] The development effort for an extensively revised, slightly revised, or completely reused module is the effort spent to modify and/or evaluate an existing module for a current project; the effort required for its original development is not included. Although some of the completely reused modules required a design inspection or some testing, 696 (84.9 percent) of them required zero hours of development effort.

Studies in general have indicated that module attributes, such as effort and various static measures, tend to correlate with module size [Boehm, 1981]. In particular, an earlier study showed this relationship to be true for data from this environment [Basili, Selby, and Phillips, 1983]. Therefore, subsequent analysis uses only module attributes that have been normalized by the final module implementation size measured in source lines. Figure 11.3 displays the module averages for total development effort per source line. Newly developed modules had the most effort per source line, modules extensively or slightly revised had the second most, and completely reused modules had the least (simultaneous $\alpha < .05$).

---

[2] In general, the discussion will focus on only those simultaneous pairwise comparisons of module origins that were statistically significant. For example, there was no statistically significant difference in development effort when newly developed modules and extensively revised modules were compared.

FIGURE 11.3
MODULE AVERAGES (AND STANDARD DEVIATIONS) FOR TOTAL
DEVELOPMENT EFFORT (IN TENTHS OF HOURS) DIVIDED BY FINAL
IMPLEMENTATION SIZE (IN SOURCE LINES), BROKEN DOWN BY MODULE
ORIGIN. OVERALL DIFFERENCE IS STATISTICALLY SIGNIFICANT ($\alpha < .0001$).
NUMBER OF MODULES IN EACH CATEGORY IS 1629, 205, 300, 820, AND
2954, RESPECTIVELY

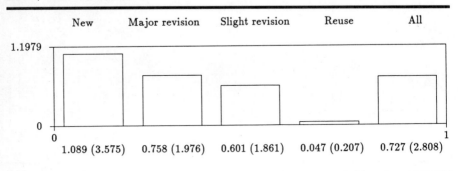

11.7 CHARACTERIZING SOFTWARE REUSE AT THE MODULE DESIGN LEVEL

Several researchers have advocated the merits of software reuse at the
design level (e.g., [Kaiser and Garlan, 1987; Biggerstaff and Richter, 1987]).
Software design information tends to be applicable across a variety of problems, while specific implementations tend to embody information customized
to individual circumstances. This section focuses on the characterization of
software reuse at the module design level. Several aspects of software design
are considered:

- [ ] interfaces that a module has with other system modules;
- [ ] interfaces that other system modules have with a module;
- [ ] interfaces that a module has with human users;
- [ ] documentation describing the functionality of a module; and
- [ ] effort spent in designing a module.

11.7.1 A Module's Interfaces with Other Modules

Two interpretations are considered for capturing the interfaces between a
given module and other modules. The first interpretation is the number of
calls that a module makes to other system modules, where utility functions
are not counted since they are relatively low-level. The second interpretation

FIGURE 11.4
MODULE AVERAGES (AND STANDARD DEVIATIONS) FOR THE NUMBER
OF CALLS TO OTHER MODULES DIVIDED BY FINAL IMPLEMENTATION
SIZE (IN SOURCE LINES), BROKEN DOWN BY MODULE ORIGIN. CALLS TO
UTILITY FUNCTIONS ARE NOT COUNTED. OVERALL DIFFERENCE IS
STATISTICALLY SIGNIFICANT ($\alpha < .0001$). NUMBER OF MODULES IN EACH
CATEGORY IS 1629, 205, 300, 820, AND 2954, RESPECTIVELY

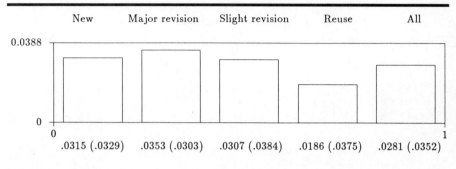

is the number of calls that a module makes just to utility functions. These
two views are intended to encompass the amount of potential interaction
that a module has with other system modules and with support modules,
respectively. These are two forms of module *fan-out*. Figures 11.4 and 11.5
present these two interpretations. Extensively revised modules had the most

FIGURE 11.5
MODULE AVERAGES (AND STANDARD DEVIATIONS) FOR THE NUMBER
OF CALLS TO UTILITY FUNCTIONS DIVIDED BY FINAL IMPLEMENTATION
SIZE (IN SOURCE LINES), BROKEN DOWN BY MODULE ORIGIN. OVERALL
DIFFERENCE IS STATISTICALLY SIGNIFICANT ($\alpha < .0001$). NUMBER OF
MODULES IN EACH CATEGORY IS 1629, 205, 300, 820, AND 2954,
RESPECTIVELY

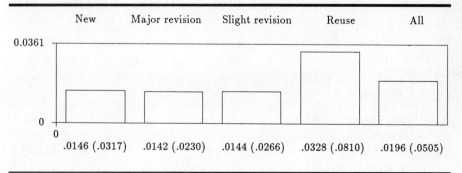

FIGURE 11.6
MODULE AVERAGES (AND STANDARD DEVIATIONS) FOR THE NUMBER OF
INPUT AND OUTPUT PARAMETERS DIVIDED BY FINAL IMPLEMENTATION
SIZE (IN SOURCE LINES), BROKEN DOWN BY MODULE ORIGIN. OVERALL
DIFFERENCE IS STATISTICALLY SIGNIFICANT ($\alpha < .0001$). NUMBER OF
MODULES IN EACH CATEGORY IS 1629, 205, 300, 820, AND 2954,
RESPECTIVELY

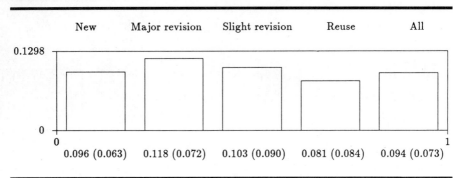

calls to other system modules, newly developed or slightly revised modules
had the second most, and completely reused ones had the fewest (Figure
11.4; simultaneous $\alpha < .05$). Completely reused modules had more calls to
utility functions than did either newly developed or slightly revised modules
(Figure 11.5; simultaneous $\alpha < .05$).

11.7.2 The Interfaces Other System Modules Have with a Module

A straightforward measure is considered for characterizing the interface
between other system modules and a given module. The measure is the number of input and output parameters in a module, including any global data
referenced. Figure 11.6 displays the module averages for the number of input
and output parameters. Modules that were extensively revised had the most
parameters, those that were either newly developed or slightly revised had
the second most, and those that were completely reused had the fewest (simultaneous $\alpha < .05$).

11.7.3 A Module's Interfaces with Human Users

Modules have interfaces not only with other modules, but also with human
users. One measure of a module's interface with humans is the number of
its input and output statements, which is the number of reads and writes.
Figure 11.7 presents the module averages for read and write statements.

FIGURE 11.7
MODULE AVERAGES (AND STANDARD DEVIATIONS) FOR THE NUMBER
OF INPUT AND OUTPUT STATEMENTS (I.E., READS AND WRITES) DIVIDED
BY FINAL IMPLEMENTATION SIZE (IN SOURCE LINES), BROKEN DOWN BY
MODULE ORIGIN. OVERALL DIFFERENCE IS STATISTICALLY SIGNIFICANT
($\alpha <$ .0001). NUMBER OF MODULES IN EACH CATEGORY IS 1629, 205,
300, 820, AND 2954, RESPECTIVELY

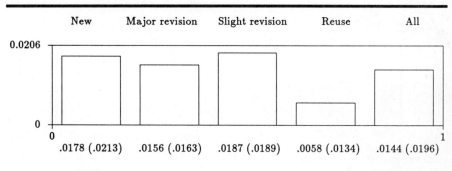

The modules that were completely reused had the fewest read and write
statements (simultaneous $\alpha <$ .05).

11.7.4 The Documentation of a Module's Functionality

In the environment being examined, a description of the intended functionality of a module is recorded in English. This description is included with the
final implementation of a module as a set of comments. One may argue that a
lengthy description enables a clear understanding of a module's functionality.
One may also argue that a lengthy description indicates a complicated specification that may be difficult to understand or implement. An approximation
for a module's ratio of commentary to functionality is the number of comments per source line in the final implementation. The distribution across
module origin for this measure is given in Fig. 11.8. Modules that were completely reused had a higher commentary-to-source-line ratio than did all other
modules (simultaneous $\alpha <$ .05).

11.7.5 Module Design Effort

Figure 11.9 displays the average percentage of module development effort
spent in module design. Modules that were newly developed had a higher
percentage of effort spent in module design than did all other modules
(simultaneous $\alpha <$ .05).

FIGURE 11.8
MODULE AVERAGES (AND STANDARD DEVIATIONS) FOR THE NUMBER
OF COMMENTS DIVIDED BY FINAL IMPLEMENTATION SIZE (IN SOURCE
LINES), BROKEN DOWN BY MODULE ORIGIN. OVERALL DIFFERENCE IS
STATISTICALLY SIGNIFICANT ($\alpha < .0001$). NUMBER OF MODULES IN
EACH CATEGORY IS 1629, 205, 300, 820, AND 2954, RESPECTIVELY

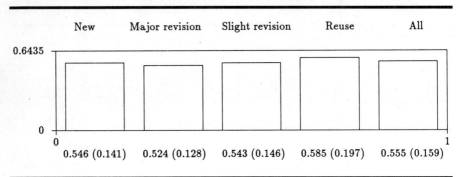

FIGURE 11.9
MODULE AVERAGES (AND STANDARD DEVIATIONS) FOR PERCENTAGE
OF DEVELOPMENT EFFORT SPENT IN DESIGN, BROKEN DOWN BY
MODULE ORIGIN. OVERALL DIFFERENCE IS STATISTICALLY SIGNIFICANT
($\alpha < .0001$). NUMBER OF MODULES IN EACH CATEGORY IS 1629, 205,
300, 124, AND 2258, RESPECTIVELY (EXCLUDED ARE THE 696
MODULES REUSED WITHOUT REVISION THAT HAD ZERO HOURS OF
DEVELOPMENT EFFORT)

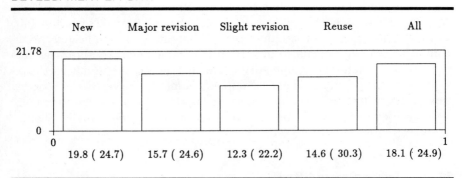

11.8 CHARACTERIZING SOFTWARE REUSE AT THE MODULE IMPLEMENTATION LEVEL

This section focuses on the characterization of software reuse at the module-implementation level. Several aspects of software implementation are considered:

☐ changes in a module;
☐ control flow structure in a module; and
☐ assignment statements ("noncontrol flow structure") in a module.

11.8.1 Module Changes

Figure 11.10 displays a simple measure of the evolution that a module undergoes—its number of changes. Newly developed modules had the most changes, modules reused with extensive or slight revision had the second most, and modules completely reused had the fewest (simultaneous $\alpha < .05$).

11.8.2 Module Control Flow

One characteristic of an implementation for a module is its control flow structure. The cyclomatic complexity metric is based on the control flow graph for a module and has provided the foundations for various software testing methods [McCabe, 1976]. Figure 11.11 gives the module averages for cyclomatic complexity divided by the number of source lines. The overall difference is not statistically significant ($\alpha > .05$). However, an earlier study

FIGURE 11.10
MODULE AVERAGES (AND STANDARD DEVIATIONS) FOR THE NUMBER OF CHANGES DIVIDED BY FINAL IMPLEMENTATION SIZE (IN SOURCE LINES), BROKEN DOWN BY MODULE ORIGIN. OVERALL DIFFERENCE IS STATISTICALLY SIGNIFICANT ($\alpha < .0001$). NUMBER OF MODULES IN EACH CATEGORY IS 1629, 205, 300, 820, AND 2954, RESPECTIVELY

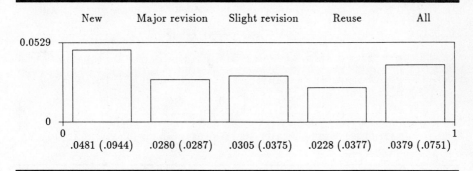

FIGURE 11.11
MODULE AVERAGES (AND STANDARD DEVIATIONS) FOR CYCLOMATIC
COMPLEXITY DIVIDED BY FINAL IMPLEMENTATION SIZE (IN SOURCE LINES),
BROKEN DOWN BY MODULE ORIGIN. OVERALL DIFFERENCE IS NOT
STATISTICALLY SIGNIFICANT ($\alpha > .05$). NUMBER OF MODULES IN EACH
CATEGORY IS 1629, 205, 300, 820, AND 2954, RESPECTIVELY

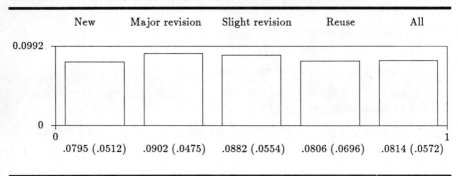

in this environment, based on a smaller data set, has indicated that cyclomatic
complexity per executable statement is the lowest for completely reused modules [Card, Church, and Agresti, 1986].

11.8.3 Module Assignment Statements

One aspect of the "noncontrol flow structure" in a module is its assignment
statements. Figure 11.12 gives the module averages for the number of assign-

FIGURE 11.12
MODULE AVERAGES (AND STANDARD DEVIATIONS) FOR THE NUMBER
OF ASSIGNMENT STATEMENTS DIVIDED BY FINAL IMPLEMENTATION SIZE
(IN SOURCE LINES), BROKEN DOWN BY MODULE ORIGIN. OVERALL
DIFFERENCE IS STATISTICALLY SIGNIFICANT ($\alpha < .0001$). NUMBER OF
MODULES IN EACH CATEGORY IS 1629, 205, 300, 820, AND 2954,
RESPECTIVELY

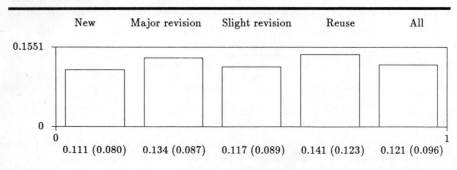

ment statements divided by the number of source lines. Modules that were either completely reused or extensively revised had more assignment statements than did newly developed modules (simultaneous $\alpha < .05$).

11.9 INTERPRETATIONS AND CONCLUSIONS

Reusing software may be the catalyst that helps the software community achieve large improvements in software productivity and quality. The goal of frequent software reuse, however, continues to challenge the software community. There are several motivations for desiring software reuse, including gains in productivity by avoiding redevelopment and gains in quality by incorporating components whose reliability has already been established. The approach presented in this study has been to provide insights through empirical analysis of an environment that actively reuses software. Twenty-five software systems ranging from 3000 to 112,000 source lines were selected for analysis from a NASA production environment. The amount of software either reused or modified from previous systems averages 32 percent per project in this environment. Nonparametric analysis-of-variance models were applied to examine a wide range of development variables across the software modules in the systems. The analysis has focused on the characterization of software reuse at the project, module design, and module implementation levels.

11.9.1 Summary of Empirical Results

To summarize the characterization of software reuse at the module design level in the environment: When compared with modules that were newly developed, extensively revised, or slightly revised, modules that were completely reused without revision had

☐ less interaction with other system modules in terms of the number of module calls per source line;

☐ simpler interfaces in terms of the number of input-output parameters per source line;

☐ less interaction with human users in terms of the number of read-write statements per source line; and

☐ higher ratios of commentary to eventual implementation size in terms of the number of comments per source line.

When compared with newly developed modules, modules that were completely reused without revision had

☐ more interaction with utility functions in terms of the number of utility function calls per source line; and

☐ a lower percentage of development effort spent in design.

To summarize the characterization of software reuse at the module-implementation level in the environment: When compared with modules that were newly developed, extensively revised, or slightly revised, modules that were completely reused without revision had

☐ smaller size in terms of the number of source lines;
☐ less total development effort in terms of the number of either total development hours or total development hours per source line; and
☐ fewer changes in terms of the number of versions per source line.

When compared with newly developed modules, modules that were completely reused without revision had more assignment statements in terms of the number of assignment statements per source line.

The project level analysis indicated that projects of larger size had a higher percentage of modules that were reused with major revision.

11.9.2 Interpretations

The empirical results from this study suggest several trends for the specific environment examined. Completely reused modules tended to be small, well-documented modules with simple interfaces and little input-output processing. There is an indication that the completely reused modules tended to be "terminal nodes" in the projects' module invocation hierarchies. This is because, when compared to newly developed modules, the completely reused modules had less interaction with other systems modules but more interaction with utility functions. The completely reused modules required little development effort or changes, and a lower proportion of the development effort was spent in design activities. This is because the design of a module from scratch requires the creation and evaluation of a new design, while the complete reuse of a module may require only a walkthrough of an existing design. There is also a suggestion that the completely reused modules had implementations of a sequential—as opposed to branching—nature because of their higher proportion of assignment statements. Regarding project size, when the developers were working on large projects, they may have been even more motivated than usual to reuse modules because of the project scale. Consequently, a higher percentage of modules in those projects ended up with extensive revisions.

Several statistically significant relationships have been outlined in this paper. For example, modules reused without revision had fewer input-output parameters. Does this result suggest that reused modules just happened to have simpler interfaces or does it mean that the simpler interfaces led to the reuse of the modules? There is a certain circularity in this question that needs to be considered before concluding the causality of effects (e.g., simpler interfaces caused the modules to be reused). In some cases the causes and effects may not be cleanly separable from one another and from the other factors affecting the projects in the environment.

Reusing software is a natural process for the developers in this environment. The reuse of software is by developer choice, not management directive. This willingness to reuse software indicates that the developers are convinced of its payoffs. Also, there is relatively low turnover of development personnel. Although the projects vary in functionality, the overall problem domain—ground support software for unmanned spacecraft control—has an established set of algorithms and processing methods. Therefore, several factors in this environment aid the developers' ability to reuse software.

Developers in this environment do not have automated tools to assist in the reuse process. Developers simply use their own experience and knowledge to accomplish software reuse. They are able to do so because of the low personnel turnover and because of the established problem domain. An open question is how such an environment would be impacted by automated systems intended to catalyze the reuse process. The development of such a system is underway.

11.9.3 Future Work

This paper has discussed an initial set of results from an empirical study of one environment. Further interpretation of the data is underway. This work is intended to suggest implications that span a variety of software development areas:

- [ ] lifecycle models incorporating reuse,
- [ ] reuse methodologies, and
- [ ] tools to support reuse.

A continuing theme in this work is the value of analyzing more than just the reuse of source code—specifically, information that relates to software reuse at the design level. Further analysis of software reuse in the projects is in progress. An expanded set of project and module attributes is being examined, including information about software errors that occurred during development. There is also some recently acquired project data about reuse in a second development organization. The continued analysis is intended to yield further information about the development, organization, and identification of reusable software objects.

ACKNOWLEDGMENT

The author is grateful to B. Agresti for his comments on an earlier version of this paper.

REFERENCES

Basili, V. R.; Selby, R. W.; and Phillips, T. Y. Metric analysis and data validation across fortran projects. *IEEE Transactions on Software Engineering*, SE-9(6): 652–663, Nov. 1983.

Basili, V. R., and Weiss, D. M. A methodology for collecting valid software engineering data. *IEEE Transactions on Software Engineering*, SE-10(6): 728–738, November 1984.

Basili, V. R.; Zelkowitz, M.V.; McGarry, Jr., F. E.; Reiter, R. W.; Truszkowski, W. F.; and Weiss, D. L. *The software engineering laboratory.* Technical report SEL-77-001, Software Engineering Laboratory, NASA/Goddard Space Flight Center, Greenbelt, Md., May 1977.

Biggerstaff, T. (ed). *Proceedings of the Workshop on Reusability in Programming*, ITT, Shelton, Conn., 1983.

Biggerstaff, T., and Perlis, A. (eds). *IEEE Transactions on Software Engineering*, SE-10(5), Special issue on software reusability, Sept. 1984.

Biggerstaff, T., and Richter, C. Reusability framework, assessment, and directions. *IEEE Software*, 4(2):41–49, March 1987.

Birtwistle, G.; Dahl, O-J.; Myhrhaug, B.; and Nygaard, K. *Simula Begin.* Berlin: Studentliteratur and Auerbach Publishers, 1973.

Bobrow, D. G., and Stefik, M. J. *Loops: An objected-oriented programming system for interlisp.* Technical report, Xerox PARC, Palo Alto, Calif., 1982.

Bobrow, D.; Kahn, K.; Kiczales, G.; Masinter, L.; Stefik, M.; and Zdybel, F. Commonloops: merging lisp and object-oriented programming. In *OOPSLA 86: Object-Oriented Programming Systems, Languages, and Applications*, pp. 17–19, 1986.

Boehm, B. W. *Software Engineering Economics.* Englewood Cliffs, N.J.: Prentice-Hall, 1981.

Booch, G. Object-oriented development. *IEEE Transactions on Software Engineering*, SE-12(2):211–221, Feb. 1986.

Brooks, F. P. *The Mythical Man-Month.* Reading, Mass.: Addison-Wesley, 1975.

Brooks, W. D. Software technology payoff: some statistical evidence. *Journal of Systems and Software*, 2:3–9, 1981.

Cannon, J. I. *Flavors.* Technical report, MIT Artificial Intelligence Laboratory, Cambridge, Mass., 1980.

Card, D. N.; Church, V. E.; and Agresti, W. W. An empirical study of software design practices. *IEEE Transactions on Software Engineering*, SE-12(2):264–271, Feb. 1986.

Card, D. N.; McGarry, F. E.; Page, J.; Eslinger, S.; and Basili, V. R. *The software engineering laboratory.* Technical report SEL-81-104, Software Engineering Laboratory, NASA/Goddard Space Flight Center, Greenbelt, Md., Feb. 1982.

Card, D. N.; Page, G. T.; and McGarry, F.E. Criteria for software modularization. In *Proceedings of the Eighth International Conference on Software Engineering*, pp. 372–377, London, August 28–30, 1985.

Cochran, W. G., and Cox, G. M. *Experimental Designs.* New York, N.Y.: John Wiley & Sons, 1950.

Conn, R. An overview of the DoD Ada software repository. *Dr. Dobbs Journal*, pp. 60–61, 86–91, Feb. 1986.

Decker, W. J., and Taylor, W. A. *Fortran static source code analyzer program (SAP) user's guide (revision 1)*. Technical report SEL-78-102, Software Engineering Laboratory, NASA/Goddard Space Flight Center, Greenbelt, Md., May 1982.

Goldberg, A., and Robson, D. *Smalltalk-80: The Language and Its Implementation*. Reading, Mass.: Addison-Wesley, 1983.

Habermann, A. N., and Notkin, D. Gandalf: software development environments. *IEEE Transactions on Software Engineering*, SE-12(12), Dec. 1986.

Hulot, J. -H. *Ceyx, version 15:1—une initiation*. Technical report 44, INRIA, France, 1984.

Kaiser, G. E., and Garlan, D. Melding software systems from reusable building blocks. *IEEE Software*, 4(4):17–24, July 1987.

McCabe, T. J. A complexity measure. *IEEE Transactions on Software Engineering*, SE-2(4):308–320, Dec. 1976.

Meyer, B. Reusability: the case for object-oriented design. *IEEE Software*, 4(2):50–64, March 1987.

Neighbors, J. The Draco approach to constructing software from reusable components. *IEEE Transactions on Software Engineering*, SE-10(5):564–573, Sept. 1984.

Osterweil, L. J. Software processes are software too. *Proceedings of the Ninth International Conference on Software Engineering*, pp. 2–13, Monterey, Calif., March 30–April 2, 1987.

Reps, T. *Generating Language-Based Environments*. Cambridge, Mass.: MIT. Press, 1983.

Scheffe, H. *The Analysis of Variance*. New York, N.Y.: John Wiley & Sons, 1959.

SEL. *Annotated bibliography of software engineering laboratory (SEL) literature*. Technical report SEL-82-006, Software Engineering Laboratory, NASA/Goddard Space Flight Center, Greenbelt, Md., Nov. 1982.

Stroustrup, B. *The C++ Programming Language*. Menlo Park, Calif.: Addison-Wesley, 1986.

Tesler, L. Object Pascal report. *Structured Language World*, 1985.

Tracz, W. Ada reusability efforts: a survey of the state of the practice. In *Proceedings of the Fifth National Conference on Ada Technology*, Arlington, Va., March 1987a.

Tracz, W. (ed). *IEEE Software*, 4(4), special issue on software reusability, July 1987b.

Vosburgh, J.; Curtis, B.; Wolverton, R; Albert, B.; Malec, H.; Hoben, S.; and Liu, Y. Productivity factors and programming environments. In *Proceedings of the Seventh International Conference on Software Engineering*, pp. 143–152, Orlando, Fla., 1984.

Walston, C. E., and Felix, C. P. A method of programming measurement and estimation. *IBM Systems Journal*, 16(1): 54–73, 1977.

Cognitive results

CHAPTER 12

EMPIRICAL STUDIES OF PROGRAMMING KNOWLEDGE

ELLIOT SOLOWAY[*]
Yale University

KATE EHRLICH
Honeywell Information Systems, Inc.

12.1 INTRODUCTION: MOTIVATION AND GOALS

What is it that expert programmers know that novice programmers don't? We would suggest that the former have *at least* two types of knowledge that the latter typically do not.

☐ *Programming plans*: Program fragments that represent stereotypic action sequences in programming, such as a RUNNING TOTAL LOOP PLAN or an ITEM SEARCH LOOP PLAN [Rich, 1981].

☐ *Rules of programming discourse*: Rules that specify the conventions in programming (for example, the name of a variable should usually agree with its function); these rules set up expectations in the minds of the programmers about what should be in the program. These rules are analogous to discourse rules in conversation.

In our view, programs are composed from programming plans that have been modified to fit the needs of the specific problem. The composition

©1984 IEEE. Reprinted, with permission, from *IEEE Transactions on Software Engineering*, Vol. SE-10, #5, September, 1984.

[*] Currently at the University of Michigan.

of those plans are governed by rules of programming discourse. Thus a program can be correct from the perspective of the problem, but can still be difficult to write and/or read because it doesn't follow the rules of discourse; that is, the plans in the program are composed in ways that violate some discourse rule(s).

Our approach to programming borrows directly from at least two converging sources: the research in text processing in artificial intelligence and psychology, and the research in problem solving with experts and novices. First, we base our claim that text comprehension research is appropriate to the task of understanding program comprehension on the following observation: Programs have a dual nature—they can be *executed* for effect, and they can be *read* as communicative entities. Viewing programs in this light, we felt that the notion of *schemas*, one of the most influential notions to have emerged from recent research on text comprehension [Bartlett, 1932; Bower *et al.*, 1979; Graesser, 1981; Rich, 1981] should be applicable to program comprehension.

> Schemas are generic knowledge structures that guide the comprehender's interpretations, inferences, expectations, and attention when passages are comprehended [Graesser, 1981].

Our notion of programming plan corresponds directly to this notion of schema.

Second, research with experts and novices in various technical domains (chess [Chase and Simon, 1973; deGroot, 1965], physics [Larkin *et al.*, 1980], electronic circuitry [Egan and Schwartz, 1979]) have shown that the experts seem to develop *chunks* that represent functional units in their respective domains, while the novices do not. Similar results have been obtained in the programming domain [Adelson, 1981; Rich, 1981; Shneiderman, 1976]. The work reported in this paper builds on and extends this research in the programming domain by examining whether programmers have and use specific programming plans and rules of programming discourse in the process of comprehending computer programs. Moreover, the work reported here extends our earlier studies on programming plans [Ehrlich and Soloway, 1984; Soloway, Ehrlich, and Bonar, 1982] by presenting a broader, more systematic empirical examination of these concepts. Note too that this work is another example of our efforts to explore the cognitive underpinnings of programming: While previously [Soloway, Bonar, and Ehrlich, 1983] we examined the cognitive fit of a particular programming language construct (Pascal's WHILE loop) to people's natural cognitive strategies, here we examine the role that various types of programming knowledge play in the comprehension of programs.

In this paper we describe two empirical studies we conducted with programmers of varying levels of expertise. The goal of these studies was to evaluate the claim that expert programmers possess programming plans and discourse rules. Programs that do not conform to such plans and discourse rules should violate the programmers' expectations; for example, if they see a variable initialized to zero **N := 0** at the top of a program, they should be surprised to see it being changed via a read statement **Read(N)** later in the program. While this type of situation will not create an unrunnable program, it certainly violates the accepted conventions of programming: (1) variables are usually updated in the same fashion as they are initialized (thus we would expect N to be updated via an assignment statement), and (2) programmers do not like to include statements that have no effect: a READ statement destroys whatever is in the variable initially, and thus the initial setting of N to zero is superfluous. We claim that these violations in expectations—the surprises due to violations of conventions—can make such programs much more difficult to comprehend. Thus if advanced programmers have knowledge about plans and discourse rules, then programs that do not conform to the rules of discourse (*unplanlike programs*) should be harder for them to understand than programs that do conform to these rules (*planlike programs*). In contrast, we would not expect novice programmers to have acquired as many of the plans and conventions in programming; by definition a novice programmer has less knowledge than an advanced programmer. Thus we would not expect novice programmers to be as sensitive to violations of conventions because they don't know what the conventions are. Therefore, in a task that requires understanding a program, we expect advanced programmers to (1) do much better than novice programmers on the programs that do conform to the plans and rules, but to (2) to perform at the level of novices when the programs violate the plans and the discourse rules.[1]

The organization of this paper is as follows: First, we present a brief description of our experimental studies; this section explains why our "stimulus materials"—the computer programs used in our experiments—were constructed in the manner that they were. Second, we present a detailed description of how and why unplanlike programs can be generated from planlike ones. In the next two major sections we present detailed descriptions of each of our empirical studies along with a discussion of the results of the studies. We close with implications from these studies for the practice of programming.

12.2 BRIEF DESCRIPTION OF BOTH EXPERIMENTAL TECHNIQUES

The first stage in both experimental procedures is as follows: First, we construct a planlike program; that is, one that uses only typical programming plans and whose plans are composed so as to be consistent with rules of

---

[1]In the second study we only used expert professional programmers as subjects, and thus we cannot look for this type of interaction. Rather, we simply want to (1) evaluate our hypothesis with professional programmers, and (2) observe whether there is a difference in performance within the experts on programs that vary along the planlike dimension.

programming discourse. Next, we construct an unplanlike version of that program by violating one (or possibly two) of the discourse rules. We will refer to the planlike version of the program as the *Alpha version*, while the unplanlike version will be referred to as the *Beta version*.[2] Examples of an Alpha version and a Beta version for a programming problem are given in Fig. 12.1. (In Section 12.3 we describe in detail how these programs were constructed and why we would consider the Beta version to be unplanlike.)

12.2.1   Brief Description of Study I: Fill in the Blank

Our first study uses a fill-in-the-blank technique: Here we take out one line of code from the program and replace that line with a blank. The task we ask of our experimental subjects, who are novice and advanced student programmers, is to fill in the blank line with a piece of code that, in their opinion, best completes the program. An example of the programs with blank lines is given in Fig. 12.1. Note carefully that we do *not* tell the subjects what problem the program is intended to solve. However, since there is only one blank line per program, a great deal of context is still left. If advanced programmers do have and use programming plans for stereotypic programming situations, then they should be able to recognize the program fragment in the planlike versions as an example of programming plan X, and they should all fill in the blank line with the same piece of code. However, in the case of the unplanlike programs, advanced programmers should be more unsure of what plan is being indicated; thus they should be less likely to complete the program in the correct fashion. On the other hand, novice programmers should not be as surprised by the unplanlike programs since they have not as yet acquired the programming conventions. Thus we expect that the advanced programmers will be more affected by the unplanlike programs than will the novices.

Notice that both the Alpha version and the beta version are runnable programs that in almost all cases compute the same values.[3] Moreover, to an untrained eye their differences may not even be apparent: They always differ by only a very few textual elements. Thus our experimental materials are not random programs, as were used in previous studies [Adelson, 1981; Rich, 1981; Shneiderman, 1976]. While those studies demonstrated the basic premise—that advanced programmers have strategies for encoding and remembering programs better than do novice programmers—we see our work as focusing on the detailed knowledge that programmers have and use.

---

[2]Clearly, the Beta versions are not totally unplanlike; in fact, they have many plans in common with the Alpha versions. The term *unplanlike* is thus meant for emphasis only.

[3] In only one program type, MAX (e.g., Fig. 12.1), do the Alpha and Beta versions compute different values.

FIGURE 12.1
EXAMPLE: PROGRAM TYPE 1

Version Alpha

```
PROGRAM Magenta(input, output);
VAR Max, I, Num INTEGER;
BEGIN
  Max = 0;
  FOR I = 1 TO 10 DO
    BEGIN
      READLN(Num);
      If Num > Max THEN Max = Num;
    END;
  WRITELN(Max);
END
```

```
PROGRAM Magenta (input, output);
VAR Max, I, Num INTEGER;
BEGIN
  Max = 0;
  FOR I = 1 TO 10 DO
    BEGIN
      READLN(Num);
                              ┌─────────┐
      If Num | | | Max THEN Max = Num;
                              └─────────┘
    END;
  WRITELN(Max);
END
```

239

FIGURE 12.1 *(Cont.)*

Version Beta

```
PROGRAM Purple(input, output);
VAR Max, I, Num INTEGER;
BEGIN
Max = 999999;
FOR I = 1 TO 10 DO
    BEGIN
    READLN(Num);
    If Num < Max THEN Max = Num;
    END;
WRITELN(Max);
END
```

```
PROGRAM Purple (input, output);
VAR Max, I, Num INTEGER;
BEGIN
Max = 999999;
FOR I = 1 TO 10 DO
    BEGIN
    READLN(Num);

             If Num | |    Max THEN Max = Num;
                    | |

    END;
WRITELN(Max);

END
```

Program type 1

Basic plan	search plan (max, min)
Discourse rule	A variable's name should reflect its function (1)
How construct	
Beta version	violate discourse rule (1)
Alpha case	variable name agrees with search function
Beta case	variable name does NOT agree with search function

12.2.2 Brief Description of Study II: Recall

In our second study, we used essentially the same stimulus materials as in Study I. This time, however, the task was a recall one, and all subjects were expert professional programmers. Subjects were presented with a complete program that they were asked to recall *verbatim*. Half the programs were planlike and half were unplanlike. Each program was presented three times. On the first trial, subjects were asked to recall as much of the program as possible. On the second and third trials, they were asked either to add to their original recall or to change any part of their recall that they felt was in error. We tracked the progression of their recall by asking them to use a different color pencil on each of the three trials. This technique of repeated presentation of the same program was developed by Kaheny [1983] for research specifically on the comprehension of computer programs. If programming plans help programmers to encode a program more efficiently we should find that experts recall more of the program earlier. However, given sufficient time, they should be able to recall as much of the unplanlike programs as the planlike ones. Again, while others have shown this to be true, our motivation is to identify specific knowledge units and to demonstrate the significant influence that planliness has on program comprehension: A change in just a few characters can result in significant differences in performance!

12.3 GENERATING PLANLIKE AND UNPLANLIKE PROGRAMS

What makes a program planlike rather than unplanlike is the way in which plans are *composed* in a program. The composition is governed by *rules of programming discourse*, which are analogous to discourse rules in ordinary conversation or discourse rules that govern the structure of stories. In Fig. 12.2 we depict a set of programming discourse rules that we have identified. Individually, they look innocuous enough, and one could hardly disagree with them. While these rules typically are not written down nor taught explicitly, we claim that programmers use these rules in the construction and comprehension of programs. If programmers do use these rules and expect other programmers to use these rules also, then we would predict that programs that violate these rules should be harder to understand than programs that do not.

One key point to notice in the ensuing subsections is that the unplanlike version (the Beta version) is *only slightly* different from the planlike version (the Alpha version). That is, the idea is to modify a planlike program ever so slightly by violating a discourse rule so as to create an unplanlike version. Both versions are executable programs that usually compute the same function. Moreover, both versions have about the same surface characteristics—about

FIGURE 12.2
RULES OF PROGRAMMING DISCOURSE

```
(1)  Variable names should reflect function.

(2)  Don't include code that won't be used.

(2a) If there is a test for a condition, then the
     condition must have the potential of being true.

(3)  A variable that is initialized via an assignment
     statement should be updated via an assignment
     statement).

(4)  Don't do double duty with code in a non-obvious way.

(5)  An IF should be used when a statement body is
     guaranteed to be executed only once, and a WHILE
     used when a statement body may need to be repeatedly
     executed.
```

---

the same number of lines of code, about the same number of operands and operations, and so forth. Thus, while more traditional methods of calculating program complexity (e.g., lines of code, or Halstead metrics [Halstead, 1977]) would predict no difference in the difficulty of understanding the two programs (the Alpha version and the Beta version), we are looking for differences in actual performance on a comprehension task.

In Sections 12.3.1 through 12.3.4 we will describe how and why we constructed the planlike and unplanlike programs for use in our empirical studies. In each of these sections we will describe a different pair of programs where the Beta version of the pair is generated by violating one (or possibly two) of the discourse rules given in Fig. 12.2. We will refer to each pair of programs as exemplifying a program type; thus we will describe four different program types:[4] (1) MAX, (2) SQRT, (3) AVERAGE, and (4) IF/WHILE.

12.3.1 Program Type 1: MAX

In Fig. 12.1, version Alpha is the planlike version of a program that finds the maximum of some numbers. In our plan jargon, it uses the MAXIMUM

---

[4]The names given to each of the four types carry no deep significance; they are meant only to aid the reader.

SEARCH LOOP PLAN, which in turn uses the RESULT VARIABLE PLAN. Notice that the RESULT VARIABLE is appropriately named Max; that is, the name of the variable is consistent with the plan's function. In contrast version Beta is unplanlike since it uses a MINIMUM SEARCH LOOP PLAN in which the RESULT VARIABLE is inconsistent with the plan's function: The program computes the minimum of some numbers using a variable name Max. To create the Beta version, we violated the first rule of programming discourse in Fig. 12.2: *Variable names should reflect function.* (See also, Weissman [1974], who did exploratory empirical studies on the role of variable names.)

The fill-in-the-blank versions of both these programs are also given in Fig. 12.1. Our hypothesis is that programmers will see the variable name *Max* and thus see the program as a MAXIMUM SEARCH LOOP PLAN. In other words, the name of the variable will color how they understand the rest of the program. Therefore, in the Beta version, where the function of the procedure is inconsistent with variable *Max*, we predict that programmers will fill in the blank with a >, rather than a <—indicating that they see the program as computing the maximum of a set of integers instead of the minimum.

12.3.2 Program Type 2: SQRT

The Alpha and Beta programs in Fig. 12.3 are both intended to produce the square root of N. Since N is in a loop which will repeat 10 times, 10 values will be printed out. The question is: How should N be set? In version Alpha the DATA GUARD PLAN constrains what should be filled into the blank line. That is, the *Sqrt* function must be protected from trying to take the square root of a negative number; thus the immediately preceding IF test checks to see if the number is negative, and makes it positive if necessary. Besides protecting the *Sqrt* function, the DATA GUARD PLAN exerts influence on what could reasonably be filled into the blank. The very presence of the DATA GUARD PLAN implies that the numbers might be negative and thus the manner in which N is set *must allow for it to be negative.* A typical way of realizing this constraint is via a **Read (N)**; the user decides what values should be entered. In contrast, setting N via an assignment statement, (e.g., **N := I**) would *never* result in a negative number—thus making the DATA GUARD PLAN totally superfluous. The influence of the DATA GUARD PLAN over the blank line stems from a rule of programming discourse: *If there is a test for a condition, then the condition must have the potential of being true.* Thus the blank line must be filled in with something that does not make the DATA GUARD PLAN superfluous (e.g., **Read (N)**).

In version Beta, however, we have added an additional constraint on the blank line: The VARIABLE PLAN for N starts off with an assignment type of initialization (**N := 0**) and sets up the expectation that N will also be

FIGURE 12.3
EXAMPLE: PROGRAM TYPE 2

Version Alpha

```
PROGRAM Beige (input, output);
  VAR Num REAL;
      I  INTEGER;
  BEGIN
    FOR I = 1 TO 10 DO
      BEGIN
        READ (Num);
        IF Num < 0 THEN Num = -Num;
        Writeln ( Num, Sqrt(Num) );
        (* Sqrt is a built-in
           function which returns the
           square root of its argument*)
      END;
  END
```

```
PROGRAM Beige(input, output);
  VAR Num REAL;
      I  INTEGER;
  BEGIN
    FOR I = 1 TO 10 DO
      BEGIN
        _____
        |                     |
        |                     |
        |                     |
        _____
        |                     |
        |                     |
        IF Num < 0 THEN Num = -Num;
        Writeln ( Num, Sqrt(Num) );
        (* Sqrt is a built-in
           function which returns the
           square root of its argument*)
      END;
  END
```

Version Beta

```
PROGRAM Violet(input, output);
  VAR Num REAL;
      I   INTEGER;
BEGIN
  Num = 0;
  FOR I = 1 TO 10 DO
    BEGIN
      Read (Num);
      IF Num < 0 THEN Num = -Num;
      Writeln ( Num. Sqrt(Num) );
      (* Sqrt is a built-in
         function which returns the
         square root of its argument*)
    END;
END.
```

```
PROGRAM Violet(input, output);
  VAR Num REAL;
      I   INTEGER;
BEGIN
  Num = 0;
  FOR I = 1 TO 10 DO
    BEGIN
      _____   _____
      _____   _____
      IF Num < 0 THEN Num = -Num;
      Writeln ( Num, Sqrt(Num) );
      (* Sqrt is a built-in function which
         returns the square root of its argument*)
    END;
END
```

Program type 2

Basic plan	guard plan, variable plan
Discourse rule	Don't include code that won't be used (2)
	If there is a test for a condition, then the condition must have the potential of being true (2a)
	A variable that is initialized via an assignment statement should be updated via an assignment statement (3)
How construct	
Beta version	include two incompatible discourse rules (2) and (3)
Alpha case	guard plan predicts read initialization
Beta case	guard plan predicts read update, but initialization plan predicts assignment update

updated via an assignment statement (**e.g., N := N + I** or **N := N + 1**). However, this expectation conflicts with the expectation set up by the DATA GUARD PLAN (namely, **Read(N)**). Moreover, there is an additional level of conflict: the expectation of the DATA GUARD PLAN is now in conflict with the initialization of N to 0. This conflict is due to a violation of the following rule of programming discourse: *A variable that is initialized via an assignment statement should be updated via an assignment statement.*

12.3.3 Program Type 3: AVERAGE

The programs in Fig. 12.4 calculate the average of some numbers that are read in; the stopping condition is the reading of the sentinel value, 99999. Version Alpha accomplishes the task in a typical fashion: variables are initialized to 0, a read-a-value/process-a-value loop [Soloway, Bonar, and Ehrlich, 1983] is used to accumulate the running total, and the average is calculated after the sentinel has been read. Version Beta was generated from version Alpha by violating another rule of programming discourse: *Do not do double duty in a nonobvious manner.* That is, in version Beta, unlike in Alpha, the initialization actions of the COUNTER VARIABLE (Count) and RUNNING TOTAL VARIABLE PLANs (Sum) in Beta serve two purposes:

☐ Sum and Count are given initial values.
☐ The initial values are chosen so as to compensate for the fact that the loop is poorly constructed and will result in an off-by-one bug: the final sentinel value (99999) will be incorrectly added in the RUNNING TOTAL VARIABLE (Sum), and the COUNTER VARIABLE (Count), will also be incorrectly updated.

We felt that using *Sum* and *Count* in this way was quite nonobvious, and would prove very hard for advanced programmers to comprehend.

12.3.4 Program Type 4: IF/WHILE

The difference between an IF statement and a WHILE statement in Pascal is that the latter executes a body of statements repeatedly, while the former only executes the body once; note both have a testing component. In looking at programs written by novice programmers, we found that novices sometimes used a WHILE statement when the body would only be executed once: it was as if novices have a rule such as *when a body needs to be executed only once,* then *either a* WHILE *or an* IF *could be used.* We felt that advanced programmers would be horrified by such a rule, and moreover, would be confused in seeing a WHILE in a situation that "clearly" called for an IF.

The programs in Fig. 12.5 were developed to test the above hypothesis. Both these programs test to see if some variable contains a number that is

FIGURE 12.4
EXAMPLE: PROGRAM TYPE 3

Version Alpha

```
PROGRAM Grey(input, output);
VAR Sum, Count, Num INTEGER;
    Average   REAL;
BEGIN
   Sum = 0;
   Count = 0;
   REPEAT
      READLN(Num);
      IF Num < > 99999 THEN
                          BEGIN
                          Sum = Sum + Num;
                          Count = Count + 1;
                          END;

   UNTIL Num = 99999;
   Average = Sum/Count;
   WRITELN (Average);
END
```

```
PROGRAM Grey (input, output);
VAR Sum, Count, Num INTEGER;
    Average   REAL;
BEGIN
   Sum = 0;


   REPEAT
      READLN(Num);
      IF Num < > 99999 THEN
                          BEGIN
                          Sum = Sum + Num;
                          Count = Count + 1;
                          END;

         UNTIL Num = 99999;
         Average = Sum/Count;
         WRITELN(average);
END
```

FIGURE 12.4 *(Cont.)*

Version Beta

```
PROGRAM Orange(input, output);
VAR Sum, Count, Num INTEGER;
    Average  REAL;
BEGIN
  Sum = -99999;
  Count = -1;
  REPEAT
    READLN(Num);
    Sum = Sum + Num;
    Count = Count + 1;
    UNTIL Num = 99999;
  Average = Sum/Count;
  WRITELN (Average);
END
```

```
PROGRAM Orange(input, output);
VAR Sum, Count, Num INTEGER;
    Average  REAL;
BEGIN
  Sum = -99999;

  REPEAT
    READLN(Num);
    Sum = Sum + Num;
    Count = Count + 1;
    UNTIL Num = 99999;
  Average = Sum/Count;
  WRITELN(average)
END
```

Program type 3

Basic plan	read/process, running total loop plan
Discourse rule	don't do double duty in a nonobvious way (4)
How construct	
Beta version	violate discourse rule (4)
Alpha case	initialize to standard values
Beta case	initialize to non-standard values to compensate for poorly formed loop.

FIGURE 12.5
EXAMPLE: PROGRAM TYPE 4

Version Alpha

```
PROGRAM Gold(input, output);
  CONST
    MaxSentence = 99;
    NumOfConvicts = 5;
  VAR
    ConvictID, I, Sentence INTEGER;

  BEGIN
    FOR I = 1 TO NumOfConvicts DO
      BEGIN
        READLN(ConvictID, Sentence);
        IF Sentence > MaxSentence
          THEN Sentence = MaxSentence;
          WRITELN(ConvictID, Sentence);
      END;
  END
```

```
PROGRAM Gold (input, output);
  CONST
    MaxSentence = 99;
    NumOfConvicts = 5;
  VAR
    ConvictID, I, Sentence INTEGER;

  BEGIN
    FOR I = 1 TO NumOfConvicts DO
      BEGIN
        READLN(ConvictID, Sentence);
        IF Sentence > MaxSentence
                    --------------
            THEN  |              |
                    --------------
              WRITELN(ConvictID, Sentence);
      END;
  END
```

FIGURE 12.5 *(Cont.)*

Version Beta

```
PROGRAM Silver(input, output);
  CONST
    MaxSentence = 99;
    NumOfConvicts = 5;
  VAR
    ConvictID, I, Sentence INTEGER;

BEGIN
  FOR I = 1 TO NumOfConvicts DO
    BEGIN
      READLN(ConvictID, Sentence);
      WHILE Sentence > MaxSentence
        DO Sentence = MaxSentence;
      WRITELN(ConvictID, Sentence);
    END;
END
```

```
PROGRAM Silver(input, output);
  CONST
    MaxSentence = 99;
    NumOfConvicts = 5;
  VAR
    ConvictID, I, Sentence INTEGER;

BEGIN
  FOR I = 1 TO NumOfConvicts DO
    BEGIN
      READLN(ConvictID, Sentence);
      WHILE Sentence > MaxSentence
               |      |
        DO     |      |
               --------
      WRITELN(ConvictID, Sentence);
    END;
END
```

Program type 4

Basic plan	reset to boundary condition
Discourse rule	An IF should be used when a statement body is guaranteed to be executed only once, and a WHILE used when a statement body may need to be repeatedly executed (5)
How construct	
Beta version	violate discourse rule (5)
Alpha case	use IF for testing and one time execution
Beta case	use WHILE for testing and one time execution

greater than a maximum, and if so, the variable is reset to the maximum. The Alpha version uses an IF test; the Beta version uses a WHILE statement. The Beta version was generated from the Alpha version by violating the following discourse rule: *An IF should be used when a statement body is guaranteed to be executed only once, and a WHILE used when a statement body may need to be repeatedly executed.* If the advanced programmers have this rule, then we predict that they would not recognize the RESET PLAN in the Beta version nearly as often as they would in the Alpha version.

12.4 DETAILED DESCRIPTION OF STUDY I: FILL IN THE BLANK

12.4.1 Subjects

A total of 139 students participated in the experiment. These students were recruited from programming classes and were paid five dollars for participating. There were 94 novice level programmers and 45 advanced level programmers. Novice programmers were students just finishing a first course in Pascal programming. The advanced level programmers had completed at least three programming courses, and most were either computer science majors or first-year graduate students in computer science; all had extensive experience with Pascal.

12.4.2 Materials

We created two pairs of programs (an Alpha version and a Beta version comprise one pair) for each of the four program types described in Section 12.3; thus there were eight pairs of programs, two pairs of programs for each program type. One instance (an Alpha-Beta pair) of each of the four program types was presented in the preceding section. Both instances of a program type were similar. For example, in Fig. 12.6 the second instance of the program type MAX is given; while the first instance of this type searched for the maximum (minimum) *integer* input (Fig. 12.1), the second instance searched from the maximum (minimum) *character* input.

12.4.3 Design: Independent and Dependent Variables

The three independent variables in this study were:

1. Version—Alpha (planlike), Beta (unplanlike).
2. Program type—(1) MAX, (2) SQRT, (3) AVERAGE, (4) IF/WHILE.
3. Level of expertise—novice or advanced.

FIGURE 12.6
EXAMPLE: PROGRAM TYPE 1—INSTANCE 2

Version Alpha

```
PROGRAM Green(input, output);
VAR I   INTEGER;
    Letter, LeastLetter   Char;
BEGIN
    LeastLetter = 'z';
    FOR I = 1 TO 10 DO
        BEGIN
        READLN(Letter);
        IF Letter < LeastLetter
            THEN LeastLetter = Letter;
        END;
    Writeln(LeastLetter);
END
```

```
PROGRAM Green (input, output);
VAR I   INTEGER;
    Letter, LeastLetter   Char;
BEGIN
    LeastLetter = 'z';
    FOR I = 1 TO 10 DO
        BEGIN
        READLN(Letter);
                        ------
        If Letter  |      |  LeastLetter
                        ------
            THEN LeastLetter = Letter;
        END;
        Writeln(LeastLetter);
END
```

Version Beta

```
PROGRAM Yellow(input, output);
VAR I  INTEGER;
    Letter, LeastLetter  Char;
BEGIN
  LeastLetter = 'a';
  FOR I = 1 TO 10 DO
    BEGIN
    READLN(Letter);
    IF Letter > LeastLetter
      THEN LeastLetter = Letter;
    END;
  WriteIn(LeastLetter);
END
```

```
PROGRAM Yellow(input, output);
VAR I  INTEGER;
    Letter, LeastLetter  Char;
BEGIN
  LeastLetter = 'a';
  FOR I = 1 TO 10 DO
    BEGIN
    READLN(Letter);
                      -------   -------
    If Letter  |     | |     |  LeastLetter
               |     | |     |  THEN LeastLetter = Letter;
                      -------   -------
    END;
  WriteIn(LeastLetter);
END
```

Program type 1 -- Instance 2

Basic plan	Search plan (max, min)
Discourse rule	A variable's name should reflect its function (1)
How construct	
Beta version	violate discourse rule (1)
Alpha case	variable name agrees with search function
Beta case	variable name does NOT agree with search function

There were two dependent variables:

1. Accuracy of the response; a correct response was one that completed the intended plan.[5]
2. Time to complete a problem.

12.4.4 Procedure

Each subject was given eight programs. In four of the problems, the subject received the Alpha version of a program, while in the other four problems, the subject received the Beta version of a program. We also counterbalanced versions within each of the four program types such that if a subject received an Alpha version for one program of a type then the subject would receive the Beta version for the other program of the same type. The test programs were presented as a booklet in which the order of the programs was randomized for each subject. Subjects were instructed to work through the booklet in the given order. As we mentioned earlier, each program was presented with one blank; subjects were not told what problems the programs were intended to solve. Subjects were given the following instruction: *Fill in the blank line with a line of Pascal code which in your opinion best completes the program.* They were given as much time to do the test as they wanted; almost all finished within an hour.

12.4.5 Results and Discussion

The main results in this study were:

☐ The experts performed better than the novices (61 percent versus 48 percent, $F_{1,137} = 17.27, p < 0.001$).

☐ Subjects answered the Alpha versions correctly more often than they did the Beta versions (88 percent versus 31 percent, $F_{1,137} = 375.22$, $p < 0.001$).

☐ The interaction between program version and expertise was significant $F_{1,137} = 6.78, p < 0.01$).

Moreover, using a Newman-Keuls test, the difference in performance between the novice and the advanced subjects for the Alpha versions was

---

[5]Strictly speaking, filling in the blank line with an answer that differs from the planlike one would not necessarily be *incorrect*. For example, filling in the blank line in Beta of Fig. 12.1 with a > would still result in a running program. However, it would be a strange program. By *correct* we actually mean the line of code that in our judgment best fulfills the overall intent of the program.

FIGURE 12.7
INTERACTION: EXPERTISE AND PROGRAM TYPE

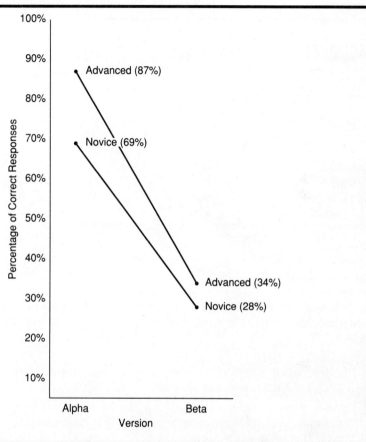

significant at the 0.05 level, while there was no significant difference between the two groups of subjects on the Beta versions. Thus the statistical analyses support the visual effect of the graph in Fig. 12.7: The performance of the advanced students was reduced to that of the novices by the Beta versions!

The magnitude of the change in performance by the advanced programmers is impressive (Fig. 12.7): The advanced programmers performed about 50 percent worse on the Beta versions that they did on the Alpha versions. (This difference was significant at the 0.01 level using a Newman-Keuls test.) Given that the only difference between the two versions was a violation of one (or possibly two) rule(s) of programming discourse, we are impressed with the enormous size of this difference. Clearly, discourse rules in pro-

TABLE 12.1
PERCENTAGE OF CORRECTNESS BY PROGRAM
TYPE

NOVICES (N = 45)		
Program Type	Alpha	Beta
1 MAX	78%	12%
2 SQRT	69%	61%
3 AVERAGE	80%	01%
4 IF/WHILE	48%	38%
ADVANCED (N = 45)		
1 MAX	93%	13%
2 SQRT	87%	84%
3 AVERAGE	96%	06%
4 IF/WHILE	73%	31%

gramming have a major effect on programmers' abilities to comprehend programs.

A breakdown by version and program type is given in Table 12.1. Here we see the percentage of subjects that correctly answered each program problem.

☐ There was a significant difference in accuracy for the four program types ($F_{3,411} = 26.81$, $p < 0.001$).

☐ Also, the differences between the Alpha and Beta programs were not constant over the four program types. This interaction between program type and version was significant ($F_{3,411} = 68.39$, $p < 0.001$).

While we had attempted to keep all the program types at about the same level of difficulty, apparently we were not successful.

There was also a significant three-way interaction between program type, version, and expertise ($F_{3,411} = 3.12$, $p < 0.05$). An intuition for this interaction can be gleaned from Table 12.1: Performance on the Beta version of the SQRT program type differed greatly from the performance on the Beta versions of the other program types. This difference was statistically significant at the 0.01 level using a Newman-Keuls test. Why was the performance on the Beta versions of this one program type so high? The most plausible explanation is based on a practice effect: Since in every other program that the subjects saw, data were input via a READ statement, subjects simply did not even see the conflict and immediately filled in the blank line with a READ.

TABLE 12.2
ERROR DATA: FILL-IN-THE-BLANK STUDY

ERRORS on Alpha and Beta Versions:

Alpha Versions:
  Total number of errors by Novice and Advanced Subjects: 140
Beta Versions:
  Total number of errors by Novice and Advanced Subjects: 390

ERRORS on only Beta Versions:

Plan-like Errors:
  Total number on Beta versions by Novice and Advanced Subjects: 257
Unplan-like Errors:
  Total number on Beta versions by Novice and Advanced Subjects: 133
                                                                         390

In Table 12.2 we display a breakdown of the number and type of errors that subjects made. There were, of course, more errors made on the Beta versions (390) than on the Alpha versions (140) ($p < 0.001$ by a sign test)[6]. More interesting, however, was the type of errors made on the Beta versions. Our theory makes a strong prediction about the type of incorrect response that subjects will make on the Beta versions: If subjects do not recognize that the Beta versions are unplanlike, and if subjects are simply using plans and discourse rules to guide their responses, then we expect them to perceive the Beta version as just being an Alpha version, *and provide the planlike response for the Alpha version.* For example, as discussed earlier (Section 12.3.1), Program Purple in Fig. 12.1 actually computes the minimum of set of inputs; however, it appears, because of the key variable name MAX to compute the maximum of some input values. The correct fill-in-the-blank answer for the Program Purple was < . However, we predicted that those subjects who fill in the blank incorrectly would do so by saying <—which *is* the correct answer for the Alpha version.

The data bear out our prediction: The difference between the planlike incorrect responses and the unplanlike incorrect responses on the Beta versions was significant ($p < .01$ by a sign test):[7] 66 percent (257/390) of the incorrect responses on the Beta versions were one specific response—the

[6]The p value of 0.001 reduces the likelihood that we are affirming a chance result from having partitioned the data.

[7]The p value of 0.01 reduces the likelihood that we are affirming a chance result from having partitioned the data.

FIGURE 12.8
TIME TO RESPOND CORRECTLY: ALPHA VERSION VS. BETA VERSION

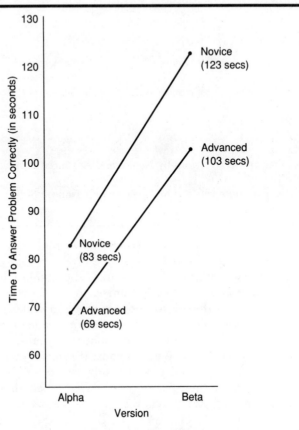

response that would have been appropriate for the corresponding Alpha version of the program.

Another view of the effect of the unplanlike Beta versions on our subjects' performance can be seen by examining the amount of time it took subjects to provide a *correct* response to the Alpha and the Beta versions. Figure 12.8 depicts this relationship. The difference in response time for the correct answers between the Alpha and Beta versions was significant ($F = 35.1$, $p < 0.001$); it took approximately 50 percent more time to respond correctly to the Beta versions than it did to respond correctly to the Alpha versions. The difference between novice and advanced programmers was also significant ($F_{1,288} = 8.6$, $p < 0.01$); however, we did not find an interaction between expertise and program version in this situation ($F < 1$).

Our interpretation of these data is that a correct response to the Alpha versions required only that programmers use their knowledge of programming plans and rules of programming discourse in a straightforward manner. However, in order to arrive at a correct answer to the Beta versions, subjects needed to employ additional processing techniques, such as trying to run the program on some sample numbers. This additional mental processing time corresponds to the increase in response time. Thus, not only do unplanlike programs reduce the accuracy of programmers, their time to respond correctly to the unplanlike programs goes up dramatically, since they need to bring in additional reasoning strategies in order to compensate for the unplanliness of the Beta versions.

12.5 DETAILED DESCRIPTION OF STUDY II: RECALL

12.5.1 Subjects

A total of 41 professional programmers participated in this study. The mean number of years experience was 7.5 (with a standard deviation of 4.8). The minimum number of years of experience was two and the maximum was 20. The company for which these programmers worked gave them time off during the workday to participate in this study. Thus we did not have to pay subjects for their participation.

12.5.2 Materials

The programs we used in this study were essentially the same as those used in the study already described; the main differences were:

☐ The programs in this study were translated from Pascal into Algol, the language used by these subjects; and

☐ Program type SQRT was eliminated; in the Beta versions, these programs simply have an extra line of code, the initialization of N, which we felt was too mild a difference from the Alpha versions.

As described in Section 12.3, each Alpha-Beta pair of programs was essentially identical[8] except for two critical lines (e.g., see lines 5 and 9 in the programs in Fig. 12.9). We have called these lines critical because they carry

---

[8]Programs of type AVERAGE were slightly different (see Fig. 12.4): The alpha versions used a process/read loop structure, while the Beta versions used a process/read structure [Soloway, Ehrlich, and Bonar, 1982]. However, the Alpha programs contain more lines than the Beta versions; thus, by more standard measures of program complexity (e.g., Halstead [1977] or lines of code) the Alpha programs should be harder to comprehend than the Beta ones.

FIGURE 12.9

EXAMPLE: CRITICAL LINES IN ALGOL PROGRAMS. THE CRITICAL LINES IN THESE PROGRAMS—THE LINES THAT ARE DIFFERENT—ARE LINES 05 AND 09

```
Program Type MAX Version Alpha

%  PROGRAM MAGENTA;
01 BEGIN
02   FILE REM (KIND = REMOTE, UNITS = CHARACTERS,
03     MAXRECSIZE = 1920, MYUSE = IO);
04   INTEGER MAX, I, NUM;
05   MAX := 0;
06   FOR I := 1 STEP 1 UNTIL 10 DO
07     BEGIN
08       READ (REM, */, NUM);
09       IF NUM > MAX THEN MAX = NUM;
10     END;
11   WRITE(REM,*/,MAX);
12 END
```

```
Program Type MAX Version Beta

%  PROGRAM PURPLE;
   BEGIN
     FILE REM (KIND = REMOTE, UNITS = CHARACTERS,
       MAXRECSIZE = 1920, MYUSE = IO);
     INTEGER MAX, I, NUM;
     MAX := 1000000;
     FOR I := 1 STEP 1 UNTIL 10 DO
       BEGIN
         READ (REM, */, NUM);
           IF NUM < MAX THEN MAX = NUM;
       END;
     WRITE(REM,*/,MAX);
   END
```

the information that makes the programs planlike or not. In the analysis, we will focus on the two critical lines in assessing whether expert programmers recall planlike programs better than unplanlike ones: We predict that the programmers should be able to recall the critical lines from the planlike programs earlier than the critical lines from the unplanlike ones. The basis for this prediction is that programmers will use their plans and discourse rules to encode a program when it is presented. In a planlike program, the critical lines are the key representatives of the program's plans, and thus they should be recalled very early on. The fact that representatives of a category are recalled first is a recognized psychological principle [Crowder, 1976]. However, in an unplanlike program, the critical lines do not represent the program's plans and as such should act no differently than the other lines in the program; thus, they should not be recalled first.

12.5.3 Design: Independent and Dependent Variables

In this study there were three independent variables:

1. Version—Alpha (planlike), Beta (unplanlike).
2. Program type—MAX, AVERAGE, IF/WHILE.
3. Trial—first, second, third presentation.

As explained in Section 12.5.4, the dependent variable was correctness of recall of the critical lines.

12.5.4 Procedure

Subjects were presented with a complete program that they were asked to recall *verbatim*. The program was presented three times, each time for 20 seconds. On the first trial, subjects were asked to recall as much of the program as possible. On the second and third trials, they were asked either to add to their original recall or to change any part of their recall that they felt was in error. We tracked the progression of their recall by asking them to use a different color pencil on each of the three trials.

Just as in the previous study, there were two Alpha-Beta program pairs for each type of program (MAX, AVERAGE, or IF/WHILE). Each subject was shown a total of six programs: three Alpha and three Beta. We also counterbalanced versions within each of the three program types such that if a subject received an Alpha version for one program of a type then the subject would receive the Beta version for the other program of the same type.

A critical line was scored as correct if and only if the line was recalled exactly as presented. If a subject recalled part of a critical line on the first

FIGURE 12.10
SUMMARY STATISTICS OF RECALL STUDY

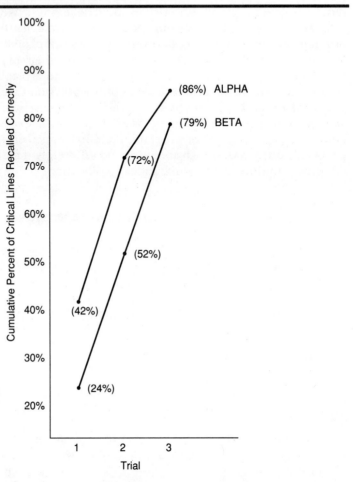

trial and the rest of the line on the third trial, then the line would be scored as being recalled on the third trial. Similarly, if a subject recalled a whole line on the first trial but the recall was wrong, and if the subject corrected the line on the third trial, then again this line would be scored as being correct on the third trial.

12.5.5   Results and Discussion

In Fig. 12.10 we present a summary of the results from the recall study. This figure shows the performance of programmers on the critical lines for all the programs. Shown are the cumulative percentages of recall for the critical lines for each of the three trials (presentations).[9] After the first trial, for example, 42 percent (101/240) of the critical lines on the Alpha versions were recalled correctly, while only 24 percent (58/240) of the critical lines on the Beta versions were recalled correctly. The effect of version was significant ($F_{1,40} = 9.05$, $p < 0.01$): More Alpha critical lines were recalled than Beta critical lines. The interaction of version and trial was also significant ($F_{2,80} = 4.72$, $p < 0.011$). The fact that the difference between the recall of the critical lines for the Alpha and the Beta versions changes over trials supports our hypothesis that the critical lines in the Alpha versions were recalled sooner than those in the Beta versions. Thus, just as in the study described previously (Section 12.4), we see the significant detrimental effect that unplanlike programs have on programmer performance.

In Table 12.3 we break down the errors and changes made by our three subjects. Of particular interest are the number of changes. Programmers made almost three times as many changes on the Beta programs as they did on the Alpha programs.[10] Moreover, the changes made on the Beta programs were consistent with our theoretical predictions: Subjects typically incorrectly recalled the planlike answer, and then changed their answer later to match what was actually being shown in the program. In particular, 22 out of 32 changes (69 percent) were from planlike but incorrect answers to the correct answer. (This difference was significant $p < 0.025$ by a sign

---

[9]The basis for this calculation is as follows: Each subject was shown three Alpha programs and three Beta programs, there were two lines per program, and there were 40 subjects. Thus there were a possible 240 critical lines in the Alpha programs and 240 critical lines in the Beta programs.

[10]All changes on the Beta programs were from incorrect to correct; one subject changed from correct to incorrect on an Alpha program.

TABLE 12.3
BREAKDOWN OF THE ERRORS AND CHANGES THAT WERE MADE

	Correctly Recalled	Errors	Unrecalled		Changes
ALPHA (Out of 240)	206	17	23		12
BETA (Out of 240)	189	24	33		32

For BETA Programs Only	
Changes Plan-like to Correct	Changes Otherwise
22	10

test.[11] For example, on program PURPLE, which is a Beta version of type MAX (Fig. 12.9), of the eight subjects who made changes to the IF line (line 9), seven of them initially wrote *Num MAX*—the response that would be correct if the program were actually finding the maximum value (see the Alpha version in Fig. 12.9)—and then changed their response on later trials to the correct *Num < Max*. Notice that these subjects were initially recalling something that *was not in the program*. Thus, just as in the fill-in-the-blank study, an analysis of incorrect responses is particularly telling: Programmers expected to see planlike programs and consistently behaved as if the programs at hand were planlike.

12.6 CONCLUDING REMARKS

The objective of these studies was to evaluate the claim that advanced programmers have and use (1) programming plans and (2) rules of programming discourse. The experiments discussed in this paper were designed to examine this question. The results of the experiments support our initial claim.

☐ In Study I, when test programs were planlike, advanced programmers performed significantly better than novice programmers; however, when the test programs were *not* planlike (i.e., the plan composition violated some rule of programming discourse), then the performance of the advanced programmers was reduced to essentially that of the novice programmers.

☐ In Study II, the performance of the expert programmers was significantly different for planlike and unplanlike programs: the critical lines in the planlike programs were recalled earlier than those in the unplanlike ones.

On the one hand, the results point to the fragility of programming expertise: Advanced programmers have *strong* expectations about what programs should look like, and when those expectations are violated (even in seemingly innocuous ways) their performance drops drastically. On the other hand, the results support our claim that the plan knowledge and the discourse rule knowledge upon which the expectations are built play a powerful role in program comprehension.

We hasten to point out that measures of surface characteristics, such as lines of code or Halstead metrics, would not predict the differences in performance we obtained. The Beta versions typically had either the same number of lines of code or slightly fewer lines of code than did the comparable

---

[11]The p value of 0.025 reduces the likelihood that we are affirming a chance result from having partitioned the data.

Alpha versions. We certainly do not dispute the results of earlier studies that show that such surface measures correlate with program complexity [Curtis *et al.*, 1979]. However, as our study vividly shows, surface feature measures do not necessarily predict complexity.

More importantly, our approach is to provide *explanations* for why a program may be complex and thus hard to comprehend. Toward this end, we have attempted to articulate the programming knowledge that programmers have and use. Thus our intent is to move beyond *correlations* between programmer performance and surface complexity as measured by Halstead metrics, lines of code, and so forth, to a more principled, cognitive explanation [Soloway, Bonar, and Ehrlich, 1983].

A potential criticism of this work is that the programs we used in the experiments were unrealistic. While our experimental programs were short, the programs produced by experts are typically much longer. One major rationale for the use of short programs was experimental control: We wanted to keep as much constant as possible and only vary one (or possibly two) discourse rule(s). Given the range of results we obtained for the different program types (see Table 12.1) we feel justified in our concern. Nonetheless, we are sensitive to this criticism. While our intuition is that the effects we observed will in fact be more pronounced in longer programs, clearly our studies need to be replicated with longer programs. While not discounting the value of this criticism, we feel that the magnitude of effects that we observed is too pronounced to be simply ignored.

In closing, our studies support the claim that knowledge of programming plans and rules of programming discourse can have a significant impact on program comprehension. In their book *The Elements of Style*, Kernighan and Plauger [1978] also identify what we would call discourse rules. Our empirical results put teeth into these rules. It is not merely a matter of aesthetics that programs should be written in a particular style. There is a psychological basis for writing programs in a conventional manner. Programmers have strong *expectations* that other programmers will follow these discourse rules. If the rules are violated, then the utility of these expectations is effectively nullified. The results described in this paper provide clear support for these claims.

ACKNOWLEDGMENTS

The authors would like to thank a number of colleagues who provided invaluable aid and comments on this research: B. Adelson, C. Seifert, D. Littman, and E. Gold. We would also like to thank the reviewers for their helpful comments.

This work was supported in part by the National Science Foundation, under NSF Grants MCS–8302382 and IST–8310659, and by a contribution from the Burroughs Corporation. However, the views expressed in this paper do not necessarily reflect those of the Burroughs Corporation. Portions of this paper appear in the *Proceedings of the Conference on the Nature of Expertise*, Carnegie-Mellon University, Pittsburgh, Pa, October 1983.

E. Soloway is with the Department of Electrical Engineering and Computer Science, University of Michigan, Ann Arbor, MI 48109.

K. Ehrlich is with Honeywell Information Systems, Inc., Waltham, MA 02154.

References

Adelson, B. Problem solving and the development of abstract categories in programming languages. *Memory and Cognition*, 9: 422–433, 1981.

Bartlett, F. C. *Remembering*. Cambridge, Mass.: Univ. Press, 1932.

Bower, G. H., J. B. Black, and T. Turner. Scripts in memory for text. *Cognitive Psychol.* 11: 177–220, 1979.

Chase, W. C., and H. Simon. Perception in chess. *Cognitive Psychol.* 4: 55–81, 1973.

Crowder, R. G. Principles of learning and memory. Lawrence Erlbaum Associates, Hillsdale, N. J., 1976.

Curtis, B.; S. Sheppard; and P. Milliman. Third time charm: Stronger prediction of programmer performance by software complexity metrics. In *Proc. 4th Int. Conf. Software Eng.*, IEEE Comput. Soc., N. Denton, Tex., 1979.

deGroot, A. D. *Thought and Choice in Chess*. Paris, France: Mouton, 1965.

Egan, D., and B. Schwartz. Chunking in recall of symbolic drawings. *Memory and Cognition* 7: 149–185, 1979.

Ehrlich, K., and E. Soloway. An empirical investigation of the tacit plan knowledge in programming. In *Human Factors in Computer Systems*, J. Thomas and M. L. Schneider (Eds.) Norwood, N. J.: Ablex Inc., 1984.

Graesser, A. C. *Prose Comprehension Beyond the Word*. New York: Springer-Verlag, 1981.

Halstead, M. M. *Elements of Software Science*. New York: Elsevier, 1977.

Kaheny, J. H. Problem solving by novice programmers. In *The Psychology of Computer Use: A European Perspective*. London, England: Academic, 1983.

Kernighan, B., and P. Plauger. *The Elements of Style*. New York: McGraw-Hill, 1978.

Larkin, J.; J. McDermott; D. Simon; and H. Simon. Expert and novice performance in solving physics problems. *Science* 208: 140–158, 1980.

McKeithen, K. B.; J. S. Reitman; H. H. Rueter; and S. C. Hirtle. Knowledge organization and skill differences in computer programmers. *Cognitive Psychol.* 13: 307–325, 1981.

Rich, C. Inspection methods in programming. MIT Artificial Intell. Lab., tech. rep. TR-604, Cambridge, Mass, 1981.

Schank, R. C., and R. Abelson. Scripts, plans, goals, and understanding. Lawrence Erlbaum Associates, Hillsdale, N. J., 1977.

Shneiderman, B. Exploratory experiments in programmer behavior. *Int. J. Comput. Inform. Sci.* 5(2): 123–143, 1976.

Soloway, E.; J. Bonar; and K. Ehrlich. Cognitive strategies and looping constructs: An empirical study. *Commun. ACM* 26: 853–861, 1983.

Soloway, E.; K. Ehrlich; and J. Black. Beyond numbers: Don't ask "how many" . . . ask "why." In *Proc. SIGCHI Conf. Human Factors in Comput. Syst.*, SIGCHI, Boston, Mass., 1983.

Soloway, E.; K. Ehrlich; and J. Bonar. Tapping into tacit programming knowledge. In *Proc. Conf. Human Factors in Comput. Syst.*, Nat. Bureau Standards, Gaithersburg, Md., 1982.

Weissman, L. Psychological complexity of computer programs: An experimental methodology. *SIGPLAN Notices* 9, June 1974.

CHAPTER 13

Cognitive Issues in Reusing Software Artifacts

BILL CURTIS
Microelectronics and Computer Technology Corporation (MCC)

13.1 INTRODUCTION

No proposal for improving software productivity would fail to mention reusability. Depending on our definition of reusable software, we have been reusing software for years, we have just started a promising program, or we need to sponsor much more research on the topic. Regardless of the definition, when programmers create software they are reusing knowledge they already possess. Often this knowledge is in the form of program fragments, design templates, or an understanding of crucial issues and constraints that guide the development process. That is, programmers do not begin with a *tabula rasa* each time they undertake to construct a new program. The hallmark of professionals is their ability to reuse knowledge and experience to perform their tasks ever more efficiently.

Among the many difficulties in reusing software artifacts are three interesting limitations created by cognitive processes. One limitation is that programmers often try to force the application requirements to fit a structure for which they know a solution, even if it fails to satisfy some of the original specifications. The second limitation is that solutions programmers know for problems in one application domain may not transfer easily to problems in another domain. A third limitation is that the form in which the application request is presented to programmers may disguise cues in the structure of the problem or the solution that would trigger the recognition of potentially reusable artifacts. These limitations are exacerbated when a programmer has only limited knowledge about a particular application area. As a foundation for methods to overcome these limitations, the next two sections will describe the cognitive aspects of programming.

13.2 WHAT DO PROGRAMMERS KNOW?

Reusable program fragments or templates can be stored either in the head or in an external medium such as a musty deck of punch cards or on a disk. Programmers will turn to reusable code fragments or design templates after they have performed enough mental analysis of the problem statement to decide that they have already written a program that can be at least partly reused or that can guide the design of a new one. In order to understand how programmers arrive at decisions about what previous artifacts may be relevant to the current programming task, we must understand how their knowledge of programming is structured and how they use it to solve programming problems. Most cognitive models of programming begin with the distinction between short- and long-term memory. Short-term memory involves the conscious processing of information while performing a task, and long-term memory involves how information is structured for storage and retrieval.

13.2.1 Short-Term Memory

Short-term memory is a limited-capacity workspace that holds and processes those items of information under our attention. It has been characterized by Miller [1956] as holding approximately seven items of information. An item is a single piece of information, although there is no requirement that it be an elementary piece resulting from the decomposition of a larger body of information. Items in short-term memory will decay and be forgotten in less than half a minute unless they are refreshed by rehearsing the item. Short-term memory imposes one of our greatest limitations in building large software systems, because it prohibits us from being able to consciously attend to and manipulate all of the interacting parts of a complex system at once.

In order to overcome the limits of short-term memory, we chunk information into units that possess greater semantic content. Thus we can retrieve larger amounts of information by retrieving a single informational unit that acts as a cue for later recalling all of the information associated with it. Building these higher-level semantic units is an important part of the learning process. For instance, during a first programming course a novice learns a conceptual unit called a *counter*, represented as:

```
COUNT := COUNT + 1;
```

In building a structure to sum an array, novices can think of needing to build a counter and consider its implementation no further, because they are confident of being able to call forth the elements of a counter statement when it comes time to write one down.

Through experience and training, programmers are able to build increasingly larger chunks based on solution patterns that emerge frequently in solving problems. They do this by interleaving statements into small routines to accomplish specific purposes. Thus a single label, such as *array sum*, can become a chunk that represents an increasingly complex set of programming instructions:

```
READ (N);
WHILE N <> 999 DO
  BEGIN
    SUM := SUM + 1;
    COUNT := COUNT + 1;
    READ (N);
  END;
```

The label *array sum* takes up far less of the limited short-term memory space than would be required for the seven lines of instructions listed above. The semantic content associated with the label can be recalled at will should the programmer need to consider it in greater depth. Further, as a programmer's knowledge base grows through experience, chunks can be incorporated into higher-order chunks to build larger structures that can be recalled with a brief label. This allows programmers to process complex information in the same short-term memory space where they could originally process only very limited programming concepts.

By recalling a series of statements from a triggering label, the programmer is mentally accomplishing the trick achieved by higher-level languages whose compilers generate many lines of machine code from a single command. Thus, in chunking, as in higher-level programming languages, there is an attempt to hide a low-level procedural implementation under a higher-level concept. As described later, the ease of reusing modules will be partly determined by the programmer's ability to label the module's function as an easily recognized concept.

Because of chunking, it can be argued that much of the code an experienced programmer produces is reused. While some modules are physically stored in piles of listings in the corner of the office, other pieces are simply stored mentally and can be referenced by the appropriate concept. Reusability is universally used to describe the former, although the latter (the reuse of programming knowledge) is the largest source of reuse in programming. These reusable chunks are stored in long-term memory, a virtually limitless database of information.

13.2.2 Long-Term Memory

An important concern in studying the representation of programming knowledge in long-term memory is how the pieces of information constituting this knowledge base are interrelated and indexed such that:

1. items in short-term memory can quickly cue the recall of appropriate chunks of information from long-term memory;
2. items in short-term memory can be linked into and transferred quickly to long-term memory for retention, and
3. information in long-term memory can cue the retrieval of additional chunks of information when appropriate.

Information in long-term memory is typically characterized as being stored in semantic nets. The nodes in these semantic networks contain knowledge about a particular concept. Knowledge about a concept is often represented as a *schema*, which can be treated as the unit of long-term memory storage [Anderson, 1980]. A schema is a generic knowledge structure that bundles together the knowledge necessary to reason about a concept [Winograd, 1977]. It specifies characteristic attributes of category membership, actual principal members of the class, and allowable operations the schema can trigger [Simon, 1979].

The primary characteristic of a schema is that it represents generic information about a concept (e.g., type or class) and contains slots for specific instantiations [Simon, 1979]. Schemas are primarily treated as declarative knowledge, that is, factual knowledge that does not necessarily provide the ability to perform a task related to the knowledge domain. However, a schema can include information about how it can be used for the attainment of a goal and about the action (procedural) elements required to accomplish the goal [Bobrow and Norman, 1975]. Programming schemata are used in guiding module development by indicating generic elements that a module should contain, such as components for initialization, processing, output, and so on. Such schemata can also be used for rapid pattern recognition of a program's components, which occurs in trying to understand a program before making changes to it.

A deeply elaborated concept may give rise to its own semantic network, since the information in a schema is often considered to be organized hierarchically. The schema for a complex topic such as sorting algorithms will have slots that are instantiated with types of sorts (e.g., quicksort, bubble sort, and hash sort). If the programmer has learned more than the name of the particular algorithm, each of these sorting algorithms will have its own schema. Thus a well-learned subject involves a deep network of these interrelated schemata. The better an idea has been learned, the more richly elaborated its associated schemata have become, and the more deeply embedded it has become in the fabric of the larger semantic network. The basis for expertise appears to be the depth and breadth of the schemata incorporated in the semantic network that represents what experts know about their topic.

13.2.3   Expertise in Programming

One of the characteristics that distinguishes experts from novices is that experts are better at encoding new information. The broader knowledge base of experts guides them to quickly identify the most important aspects of new information, to analyze them, and to relate them to the appropriate schema in long-term memory. This effect has been replicated for programming knowledge [Shneiderman, 1976; Barfield, 1986; and McKeithen *et al.*, 1981]. Developing technical skill is not merely the learning of a long list of facts. Rather, it involves an effort to learn the underlying structure of the knowledge base. McKeithen *et al.* observed greater similarity among the knowledge structures developed by experts than among those developed by intermediates or novices. Thus, as expertise increases, programmers tend to gravitate toward a similar structuring of domain knowledge. The development of this structure enhances the ability of advanced programmers to assimilate new information.

Weiser and Shertz [1983] demonstrated that novices comprehend a problem statement based on its surface structure; that is, the particular application domain of the problem, such as banking or avionics. Experts, however, analyze a problem by the solution or algorithmic structure of the program that would satisfy its requirements. Similarly, experts are able to remember the keywords of a computer language by their position in the structure of the language [McKeithen *et al.*, 1981]. Novices, not having an adequate mental representation of the language structure, often use mnemonic tricks to remember command names. Adelson [1981] demonstrated that while learning to program, novices first key on the syntactic aspects of single computer instructions and their function in isolation from the rest of a program. Later they learn to comprehend the role of an instruction in a larger functional unit that integrates several types of instructions.

Shneiderman and Mayer [1979] described the structure of programming knowledge in long-term memory as containing separate syntactic and semantic knowledge components. Semantic knowledge concerns conceptual relationships in the application domain and the algorithms appropriate for making them computational. Semantic knowledge is independent of the programming language in which a program is written. Syntactic knowledge involves the procedural idiosyncrasies of a given programming language. An important implication of this model is that the development of programming skill requires the integration of knowledge from several different knowledge domains [Brooks, 1983]. For instance, the programming of an onboard aircraft guidance system may require knowledge of

1. aeronautical engineering,
2. radar and sensors technology,
3. the design of an onboard microprocessor,
4. the development computer and its software tools,
5. a high-level programming language,
6. an assembly language, and
7. a library of reusable avionics modules.

Each of these is a separate domain of knowledge, and some of them require years of training and experience to master. Thus, much of programming skill is specific to the application being considered. One can be a talented avionics programmer and still be a novice at programming large multiuser transaction processing systems.

Several efforts have been made to model the structure of programming knowledge at a level deeper than that of Shneiderman and Mayer. Brooks [1977] used Newell and Simon's [1972] production systems approach to model the rules a programmer would use in writing a program. These rules are of the type "If the following conditions are satisfied, then produce the following action." After analyzing a programmer's verbal protocol, Brooks identified 73 rules that were needed to model the coding process of a single, and relatively simple, problem solution. Brooks estimated that the number of production rules needed to model the performance of an expert programmer was in the tens or hundreds of thousands.

13.2.4 Programming as the Interleaving of Plan Knowledge

Soloway and Ehrlich [1984] argue that programming knowledge is organized into two basic components: rules of programming discourse and programming plans. Rules of programming discourse describe stylistic guides to the development of programs, guides that are independent of particular languages or applications; (e.g., "variable names should reflect their function"; "don't do double duty with code in an obscure way"; or "a variable initialized by an assignment statement should be updated via an assignment statement"). A programming plan is an abstract structure containing a decomposition of goals that must be achieved to accomplish the function of the program. A programming plan links the bottom-level goals to specific computational structures for performing the function. Most programs are composed of plans that have been composed by interleaving lower level plans. An example plan structure compiled from Soloway and his colleagues [Soloway *et al.*, 1982; Soloway and Ehrlich, 1984; and Soloway, 1986] is provided in Figure 13.1. Severely violating rules of programming discourse or programming plans can produce code that is understood no better by experts than by novices.

FIGURE 13.1
SOLOWAY AND COLLEAGUES' INTERLEAVING OF PROGRAMMING PLANS

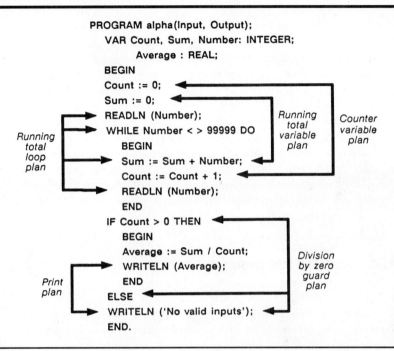

One of the difficult tasks in learning how to program is learning how to select the plans that will be required to perform a computational task and how then to interleave them into a correct program. Soloway and his colleagues have provided excellent demonstrations of how novices learn to use plan structures in writing simple programs. These plan structures correspond to the schemata that programmers use during programming. Notice in Fig. 13.1 that a lower-level plan structure (e.g., the division-by-zero guard plan) constitutes a schema and is also a component of a higher-level schema for how to construct a program for calculating a mean. Once programmers have acquired this schema, they will not need to think in terms of the various subplans that had to be interleaved to create it. Instead, the entire schema for calculating a mean can be called forth as a single unit when programmers require it. At other times, they can simply use the plan label "mean" without having to retrieve all of the elements included in the schema for a mean.

The plans that constitute programming knowledge consist, in part, of a set of subgoals that are to be accomplished in applying the plan. Some of these subgoals may be complex and require the retrieval of a plan for accomplishing a specific subgoal. For instance, a plan for finding a mean value contains subgoals for counting the number of cases, summing their values, and dividing the former by the latter. Furthermore, the plan for this division is complex in that it must contain a subgoal for ensuring that the program does not attempt to divide by zero. When programmers call forth a set of relevant plans, they must interleave the code that instantiates them in a way that does not violate the rules of programming discourse. These rules act as constraints on the methods for interleaving plans.

There is less evidence about how higher-level plan structures are created for interleaving large segments of a system. For example, most programmers do not have a relevant plan schema for the flight control portion of avionics software. The process of selecting and interleaving plan segments into a larger plan is a crucial issue in reusable computational structures. Programmers must be able to retrieve units of code or design templates that correspond to the plan chunks that they manipulate mentally when designing software. Furthermore, these plan fragments must be capable of being interleaved into larger plan segments. This issue will become clearer in discussing problem solving during software design.

13.3 HOW DO PROGRAMMERS DESIGN SOFTWARE?

If programmers are to reuse software artifacts effectively, a process must be defined for incorporating knowledge of these artifacts into their design behavior. In order to understand how to include reusable artifacts as an ordinary component of the design process, we must understand how programmers go about the task of designing software under current circumstances.

In studying the program design process, Jeffries, Turner, Polson, and Atwood [1981] noted that programmers with greater experience decomposed a problem more fully into minimally interacting parts. The design knowledge of novices did not appear sufficient to provide for a full decomposition. In particular, more experienced programmers spent greater time evaluating the problem structure prior to beginning the design process. Observations similar to these were also made by Nichols [1981], who concluded that expert programmers will retrieve a stored program plan from memory, intermediate programmers will have to construct a plan from interleaved parts, and novices will conduct an exhaustive search for a solution since they have few schemata containing design information.

Jeffries *et al.* [1981] hypothesized that there is the equivalent of a mental design executive. This executive attempts to recursively decompose the problem statement and relate the components emerging from the decomposition to patterns in the programming knowledge base in long-term memory. The shallowness of the novice's decomposition reflects the shallowness of the knowledge base against which they attempt to compare pieces of the problem statement. The richer knowledge base of experts allows them to make a fuller decomposition of the problem statement. Experts terminate the decomposition process for a particular aspect of the problem when it has been decomposed to a level at which the programmer can retrieve a known solution pattern.

Kant and Newell [1984] studied university faculty members at work in creating an algorithm to solve the convex hull problem. They observed that participants rapidly chose a problem-solving schema, such as generate-and-test or divide-and-conquer, and pursued this strategy until they had reached a solution. The participants rarely considered alternative solution schemata before selecting an approach, and they usually only considered the alternatives if the initial schema failed to produce satisfactory results. Kant and Newell postulated that two cognitive spaces were important in the process of searching for a solution. The first space contained knowledge of the application domain. The second space contained information about the emerging solution, representing it as a set of increasing complete data-flow diagrams where the nodes represented pieces of algorithms. The crucial insights required to solve problems emerged when relations in the application domain were seen in a new light and ascribed new meaning. However, the insight did not occur unless the solution space had been developed to a sufficient extent that this new insight was meaningful in the context of the emerging solution. Thus, insights in design are fragile, because they require a mapping between an act of recognition in two separate knowledge domains.

In studying expert and novice design behavior, Adelson and Soloway [1985] have articulated a goal tree that represents part of the control function of the design executive postulated by Jeffries *et al.* They maintain that the design process is driven by a metascript that is composed of three goals: checking the current state of the design for sufficiency, checking the current state of the design for consistency, and expanding the design to the next level of specificity. They identified six characteristic design behaviors controlled by the design executive in the process of satisfying these goals:

1. *Formulation of mental models* to support mental simulation of the emerging program,
2. *Mental simulation* to check unforeseen interactions and external consistency with the specifications,
3. *Systematic expansion of components to* aid simulation by ensuring equal levels of detail across functional components that interact,
4. *Representation of constraints* to aid in simulating unfamiliar elements,
5. *Retrieval of plan labels* to reduce the load on memory and terminate exhaustive searches, and
6. *Note making* to capture and save issues relevant to a different component or hierarchical level of the design.

They observed simulation and note making only when the designer had sufficient domain knowledge. Without sufficient experience with the object under design, constraints were placed on the design to gain enough specificity to support simulation. When designers had an adequate plan for the solution, they would use it rather than formulating constraints, performing simulations, and taking notes.

In more recent research, Guindon and Curtis [1988] observed that the software design process was opportunistic in the same sense that Hayes-Roth and Hayes-Roth [1979] described planning as an opportunistic process. Design was opportunistic in that many aspects of the design problem vied simultaneously for the attention of the designer. Thus, designers not only needed problem-specific design schemata, but also a metaschema to control the contention for cognitive resources (i.e., a design executive). If the designer possessed a problem-specific schema relevant to the design solution, the design process could proceed in a systematic top-down expansion of the design. However, designers typically focused on issues that had been important in designs they had previously participated in, and they organized their problem solving behaviors to satisfy the requirements within the boundaries created by these constraints. For instance, one designer creating a control structure for a set of elevators focused early on not allowing the system to possess a single point of failure. This goal quickly led the designer to select a distributed architecture. The breakdowns observed in the design process involved either the lack of relevant design schemata in long-term memory or the capacity limits to processing in short-term memory [Guindon, Krasner, and Curtis, 1987].

13.4 HOW CAN PROGRAMMERS REUSE SOFTWARE ARTIFACTS?

There are many means of reusing software artifacts: subroutine calls, Ada packages, program generators, code skeletons, design templates, and easily reconfigured systems, to name a few. Nevertheless, there are several cognitive processes involved in the software reuse process regardless of the method through which an artifact is obtained. For instance, the programmer must comprehend the customer's requirements and the specification to be able to determine what artifacts will be relevant and how some reusable components must be altered. The programmer must be aware of the artifact's existence regardless of whether it is a subroutine, an abstract data type, or a program that can be modified. The programmer must be able to determine how well the reusable artifact matches the functional specification of the required software. Thus the programmer must be able to comprehend the attribute's functional behavior. Finally, the programmer must be able to comprehend the computational structure of the existing artifact, especially the interleaving of its plan structures, if it is to be modified.

Recent exploratory studies suggest that these processes are not as simple as might be believed [Woodfield et al., 1987]. Fischer [1987] describes how a Lisp programming environment might be structured to encourage reuse of artifacts. The discussion in the following sections will focus on reusing artifacts such as routines, packages, or templates that can be stored in a library or similar repository, and can be the object of queries or other search techniques.

13.4.1   Problems in Retrieving Reusable Components

In order for programmers to make the best use of a reusable library, they must be able to determine quickly what is available. The presentation of a library's contents should provide quick location of relevant components. Such a presentation is not typical of reusable libraries. For instance, several years ago I was searching for a particular statistical procedure in a library of subroutines. The manual clustered the routines according to functional area (e.g., regression, nonparametric statistics, etc.), and the table of contents of this manual presented the 17 clusters in alphabetical order with statistical, mathematical, and other types of clusters intermingled as follows:

A—Analysis of variance
B—Basic statistics
C—Categorized data analysis
D—Differential equations
E—Eigensystem analysis
F—Forecasting
G—Generation and testing of random numbers
I—Interpolation
L—Linear algebraic equations
M—Mathematical and statistical special functions
N—Nonparametric statistics
O—Observation structure
R—Regression analysis
S—Sampling
U—Utility functions
V—Vector-matrix arithmetic
Z—Zeros and extrema.

If users could not guess the label used for the module cluster they wanted to find, they were in for a difficult search, since no further organizational schema was provided.

For instance, if one wanted to perform a discriminate analysis, one found little help looking under *D* (Differential Equations). One needed enough statistical knowledge to know that discriminate analysis was a multivariate statistical technique. So, look under *M*, right? Wrong, the *M*s were devoted to

Mathematical and Statistical Special Functions. In reading down the list, one needed to realize that multivariate statistics provide an analysis of the latent structure underlying a set of observations. Therefore, for discriminate analysis one must go to the *O*s. One finds there a procedure for "multivariate normal linear discriminate analysis among several known groups" with the curious title of ODNORM. After such an experience, one feels more like a detective than a programmer.

This example, although a bit overdrawn, serves to emphasize the importance of organizing information in ways that reflect the user's mental model of the domain, that is, the way the user mentally organizes knowledge about the domain's contents. Such an organization will expedite the search processes of expert users and will assist novices in developing more effective structures for organizing information about the application domain of the artifacts. The effective use of a reusable library will require an indexing scheme similar to the knowledge structures possessed by most programmers working in an application area. The challenge to such indexing schemes is that the organization of a programmer's knowledge will change with increased experience.

The Dewey decimal and Library of Congress indexing schemes offer models of how indexing systems can be structured. Although they attempt to cluster similar topics, one still finds books on related topics classified in ways that spread them to the far ends of the building. Thus the type of multiattribute search capabilities represented in a card catalog may be necessary to locate relevant components in large, complex application areas. However, these indexing schemes are monolithic and hard to adapt to the users' understanding of the domain.

13.4.2   Prieto-Díaz's Software Classification Scheme

Prieto-Díaz postulated that retrieving reusable components was analogous to finding materials in a library [Prieto-Díaz, 1985; Prieto-Díaz and Freeman, 1987]. Consequently, he used principles developed in library science to design a classification and retrieval scheme for reusable components that, from a cognitive perspective, has many appealing features. First, he avoided focusing on the strictly hierarchical relationships among objects (those expressing subordination or inclusion) in favor of a scheme that captures the syntactic or attribute-level relationships among objects that might be classified into different hierarchies. Second, he stressed building up the classification scheme not by enumerating objects into smaller and smaller classes organized hierarchically, but by the bottom-up analysis of the attributes of objects, synthesizing objects into compound classes called *facets*, each composed of a set of elements called *terms*.

Prieto-Díaz created a classification scheme that consisted of six facets: three related to the functionality of the component and three related to its environment. The three functionality facets concern the actual computational function performed, the object on which the function would be performed, and the medium through which the function would be applied to the object. The environmental facets have to do with the role of the function within the system, the functional area of the application, and the external setting in which the function will be used. Within these facets are numerous terms describing how the system could be classified on that facet. The search for a reusable component is accomplished by entering a query with six terms into a relational database that contains components, documentation, and so forth. Synonyms for a term are not allowed in a query, but a thesaurus is provided to aid search for the correct term.

Within a facet, terms are structured around certain supertypes that represent organizing concepts. The conceptual distance between two terms can be measured as the cumulative distance between the two terms and the supertype to which they both belong. These distances are assigned by the user, and the conceptual graph can be used during a component search session to find a reasonable alternative component description to search for if the original query failed to produce a component. The development of individually weighted conceptual graphs relies on programmers' willingness to input the data needed to construct them. Even so, there are quantitative methods for studying these conceptual spaces to determine the facets, the supertypes within facets, and the relation of terms to supertypes, and to determine how much commonality there is to the cognitive structures among programmers that give rise to them.

13.4.3 Matching Indexing Schemes to Cognitive Structures

As discussed earlier, knowledge structures of inexperienced programmers are quite dissimilar [McKeithen et al., 1981]. As programmers gain experience, their understanding of the knowledge in a particular domain gravitates toward a common structure. Thus, while one organizational structure will not suit all users, it appears that we can find a generic structure for a particular domain that will become increasingly suitable for programmers as they gain experience. This is the structure that most resembles the organization of knowledge held by experts in the application area.

There are several methods for identifying the cognitive structures that represent an individual's organization of knowledge about a particular domain. One such method involves a multidimensional scaling analysis of concepts from the application domain. For instance, in statistics we might generate a list of statistical routines. Next we would ask a number of experienced statistical programmers to rate the similarity of each possible pair of concepts on a scale of 1 to 9. These similarity ratings would then be input to a multidimensional scaling program such as INDSCAL [Carroll and Chang, 1968; Carroll and Chang, 1970]. This analysis presents a multidimensional representation of the structure of this domain of knowledge based on the similarity of the concepts. The dimensions are ordered in terms of the amount of variation they account for in the respondents' data. Furthermore, differences in how each individual weights these dimensions in constructing their own semantic space can be assessed. Such scaling analyses provide data on a generic cognitive information space and on how broad the individual differences are in structuring this information. An organization that matches expert knowledge offers one method of organizing an index structure for the components in a library to support knowledgeable users. An important research question raised by Prieto-Díaz's scheme is how self-tailorable the classification scheme should be made to suit the ways less knowledgeable users structure their understanding of a domain.

A cognitive analysis provides a model of the information structures that will be useful in assisting programmers to navigate a reusable library. This information can be used to provide an indexing scheme for retrieving artifacts. It will also provide guidance on the information that should be included in a manual describing the contents of the library. Detailed follow-up interviews with expert programmers will indicate nuances of different computational structures or their options that the novice must be made aware of before selecting a particular artifact.

13.4.4 Interactive Aids for Searching Libraries

The retrieval scheme proposed by Prieto-Díaz is a database query approach using sextuples of descriptive terms. This technique is most successful when users know what is in the library and how the data they must use in building a query is structured. However, for novice users of such information systems there is usually a major vocabulary barrier to efficient use [Furnas et al., 1983]. Furnas [1985] describes an interactive system for developing an adaptive indexing scheme. Structuring a sextuple query also assumes that programmers understand the issues behind important decisions they must make in deciding which terms to include in the query. For less experienced users of the library, assistance based on the issues required to determine the correct component could be provided to help guide selection of appropriate terms for the query.

Once the structure of the knowledge domain has been determined, it can guide the design of an aid for finding information. One possible retrieval aid for a statistical library would be a decision tree with questions such as

1. Is there a criterion variable?
2. Should the analysis be univariate or multivariate?
3. Are the variables normally distributed?
4. Are we testing for group differences?

Such a decision structure partially models some of the search strategies employed by experienced users of statistical libraries. A question-driven search assistant has been demonstrated [Burton et al., 1987] for selecting components from a reusable software library. The system requires that components be described in terms of a set of attributes that are then the source of questions to programmers searching for a relevant component.

Users typically develop characteristic patterns of library use. The structural characteristics that help novices navigate the library will often not be beneficial to the expert user, because these aids are redundant with knowledge structures that the expert already possesses. Thus, the library interface and retrieval aids need to be flexible in order to serve both novice and expert users.

When more efficient ways are available for finding a component than those being used, it is possible to identify weaknesses in a programmer's mental model of either the library's organization or of the application. However, when inefficient usage patterns characterize a number of users, cues may need to be highlighted that will lead users to more efficient strategies. Thus reusable libraries need to be implemented with a data collection facility that can monitor usage patterns. Jones [1986] described how interactively collected data could be used to improve the retrieval performance of a personal filing system. These data can also become an important tool in helping designers identify ways to improve the usability of the library.

Another possibility is to build an explanation system that understands semantic information about the contents of the library. This intelligent interface may prove an invaluable aid during early library use, when it can provide a tutorial about the library's contents. An intelligent tutoring system [Clancey, 1987] hidden behind the interface should help programmers learn enough about the library's structure and contents for them to be able to eventually access a useful component rapidly without assistance. However, they will remain novices to areas of the library that they use infrequently. Thus, even experts may require assistance in finding components in portions of the library where they venture infrequently.

13.4.5 The Interaction of Experience and Reusability

Based on the model of programming knowledge presented in this paper, there are different reusability problems for programmers at different levels of experience. Prieto-Díaz, for example, identified experience as a fuzzy modifier of the relationship between the size of a component and the difficulty a programmer will have in reusing it. Basili and Hutchens [1983] presented data from a software metrics study that supports this relationship between size and effort and suggests that there may be several individual difference factors that affect it. Let us consider separately the reusability issues facing novice, intermediate, and expert programmers.

Because their knowledge of alternative ways for implementing a function is meager, novice programmers often have difficulty correctly selecting from among several reusable modules whose functions are similar. Their difficulty will increase if they do not understand the structure of the application domain and therefore miss clues to the correct choice. For instance, nonstatistical programmers looking at a statistical package will not understand which regression routine to select for their business application if they find several listed (simple, multiple, stepwise, polynomial, etc.). Without sufficient knowledge about the application area, novices will have difficulty in selecting and integrating the correct artifacts.

If a reusability system is intelligent enough to reason about a high-level functional specification of what should be developed and then select methods to transform these specifications into operational code, then the productivity of novices may be enhanced by reusing existing components. However, this level of transformational technology is still in its infancy and most novices will be only minimally assisted by reusable artifacts. Their problem is not in having things to reuse, but in correctly specifying what should be done in the first place or in selecting among the things that purport to do it.

For novices a library of reusable artifacts can provide an educational experience. If some of the artifacts in the library consist of past designs and the rationale behind the design decisions made, then novices can be quickly exposed to the crucial issues involved in designing such a system. Even for experienced designers, reusable design templates and rationale from previous efforts can save some of the expense in learning information often obtained through trial and error prototyping.

If an intelligent tutoring system could be superimposed on a reusable library, novices might be brought up to speed in a new application area much quicker. Even if such tutoring aids were too difficult or expensive to build for a particular area, the artifacts and their documentation should be sufficiently easy to call forth that novices are invited to explore the available routines without regard to their immediate usefulness. Incidental learning of this type will prove valuable in expanding their repertoire of available solution strategies for later programming tasks.

Reusable artifacts may not always be used effectively by intermediate programmers whose partial knowledge of an application area leads them to believe they have solved a problem simply because they have found an existing module with the right title. Programmers with intermediate experience in an area often massage the specifications to conform to a solution strategy they understand (a schema they already possess). This tendency may be encouraged by the existence of reusable artifacts, since considerable effort is reduced by making the problem fit the available solution. However, only the user or customer can decide if the costs of reusing components that do not completely satisfy the specifications offset the cost of developing new software.

Although reusable libraries may improve the productivity of most programmers when measured by output per unit of time, their most successful use will require programmers with substantial application knowledge. Further, reusable artifacts will be helpful primarily for those programmers who have sufficient background to know what they are looking at when they read descriptions of several different modules purported to do similar things.

Reducing or eliminating coding and module testing reduces the number of jobs normally assigned to less experienced programmers. Increased emphasis will be placed on design, interface control, and system testing—jobs that require skilled programmers. Thus the need for programmers and analysts with specialized skills will not be reduced by the availability of reusable artifacts.

REFERENCES

Adelson, B. Problem solving and the development of abstract categories in programming languages. *Memory and Cognition.* 9(4): 422–433, 1981.

Adelson, B., and Soloway, E. The role of domain experience in software design. *IEEE Transactions on Software Engineering.* 11(11): 1351–1360, 1985.

Anderson, J. R. Concepts, propositions, and schemata: What are the cognitive units? *Nebraska Symposium on Motivation* 28: 121–162, 1980.

Atwood, M. E., and Ramsey, H. R. *Cognitive structures in the comprehension and memory of computer programs: An investigation of computer program debugging.* Tech. rep. TR-78-A21. Alexandria, Va.: Army Research Institute, 1978.

Atwood, M. E.; Turner, A. A.; Ramsey, H. R.; and Hooper, J. N. *An Exploratory Study of the Cognitive Structures Underlying the Comprehension of Software Design Problems.* Tech. rep. 392. Alexandria Va.: Army Research Institute, 1979.

Barfield, W. Expert-novice differences in software: Implications for problem solving and knowledge acquisition. *International Journal of Man-Machine Studies* 5(1): 15–29, 1986.

Basili, V. R., and Hutchens, D. H. An empirical study of a syntactic complexity family. *IEEE Transactions on Software Engineering,* 9(6): 664–672, 1983.

Bobrow, D. G., and Norman, D. A. Some principles of memory schemata. In *Representation and Understanding: Studies in Cognitive Science*, D. G. Bobrow and A. Collins (eds.), pp. 131–149. New York: Academic, 1975.

Brooks, R. Towards a theory of cognitive processes in computer programming. *International Journal of Man-Machine Studies* 9: 737–751, 1977.

———. Towards a theory of the comprehension of computer programs. *International Journal of Man-Machine Studies* 18: 543–554, 1983.

Burton, B. A.; Aragon, R. W.; Bailey, S. A.; Koehler, K. D.; and Mayes, L. A. The reusable software library. *IEEE Software* 4(4): 25–33, 1987.

Carroll, J. D., and Chang, J. J. *Program INDSCAL.* Murray Hill, N. J.: AT&T Bell Laboratories, 1968.

———. Analysis of individual differences in multidimensional scaling via an N-way generalization of the Eckert-Young decomposition. *Psychometrika* 35: 283–319, 1970.

Clancey, W. J. *Knowledge-Based Tutoring: The GUIDON Program.* Cambridge, Mass: MIT Press, 1987.

Curtis, B. *Human Factors in Software Development.* 2nd Ed. Washington, D.C.: IEEE Computer Society, 1985.

Fischer, G. Cognitive view of reuse and redesign. *IEEE Software* 4(4): 60–72, 1987.

Furnas, G. W. Experience with an adaptive indexing scheme. *Proceedings of CHI '85: Human Factors in Computer Systems*. New York: ACM, 131–135, 1985.

Furnas, G. W.; Landauer, T. K.; Gomez, L. M.; and Dumais, S. T. Statistical semantics: Analysis of the potential performance of keyword information access systems. *Bell System Technical Journal* 62: 1753–1806, 1983.

Guindon, R., and Curtis, B. Control of cognitive processes during software design: What tools are needed. *Proceedings of CHI '88*. New York: ACM, 263–268, 1988.

Guindon, R.; Krasner, H.; and Curtis, B. Breakdowns and processes during early activities of software design by professionals. In *Proceedings of the Second Workshop on Empirical Studies of Programmers*, G. M. Olson, E. Soloway, and S. Sheppard, pp. 65–82, Norwood, N. J.: Ablex, 1987.

Hayes-Roth, B., and Hayes-Roth, F. A cognitive model of planning. *Cognitive Science* 3(4): 275–310, 1979.

Jeffries, R.; Turner, A. A.; Polson, P. G.; and Atwood, M. E. The processes involved in designing software. In *Cognitive Skills and Their Acquisition*, in J. R. Anderson (ed.), pp. 255–283. Hillsdale, N. J.: Erlbaum, 1981.

Jones, W. P. On the applied use of human memory models: The memory extender personal filing system. *International Journal of Man-Machine Studies* 25(2): 191–228, 1986.

Kant, E., and Newell, A. Problem solving techniques for the design of algorithms. *Information Processing and Management* 28(1): 97–118, 1984.

McKeithen, K. B.; Reitman, J. S.; Rueter, H. H.; and Hirtle, S. C. Knowledge organization and skill differences in computer programmers. *Cognitive Psychology* 13: 307–325, 1981.

Miller, G. A. The magical number seven plus or minus two: Some limits on our capacity to process information. *Psychological Review* 63: 81–97, 1956.

Newell, A., and Simon, H. A. *Human Problem Solving*. Englewood Cliffs, N. J.: Prentice-Hall, 1972.

Nichols, J. A. Problem solving strategies and organization of information in computer programming. *Dissertation Abstracts International*. Ann Arbor, Mich.: University Microfilms International, 1981.

Prieto-Díaz, R. A software classification scheme. *Dissertation Abstracts International*. Ann Arbor, Mich.: University Microfilms International, 1985.

Prieto-Díaz, R., and Freeman, P. Classifying software for reusability. *IEEE Software*, 4(1): 6–16, 1987.

Shneiderman, B. Exploratory experiments in programmer behavior. *International Journal of Computer and Information Sciences* 5: 123–143, 1976.

———. Control flow and data structure documentation: Two experiments. *Communications of the ACM* 25(1): 55–63, 1982.

Shneiderman, B., and Mayer, R. E. Syntactic/semantic interaction in programmer behavior: A model and experimental results. *International Journal of Computer and Information Sciences* 8: 219–238, 1979.

Simon, H. A. Information processing models of cognition. In *Annual Review of Psychology*, M. R. Rosenzweig and L. W. Porter (eds.), vol. 30, pp. 363–396. Palo Alto, Calif.: Annual Reviews, 1979.

Soloway, E. Learning to program = Learning to construct mechanisms and explanations. *Communications of the ACM* 29(9): 850–858, 1986.

Soloway, E., and Ehrlich, K. Empirical studies of programming knowledge. *IEEE Transactions on Software Engineering* 10(5): 595–609, 1984.

Soloway, E.; Ehrlich, K.; and Bonar, J. Tapping into tacit programming knowledge. In *Proceedings of Human Factors in Computer Systems*. New York: ACM, 52–57, 1982.

Weiser, M., and Shertz, J. Programming problem representation in novice and expert programmers. *International Journal of Man-Machine Studies* 19: 391–398, 1983.

Winograd, T. A framework for understanding discourse. In *Cognitive Processes in Comprehension*, P. A. Carpenter and M. A. Just (eds.), pp. 63–88, Hillsdale, N. J.: Erlbaum, 1977.

Woodfield, S. N.; Embley, D. W.; and Scott, D. T. Can programmers reuse software? *IEEE Software* 4(4): 52–59, 1987.

CHAPTER **14**

A FIFTEEN-YEAR PERSPECTIVE ON AUTOMATIC PROGRAMMING

ROBERT BALZER

USC/Information Sciences Institute

14.1 INTRODUCTION

The notion of automatic programming has fascinated our field since at least 1954 when the term was used to describe early Fortran compilers. The allure of this goal is based on the recognition that programming was, and still is, the bottleneck in the use of computers. Over this period we have witnessed phenomenal improvements in hardware capability with corresponding decreases in cost. These price/performance gains reached the point in the early 1980s that individual dedicated processes became cost-effective, giving birth to the personal computer industry. This hardware revolution apparently will continue for at least the rest of the decade.

Software productivity has progressed much more slowly. Despite the development of high-level, and then higher-level, languages, structured methods for developing software, and tools for configuration management and tracking requirements, bugs, and changes, the net gain is nowhere close to that realized in hardware.

But the basic nature of programming remains unchanged. It is largely an informal, person-centered activity that results in a highly detailed formal object. This manual conversion from informal requirements to programs is error-prone and labor-intensive. Software is produced via some form of the waterfall model in which a linear progression of phases is expected to yield correct results. Rework and maintenance are afterthoughts.

Unfortunately, this existing software paradigm contains two fundamental flaws which exacerbate the maintenance problem.

First, there is no technology for managing the knowledge-intensive activities that constitute the software development processes. These processes, which convert a specification into an efficient implementation, are informal, human-intensive, and largely undocumented. It is just this information, and the rationale behind each step, that is crucial but unavailable for maintenance. (This failure also causes problems for the other life cycle phases but is particularly acute for maintenance because of the time lag and personnel changeover normally involved, which precludes reliance on the informal mechanisms, such as "walking down the hall," typically used among the other phases.)

Second, maintenance is performed on source code (i.e., the implementation). All of the programmer's skill and knowledge has already been applied in optimizing this form (the source code). These optimizations spread information; that is, they take advantage of what is known elsewhere and substitute complex but efficient realizations for (simple) abstractions.

Both of these effects exacerbate the maintenance problem by making the system harder to understand, by decreasing the dependencies among the parts (especially since these dependencies are implicit), and by delocalizing information.

With these two fundamental flaws, plus the fact that we assign our most junior people to this onerous task, it is no wonder that maintenance is such a major problem with the existing software paradigm.

Against this background, it is clear why automatic programming commands so much interest and appeal. It would directly obviate both these fundamental flaws through full automation of the compilation process.

But programming is more than just compilation. It also involves some means of acquiring the specification to be compiled and some means of determining that it is the intended specification. Furthermore, if one believes, as we do, that optimization cannot be fully automated, it also involves some interactive means of translating this high-level specification into a lower-level one that can be automatically compiled.

This is the extended automatic programming problem, and the main issue is how to solve it in a way that still obviates the two fundamental flaws in the current paradigm.

ISI's Software Sciences Division has been pursuing this goal for nearly 15 years. This paper describes the perspective and approach of this group to the automatic programming problem and justifies it in terms of the successes and failures upon which it was built.

14.2 THE EXTENDED AUTOMATIC PROGRAMMING PROBLEM

Automatic programming has traditionally been viewed as a compilation problem in which a formal specification is compiled into an implementation. At any point in time, the term has usually been reserved for optimizations that are beyond the then current state of the compiler art. Today, automatic register allocation would certainly not be classified as automatic programming but automatic data structure or algorithm selection would be.

Thus automatic programming systems can be characterized by the types of optimizations they can handle and the range of situations in which those optimizations can be employed. This gives rise to two complementary approaches to automatic programming. In the first (bottom-up) approach, the field advances by the addition of an optimization that can be automatically compiled and by the creation of a specification language that allows the corresponding implementation issue to be suppressed from specifications. In the second (top-down) approach, which gives up full automation, a desired specification language is adopted, and the gap between it and the level that can be automatically compiled is bridged interactively. It is clear that this second approach builds upon the first and extends its applicability by including optimizations and/or situations that cannot be handled automatically.

Hence there are really two components of automatic programming: a fully automatic compiler and an interactive front end that bridges the gap between a high-level specification and the capabilities of the automatic compiler. In addition, there is the issue of how the initial specification was derived. It has grown increasingly clear that writing such formal specifications is difficult and error-prone. Even though these specifications are much simpler than their implementations, they are nonetheless sufficiently complex that several iterations are required to get them to match the user's intent. Supporting this acquisition of the specification constitutes the third and final component of the extended automatic programming problem.

This paper is organized into sections corresponding to each of these three components of the extended automatic programming problem, captured as a software development paradigm, as shown in Fig. 14.1. Throughout this

FIGURE 14.1
EXTENDED AUTOMATIC PROGRAMMING PARADIGM (INITIAL VERSION)

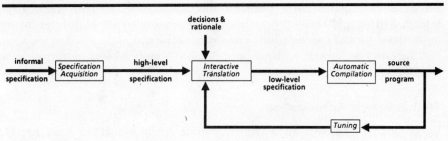

paper we will elaborate this diagram to obtain our goal software life cycle paradigm. In fact, our group has focused its efforts much more on the specification acquisition and interactive translation components than it has on the traditional automatic compiler task.

14.3 SPECIFICATION ACQUISITION

14.3.1 Informal to Formal

Our entry into this field was preceded by a survey [Balzer, 1983] that categorized then current work. We identified specification acquisition as a major problem and decided to focus our initial efforts on the earliest aspects of this task—namely, converting informal specifications into formal ones. Our SAFE project [Balzer, Goldman, and Wile, 1978] in the early 1970s took a (parsed) natural language specification as input and produced a formal specification as output. This system was able to handle correctly several small (up to a dozen sentences) but highly informal specifications (Fig. 14.2).

The basis for its capability was its use of semantic support to resolve ambiguity. Its input was assumed to be an informal description of a well-formed process. Hence it searched the space of possible disambiguations for a well-formed interpretation. This search space was incrementally generated because each informal construct was disambiguated as it was needed in the dynamic execution context of the hypothesized specification. This dynamic execution context was generated via symbolic evaluation.

This use of the dynamic execution context as the basis of semantic disambiguation was strong enough that, at least for the simple specifications on which the system was tested, most ambiguities were locally resolved, and rather little (chronological) backtracking was needed.

Many key aspects of our approach to automatic programming (as explained later in the paper) found their first expression in this system: executable specifications and the use of symbolic evaluation to analyze each execution, an explicit domain model (constructed by the system), and the database view as a specification abstraction of software systems (as embodied in AP3 [Goldman, 1983a], the knowledge representation system for SAFE).

Our modest success with SAFE led us to consider the problems of scaling the system up to handle realistically sized specifications. We recognized that we were solving two hard problems simultaneously: the conversion from informal to formal specification, and the translation from high-level formal to low-level formal specification. The first was the task we wanted to work on, but the latter was required because a suitable high-level formal specification language did not exist.

14.3.2 Formal Specification

We decided to embark on a "short" detour (from which we have not yet emerged) to develop an appropriate high-level specification language. The

FIGURE 14.2a
ACTUAL INPUT FOR MESSAGE PROCESSING EXAMPLE

```
* ((MESSAGE ((RECEIVED) FROM (THE ''AUTODIN-ASC''))) (ARE PROCESSED)
FOR (AUTOMATIC DISTRIBUTION ASSIGNMENT))

* ((THE MESSAGE) (IS DISTRIBUTED) TO (EACH ((ASSIGNED)) OFFICE))

* ((THE NUMBER OF (COPIES OF (A MESSAGE) ((DISTRIBUTED) TO (AN
OFFICE)))) (IS) (A FUNCTION OF (WHETHER ((THE OFFICE) (IS ASSIGNED)
FOR ((''ACTION'') OR (''INFORMATION''))))))

* ((THE RULES FOR ((EDITING) (MESSAGES))) (ARE) (: ((REPLACE) (ALL
LINE-FEEDS) WITH (SPACES)) ((SAVE) (ONLY (ALPHANUMERIC CHARACTERS)
AND (SPACES))) ((ELIMINATE) (ALL REDUNDANT SPACES))))

* (((TO EDIT) (THE TEXT PORTION OF (THE MESSAGE))) (IS) (NECESSARY))

* (THEN (THE MESSAGE) (IS SEARCHED) FOR (ALL KEYS))

* (WHEN ((A KEY) (IS LOCATED) IN (A MESSAGE)) ((PERFORM) (THE ACTION
((ASSOCIATED) WITH (THAT TYPE OF (KEY))))))

* ((THE ACTION FOR (TYPE-8 KEYS)) (IS) (: (IF ((NO OFFICE) (HAS BEEN
ASSIGNED) TO (THE MESSAGE) FOR (''ACTION'')) ((THE ''ACTION'' OFFICE
FROM (THE KEY)) (IS ASSIGNED) TO (THE MESSAGE) FOR (''ACTION'')))
(IF ((THERE IS) ALREADY (AN ''ACTION'' OFFICE FOR (THE MESSAGE)))
((THE ''ACTION'' OFFICE FROM (THE KEY)) (IS TREATED) AS (AN
''INFORMATION'' OFFICE))) (((LABEL OFFS: (ALL ''INFORMATION'' OFFICES FROM
(THE KEY))) (ARE ASSIGNED) TO (THE MESSAGE)) IF ((REF OFFS: THEY)
(HAVE (NOT) (ALREADY) BEEN ASSIGNED) FOR ((''ACTION'') OR (''INFOR-
MATION''))))))

* ((THE ACTION FOR (TYPE-1 KEYS)) (IS) (: (IF ((THE KEY) (IS) ((FIRST
TYPE-1 KEY ((FOUND) IN (THE MESSAGE)))) THEN ((THE KEY) (IS USED)
TO ((DETERMINE) (THE ''ACTION'' OFFICE)))) (OTHERWISE (THE KEY) (IS
USED) TO ((DETERMINE) (ONLY ''INFORMATION'' OFFICES))))))
```

result of this effort was the Gist language [Balzer, Cohen, Feather, Goldman, Swartout, and Wile, 1983; Goldman and Wile, 1980].

Gist differs from other formal specification languages in its attempt to minimize the translation from the way we think about processes to the way we write about them by formalizing the constructs used in natural language. We designed Gist from an explicit set of requirements [Balzer and Goldman, 1979] that embodied this goal and the goal of using such specifications in an automation-based software life cycle (evolved from Fig. 14.1). It is indeed surprising and unfortunate that so few languages have been designed this way.

This requirements-based design resulted in a language with a novel combination of features.

FIGURE 14.2b

HAND ANNOTATED AMBIGUITIES IN MESSAGE PROCESSING EXAMPLE (BY CONVENTIONAL PROGRAMMING STANDARDS)

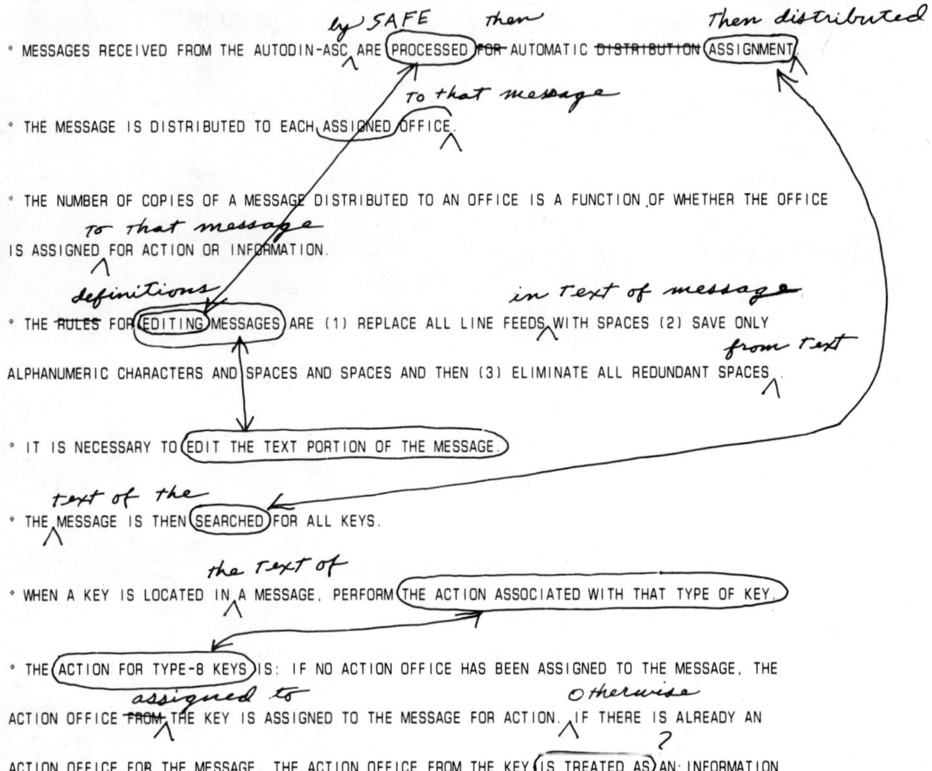

[handwritten: by SAFE] *[handwritten: then]* *[handwritten: Then distributed]*

° MESSAGES RECEIVED FROM THE AUTODIN-ASC ARE (PROCESSED) ~~FOR~~ AUTOMATIC ~~DISTRIBUTION~~ (ASSIGNMENT).

[handwritten: To that message]

° THE MESSAGE IS DISTRIBUTED TO EACH ASSIGNED OFFICE.

° THE NUMBER OF COPIES OF A MESSAGE DISTRIBUTED TO AN OFFICE IS A FUNCTION OF WHETHER THE OFFICE

[handwritten: To that message]

IS ASSIGNED FOR ACTION OR INFORMATION.

[handwritten: definitions] *[handwritten: in Text of message]*

° THE (RULES FOR (EDITING) MESSAGES) ARE (1) REPLACE ALL LINE FEEDS WITH SPACES (2) SAVE ONLY

[handwritten: from Text]

ALPHANUMERIC CHARACTERS AND SPACES AND SPACES AND THEN (3) ELIMINATE ALL REDUNDANT SPACES.

° IT IS NECESSARY TO (EDIT THE TEXT PORTION OF THE MESSAGE.)

[handwritten: text of the]

° THE MESSAGE IS THEN (SEARCHED) FOR ALL KEYS.

[handwritten: the Text of]

° WHEN A KEY IS LOCATED IN A MESSAGE, PERFORM (THE ACTION ASSOCIATED WITH THAT TYPE OF KEY.)

° THE (ACTION FOR TYPE-8 KEYS) IS: IF NO ACTION OFFICE HAS BEEN ASSIGNED TO THE MESSAGE, THE

[handwritten: assigned to] *[handwritten: Otherwise]*

ACTION OFFICE ~~FROM~~ THE KEY IS ASSIGNED TO THE MESSAGE FOR ACTION. IF THERE IS ALREADY AN

[handwritten: ?]

ACTION OFFICE FOR THE MESSAGE, THE ACTION OFFICE FROM THE KEY (IS TREATED AS) AN INFORMATION

[handwritten: for Key] *[handwritten: for information]*

OFFICE. ALL INFORMATION OFFICES FROM THE KEY ARE ASSIGNED TO THE MESSAGE IF THEY HAVE NOT

[handwritten: To the message]

ALREADY BEEN ASSIGNED FOR ACTION OR INFORMATION.

° THE ACTION FOR TYPE-1 IS: IF THE KEY IS THE FIRST TYPE-1 KEY FOUND IN THE MESSAGE THEN

[handwritten: ?] *[handwritten: of the message]* *[handwritten: ?]*

THE KEY IS (USED TO DETERMINE) THE ACTION OFFICE, OTHERWISE THE KEY IS (USED TO DETERMINE ONLY)

[handwritten: of the message]

INFORMATION OFFICES.

Global Database. We conceive the world in terms of objects, their relationships to one another, and the set of operations that can be performed on them. At the specification level, all these objects must be uniformly accessible.

Operational. Gist specifications are operational (i.e., have an executable semantics) because they describe systems that display behavior (i.e., modify the objects defining some environment). These systems are defined in terms of a set of interacting agents (i.e., concurrent processes) that contribute to the system's overall behavior. The Gist specification must constructively generate this set of intended system behaviors. This operational semantics also allows the specification to be reasoned about as programs (although highly inefficient ones).

Perfect Knowledge. The distinction between explicit and implicit information must be hidden at the specification level. (This is an optimization issue.) It must appear that all derivable information is already contained in the global database. This implies the need for inference and/or derivation rules that are self-organizing (used as needed). Thus any computation which does not change state, but merely the form of information, is expressed via such rules (as in Prolog).

Descriptive Reference. This is the ability to access objects via a description of their relationships with other objects. Since the relationships may be used to access any of the objects participating in the relationship, associative retrieval is implied. If the description is underconstrained, then one member of the set of described objects is nondeterministically selected.

Historical Reference. Just as descriptive reference is used to access objects by descriptions from the current state, historical reference allows this same access capability from previous states. The absence of such a capability forces the specifier to create memory structures to hold needed historical information and to maintain them dynamically. Such compilation activities should have no place in specifications.

Constraint Avoidance. The semantics of Gist is that the generated set of behaviors does not violate any constraints. Gist specifications normally contain much nondeterminism (in descriptive and historical references, and in the interleaving of concurrent processes), which generates alternative possible behaviors. Only those behaviors that do not violate any constraints are actually generated. Thus constraints can be thought of as pruning a set of overly general behaviors to the acceptable subset. Gist specifications usually specify a simple, overly general process for performing some task and then some constraints that "force" it to generate only the desired behaviors.

Closed System. In order to define the interactions of the specified system with its environment, that environment must also be specified. This allows the entire specification to be simulated and analyzed.

The resulting language was used to specify several real applications [Feather, 1980b, 1980c] and has recently been adopted as the specification language for a software development environment being built by a software engineering course at USC. An example of a Gist specification is given in Fig. 14.3.

14.3.3 Specification Readability

We believe that Gist successfully allows specifiers to create formal specifications that are cognitively close to their conceptualization of the specified system. We had assumed that this cognitive closeness would result in specifications that were also easy to read.

Unfortunately, this assumption was false. Gist specifications were nearly as hard to read as those in other formal specification languages. We soon realized that the problem was not particular to Gist, but extant across the entire class of formal specification languages. In their effort to be formal, all these languages have scrubbed out the mechanisms that make informal languages understandable, such as summaries and overviews, alternative points of view, diagrams, and examples.

To partially overcome this problem, we built a paraphraser [Swartout, 1982] that takes a formal Gist specification as input and produces a natural language paraphrase as output. This paraphrase both summarizes and reorganizes the specifications to provide an alternative point of view. Figure 14.3 shows an example of a Gist specification and its paraphrase.

As can readily be seen from this example, the paraphraser produces a remarkable improvement in readability. In fact, it does better than that. It also helps uncover errors in the specification (places where the specification differs from intent). We found such errors in specifications we had carefully constructed and "knew" were correct. The paraphraser made it obvious that the formal specification did not match our intent (the paraphraser cannot detect such problems itself, but it makes it easy for us to do so).

We are starting a joint effort with TRW to convert the current laboratory prototype paraphraser into a practical tool and to make it applicable to their specification language, RSL [Bell and Bixler, 1976].

14.3.4 Symbolic Evaluation and Behavior Explanation

The paraphraser pointed out that what we write is often not what we had intended. But it does not help uncover mismatches between our intent and what we really wanted. A specification, after all, is really a generator of behaviors, and the real question is whether the intended set of behaviors was generated. While the paraphraser can help us detect some of these mismatches by making the generator (i.e., the specification) more understandable, many mismatches can be detected only by examining the behaviors themselves.

FIGURE 14.3
EXAMPLE OF A GIST SPECIFICATION

<u>type</u> **location** () <u>supertype</u> <u>of</u>
  < **source**(SOURCE_OUTLET | **pipe**);
    pipe(CONNECTION_TO_SWITCH_OR_BIN | (**switch** <u>union</u> **bin**) :: <u>unique</u>);
    switch(SWITCH_OUTLET | **pipe** :2, SWITCH_SETTING | **pipe**)
        <u>where</u> <u>always</u> <u>required</u>
            switch:SWITCH_SETTING = *switch*:SWITCH_OUTLET <u>end</u>;
    bin()
  > ;
  Packages - the objects moving through the network
  <u>type</u> **package**(LOCATION | **location,** DESTINATION | **bin**) ;
There are packages, sensors, package_routers and environments.
Bins, switchs, pipes and sources are locations.
      Each switch has 2 switch_outlets which are pipes.   Each switch has one
      switch_setting which is a pipe.
          Always required:
              The switch_setting of a switch must be a switch_outlet of the switch.
      Each pipe has one connection_to_switch_or_bin which is a switch or bin.
      Each switch or bin is the connection_to_switch_or_bin of one pipe.
      Each source has one source_outlet which is a pipe.
Each package has one location. Each package has one destination which is a bin.
Bins and switchs are sensors.

There are three classes of tools relevant to this task. The first is a theorem prover. It could be used to prove that all behaviors have some desired set of properties. We have not investigated this approach because it is hard to completely characterize the intended behavior via such properties, and because this approach only checks the expected. A major problem is that unexpected behaviors occur. The remaining two classes directly examine behaviors and so are able to detect these unexpected behaviors.

The second class of tools is an interpreter for the specification language. Since we have required that our specification language be operational, all specifications are directly executable (although potentially infinitely inefficient). The major advantage of this type of tool is that it provides a means for augmenting and testing the understanding of the specification through examples. Its major problem is the narrow, case-by-case feedback that it provides.

This has caused us to focus our efforts on the remaining class of tools: symbolic evaluation. Symbolic evaluation differs from normal evaluation by allowing the test case to be partially specified [Cohen, 1983]. Those aspects not specified are treated symbolically with all cases (relevant to the specification) automatically explored. This provides a means of exploring entire classes of test cases simultaneously. These cases are only subdivided to the extent that the specification makes such distinctions. These subcases are automatically generated and explored. The size of the test case explored by symbolic eval-uation is determined by the degree to which it is only partially specified (in the limit, when the case is completely specified, symbolic evaluation reduces to normal interpretation).

We have built a prototype evaluator for Gist. It produces a complex case-based exploration of the symbolic test case. It retains only the "interesting" (as defined by a set of heuristics) consequences of the behavior generated for the test case. To make this behavior understandable, we have also built a natural language behavior explainer (see [Swartout, 1983b] for details of this work).

Our intent is to provide both static (via the specification paraphraser) and dynamic (via the symbolic evaluator) means for validating a specification. We imagine an intense iterative cycle during the creation of a specification in which the validation cycles progress from the static feedback provided by the specification paraphraser to the dynamic feedback provided by the symbolic evaluator. During this period the specification is being used as a fully functional (although highly inefficient) prototype of the target system. These augmentations to the software life cycle are shown in Fig. 14.4.

14.3.5 Maintenance

We also realized that the revisions made to the specification during this val-idation cycle are just like those that arise during maintenance. This realiza-tion suggested a radical change in how maintenance is accomplished: Modify the specification and reimplement. This change in the software life cycle (as shown in Fig. 14.5) resolves the fundamental flaw in the current life cycle. By performing maintenance directly on the specification, where information is localized and loosely coupled, the task is greatly simplified because the opti-mization process, which spreads information and builds up (largely implicit) interconnections between the parts, has not yet occurred. In the current life cycle, we attempt to maintain the optimized source code, with predictable consequences.

FIGURE 14.4
EXTENDED AUTOMATIC PROGRAMMING PARADIGM (INTERMEDIATE
VERSION 1)

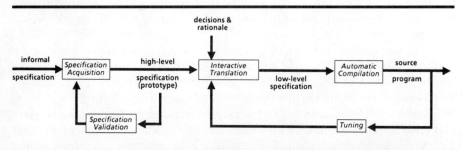

FIGURE 14.5
EXTENDED AUTOMATIC PROGRAMMING PARADIGM (INTERMEDIATE
VERSION 2)

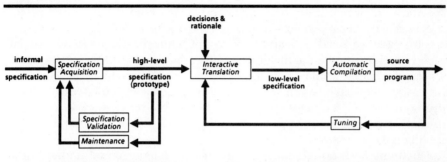

At the specification level, such maintenance is almost always simple (if not trivial)—usually explainable in a few sentences. This corresponds to the fact that the logical trajectory of a system changes slowly, in part limited by users' ability to absorb such changes. It is only at the implementation level that these small logical changes can have large, global, and complex effects. However, rather than trying to "patch" the previous implementation to obtain the next one, these problems are avoided by deriving the new implementation from the revised specification. To the extent that the implementation process is automated and guaranteed to produce valid implementations, this option becomes feasible. Notice that this is what we have always done with compilers. (It is just that currently much of the optimization process has already been manually performed because existing compilers only accept lower-level implementation-oriented languages, and maintaining this portion manually is difficult and error-prone.)

14.3.6 Incremental Specification

We have noted that maintenance modifications can usually be explained in a few sentences. This is because natural language provides us with a metalanguage mechanism that enables previous utterances to be modified. This capability is crucial for our major explanation strategy: gradual elaboration. We explain things by starting with a simplified kernel, which is repeatedly elaborated and revised. Each cycle is a better approximation of the final description. We simplify earlier stages to improve comprehension, and in so doing, tell "white lies," which are corrected by later revisions.

These simplified overview approximations are central to our ability to communicate with one another but, as noted earlier, are totally lacking in our formal specification languages. The lack of this capability, and the metalevel mechanisms for modifying previous utterances upon which it depends, constrains the current generation of formal specification languages to a "batch" semantics in which the information is order independent. Hence the entire specification must be understood at once, and desired changes must be added to the specification by rewriting the whole specification with the change integrated in. This "compilation" process produces a larger, more complex batch specification, which must be understood as a whole. Clearly, this process breaks down after a certain size and complexity are reached.

Instead, we need to learn how to tell white lies in these formal languages and how to define metamechanisms that modify previous utterances. These capabilities would create a new generation of incremental specification languages. We have begun to explore the dimensions along which change can occur in such languages [Goldman, 1983b], and to define a complete set of high-level modifications to the domain model portion of specifications in such languages [Balzer, 1985].

Defining such an incremental specification language and understanding its implications on our automated software development life cycle is our major specification goal.

14.3.7 Interactive Translation

After obtaining a valid high-level specification via the iterative and/or incremental derivation process described above, this high-level specification must be interactively translated into a low-level specification that can be automatically compiled. The amount of work involved in this phase is dependent on the distance between these two specification levels.

In our efforts, this gap is quite large because we have consciously defined Gist to minimize the difference between the way we think about processes and the way we write about them. This decision maximized the work involved in this iterative translation phase. It includes "traditional" automatic programming issues of representation and algorithm selection as well as several issues specific to Gist, such as algorithm organization (to guarantee the nonviolation of constraints), cache detection and organization (to handle inferencing), state saving (to handle historical reference), and algorithm decomposition (to break the single Gist specification and its global database into tractable modules).

Any transformation-based approach such as ours is inevitably drawn to the notion of a wide-spectrum language, as first enunciated by Bauer [1976], in which a single language contains both specification and implementation constructs. Each translation is from and into the same language because each affects only a small portion of the specification (the transformations generally either replace higher-level constructs with lower-level ones within the same language, or they reorganize constructs at the same level). Use of a wide-spectrum language has two other pragmatic benefits. First, it allows transformations to be less order dependent (if there is a succession of languages, then transformations can only be employed while their language is in effect). Second, it avoids having to build separate transformation languages and analysis packages for each language.

Finally, it should be noted that combining a wide-spectrum language with an operational semantics allows a single program semantics and its associated analysis to be used throughout a transformational implementation.

Our first transformation efforts were based on manually applied transformations [Balzer, 1981]. It was immediately apparent that the clerical work involved was untenable and that the transformations had to be applied by the system.

We decided to embed such a capability in Popart [Wile, 1981], a grammar-driven development system we were creating. This was a most fortunate choice because this grammar-driven aspect was central to our first major advance in transformations, both in its implementation and in our recognizing the opportunity and need for this capability.

14.3.8 Formal Development Structure

We recorded the sequence of transformation applications to provide a derivation history. To examine this history, it was natural to use the Popart editor. This necessitated building a grammar for this structure, which in turn forced us to consider the language for expressing such structures. This led to the observation that, rather than representing the derivation history directly, we should describe how to generate that history; that is, a program for transformational derivation (called a formal development).

The resulting language, Paddle [Wile, 1983], enabled us to operationally specify the structure of the sequence of transformations needed to implement some system. That specification could be executed to obtain the implementation. However, we could also use the Popart editor to modify the formal development and then reexecute it.

Paddle's contribution lies in the combination of these two capabilities. It formally represented a structured transformational derivation, and the fact that this representation was generative provided us with the insight that such derivations should be iteratively and incrementally developed.

In fact, it is also the basis for our approach to maintenance. As we described previously, we believe that maintenance should be performed by modifying the specification and rederiving the implementation. This strategy is ideal when the implementation is fully automatic because the modified specification then only needs to be "recompiled."

14.3.9 Replay

However, in an interactive translation approach such as our own, while much of the effort has been automated, there is still considerable human involvement. This makes it unfeasible to rederive the entire implementation each time the specification is modified. However, most of the implementation decisions remain unchanged from one cycle to the next, so rather than rederiving the implementation from the specification, we modify the Paddle program that generated the previous implementation to alter only appropriate implementation decisions and then replay (i.e., rerun) it to generate the new implementation.

Reimplementing a specification by modifying the formal development (the Paddle program) and replaying it represents the final elaboration to our extended automatic programming paradigm (see Fig. 14.6). The formal development becomes an output of interactive translation in addition to the low-level specification that is fed to the automatic compiler. This formal development is also an additional input to the next cycle of interactive translation, in which it is modified and replayed to generate the next version of the low-level specification.

This replay mechanism, and the formal development on which it is based, is the means by which this paradigm still eliminates the two fundamental flaws in the current software paradigm without requiring the unachievable goal of full automation. The flaw of informal and undocumented translations is eliminated by the formal development that formally documents and records the optimization decisions made by the human developer, thus making them accessible to other developers for later maintenance or enhancement of the system. The flaw of trying to modify optimized source code is eliminated by replay, which provides enough automation of the optimization process that a new implementation can feasibly be rederived directly from the specification.

An earlier version of this extended automatic programming paradigm, which did not differentiate between the interactive translation and automatic compilation phases, was adopted for the Knowledge-Based Software Assistant [Green *et al.*, 1983] and included as a long-range objective of the Stars program [Balzer, Green, and Cheatham, 1983].

14.3.10 Automating Interactive Translation

Achieving such a replay capability is our major transformation goal. The main impediment is the operational rather than specificational nature of Paddle. We currently define how to accomplish the translation from high- to low-level specification rather than describe our optimization decisions directly. We need to define a much higher level language than Paddle for describing these

FIGURE 14.6
EXTENDED AUTOMATIC PROGRAMMING PARADIGM

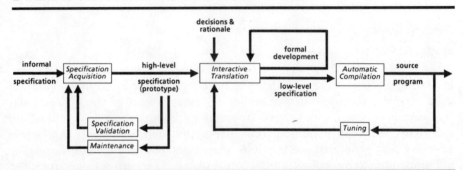

decisions, and just as with conventional computer languages, back them up with correspondingly high-level translation. Here, this translation involves a problem solver, which satisfies optimization goals by constructing appropriate transformation sequences.

A first step in this direction is the Glitter system [Wile, 1983]. In a narrowly defined and restricted domain, it was able to achieve an order of magnitude decrease in the need for interactive input. This type of automation is triply effective. It not only automates the initial development of the implementation, but even more importantly, it enhances its replay capability in two ways. By raising the formal development's level of description and reducing its operational character, it becomes easier both to understand and to modify. The biggest effect, however, is that the formal development often may be replayed without modification because the changes in its operational expansion, necessitated by the revision of the program specification, are being filled in by the problem solver rather than being an explicit part of the Paddle specification, and they can be automatically rederived by the problem solver to fit the new situation.

The creation, modification, and implementation of Paddle's formal development structure is exactly analogous to that of program specifications themselves. It is therefore reasonable to ask whether automatic compilation (the transformation problem solver) can be any more successful here than we argued it could be with program specifications in general. Our answer is that it cannot. Just as with program specification, we will inevitably want to write formal development specifications that are beyond the automatic compilation state of the art. We will therefore need an interactive translation facility to bridge this gap.

In fact, we need to employ our entire extended automatic programming paradigm to create and maintain the formal development. This potentially endless recursion is broken, as always, by the human inability to tolerate more than one or two recursive levels. On an engineering basis, we will limit our specifications at some level to the capabilities of that level's automatic compiler. The price is the corresponding locking of the strategies of that level into an explicit operational structure that must be manually maintained [Mostow, 1986].

Thus our entire approach to interactive translation is based on the ability to represent the translation in a language that is executable and upon which our development tools and technology can be applied. We are indeed fortunate that our initial efforts with Popart led us in this direction.

14.3.11 Transformations

While most of our effort on transformations has focused on the technology (language, tools, control structure, etc.) rather than on individual transformations, we have developed some transformations for areas of special interest for Gist. These transformations map away the specification freedoms provided by

Gist: specifically, historical reference, derived relations, demons, associative retrieval, and angelic evaluation (nondeterministic execution that proceeds in such a way that constraints will not be violated) [London and Feather, 1982].

We have also investigated how constraints defined on a system can be refined into constraints on the parts of that system [Feather, 1985]. As with most of the areas listed above, this issue has not received much attention because, along with other specification languages, it had to be resolved before a formal specification could be written. Gist allows these issues to remain unresolved in the formal specification; that is, to be a specification freedom.

In general, for each of these freedoms we have identified the implementation issues involved, characterized the space of alternatives, and provided a few example transformations to map a subset of the instances of the freedom into an implementation. We have not attempted the much larger task of building a comprehensive library of such transformations.

One area where we did attempt to build such a comprehensive set of transformations was for implementing derived relations in software caches. We observed that much of the complexity of our programs was due to building and maintaining caches of various kinds. We therefore decided to try to build a system which automated this aspect of programming [Mostow, 1985].

This system employed a comprehensive set of transformations for creating and maintaining a variety of different types of caches. Furthermore, it automatically determined when, where, and how to install them (based on an analysis of costs compiled from interactively acquired data). It extends previous work on caching by dealing with real Lisp programs that have side effects and shared list structure and that evolve (via an editor). It was able to cache several Lisp programs, including itself.

However, our decision to have it work on arbitrary Lisp programs greatly complicated its analysis and limited its ability to safely install caches. Revising it to work in the more structured Gist environment should alleviate this difficulty.

14.4 AUTOMATIC COMPILATION

As indicated earlier, most of our group's effort has focused on the specification derivation and interactive translation phases. However, recently we have started two significant efforts in automatic compilation: explainable expert systems and annotations.

14.4.1 Narrowed Focus

The Explainable Expert Systems project [Swartout, 1983a] is specializing our general software development paradigm to the narrower area of expert system construction. This focus, and the fact that the structure of these systems is regular and declarative, has allowed us to match the specification language with the automatic compiler and (attempt to) eliminate the need for interactive translation. The basis for this effort is Swartout's thesis [Swartout, 1981, 1983c], in which he observed that good explanations of the behavior of a system required not only an ability to paraphrase the code of the system, but also an ability to describe the relationship of the implementation to the (possibly implicit) specification from which it was derived and the rationale behind the design decisions employed in the translation.

Rather than attempting to extract this much information from a human designer, he built a special-purpose automatic programmer that dropped mental bread crumbs along the way (i.e., it recorded its design decisions in a development history). We are extending this automatic compiler to build rules from domain principles applied to specific domain facts and to integrate rules together into methods. Each such capability that the automatic compiler can handle can be removed from the input specification. Since so little effort has yet occurred in specifying rather than programming expert systems, considerable progress can be made before we reach the limits of our ability to extend the automatic compiler.

14.4.2 Annotations

Our annotation effort is exploring a quite different approach to automatic compilation. Rather than extending the compiler's ability to make optimization decisions automatically, we are attempting to extend its ability to carry out the decisions of a human designer. These decisions are represented as declarative annotations of the specification. The human designer is interested only in the eventual achievement of these decisions, not in interactively examining the resulting state and using it as the basis for further decisions.

Thus this annotation approach is really the logical limit of our attempts to get more declarative specifications of the formal development. Our reason for considering it here is that it basically trivializes the interactive translation phase to make syntactic annotations while enhancing the role of the automatic compiler, which follows the guidance provided by those annotations.

We believe that the annotation approach has great promise because it enables the human designer to make decisions in a nonoperational way, which facilitates enhanced replay, decreases the need to interactively examine intermediate states of the implementation, and allows the automatic compiler to consider these decisions in any order, or even jointly.

Our first target of opportunity for annotation is representation selection. Towards this end, we are constructing a new knowledge representation system, AP5 [Cohen, 1985], to replace AP3. Besides cleaning up the semantics of AP3, its main purpose is to allow heterogeneous representations of knowledge. AP5 defines relations, its basic unit of representation, as an abstract data type. Any implementation that satisfies the formal interface thus defined is acceptable. Annotations allow the user to select among several predefined implementations, or to define new, special-purpose ones. The

AP5 compiler is concerned with translating specifications that use the abstract knowledge base interface to access and manipulate logical data into efficient programs [Cohen and Goldman, 1985]. The term *virtual database* has been coined to describe such data and knowledge bases that logically hold and manage data, which are actually represented heterogeneously and directly accessed and manipulated by compiled database applications. We expect large improvements in efficiency in such applications over the homogeneous and actual (as opposed to virtual) interface currently employed in AP3 programs.

14.5 FORMALIZED SYSTEM DEVELOPMENT

Nearly three years ago, we confronted the realization that although we had broadly explored the extended automatic programming problem and conceived a new paradigm for automated software development, all of our insight and experience was based on pedagogical examples. None of our tools or technology had progressed to a usable state.

We believe very strongly in the evolution notion, embedded in our software paradigm, that large, complex systems cannot be predesigned, but rather must grow and evolve on the basis of feedback from use of earlier simpler versions. We know that our insights and perceptions are necessarily limited and preliminary, and that only by actually experiencing such an environment would they significantly deepen. We also felt that enough pieces of technology had been developed that we could begin to benefit from their use.

We therefore committed ourselves to building an operational testbed capable of supporting our own software department. This testbed will be used to experiment with tools and technologies for supporting our software paradigm and for studying alterations to it. The testbed became operational in January 1984 and since then is the only system we have used for all our computing needs. It is available to the research community as a framework for development and evolution of Common Lisp systems.

To build this testbed, called formalized system development (FSD) [Balzer, Dyer, Morgenstern, and Neches, 1983], we had to overcome two major obstacles to using our new software paradigm. The first was establishing a connection between our high and low levels of specification. Because we attempted to minimize the difference between the way we think about processes and the way we write about them, we created a large gap between these two levels of specification. We still have a long way to go in creating an appropriate interactive translation framework, stocking it with a suitable and comprehensive set of translations, and providing an adequate level of automation to obtain a usable interactive translation facility, even for quite sophisticated programmers.

This lack of connection has bedeviled our efforts right from the start (with SAFE [Balzer, Goldman, and Wile, 1978]) and has been the major impediment to our use of this new paradigm. It has isolated our high-level specification language from our technology and relegated its use to pedagogical examples.

Overcoming this problem is simple but philosophically painful. By suitably lowering the level of our high-level specification (hereafter called the prototype specification), we can bring it close enough to the lower level of specification to bridge via interactive translation. The cost of such a lowering of the input prototyping specification is that more optimization issues must be handled manually outside the system, thus complicating maintenance.

We decided to initially limit interactive translation to providing annotations for the automatic compiler (as discussed in the annotations section). We believe we currently understand how to annotate data representations, inference rules, and demon invocations, and how to compile those annotations. This then defines the initial difference between the prototyping and low-level specifications.

The rest of the high-level specification is therefore determined by the capabilities of our automatic compiler. This brings us to a second major obstacle to using our new software paradigm: automatic compilation. The issue is both what can be compiled and what constitutes an adequate level of optimization.

From the very start of our efforts, we were writing our tools in terms of a knowledge representation system, FSD [Goldman, 1983a], which directly incorporated many aspects of our specification semantics. We found that AP3's direct implementation of these semantic constructs, while far from what could be produced by hand, still provided adequate response. Major portions of the FSD testbed are constructed this way, with the same acceptable performance result. We therefore decided that, in general, this is an appropriate target level for our automatic compiler. This compiler will actually be a two-phase compiler. The first phase will translate the annotated low-level specification language into calls on the AP5 knowledge-base system. The AP5 compiler will then use the annotations to perform any further indicated optimizations. A major reason for our shift from AP3 to AP5 is the latter's capability to compile annotations into heterogeneous representations. We believe that this additional, directed level of optimization will enable us to write the entire FSD system in the prototyping specification language.

We have not yet addressed the simplifications required to convert Gist into a compilable prototyping language. These simplifications are defined by the capabilities of the first phase of the automatic compiler. Because so much of the semantics of Gist is directly captured by AP5, most of the compilation is straightforward. The remaining difficult aspects are all related to specific language constructs.

The most problematical is Gist's constraints. These constraints limit nondeterministic behavior so that the constraints are never violated. This requires indefinite look-ahead, and no effective general implementation is known. Instead, this construct has been replaced by two lower-level ones: a simple constraint that merely signals an error when its pattern is violated, and a consistency rule. Like the simple constraint, the consistency rule specifies, through a knowledge-base pattern, some relationships that are always supposed to be satisfied. However, when this pattern is violated, the consistency rule attempts to patch the state, via a set of repair rules that have access to both the old and the new state. If it is successful in reestablishing the relationship in the new state, then the computation continues (with the extra modifications made by the repair rule merged with those of the original transition as a single atomic step, so that the intermediate state, which violated the consistency rule, is not visible). This allows the system to automatically maintain consistency relationships expressed via these rules in an electron-like manner. Like Prolog [Kowalski, 1979] rather than spreadsheets, these rules can involve logical as well as numeric relationships, and can be used multidirectionally.

14.5.1 Prototyping the Prototype

In 1985 the FSD testbed was fully operational and in daily use within our group at ISI. It supported the semantics of the prototyping specification language described above. However, the syntax of this language was not yet in place. Instead, we wrote in a macro and subroutine extension to AP3.

FSD was then converted to AP5, putting the second phase of the automatic compiler in place. Work was then begun to bring up the first phase, which translates the Gist-like syntax of the prototyping specification language into AP5.

We originally intended FSD to be just a testbed for software development. However, when we considered the semantic base we were installing for it, we found nothing in it that was particular to software development. Rather, this semantic base defined the way we wanted to interact with computer systems in general. We therefore decided to extend FSD from a software development environment to a general computing environment in which we could also read and compose mail, prepare papers, and maintain personal databases, because such an extension merely involved writing these additional services. Furthermore, the creation and evolution of these extra services would give us an additional insight into the strengths and weaknesses of our software development capabilities.

The FSD environment presents the user with a persistent universe of typed objects (instead of a file-based world), which can be accessed via description (i.e., associatively) and modified by generic operations. All the metadata defining the types, attributes, inheritance, viewing, and printing mechanisms are also represented as manipulable objects in this persistent universe. Consistency rules invisibly link objects to one another so that the consistency conditions are automatically maintained as the objects are modified, either directly by the user or by some service. Automation rules (demons) provide a way of transferring clerical activities to the system so that it gradually becomes a specialized personal assistant.

More and more of our tools and technology are being integrated into this method. This effort is providing us with a wealth of prototyping experience for use on later versions. Our long-term goal is to understand the rules that govern (or should govern) software development and evolution, and to embed them within our system and paradigm.

14.6 SUMMARY

We have incrementally elaborated the simple notion of an automatic compiler into a paradigm for automated software development. These elaborations recognize that

1. the specifications have to be acquired and validated;
2. the validation requires an operational semantics;
3. an interactive translation facility is needed to obtain the lower-level specification that can be automatically compiled;
4. the decisions employed in that interactive translation must be documented and recorded in a formal structure; and
5. this formal development is the basis for a replay facility that enables implementations to be rederived from the revised specification on each maintenance cycle.

We showed how this paradigm, even without full automation, eliminated the two fundamental flaws in the current paradigm.

We also described the wide variety of research we have undertaken in support of this paradigm and characterized our successes and failures. Our chief successes are

1. Gist, its validation (via paraphrase, symbolic evaluation, and behavior explanation);
2. Paddle (formal development structure);
3. explication of the paradigm itself; and
4. development of FSD (operational testbed).

Our chief failures were

1. the unreadability of Gist (partially resolved by the Gist paraphraser);
2. replay;
3. automatic compilation leverage provided by a narrower focus (explainable expert systems) and by annotations; and
4. explication of the rules that govern software development and evolution, and embedding them within an operational testbed (FSD).

Acknowledgment

The work reported here is the result, over nearly 15 years, of many colleagues who have participated with the author in this joint endeavor to understand, formalize, and automate the software process. We are grateful to all of these colleagues for making this effort so exciting, rewarding, and productive. We are particularly indebted to N. Goldman for his contributions to SAFE and the formalization of Gist, to D. Wile for his development of Popart and Paddle, to B. Swartout for bringing explanation into our group and exploring the use of our paradigm for developing expert systems, to D. Cohen for his work on symbolic evaluation and the development of AP5, and to M. Feather for developing Gist transformations and formalizing its semantics. Finally, we would like to thank all the members of our group for their help in making FSD an operational testbed in which they can explore our software paradigm and the utility of their tools and technology.

References

Balzer, R. Transformational implementation: an example. IEEE Trans. *Software Eng.*, vol. SE-7, pp. 3–14, Jan. 1981. See also Balzer, Res. rep. RR-79-79, Inform. Sci. Inst., Univ. Southern Calif., Marina del Rey, May 1981.

———. A global view of automatic programming. In *Proc. Third Int. Joint Conf. Artif. Intell.*, pp. 494–499, Aug. 1983.

———. Automated enhancement of knowledge representations. In *Proc. Ninth Int. Joint Conf. Artif. Intell.*, Los Angeles, Calif., Aug. 18–23, 1985.

Balzer, R.; Cohen, D.; Feather, M.; Goldman, N.; Swartout, W.; and Wile, D. Operational specification as the basis for specification validation. In *Theory and Practice of Software Technology*, Ferrari, Bolognani, and Goguen, eds. Amsterdam, The Netherlands: North-Holland, 1983.

Balzer, R.; Dyer, D.; Morgenstern, M.; and Neches, R. Specification-based computing environments. In *Proc. Nat. Conf. Artif. Intell. AAAI-83*, Inform. Sci. Inst., Univ. Southern Calif., Marina del Rey, Calif., 1983b.

Balzer, R., and Goldman, N. Principles of good software specification and their implications for specification languages. In *Proc. Specifications Reliable Software Conf.*, pp. 58–67, Boston, Mass., Apr. 1979. See also *Proc. Nat. Comput. Conf.*, 1981.

Balzer, R.; Goldman, N.; and Wile, D. Informality in program specifications. *IEEE Trans. Software Eng.*, vol. SE-4, pp. 94–103, Feb. 1978.

Balzer, R.; Green, C.; and Cheatham, T. Software technology in the 1990's using a new paradigm. *Computer*, pp. 39–45, Nov. 1983.

Bauer, F. L. Programming as an evolutionary process. In *Proc. Second Int. Conf. Software Eng.*, pp. 223–234, Oct 1976.

Bell, T. E., and Bixler, D. C. A flow-oriented requirements statement language. In *Proc. Symp. Comput. Software Eng.* MRI Symp. Series. Brooklyn, N. Y.: Polytechnic Press, 1976. See also TRW-SS-76-02, TRW Software Series.

Cohen, D. Symbolic execution of the Gist specification language. In *Proc. Eighth Int. Joint Conf. Artif. Intell., IJCAI-83,* pp. 17–20, 1983.

Cohen, D., and Goldman, N. Efficient compilation of virtual database specifications. Jan. 1985.

———. *AP5 Manual.* Inform. Sci. Inst., Univ. Southern Calif., Marina del Rey, draft, 1985.

Feather, M. *Formal specification of a real system.* Working paper, Nov. 21, 1980a.

———. *Formal specification of a source-data maintenance system.* Working paper, Nov. 21, 1980b.

———. *Package router description and four specifications.* Working paper, Dec. 1980c.

———. *Language support for the specification and development of composite systems.* Draft, Jan. 1985.

Goldman, N. *AP3 Reference Manual.* Inform. Sci. Inst., Univ. Southern Calif., Marina del Rey, 1983a.

Goldman, N. M. *Three dimensions of design development.* Inform. Sci. Inst., Univ. Southern Calif., Marina del Rey, tech. rep. RS-83-2, July 1983b.

Goldman, N., and Wile, D. *Gist language description.* Draft, 1980.

Green, C.; Luckham, D.; Balzer, R.; Cheatham, T.; and Rich, C. *Report on a knowledge-based software assistant.* Rome Air Develop. Cent. tech. rep. RADC-TR-83-195, Aug. 1983.

Kowalski, R. *Logic for Problem Solving.* Amsterdam, The Netherlands: Elsevier North-Holland, 1979.

London, P., and Feather, M. S. Implementing Specification Freedoms. Inform. Sci. Inst., Univ. Southern Calif., Marina del Rey, Calif., tech. rep. RR-81-100. See also *Sci. Comput. Programming,* 1982.

Mostow, J. Why are design derivations hard to replay? To be published in *Machine Learning: A Guide to Current Research,* T. Mitchell, J. Carbonell, and R. Michalski, eds. Hingham, Mass.: Kluwer, 1986.

———. Automating program speedup by deciding what to cache. In *Proc. 9th Int. Joint. Conf. Artif. Intell.,* 1985.

Swartout, W. *Producing explanations and justifications of expert consulting systems.* Mass. Inst. Technol., Cambridge, tech. rep. 251, 1981.

———. Gist English generator. In *Proc. Nat. Conf. Artif. Intell. AAAI-82,* 1982.

———. Explainable expert systems. In *Proc. MEDCOMP-83,* Oct. 1983a.

———. The Gist behavior explainer. In *Proc. Nat. Conf. Artif. Intell., AAAI-83,* Marina del Ray, Calif.: Inform. Sci. Inst., Univ. Southern Calif., 1983b. See also Inst. Inform. Sci., RS-83-3.

———. XPLAIN: A system for creating and explaining expert consulting systems. *Artif. Intell.,* vol. 21, no. 3, pp. 285–325, Sept. 1983c. See also RS-83-4, Inst. Inform. Sci., Univ. Southern Calif., Marina del Rey.

Wile, D. *POPART: Producer of Parsers and Related Tools, System Builders' Manual.* Marina del Ray, Calif.: Inform. Sci. Inst., Univ. Southern Calif., 1981.

———. Program development: Formal explanations of implementations. *Commun., ACM,* pp. 902–911, 1983. See also ISI RR-82-99.

CHAPTER 15

FORMALIZING REUSABLE SOFTWARE COMPONENTS IN THE PROGRAMMER'S APPRENTICE

CHARLES RICH *and* **RICHARD C. WATERS**
The Artificial Intelligence Laboratory
Massachusetts Institute of Technology

There has been a long-standing desire in computer science for a way of collecting and using libraries of standard software components. Unfortunately, there has been only limited success in actually doing this. The lack of success stems not from any resistance to the idea, nor from any lack of trying, but rather from the difficulty of choosing an appropriate formalism for representing components.

15.1 THE WIDE VARIETY OF COMPONENTS

The biggest problem one faces when developing a formalization for components is that there are many different kinds of things that it would be beneficial to express as components. Essentially, any kind of knowledge shared between distinct programs is a candidate to become a reusable component.

313

As an illustration of the diversity of potential components, consider the following six examples. In each case, it is important to consider not only what information is contained in the component, but also the kinds of information that are not properly part of the component.

Matrix add — the algorithm for adding together two matrices. This algorithm is independent of the data representation for the matrices and the type of matrix elements.

Stack — the stack data structure and its associated operations PUSH and POP. Both the representation and the operations are independent of the type of stack element.

Filter positive — the idea of selecting the positive elements of a temporal sequence of quantities available in a loop. For example, in the following fragmentary loop, the if statement implements a filter positive.

```
do ...
  X = ...;
  if X>0 then ... X ...;
end;
```

This idea is independent of the type of sequence element and the sequence creation method. In particular, the idea is applicable to both loops and recursive programs.

Master file system — the idea of having a cluster of programs (reports, updates, audits, etc.) that operate on a single *master* file that is the sole repository for information about some topic. This idea is essentially a set of constraints on the programs and how they interact with the file. It is independent of the kind of data to be stored in the file and the details of the computation to be performed by the programs.

Deadlock free — the idea that a set of asynchronously interacting programs have the property that they are guaranteed not to reach a state where each program is blocked waiting for some other program to act. This idea places restrictions on the ways in which the programs can interact. However, it is independent of the details of computations to be performed by the programs.

Move invariant — the idea that the computation of an expression can be moved from inside a scope of repetitive execution to outside the repetitive scope as long as it has no side effects and all of the values it references are constants within the repetitive scope. This idea is independent of the specific computation being performed by the expression and by the rest of the repetitive scope. In addition, the idea is applicable to both loops and recursive programs.

The example components above differ from each other along many dimensions. *Matrix add* is primarily a computational component that specifies a particular combination of operations, while *stack* is a data component that primarily specifies a particular combination of data objects. *Matrix add* and *stack* also differ in that *matrix add* is a concrete algorithm while *stack* is much more of an abstract concept. Another dimension of difference between components is that while *matrix add* can be used in a program as a simple subunit, *filter positive* is fragmentary and must be combined with fragments that generate and use temporal sequences before it can perform a useful computation.

The first three components are all low-level, localized units. In contrast, *master file system* and *deadlock free* are high-level, diffuse concepts that correspond more closely to sets of constraints than to computational units. These two components differ in that *master file system* is a relatively straightforward set of constraints that can be satisfied individually, while *deadlock free* is a property of an entire system of programs and critically depends on each detail of the interaction between the programs.

Move invariant differs from all of the other components in that it is an optimization achieved by a standardized transformation on programs rather than a standardized computation performed by programs.

15.2 DESIDERATA FOR A FORMALIZATION

Many properties are required of a formalization in order for it to be an effective representation for reusable components. The following five desiderata stand out as being of particular importance.

Expressiveness — The formalism must be capable of expressing as many different kinds of components as possible.

Convenient combinability — The methods of combining components must be easy to implement and the properties of combinations should be evident from the properties of the parts.

Semantic soundness — The formalism must be based on a mathematical foundation that allows correctness conditions to be stated for the library of components.

Machine manipulability — It must be possible to manipulate the formalism effectively using computer tools.

Programming language independence — The formalism should not be dependent on the syntax of any particular programming language.

Given the wide range of components that it would be useful to represent, the expressiveness of a formalization is paramount. Though hard to assess, an important aspect of this is *convenience*. It is not sufficient that a formalism merely be *capable* of representing a given component. To be truly useful, the formalization must be able to represent the component in a straightforward way that supports the other desiderata rather than representing it via a circumlocution that impedes the other desiderata.

Convenient combination properties are also essential, since they are the way in which components are in fact reused. An important part of this is the desire for *fine granularity* in the representation. The goal is to have each component embody only a single idea or design decision so that users have the maximum possible freedom to combine them as they choose.

A firm semantic basis is needed for a good formalization so that it is possible to be certain of what is being represented by a given component and certain that the combination process preserves the key properties of components. The semantic basis does not need to make totally automatic verification possible; although it is less convenient, machine-aided (or even manual) verification of library components is sufficient in many situations.

Machine manipulability of a formalization is a key issue. There are thousands of programming ideas that it would be useful to express as components. In order to be able to deal effectively with such a large library, tools need to be developed to support the automatic creation, modification, selection, and combination of components.

A major problem with previous formalisms has been the focus on existing programming languages as the basis for defining reusable components, when there are in fact important differences between the original goals of these programming languages and the goals of work on reusable components. Existing programming languages are designed primarily to express complete programs in a form that is easily readable by the programmer and that can be effectively executed by a machine. In contrast, the challenge in reusability is to express the fragmentary and abstract components out of which complete programs are built.

The most obvious benefit of a language-independent formalism is that it makes it possible to represent components in such a way that they can be reused in many different language environments. Another point of equal importance is that in general, a language-dependent formalism forces components to be represented in terms of specific control flow and data flow constructs. These constructs are typically not an essential part of the component and may limit the way it can be combined with other components. For example, if you specify the PUSH operation for a stack in a language-dependent way, you typically have to specify particular variable names to be used and whether the operation should be coded in-line or out-of-line when it is used.

15.3 APPROACHES TO FORMALIZATION

The following sections discuss a number of approaches to the formalization of components. (For a more in-depth discussion see the articles in [Rich and Waters, 1986], many of which are referenced individually in this chapter.) The relative strengths and weaknesses of the approaches are evaluated in the light of the five desiderata. The central theme that ties the sections to-gether is the search for formalisms capable of expressing the wide range of components desired without sacrificing the other desiderata.   Figure 15.1 summarizes graphically the major flow of ideas between the approaches discussed.

As a point of comparison for other formalisms, one must consider free-form English text. Much of the knowledge that needs to be formalized is already captured informally in the vocabulary of programmers and in text-books on programming (e.g., [Aho *et al.*, 1974; Knuth, 1968]). The great strength of English text is expressiveness. It is capable of representing any kind of component.   Moreover, it is programming language independent. Unfortunately, English text does not satisfy any of the other desiderata. There is no theory of how to combine textual fragments together; there is no seman-tic basis that makes it possible to determine whether a piece of English text means what you think it means; and free-form English text is not machine manipulable in any significant way.

FIGURE 15.1
APPROACHES TO FORMALIZATION

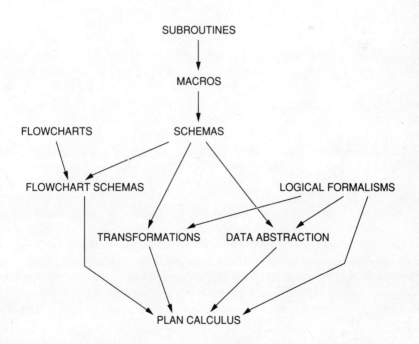

15.3.1 Subroutines

Subroutines have many advantages as a representation for components. They can be easily combined by writing programs that call them. They are machine manipulable in that high-level language compilers and linkage editors directly support their combination. Furthermore, they have a firm semantic basis via the semantics of the programming language they are written in.

Unfortunately, subroutines are limited in their expressiveness. They are really only convenient for expressing localized computational algorithms, such as *matrix add*. They cannot represent data components, such as *stack*, fragmentary components such as *filter positive*, diffuse high-level components such as *master file system*, or transformational components, such as *move invariant*. In addition, they lack fineness of granularity. It is difficult to write a subroutine without gratuitously specifying numerous details that are not properly part of the component. For example, in most languages, there is no convenient way to write a subroutine representing *matrix add* without specifying the data representation for the matrices and the numbers in them.

15.3.2 Macros

A subroutine specifies a fixed piece of program text corresponding to a component. The only variability allowed is in the arguments passed to the subroutine. In contrast, a macro specifies an arbitrary computation that is used to create a piece of program text corresponding to a use of a component. Due to the provision for arbitrary computation, macros are a considerable improvement over subroutines in expressiveness. They can be used to represent data components and fragmentary components. In addition, they can represent components at a much finer granularity. For example, it is straightforward to write a macro that represents *matrix add* independently of the data structures it operates on. Note however, that macros are still not suited to represent diffuse components or transformational ones.

Like subroutines, macros are machine manipulable in that macro processors directly support the evaluation of macro calls and the integration of the resulting program text into the program as a whole. Unfortunately, macros are less satisfactory than subroutines in other respects. Though macro calls are combined syntactically in essentially the same way as subroutine calls, their combination properties are not as simple. For example, since a macro can perform arbitrary computation utilizing its calling form in order to create the resulting program text, there is no guarantee that nested macro calls will operate as they are intended. The macro writer must take extreme care in order to ensure that flexible combination is possible. Unfortunately, this militates against the increased expressiveness that is the primary advantage of macros.

The paramount problem with macros is that they lack any firm semantic basis. Because they allow arbitrary computation, it is very difficult to verify that a macro accurately represents a given component. It is even more difficult to show that a pair of macros can be combined without destructive interaction.

15.3.3 Program Schemas

There has been a considerable amount of theoretical investigation into the benefits of program schemas as a vehicle for representing components [Basu and Misra, 1976; Gerhart, 1975; Wirth, 1973]. Program schemas are essentially templates with holes in them that can be filled in with user-supplied program text. As such, they can be viewed as a compromise between subroutines and macros. The main improvement of program schemas over macros is that, like subroutines, they have a firm semantic foundation in the semantics of the programming language they are written in, and their combination properties are relatively straightforward.

There has not been very much activity directed towards creating an actual programming environment incorporating a library of program schemas. However, there is no reason to believe that program schemas are not at least as machine manipulable as macros. For example, one could create a programming environment supporting program schemas by taking a standard macro processor and limiting the macros that could be written to ones that were essentially program schemas.

Unfortunately, though program schemas are an improvement in expressiveness over subroutines, they are significantly less expressive than macros. Like macros, program schemas are of some use in representing data components, such as *stack,* and can represent components at a finer granularity than subroutines. In addition, they could be used to represent *matrix add* independently of the representation for the matrices it operates on. However, unlike macros, program schemas cannot in general be used to represent fragmentary components such as *filter positive.* Going beyond this, they are no more useful than macros at representing diffuse or transformational components.

15.3.4 Flowcharts and Flowchart Schemas

A limitation shared by subroutines, macros, and program schemas is programming language dependence. One way to alleviate this problem would be to write components in a programming language-independent representation, such as a flowchart. Flowcharts use boxes and control flow arrows in order to specify control flow independently of any particular control flow construct. Similarly, data flow arrows can be used to represent data flow independently of any particular data flow construct [Dennis, 1974].

A flowchart using data and control flow arrows is basically equivalent to a subroutine and has the same level of expressiveness. Through analogy with program schemas one can gain additional expressiveness by using flowchart schemas [Ianov, 1960; Manna, 1974]—flowchart templates with holes in them where other flowcharts can be inserted. Just as a programming language can be given a rigorous semantic foundation, a flowchart language can be given a semantic foundation to serve as a semantic basis for components. In addition, flowcharts and flowchart schemas can be combined together in the same semantically clean way that subroutines and program schemas can be.

To date, flowcharts with data and control flow arrows have primarily been used as a documentation and design aid and have not been given much machine support. However, there is no reason they cannot be represented in a machine-manipulable form and used as part of a programming environment. All that is needed is modules to translate back and forth between flowcharts and various programming languages.

Flowcharts and flowchart schemas are a significant improvement over subroutines and program schemas in that they are programming language-independent. However, with regard to the other desiderata, they are basically identical to subroutines and program schemas. In particular, they are no more expressive. As a result, they are still not fully satisfactory as a representation for reusable components.

15.3.5 Logical Formalisms

With the exception of some macros, the formalisms discussed previously are all *algorithmic* in that they represent a component by giving an example (or template) of it in a programming (or flowchart) language. Using these formalisms, the only way a component can be used is by placing it somewhere in a program. This fundamentally limits the expressiveness of these formalisms. They can only represent localized algorithmic components because the languages used are only capable of representing algorithms and the way the components are used requires them to be localized.

The extensive work on specifying the semantics of programming languages suggests a completely different approach to the problem of specifying components—using logical formalisms (e.g., the predicate calculus) to represent components. A key advantage of logical formalisms is semantic soundness. (In the role of providing a semantic basis for programming languages, logical formalisms are the ultimate semantic basis for all the formalisms already discussed.) An implicit part of this is that logical specifications must be provided for components so that they can be verified (by hand if necessary).

Another important advantage of logical formalisms is in the area of expressiveness. In contrast to the algorithmic formalisms, logical formalisms have no trouble representing diffuse, high-level components such as *master file system* and *deadlock free*. The usefulness of such components is enhanced by the fact that logical formalisms also have very convenient combination properties. Specifically, the theory generated by the union of two axiom systems is always either the union of the theories of the two component systems or a contradiction, but never some third, unanticipated theory. An additional advantage of logical formalisms is that they are inherently programming language independent.

However, logical formalisms are quite cumbersome when it comes to representing an algorithmic component such as *matrix add* (as opposed to representing the specification for an algorithmic component). Given a component such as *stack,* which combines some nonalgorithmic aspects with some algorithmic aspects, logical formalisms are convenient for the former, but not the latter. This suggests that logical formalisms are best used as an adjunct to, rather than a replacement for, algorithmic formalisms.

The greatest weakness of logical formalisms is in the area of machine manipulability. It is not hard to represent logical formulas in a machine-manipulable way. However, at the current state of the art, practical automatic theorem provers are only capable of relatively simple logical deductions. As a result, it is hard to do anything useful with logical formulas. For example, if a programming system were to be based on the combination of components represented as logical formulas, the system would need to have a module that could produce program text corresponding to sets of logical formulas. Unfortunately, although this kind of automatic programming has been demonstrated on small examples [Manna and Waldinger, 1980a] it has not yet progressed to the point where it is at all practical.

This problem again suggests that it might be fruitful to combine logical and algorithmic formalisms in order to reduce the amount of deduction that must be performed. Unfortunately, it is not clear how helpful this can be with regard to components, such as *master file system* and *deadlock free,* which have little or no algorithmic aspects. Presumably, if one includes *deadlock free* as one of the components describing a set of programs, one would like the programming system to be of some assistance in producing programs safe from deadlock, or at the very least, to be able to detect when deadlock is possible. However, it is not clear that even the latter goal is achievable given the current state of the art of automatic theorem proving.

15.3.6 Data Abstraction

An interesting area of inquiry that has combined logical and algorithmic formalisms is data abstraction. The contribution of data abstractions is that they extend the expressiveness of algorithmic formalizations into the realm of components with data structure aspects. For example, data abstraction can be used to represent *stack* in full generality and to represent *matrix add* without specifying the data representation to be used for the matrices.

A considerable amount of research has been done on how to state the specifications for a data structure and its associated access functions [Goguen *et al.,* 1978; Guttag *et al.,* 1978; Liskov and Zilles, 1977b]. This provides a semantic basis for data abstractions and for methods of combining them.

In addition, languages such as Alphard [Wulf *et al.*, 1976], CLU [Liskov *et al.*, 1977], and Ada [U.S. Defense Dept., 1983] have been developed with constructs that directly support data abstraction. This demonstrates the ease with which data abstractions can be represented in a machine-manipulable (though language-dependent) form.

15.3.7 Program Transformations

Neither algorithmic nor logical formalisms are particularly well suited to representing components like *move invariant*. These components (and many other kinds as well) can be represented as program transformations [Balzer, 1981; Broy and Pepper, 1981; Standish *et al.*, 1976].

A transformation matches against some section of program text (or more usually its parse tree) and replaces it by a new section of program text (or parse tree). A typical transformation has three parts. It has a pattern that matches against the program in order to determine where to apply the transformation. It has a set of logical applicability conditions that further restrict the places where the transformation can be applied. Finally, it has a (usually procedural) action that creates the new program section based on the old section. Note that when applied to small localized sections of a program, program transformations are very much the same as macros.

An important aspect of program transformations is the idea of a *wide-spectrum language*. In contrast to ordinary high-level languages, wide-spectrum languages contain syntactic and semantic extensions that are not directly executable. In some cases these higher-level constructs have a semantics independent of the transformation system, but often they are defined only in terms of the transformations that convert them into executable constructs.

The most interesting contribution of transformations is that they view program construction as a process. Rather than viewing a program solely as a static artifact that may be decomposed into components the way a house is made up of a floor, roof, and walls, transformations view a program as evolving through a series of construction steps that utilize components that may not be visible in the final program, just as the construction of a house requires the use of scaffolding and other temporary structures. This point of view enables transformations to express components, such as *move invariant*, that are common steps in the construction of a program rather than common steps in the execution of a program.

Another important aspect of transformations is that they can be combined quite differently from the other formalisms. As mentioned above, many simple transformations are basically just macros that specify how to implement particular high-level constructs in a wide-spectrum language. These transformations are only triggered when instances of their associated high-level constructs appear; thus they only operate where they are explicitly requested, and they combine in much the same way as macros.

However, other transformations are much less localized in the way they operate. For example, a transformation representing *move invariant* would have applicability conditions (e.g., that the expression is invariant) that must look at large parts of the program. In addition, such transformations are not intended to be applied only when explicitly requested by the user. Rather, they are intended to be used whenever they become applicable for any reason. This makes powerful synergistic interaction between transformations possible.

Unfortunately, if transformations are allowed to contain arbitrary computation in their actions, they have the same difficulty with regard to semantic soundness and convenient combinability that macros have. The transformation writer has to take great care in order to ensure that the interaction between transformations will in fact be synergistic rather than antagonistic. In order to have a semantic basis, a transformation must include a logical description of what it is doing. One important way that this has been done is to focus on transformations that are correctness preserving—ones that, from a logical perspective, do nothing.

A number of experimental systems have demonstrated that transformations are machine manipulable [Barstow, 1979; Cheatham, 1984; Darlington, 1981]. All of these systems support the automatic application of transformations. Some of them go beyond this to attack the harder problem of automatically selecting the transformations to apply.

A difficulty with transformations is that, as generally supported, they are very much programming language dependent. This not only limits the portability of components represented as transformations, it also limits the way transformations can be stated by requiring that every intermediate state of a program being transformed fit into the syntax of the programming language. One way to alleviate these problems would be to apply transformations to a programming language-independent representation, such as flowcharts.

15.4 THE PLAN CALCULUS

As part of the Programmer's Apprentice project, a formalism has been developed that seeks to satisfy all of the desiderata by combining several of the techniques previously discussed. In this formalism, called the Plan Calculus [Rich, 1981], components (which are referred to as *clichés*) are represented as plans. Plans contain three kinds of information: *plan diagrams, logical annotation,* and *overlays*.

A plan diagram contains information about the algorithmic aspects of a plan. In order to achieve language independence, plan diagrams are represented as hierarchical data flow schemas. In a plan diagram, computations are represented as boxes with input and output ports, while control flow and data flow are both represented using arcs between ports. In addition, plan diagrams are hierarchical—a box in a diagram can contain an entire subdiagram.

Furthermore, the diagrams are schematic—they can contain empty boxes (called roles) to be filled in later.

As an example of a plan diagram, Fig. 15.2 shows the algorithmic part of a plan for computing the absolute value of a number. In the figure, data flow arcs are drawn as solid lines and control flow arcs as hatched lines. The diagram is composed of an operation box (**action**) whose output is the negation of its input, a test box (**if**) that splits control based on whether its input is negative, and a join box (**end**) that rejoins the control split by the test. The output of the join is determined by the control flow path used to enter it.

The nonalgorithmic aspects of a plan are represented using predicate calculus assertions. These assertions are attached as annotations on the plan diagram. Each box in a plan diagram is annotated with a set of preconditions and postconditions. In addition, logical constraints between roles are used to limit the way the roles can be filled in. Finally, dependency links summarize a

FIGURE 15.2
AN EXAMPLE PLAN

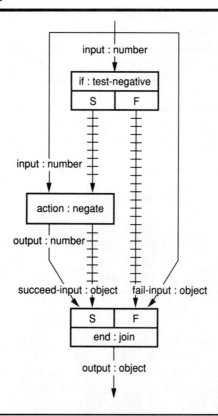

proof that the specifications of the plan as a whole follow from the specifications of the inner boxes and the way these boxes are connected. Components, such as *master file system* and *deadlock free,* that have little or no algorithmic aspect are represented by plans consisting almost entirely of predicate calculus assertions with little or no diagrammatic information.

In order to unify the concept of a plan for an algorithm with the concept of a plan for a data structure, the basic flowchartlike ideas behind plan diagrams are extended so that plan diagrams can contain parts that correspond to data objects as well as to subcomputations. Data parts can be left unspecified as data roles, and they can be annotated with specifications, constraints, and dependencies. Given these extensions, plans are capable of representing the same kinds of information as data abstraction mechanisms. For example, the plan for *stack* consists of a number of logically interrelated plan diagrams, one of which represents the stack data object and the rest of which represent the operations on a stack.

The transformational aspects of a plan are represented as *overlays.* An overlay is a mapping between two plans. It specifies a set of correspondences between the roles of the plans. Overlays are similar to transformations in which both the left- and right-hand sides are plans. However, overlays differ from program transformations in two ways: They are bidirectional, and their actions are declarative as opposed to procedural. The fact that overlays are bidirectional means that, like grammar rules, they can be used for both analysis and synthesis. The fact that overlays are totally declarative gives them a firm semantic basis and makes it easier to reason about them as opposed to merely using them.

Figure 15.3 shows an example of an overlay that specifies how to transform a tail-recursive program that accumulates a value "on the way down" into a recursive program that accumulates the same result "on the way up," and vice versa. This overlay captures the commonality between the programs SUM_UP and SUM_DOWN shown below.

```
SUM_DOWN(L) = SUM_DOWN2(L,0);
SUM_DOWN2(L,S) = if EMPTY(L) then S else SUM_DOWN2(TAIL(L),S+HEAD(L));
SUM_UP(L) = if EMPTY(L) then 0 else SUM_UP(TAIL(L))+HEAD(L);
```

The plan diagrams in Fig. 15.3 are drawn in the same way as in Fig. 15.2. However, three new features are shown. Dashed boxes are used to group diagrams hierarchically. Looping lines are used to indicate that a dashed box in a diagram is identical to the dashed box containing it. (The right and left diagrams in the figure are both infinite.) Finally, hooked lines are used to indicate the overlay relationship between the two diagrams.

The plan on the left side of Fig. 15.3 represents accumulation of a result on the way up, while the plan on the right side of the figure represents tail-recursive accumulation. The four hooked lines specify correspondences. Unlabeled correspondences are equalities. The initialization (**init**), accumu-

FIGURE 15.3
AN EXAMPLE OVERLAY

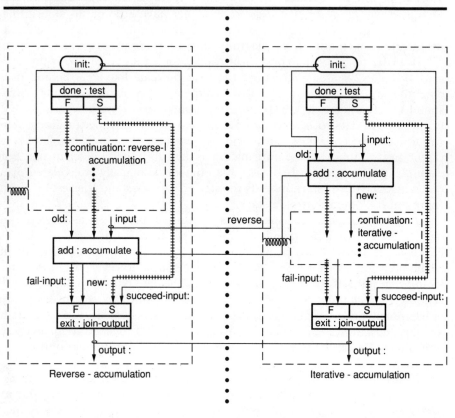

Reverse - accumulation   Iterative - accumulation

lation (**add**), and output values in the two plans correspond directly. The
correspondence labeled **reverse** is more complex. It specifies that the order
of the input elements on the right-hand side is the reverse of the order of the
input elements on the left-hand side. (The storage of elements on the function
invocation stack performs the reversal.) A logical assertion (not shown in the
figure) indicates that the final output in the two plans is not equal unless the
add operation is associative.

In order to give plan diagrams a precise definition, each aspect of plan
diagrams is defined in terms of a version of the situational calculus [Green,
1969]. Manna and Waldinger have used the situational calculus in a similar way to specify certain problematic features of programming languages
[Manna and Waldinger, 1980b].

Since the situational calculus is essentially just predicate calculus with
some conventions applied, a plan diagram can be viewed as the abbreviation

for a set of predicate calculus assertions. Given that the logical annotation in a plan consists directly of predicate calculus assertions and that overlays are just mappings between plans, this implies that everything in a plan can be reduced to a set of logical assertions.

In summary, the Plan Calculus combines the expressiveness of hierarchical data flow schemas, logical formalisms, and transformations. Given that each of these mechanisms is programming language independent, the Plan Calculus is language independent as well. The fact that plans can, in principle, be translated into predicate calculus gives the Plan Calculus the same kind of rigorous semantic foundation that any logical formalism has. In addition, the combination of two plans amounts semantically to the union of axioms and is therefore convenient from a theoretical viewpoint. Finally, since any plan can be represented as a set of assertions, the Plan Calculus is, in principle, machine manipulable by an automatic reasoning system. The only question that remains unanswered is whether the Plan Calculus is machine manipulable in practice.

15.4.1 A Hybrid Reasoning System for Plans

The weakness of current automatic reasoning systems implies that general-purpose deduction cannot be used by itself to manipulate a complex representation, such as the Plan Calculus. Experimentation has shown that a hybrid system that combines special-purpose techniques with general-purpose logical reasoning is required.

Special-purpose representations and algorithms are essential to avoid the combinatorial explosions that typically occur in general-purpose reasoning systems. On the other hand, logic-based reasoning is very valuable when used under strict control as the "glue" between inferences made in different special-purpose representations.

A hybrid reasoning system called CAKE [Rich, 1985; Feldman and Rich, 1986] is being implemented that is tailored specifically for reasoning about plans. Figure 15.4 shows the architecture of CAKE. The bottom layers of CAKE

FIGURE 15.4
THE LAYERS OF CAKE

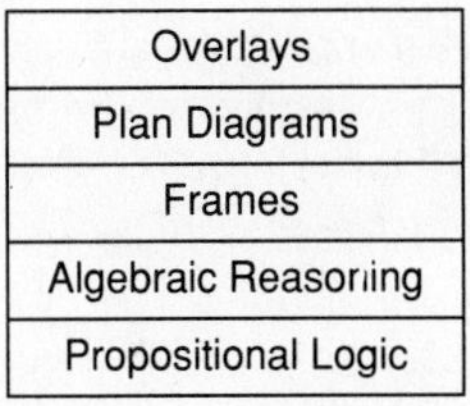

Overlays
Plan Diagrams
Frames
Algebraic Reasoning
Propositional Logic

support general-purpose logical reasoning while the top two layers support special-purpose reasoning about plans.

Although the information in a plan that is represented by means of plan diagrams and overlays could be converted into logical assertions, it is for the most part not converted. Rather, this information is represented in terms of graphical data structures that can be manipulated by means of special-purpose procedures. For example, the combination of plan diagrams can be performed by substituting one diagram into the other. General-purpose reasoning is necessary only for the much simpler task of checking whether the relevant preconditions and constraints permit the substitution to take place.

At the current time, the three lowest layers of CAKE have been completed. Figure 15.5 is a short transcript of some of the facilities provided. (Line numbers in the ensuing discussion refer to Fig. 15.5.)

The propositional layer of CAKE provides three principal facilities. First, it automatically performs simple one-step deductions (lines 1–3). Second, it acts as a recording medium for dependencies and thus supports explanation (line 3) and retraction (lines 4–5). Third, this layer detects contradictions (lines 6–7). Contradictions are represented explicitly in such a way that reasoning can continue with other information not involved in the contradiction. This is important for allowing a user to postpone dealing with problems.

FIGURE 15.5
A TRANSCRIPT SHOWING CAKE IN ACTION

```
1> (Assertq P)
2> (Assertq (Implies P Q))
3> (Whyq Q)
   Q is TRUE by Modus Ponens from:
      1. (IMPLIES P Q) is TRUE as a premise.
      2. P is TRUE as a premise.
4> (Retractq P)
5> (Whyq Q)
   I don't know whether or not Q is true.
6> (Assertq (And P (not Q)))
   >>Contradiction: There is a conflict between the premises:
      1. (AND P (NOT Q)) is TRUE.
      2. (IMPLIES P Q) is TRUE.
   s-A, Resume:    Ignore this contradiction.
   s-B:            Retract one of the premises.
7> s-B Retract one of the premises.
   Premise to retract: 1
   Retracting (AND P (NOT Q)) being TRUE...
   #<Node (AND P (NOT Q)): False>
8> (Assertq (= I J))
9> (Whyq (= (F I) (F J)))
   (= (F I) (F J)) is TRUE by Equality from:
      1. (= I J) is TRUE as a premise.
10> (Assertq (Transitive R))
```

FIGURE 15.5 (*Cont.*)

```
11> (Assertq (R W X)) (Assertq (R X Y)) (Assertq (R Y Z))
12> (Whyq (R W Z))
    (R W Z) is TRUE by Transitivity from:
       1. (R W X) is TRUE as a premise.
       2. (R X Y) is TRUE as a premise.
       3. (R Y Z) is TRUE as a premise.
       4. (TRANSITIVE R) is TRUE as a premise.
13> (Assertq (Subset A B))
14> (Assertq (Member X A))
15> (Whyq (Member X B))
    (MEMBER X B) is TRUE by Subsumption from:
       1. (SUBSET A B) is TRUE as a premise.
       2. (MEMBER X A) is TRUE as a premise.
16> (Deftype Address (:Specializes Number))
17> (Deframe Interrupt (:Roles (Location Address) Program))
18> (Deframe Device (:Roles (Transmit Address) (Receive Address)))
19> (Deframe Interface
       (:Roles (Target Device) (From Interrupt) (To Interrupt))
       (:Constraints (= (Location ?From) (Receive ?Target))
                     (= (Location ?To) (Transmit ?Target))))
20> (FInstantiate 'Interface :Name 'K7)
21> (FPut (>> 'K7 'Target 'Receive) 777777)
22> (FGet (>> 'K7 'From 'Location))
    777777
23> (Why ...)
    (= 777777 (LOCATION (FROM K7))) is TRUE by Equality from:
       1. (= (LOCATION (FROM K7))
             (RECEIVE (TARGET K7))) is TRUE.
       2. (= (RECEIVE (TARGET K7)) 777777) is TRUE as a premise.
```

The algebraic layer of CAKE is composed of special-purpose decision procedures for congruence closure, common algebraic properties of operators (i.e., commutativity, associativity, and transitivity), and the algebra of sets. The congruence closure algorithm in this layer determines whether or not terms are equal by substitution of equal subterms (lines 8–9). The decision procedure for transitivity (lines 10–12) determines when elements of a binary relation follow by transitivity from other elements. The algebra of sets (lines 13–15) involves the theory of membership, subset, union, intersection, and complements. (The propositional layer and the congruence closure algorithm of the algebraic layer are derived from McAllester's Reasoning Utility Package [McAllester, 1982].)

The frames layer, which is built using facilities from the layers below it, supports the conventional frame notions of inheritance (:Specializes in line 16), slots (:Roles in lines 17–19), and instances (line 20). A notable feature of CAKE's frame system is that constraints are implemented in a general way. For example, the definition of an Interface (line 19) has constraints between the roles of the frames filling its roles. When an instance of this frame is created (line 20) and a particular value (777777) is put into one of its roles (line 21), the same value can be retrieved from the other constrained role (line 22). This propagation is not achieved by ad hoc procedures, but by the operation of the underlying logical reasoning system, including dependencies (line 23).

It should be realized that CAKE's general-purpose reasoning capabilities are relatively weak. Therefore, the practicality of CAKE as a tool for manipulating the Plan Calculus depends on whether most of the information in a plan is represented diagrammatically as opposed to logically. As a result, it is unlikely that CAKE will be able to deal effectively with components, such as *deadlock free*, that have little or no algorithmic aspect and that require complex reasoning. However, it should be able to effectively manipulate all of the other kinds of components cited as examples above.

15.5 THE KNOWLEDGE-BASED EDITOR IN EMACS

The Knowledge-Based Editor in Emacs (KBEmacs) is the demonstration system currently implemented as part of the Programmer's Apprentice project. KBEmacs [Waters, 1985] is a program editor that makes it possible to construct programs rapidly and reliably by combining algorithmic components called *clichés*. From the point of view of the current discussion, the key feature of KBEmacs is that it demonstrates the machine manipulability of plan diagrams.

KBEmacs is implemented on the Symbolics Lisp Machine [*Lisp*, 1984]. Figure 15.6 shows the architecture of the system. KBEmacs maintains two representations for the program being worked on: program text and a plan. KBEmacs is based on a simple, early plan representation that corresponds to the plan diagram portion of the Plan Calculus with the addition of support for procedural constraints. While KBEmacs was under construction, this simple plan representation evolved into the Plan Calculus.

At any moment, the programmer can modify either the program text or the plan. To modify the program text, the programmer can use the standard Emacs-style Lisp Machine editor. This editor supports both text-based and syntax-based program editing. To modify the plan, the programmer can use the *knowledge-based editor* module. This module supports several commands for instantiating and combining components. Each command is supported by a special-purpose procedure that operates directly on the plan representation. The knowledge-based editor also provides support for maintaining the consistency of procedurally represented constraints. However, it does not have any general-purpose reasoning abilities.

The components themselves are represented as plans and stored in the component library. New components can be defined by the user by using a programming language–like representation.

FIGURE 15.6
THE ARCHITECTURE OF KBEMACS

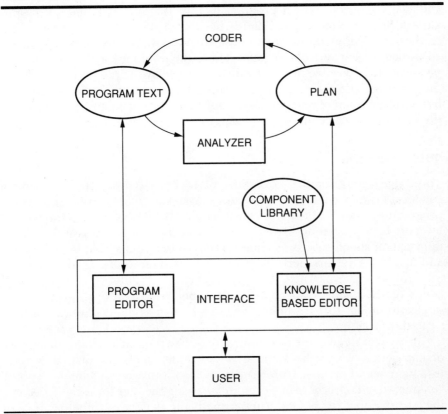

An interface unifies ordinary program editing and knowledge-based editing so that they can both be conveniently accessed through the standard Lisp
Machine editor. The knowledge-based commands are supported as an extension of the standard editor command set and the results of these commands
are communicated to the programmer by altering the program text in the
editor buffer. The effect is the same as if a human assistant were sitting at
the editor modifying the text under the direction of the programmer.

Whenever the plan is modified, the *coder* module is used to create new
program text. The coder operates in three steps. First, it examines the plan
to determine how the control flow should be implemented, that is, where
conditional and looping constructs should be used. Second, it determines
how the data flow should be implemented, that is, when variables should be
used and what names should be used for them. Third, it constructs program
text based on these two decisions and then applies various transformations
to improve the readability of the result. The complexity of the coder stems
not from the need to create correct code (this is relatively easy) but from the
need to create aesthetic code.

Whenever the program text is modified, the *analyzer* module is used to create a new plan. The analyzer is similar to the front end of an optimizing compiler. It operates on a program in four stages. First, the program is parsed. Second, macro expansion is used to express the various constructs of the language in terms of primitive operations. For example, all control constructs are expanded into **gotos**. Third, the resulting intermediate form is processed to determine the basic functions called by the program, the roles in the program, and the data flow and control flow between them. This results in the construction of a simple plan. Fourth, the plan is analyzed to determine the hierarchical structure of the program.

15.5.1 Scenario

To give a feeling for the capabilities of KBEmacs, this section presents a condensed summary of the scenario in [Waters, 1985]. In that scenario, a programmer uses KBEmacs to construct an Ada program in the domain of business data processing. It is assumed that there is a database containing information about various machines (referred to as units) sold by a company and about the repairs performed on each of these units. In the scenario, the programmer constructs a program called UNIT_REPAIR_REPORT, which prints out a report of all of the repairs performed on a given unit. The directions in Fig. 15.7 might be given to a human assistant who was asked to write this program.

A key feature of these directions is that they refer to a significant amount of knowledge, which the assistant is assumed to possess. First, they refer to a number of standard programming algorithms (e.g., "simple report," "enumerating the records in a chain," "querying the user for a key"). Second, they assume that the assistant understands the structure of the database of units and repairs. Another feature of the directions is that, given that the assistant has a precise understanding of the algorithms to be used and of the database, little is left to the assistant's imagination. Essentially every detail of the algorithm is spelled out, including the exact Ada code to use when printing the title.

Using KBEmacs, the commands shown in Fig. 15.8 can be used to construct the program UNIT_REPAIR_REPORT. The Ada program that results from these commands is shown in Fig. 15.9.

FIGURE 15.7
HYPOTHETICAL DIRECTIONS FOR A HUMAN ASSISTANT

Define a simple report program UNIT_REPAIR_REPORT. Enumerate the chain of repairs associated with a unit record, printing each one. Query the user for the key (UNIT_KEY) of the unit record to start from. Print the title ("Report of Repairs on Unit " & UNIT_KEY). Do not print a summary.

FIGURE 15.8
KBEmacs COMMANDS

Define a simple_report procedure UNIT_REPAIR_REPORT.
Fill the enumerator with a chain_enumeration of UNITS and REPAIRS.
Fill the main_file_key with a query_user_for_key of UNITS.
Fill the title with ("Report of Repairs on Unit " & UNIT_KEY).
Remove the summary.

FIGURE 15.9
THE ADA PROGRAM UNIT_REPAIR_REPORT

```
with CALENDAR, FUNCTIONS, MAINTENANCE_FILES, TEXT_IO;
use CALENDAR, FUNCTIONS, MAINTENANCE_FILES, TEXT_IO;
procedure UNIT_REPAIR_REPORT is
    use DEFECT_IO, REPAIR_IO, UNIT_IO, INT_IO;
    CURRENT_DATE: constant STRING := FORMAT_DATE(CLOCK);
    DEFECT: DEFECT_TYPE;
    REPAIR: REPAIR_TYPE;
    REPAIR_INDEX: REPAIR_INDEX_TYPE;
    REPORT: TEXT_IO.FILE_TYPE;
    TITLE: STRING(1..33);
    UNIT: UNIT_TYPE;
    UNIT_KEY: UNIT_KEY_TYPE;
    procedure CLEAN_UP is
        begin
            SET_OUTPUT(STANDARD_OUTPUT);
            CLOSE(DEFECTS); CLOSE(REPAIRS); CLOSE(UNITS); CLOSE(REPORT);
        exception
            when STATUS_ERROR => return;
        end CLEAN_UP;
begin
    OPEN(DEFECTS, IN_FILE, DEFECTS_NAME); OPEN(REPAIRS, IN_FILE, REPAIRS_NAME);
    OPEN(UNITS, IN_FILE, UNITS_NAME); CREATE(REPORT, OUT_FILE, "report.txt");
    loop
        begin
            NEW_LINE; PUT("Enter UNIT Key: "); GET(UNIT_KEY);
            READ(UNITS, UNIT, UNIT_KEY);
            exit;
        exception
            when END_ERROR => PUT("Invalid UNIT Key"); NEW_LINE;
        end;
    end loop;
    TITLE := "Report of Repairs on Unit" & UNIT_KEY;
    SET_OUTPUT(REPORT);
```

FIGURE 15.9 (*Cont.*)

```
   NEW_LINE(4); SET_COL(20); PUT(CURRENT_DATE);
   NEW_LINE(2); SET_COL(13); PUT(TITLE); NEW_LINE(60);
   READ(UNITS, UNIT, UNIT_KEY); REPAIR_INDEX := UNIT.REPAIR;
   while not NULL_INDEX(REPAIR_INDEX) loop
      READ(REPAIRS, REPAIR, REPAIR_INDEX);
      if LINE > 64 then
         NEW_PAGE; NEW_LINE; PUT("Page: "); PUT(INTEGER(PAGE-1), 3);
         SET_COL(13); PUT(TITLE); SET_COL(61); PUT(CURRENT_DATE); NEW_LINE(2);
         PUT("  Date      Defect    Description/Comment"); NEW_LINE(2);
      end if;
      READ(DEFECTS, DEFECT, REPAIR.DEFECT);
      PUT(FORMAT_DATE(REPAIR.DATE)); SET_COL(13); PUT(REPAIR.DEFECT);
      SET_COL(20); PUT(DEFECT.NAME); NEW_LINE;
      SET_COL(22); PUT(REPAIR.COMMENT); NEW_LINE;
      REPAIR_INDEX := REPAIR.NEXT;
   end loop;
   CLEAN_UP;
exception
   when DEVICE_ERROR | END_ERROR | NAME_ERROR | STATUS_ERROR =>
      CLEAN_UP; PUT("Data Base Inconsistent");
   when others => CLEAN_UP; raise;
end UNIT_REPAIR_REPORT;
```

A key feature of the commands in Fig. 15.8 is that they refer to a number of components known to KBEmacs (*simple-report, chain-enumeration,* and *query-user-for-key*). In addition, they assume an understanding of the structure of the database. (KBEmacs understands the database because it can understand the Ada package that defines the database.) The Fill commands specify how to fill in the roles of the plan for *simple-report*.

Without discussing either the commands or the program produced in any detail, two important observations can be made. First, the commands used are very similar to the hypothetical directions for a human assistant. Second, a set of 5 commands produces a 55-line program. (The program would be even longer if it did not make extensive use of data declarations and functions defined in the packages FUNCTIONS and MAINTENANCE_FILES.)

The KBEmacs commands and the hypothetical directions differ in grammatical form but not in semantic content. This is not surprising in light of the fact that the hypothesized commands were in actuality created by restating the knowledge-based commands in more free-flowing English.

The purpose of this translation was to demonstrate that although the KBEmacs commands may be syntactically awkward, they are not semantically awkward. The commands are neither redundant nor overly detailed. They specify only the basic design decisions underlying the program. There is no reason to believe that any automatic system (or for that matter a person) could be told how to construct the program UNIT_REPAIR_REPORT without being told at least most of the information in the commands shown.

The leverage that KBEmacs applies to the program construction task is illustrated by the order of magnitude difference between the size of the set of commands and the size of the program. A given programmer seems to be able to produce a more or less constant number of lines of code per day regardless of the programming language being used. As a result, there is reason to believe that the order of magnitude size reduction provided by the KBEmacs commands would translate into an order of magnitude reduction in the time required to construct the program. It should be noted that since program construction is only a small part (around 10 percent) of the programming life cycle, this does not translate into an order of magnitude savings in the life cycle as a whole.

Another important advantage of KBEmacs is that using standard components (such as *simple-report* and *chain-enumeration*) enhances the reliability of the programs produced. Since the components known to KBEmacs are intended to be used many times, it is economically justifiable to lavish a great deal of time on them to ensure that they are general-purpose and bug free. This reliability is inherited by the programs that use the standard algorithms.

When using an ordinary program editor, programmers typically make two kinds of errors: picking the wrong algorithms to use and incorrectly instantiating these algorithms (i.e., making mistakes when combining the algorithms and rendering them as appropriate program code). KBEmacs eliminates the second kind of error.

15.5.2 Combining Components

As an illustration of the way KBEmacs supports the combination of components represented as plans, we discuss two steps in the creation of the program in Fig. 15.9.

Figure 15.10 shows the program text produced by KBEmacs after the first command in Fig. 15.8. This code comes almost entirely from the component *simple-report*. This component specifies the high-level structure of a simple reporting program. The component has several roles represented using the notation { ...}.

The *title* role is printed on a title page and, along with the page number, at the top of each succeeding page of the report. The *enumerator* enumerates the elements of some aggregate data structure. The *print-item* is used to print out information about each of the enumerated elements. The *column-headings* are printed at the top of each page of the report to explain the output of the *print-item*. The *summary* prints out some summary information at the end of the report. The *print-item, column-headings,* and *summary* roles are all computations that modify the report file (used as the value of STANDARD_OUTPUT) by sending output to it.

The *enumerator* is different from the other roles in that it is *compound* — consisting of four subroles distributed through the program. Compound roles

FIGURE 15.10

RESULTS OF "DEFINE A SIMPLE_REPORT PROGRAM UNIT_REPAIR_REPORT"

```
with CALENDAR, FUNCTIONS, TEXT_IO;
use CALENDAR, FUNCTIONS, TEXT_IO;
procedure UNIT_REPAIR_REPORT is
   use INT_IO;
   CURRENT_DATE: constant STRING := FORMAT_DATE(CLOCK);
   DATA: {};
   REPORT: TEXT_IO.FILE_TYPE;
   TITLE: STRING(1..{});
   procedure CLEAN_UP is
      begin
         SET_OUTPUT(STANDARD_OUTPUT);
         CLOSE(REPORT);
      exception
         when STATUS_ERROR => return;
      end CLEAN_UP;
begin
   CREATE(REPORT, OUT_FILE, "report.txt");
   TITLE := {the title};
   SET_OUTPUT(REPORT);
   NEW_LINE(4); SET_COL(20); PUT(CURRENT_DATE); NEW_LINE(2);
   SET_COL(13); PUT(TITLE); NEW_LINE(60);
   DATA := {the input structure of the enumerator};
   while not {the empty_test of the enumerator}(DATA) loop
      if LINE > 64 then
         NEW_PAGE; NEW_LINE; PUT("Page: "); PUT(INTEGER(PAGE-1), 3);
         SET_COL(13); PUT(TITLE); SET_COL(61); PUT(CURRENT_DATE); NEW_LINE(2);
         {the column_headings}({CURRENT_OUTPUT, modified});
      end if;
      {the print_item}({CURRENT_OUTPUT, modified},
                       {the element_accessor of the enumerator}(DATA));
      DATA := {the step of the enumerator}(DATA);
   end loop;
   {the summary}({CURRENT_OUTPUT, modified});
   CLEAN_UP;
exception
   when DEVICE_ERROR | END_ERROR | NAME_ERROR | STATUS_ERROR =>
      CLEAN_UP; PUT("Data Base Inconsistent");
   when others => CLEAN_UP; raise;
end UNIT_REPAIR_REPORT;
```

are used when the syntactic limitations of a programming language prevent a logical unit from being expressed as a syntactic unit. To facilitate component combination, the *enumerator* is represented as a single box in the plan for *simple-report*.

The *input structure* of the *enumerator* corresponds to the aggregate structure to be enumerated. The *empty-test* determines whether all of the elements in the aggregate structure have been enumerated and therefore whether the enumeration should be terminated. The *element-accessor* accesses the current element in the aggregate. The *step* steps from one element of the aggregate structure to the next.

There is an additional role of the component *simple-report* that is of particular importance. This role is called the *line-limit* and is used to determine when a page break should be inserted in the report. The presence of this role is not obvious in Fig. 15.10 because it has already been filled in with the default value 64. This value was generated by a constraint.

The most interesting feature of the component *simple-report* is that it contains the constraints shown in Fig. 15.11. The first constraint specifies that the *line-limit* is constrained to be 66 minus the number of lines printed by the *print-item* and the number of lines printed by the *summary*. Under the assumption that there is room for 66 lines on a page of output, the constraint guarantees that whenever the line number is less than or equal to the *line-limit*, there will be room for both the *print-item* and the *summary* to be printed on the current page. Because the *line-limit* role is derived by this constraint, the programmer never has to fill it in explicitly, and the role will be automatically updated whenever either the *print-item* or the *summary* is changed.

The other two constraints specify default values for the *print-item* and *column-headings* roles. The function CORRESPONDING_PRINTING determines what should be used to fill in the *print-item* role based on the type of object being enumerated. The function CORRESPONDING_HEADINGS determines what headings should be used based on the way the *print-item* is filled in.

FIGURE 15.11
CONSTRAINTS IN THE COMPONENT *SIMPLE-REPORT*

```
constraints
   DERIVED(the line_limit,
           66-SIZE_IN_LINES(the print_item)
             -SIZE_IN_LINES(the summary));
   DEFAULT(the print_item,
           CORRESPONDING_PRINTING(the enumerator));
   DEFAULT(the column_headings,
           CORRESPONDING_HEADINGS(the print_item));
end constraints;
```

The functions CORRESPONDING_PRINTING and CORRESPONDING_HEAD-INGS operate in one of two modes. In general, components will have been defined that specify how to print out a given type of object in a report and how to print the corresponding headings. If this is the case, then the functions CORRESPONDING_PRINTING and CORRESPONDING_HEADINGS merely retrieve the appropriate components. However, if there are no such components, then the functions CORRESPONDING_PRINTING and CORRES-PONDING_HEADINGS use a simple program generator to construct appropriate code based on the definition of the type of object in question.

Figure 15.12 shows the program code produced by KBEmacs after the second command in Fig. 15.8. Change indicators in the left margin of the figure indicate the lines where something has changed in comparison with Fig. 15.10. These changes, which result from combining the components *simple-report* and *chain-enumeration,* are spread throughout the program.

The lines marked with 1 indicate changes that come directly from the component *chain-enumeration.* This includes code for each of the subroles of the *enumerator.*

FIGURE 15.12
RESULTS OF "FILL THE ENUMERATOR WITH A CHAIN_ENUMERATION OF ..."

```
5 with CALENDAR, FUNCTIONS, MAINTENANCE_FILES, TEXT_IO;
5 use CALENDAR, FUNCTIONS, MAINTENANCE_FILES, TEXT_IO;
  procedure UNIT_REPAIR_REPORT is
5    use DEFECT_IO, REPAIR_IO, UNIT_IO, INT_IO;
     CURRENT_DATE: constant STRING := FORMAT_DATE(CLOCK);
5    DEFECT: DEFECT_TYPE;
5    REPAIR: REPAIR_TYPE;
5    REPAIR_INDEX: REPAIR_INDEX_TYPE;
     REPORT: TEXT_IO.FILE_TYPE;
     TITLE: STRING(1..{});
5    UNIT: UNIT_TYPE;
     procedure CLEAN_UP is
        begin
           SET_OUTPUT(STANDARD_OUTPUT);
5          CLOSE(DEFECTS); CLOSE(REPAIRS); CLOSE(UNITS); CLOSE(REPORT);
        exception
           when STATUS_ERROR => return;
        end CLEAN_UP;
  begin
2    OPEN(DEFECTS, IN_FILE, DEFECTS_NAME);
1    OPEN(REPAIRS, IN_FILE, REPAIRS_NAME); OPEN(UNITS, IN_FILE, UNITS_NAME);
     CREATE(REPORT, OUT_FILE, "report.txt");
     TITLE := {the title};
     SET_OUTPUT(REPORT);
     NEW_LINE(4); SET_COL(20); PUT(CURRENT_DATE); NEW_LINE(2);
     SET_COL(13); PUT(TITLE); NEW_LINE(60);
```

FIGURE 15.12 (*Cont.*)

```
1    READ(UNITS, UNIT, {the main_file_key});
1    REPAIR_INDEX := UNIT.REPAIR;
1    while not NULL_INDEX(REPAIR_INDEX) loop
1      READ(REPAIRS, REPAIR, REPAIR_INDEX);
4      if LINE > 63 then
           NEW_PAGE; NEW_LINE; PUT("Page: "); PUT(INTEGER(PAGE-1), 3);
           SET_COL(13); PUT(TITLE); SET_COL(61); PUT(CURRENT_DATE); NEW_LINE(2);
3          PUT(" Date     Defect    Description/Comment"); NEW_LINE(2);
       end if;
2      READ(DEFECTS, DEFECT, REPAIR.DEFECT);
2      PUT(FORMAT_DATE(REPAIR.DATE)); SET_COL(13); PUT(REPAIR.DEFECT);
2      SET_COL(20); PUT(DEFECT.NAME); NEW_LINE;
2      SET_COL(22); PUT(REPAIR.COMMENT); NEW_LINE;
1      REPAIR_INDEX := REPAIR.PREVIOUS;
     end loop;
     {the summary}({CURRENT_OUTPUT, modified});
     CLEAN_UP;
   exception
     when DEVICE_ERROR | END_ERROR | NAME_ERROR | STATUS_ERROR =>
         CLEAN_UP; PUT("Data Base Inconsistent");
     when others => CLEAN_UP; raise;
   end UNIT_REPAIR_REPORT;
```

Once the *enumerator* has been specified, the constraints (described previously) in the component *simple-report* fill in most of the rest of the program UNIT_REPAIR_REPORT. It is assumed that two components (*print-repair* and *print-repair-headings*) exist that specify how to print a repair record and the associated column headings. (The lines marked with 2 and 3 come from these two components respectively.)

When the *print-item* is filled in, the *line-limit* is changed from 64 to 63, since the code used to fill the *print-item* generates two lines of output, whereas the default assumption used by the constraint function SIZE_IN_LINES is that only one line of output will be produced. (This change is marked with a 4.)

The automatic updating of the *line-limit* role is a good example of the way KBEmacs can enhance program reliability. The main leverage KBEmacs applies to the reliability problem is that each component is internally consistent. The use of constraints can help maintain this consistency.

If KBEmacs had not updated the *line-limit* role, the programmer might not have realized that it needed to be updated. The resulting bug, though minor, would have the pernicious quality of being rather hard to detect during program testing since it would only manifest itself when the program attempted to print the summary at the very bottom of a page.

A final thing to note about the code in Fig. 15.12 is that a number of variable declarations and the like have been added to the program (the lines marked with 5). This is an example of the way that KBEmacs can automatically take care of several kinds of programming details. It is interesting to note that the data types in these declarations are not specified as part of the components used. Rather, KBEmacs computes what data types should be used based on the definitions of the relevant files and the specifications for the procedures that operate on the variables.

After specifying the *enumerator* in Fig. 15.12, the only roles left unfilled are the *title, main-file-key,* and *summary*. These roles are dealt with by the last three commands in Fig. 15.8.

15.5.3 Automatically Generated Documentation

As a final example of the capabilities of KBEmacs, Fig. 15.13 shows an automatically generated comment for the program UNIT_REPAIR_REPORT. The comment is in the form of an outline. The first line specifies the top-level component in the program. The subsequent lines describe how the major roles in this component have been filled in. The comment is constructed based on the components that were used to create the program.

The comment generation capability currently supported by KBEmacs is only intended as an illustration of the kind of comment that could be produced. Many other kinds of comments, containing either more or less information, could just as well have been produced. For example, KBEmacs could easily include a description of the inputs and outputs of the program in the comment. The form of comment shown was chosen because it contains a significant amount of high-level information that is not explicit in the program code. As a result, it should be of genuine assistance to a person who is trying to understand the program.

FIGURE 15.13
AUTOMATICALLY GENERATED COMMENT FOR UNIT_REPAIR_REPORT

```
-- The procedure UNIT_REPAIR_REPORT is a simple_report:
--    The file_name is "report.txt".
--    The title is ("Report of Repairs on Unit " & UNIT_KEY).
--    The enumerator is a chain_enumeration.
--        It enumerates the chain records in REPAIRS starting from the
--        the header record indexed by UNIT_KEY.
--    The column_headings are a print_repair_headings.
--        It prints headings for printing repair records.
--    The print_item is a print_repair.
--        It prints out the fields of REPAIR.
--    There is no summary.
```

A key feature of the comment in Fig. 15.13 is that, since it is generated from the knowledge underlying the program, it is guaranteed to be complete and correct. In contrast, much of the program documentation one typically encounters has been rendered obsolete by subsequent program modifications. Although it is not currently supported, it would be easy for KBEmacs to generate a new program comment every time a program was modified.

The fact that KBEmacs can generate the comment shown highlights the fact that KBEmacs always maintains a plan for the program being edited and that this plan contains complete information about what components were used to construct it. This gives the approach taken by KBEmacs significant leverage on program maintenance as well as program construction.

15.6 FUTURE DIRECTIONS OF THE PROGRAMMER'S APPRENTICE PROJECT

The work described in this chapter is being extended in several directions. To start with, work is progressing rapidly toward the implementation of the topmost layers of CAKE. When CAKE is completed, it will be used as the basis for a new demonstration system called the Design Apprentice [Rich and Waters, 1987]. The Design Apprentice will incorporate all of the capabilities of KBEmacs. In addition, since it will contain a general-purpose reasoning module (CAKE), it will be able to assist in a greater portion of the programming process. With the assistance of the programmer, the Design Apprentice will be able to create programs based on detailed low-level specifications similar to the comment in Fig. 15.13. As part of this, the Design Apprentice will be able to deduce implicit design decisions that follow from explicit decisions made by the user. The Design Apprentice will also be able to detect many kinds of specification errors.

Work has also begun on a separate system called the Requirements Apprentice [Rich, Waters, and Reubenstein, 1987]. The Requirements Apprentice will assist an analyst in the creation and modification of software requirements. Productivity will be enhanced by allowing an analyst to rapidly build up a requirement by combining standard requirements fragments. Reliability will be enhanced through the use of general-purpose reasoning to detect contradictions and ambiguities in the evolving requirement. Like the Design Apprentice, the Requirements Apprentice will be based on CAKE. However, significant extensions will have to be made in the Plan Calculus so that it can represent reusable requirements components as well as reusable program components.

The long-term goal is for the Requirements Apprentice to link up with the Design Apprentice, providing support for the entire programming process. However, as currently envisioned, there is a significant gap between the capabilities of these two systems. This gap corresponds to high-level system design. Work on the Design Apprentice will assume that a high-level design has already been obtained and will focus on the problem of detailed design.

Acknowledgments

This report describes research done at the Artificial Intelligence Laboratory of the Massachusetts Institute of Technology. Support for the laboratory's artificial intelligence research has been provided in part by the IBM Corporation, in part by the Sperry Corporation, in part by National Science Foundation grant MCS-7912179, and in part by the Advanced Research Projects Agency of the Department of Defense under Office of Naval Research contract N00014-85-K-0124.

References

Aho, A.; Hopcroft, J.; and Ullman, J. *The Design and Analysis of Computer Algorithms.* Reading, Mass.: Addison-Wesley, 1974.

Balzer, R. Transformational implementation: An example. *IEEE Trans. on Software Eng.* 7(1):3, 1981.

Barstow, D. An experiment in knowledge-based automatic programming. *Artificial Intelligence* 12(1):73, 1979.

Basu, S., and Misra, J. Some classes of naturally provable programs. *Second Int. Conf. on Software Eng.,* San Francisco, Calif., October 1976.

Broy, M., and Pepper, P. Program development as a formal activity. *IEEE Trans. on Software Eng.* 7(1):14, 1981.

Cheatham, T. Reusability through program transformation. *IEEE Trans. on Software Eng.* 10(5):589, 1984.

Darlington, J. An experimental program transformation and synthesis system. *Artificial Intelligence* 16(1):1, 1981.

Dennis, J. First version of a data flow procedure language. *Proc. of Symposium on Programming,* Institute de Programmation, University of Paris, April 1974.

Feldman, Y., and Rich, C. Reasoning with simplifying assumptions: A methodology and example. In *Proc. Fifth National Conference on Artificial Intelligence.* Los Altos, Calif.: Morgan Kaufmann, 1986.

Gerhart, S. Knowledge about programs: A model and case study. *Int. Conf. on Reliable Software,* June 1975.

Goguen, J.; Thatcher, J.; and Wagner, E. An initial algebra approach to the specification, correctness, and implementation of abstract data types. In R. Yeh (ed.), *Current Trends in Programming Methodology,* vol 4. Englewood Cliffs, N. J.: Prentice-Hall, 1978.

Green, C. Theorem proving by resolution as a basis for question-answering systems. In D. Michie and B. Meltzer (eds.), *Machine Intelligence,* vol 4. Edinburgh, Scotland: Edinburgh University Press, 1969.

Guttag, J.; Horowitz, E.; and Musser, R. Abstract data types and software validation. *Comm. of the ACM* 21(12):1048, 1978.

Ianov, Y. The logical schemes of algorithms. In *Problems of Cybernetics,* vol 1. New York, N. Y.: Pergamon Press, 1960.

Knuth, D. *The Art of Computer Programming*. Vols. 1–3. Reading, Mass.: Addison-Wesley, 1968–1973.

Liskov, B.; Snyder, A.; Atkinson, R; and Schaffert, C. Abstraction mechanisms in CLU. *Comm. of the ACM* 20(8):564, 1977.

Liskov, B., and Zilles, S. An introduction to formal specifications of data abstractions. In R. Yeh (ed.), *Current Trends in Programming Methodology*, vol. 1. Englewood Cliffs, N. J.: Prentice-Hall, 1977.

Lisp Machine Documentation. (Release 4.) Cambridge Mass.: Symbolics Inc., 1984.

Manna, Z. *Mathematic Theory of Computation*. New York, N.Y.: McGraw-Hill, 1974.

Manna, Z., and Waldinger, R. A deductive approach to program synthesis. *ACM Trans. on Programming Languages and Systems* 2(1):90, 1980a.

———. *Problematic Features of Programming Languages: A Situational-Calculus Approach*. Part 1. *Assignment Statements*. Artificial Intelligence Center, Stanford Univ., Palo Alto, Calif., 1980b.

McAllester, D. Reasoning utility package user's manual. Technical report MIT/AIM-667, Artificial Intelligence Laboratory, Massachusetts Institute of Technology, Cambridge, Mass., 1982.

Rich, C. A formal representation for plans in the Programmer's Apprentice. In *Proc. Seventh Int. Joint Conf. on Artificial Intelligence*. Los Altos, Calif.: Morgan Kaufmann, 1981.

———. The layered architecture of a system for reasoning about programs. In *Proc. Ninth Int. Joint Conf. on Artificial Intelligence*. Los Altos, Calif.: Morgan Kaufmann, 1985.

Rich, C., and Waters, R. (eds). *Readings in Artificial Intelligence and Software Engineering*. Los Altos, Calif.: Morgan Kaufmann, 1986.

Rich, C., and Waters, R. A scenario illustrating a proposed program design apprentice. Technical report MIT/AIM-933, Artificial Intelligence Laboratory, Massachusetts Institute of Technology, Cambridge, Mass., 1987.

Rich, C.; Waters, R.; and Reubenstein, H. Toward a requirements apprentice. *Fourth Int. Workshop on Software Specification and Design*, Monterey, Calif., April 1987.

Standish, T.; Harriman, D. C.; Kibler, D. F.; and Neighbors, J. M., The Irvine program transformation catalogue. Technical report, Computer Science Department, Univ. of California, Irvine, Calif., 1976.

United States Department of Defense. *Military Standard Ada Programming Language*. ANSI/MIL-STD-1815A-1983. Washington, D.C.: U.S. Government Printing Office, 1983.

Waters, R. The programmer's apprentice: A session with KBEmacs. *IEEE Trans. on Software Eng.* 11(11):1296, 1985.

Wirth, N. *Systematic Programming: An Introduction*. Englewood Cliffs, N. J.: Prentice-Hall, 1973.

Wulf, W.; London, R.; and Shaw, M. An introduction to the construction and verification of Alphard programs. *IEEE Trans. on Software Eng.* 2(4):253, 1976.

CHAPTER 16

ADDRESSING SOFTWARE REUSE THROUGH KNOWLEDGE-BASED DESIGN

MITCHELL D. LUBARS
Microelectronics and Computer Technology Corporation (MCC)

MEHDI T. HARANDI
Department of Computer Science
University of Illinois at Urbana-Champaign

16.1 INTRODUCTION

The reuse of available software components is one important method for improving the productivity of new software product development. Software reuse benefits are especially apparent in the early portions of software development (requirements, specification, and design) since that is where the foundations are established for the development and maintenance of the software product. These foundations can be traced through the software development process, providing links for addressing later reuse issues. Thus the early reuse focus provides leverage for the entire process. For example, the reuse of requirements and specification concepts facilitates the use of existing mappings from those concepts to design alternatives. These concepts and mappings provide a common vocabulary for communicating about the problem domain and a link to the design and other reusable software development components. The reuse of good designs ensures that fewer flaws will creep in during later parts of the software development process, where they are especially expensive to correct [Lubars, 1986a]. Furthermore, design reuse can provide a handle on locating and incorporating reusable code.

Effective reuse of software designs requires a collection of good design components and knowledge about how to locate and combine appropriate components into a particular software design. Indeed, experienced software engineers generally benefit from this kind of expertise [Adelson et al., 1985]. Other studies indicate large differences in the abilities of different software developers [Sackman et al., 1968; Curtis, 1981], and a number of techniques have been proposed to take the best advantage of the more experienced software engineers [Baker, 1972; Brooks, 1978]. The application of expert system technology to software engineering is one mechanism through which reusability of software components might be achieved. By encoding and abstracting the expertise of experienced software engineers into knowledge bases, their expertise can be made readily available to nonexpert system developers.

A knowledge-based design environment, IDeA (Intelligent Design Aid), has been developed to support the reuse of software designs and other early software process concepts for requirements and specifications. In IDeA, software design components are abstracted into the form of *design schemas* to enhance their reusability. Other reusable information that is encoded into IDeA's knowledge base includes rules for design specialization and refinement, domain-oriented data object descriptions, domain attributes for data objects and design schemas, and pointers to reusable templates and code. These types of reusable information are organized into abstraction hierarchies that facilitate the search, selection, and application of reusable components.

There are two key steps in reusing software components: locating the reusable components and customizing them to fit the particular application. IDeA assists with both of these steps by providing schema selection strategies for finding the reusable components and by applying various rules for specializing and refining instances of those components. IDeA provides an environment in which the user can concentrate on supplying the requirements and specifications of the desired software product and is assisted in the location and incorporation of the reusable components to construct the desired software design. In this way, IDeA helps support a paradigm of software development where software specification and design aspects occur in parallel [Harandi et al., 1986]. The reusable domain concepts thus provide a common vocabulary in which the user and IDeA communicate the necessary information for jointly constructing software designs.

In this paper, we will examine some representations for organizing reusable design schemas and software objects and describe the techniques employed by IDeA to support software reusability.

16.2 OVERVIEW OF IDeA AND SUPPORT FOR DATA FLOW METHODOLOGIES

IDeA was developed to demonstrate the principles of schema-based design reuse in an integrated environment. Its fundamental methodology is based on the refinement-based software development paradigm. Figure 16.1 illustrates

FIGURE 16.1
THE OVERALL STRUCTURE OF IDeA

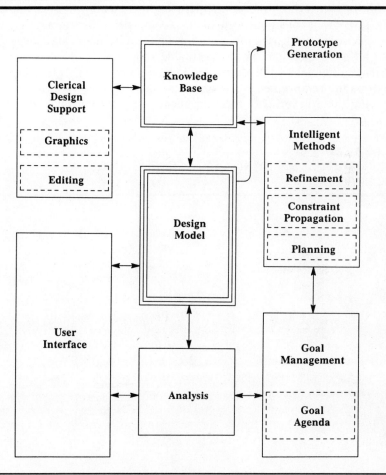

IDeA's major components. The central function of IDeA is to construct a design model of a system that corresponds to the user's specifications. To accomplish this, IDeA applies a variety of techniques that retrieve reusable components from its knowledge base, assemble them into the design model, and refine the design to a very detailed level. Once the design is completed, a prototype of the system can be generated by assembling reusable code with the assistance of a module interconnection language and supporting architecture [Purtilo, 1985]. IDeA also assists the user by managing various design goals, evaluating and maintaining the consistency of the design, and supporting the user's graphical and editing requirements.

The concepts and techniques underlying IDeA are independent of any particular representation or design methodology. However, in order to demonstrate the concepts in operation, IDeA was constructed around the data flow representation and its associated analysis and design methodologies. One of the primary motivations for choosing the data flow representation was that it provides a consistent view of the system being developed throughout the entire software process, from the initial requirements and specifications through the development of an executable prototype.

Structured analysis [DeMarco, 1978; Gane *et al.*, 1977] is frequently used to express the requirements and specifications of certain types of systems by describing them in terms of their input and output data flows and transfor-

FIGURE 16.2a

THE *UPDATE AND NOTIFY STUDENT RECORDS* PROBLEM—TOP LEVEL DESCRIPTION

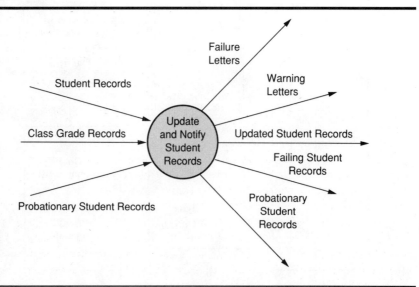

FIGURE 16.2b
THE *UPDATE AND NOTIFY STUDENT RECORDS* PROBLEM—FIRST LEVEL
DESIGN DECOMPOSITION

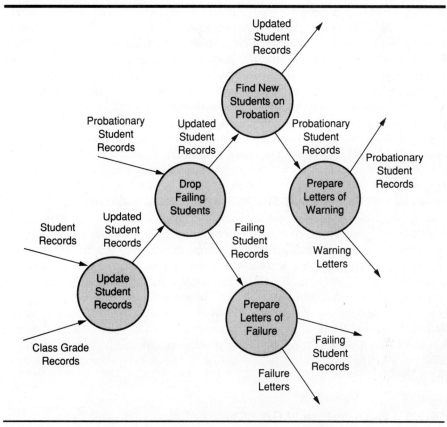

mations on those data flows. These descriptions are then structurally decomposed into more and more detailed data flow specifications and designs. Figure 16.2a shows the top level description of a system for updating student records with class grades in order to determine which students are failing and which students should be placed on probation. In addition, the system prepares letters to be sent to those failing and probationary students. The next step is to decompose (*level*) the transformations of the resulting data flow diagram (DFD). Figure 16.2b shows the next level decomposition of the *Update and Notify Student Records* example. The eventual result of the refinement process is a detailed set of leveled data flow diagrams, with the lowest level transformations corresponding to easily codable modules or pointers to reusable code. This design could then be converted to a structured design using techniques such as transform and transaction analysis [Yourdon *et al.*,

1979], or it could be interpreted as a process graph for the purpose of proto-typing.

IDeA supports the data flow methodologies by helping the user describe desired systems in terms of reusable domain concepts, finding and instantiating reusable abstract design schemas (expressed as data flow transformations), and applying reusable refinement rules to level the data flow diagrams. IDeA provides additional support for the user by tracking and managing various design goals and by checking the consistency and completeness of specifications against the current design state and selected schemas. Thus IDeA serves to guide the user through the refinement-based software development paradigm. Since the lowest level data flow transformations correspond to schemas associated with reusable code portions, IDeA assists in generating executable prototypes of the designed systems.

16.3 STRUCTURING THE REUSABLE INFORMATION

Several different kinds of reusable components are organized in IDeA's knowledge base to permit users to convey different types of information necessary for constructing software systems. These include abstract design schemas, data object definitions, and data object features. The information is organized into abstraction hierarchies. This permits the sharing of common component features in abstract parent nodes and facilitates the user's navigation through the component libraries and selection of desired components. We shall see in this section how the abstraction hierarchies are organized to represent the conceptual relationships of the different types of reusable information.

16.3.1 Representation of Data Objects, Data Types, and Type Constraints

Data objects represent the structures that are operated on by the functional components of the designed system. They tend to be domain-oriented and comprise the data flows of the leveled data flow diagrams in IDeA. In the above example, *student records*, *class grade records*, and *failure letters* are data objects.

Data objects typically contain a number of features that are important for understanding the object's conceptual functions and for distinguishing them from each other. Data objects with common or related features are grouped together into abstract categories to represent this relationship. In fact, when these common features include methods for operating on those data objects, the organization is considered to be *object-oriented*. The various features of data objects can also be used in their classification. Such *faceted* classification schemes offer flexibility in terms of locating desired data objects [Prieto-Díaz *et al.*, 1987].

Once a data object abstraction hierarchy has been constructed, a particular data object can be identified in terms of a more abstract parent and one or more features that distinguish it from other specializations of its parent. In essence, such features *constrain* the object's description. The representation of features in IDeA focuses on this constraint notion and its applicability to locating particular data objects. In fact, within IDeA, such features are referred to as *constraints*.

The Organization of Constraints. Constraints represent the independent features and feature values of data objects. They are organized into their own abstraction hierarchy, with the structure resembling a forest of trees. A portion of a constraint abstraction hierarchy used for revenue-related problems is shown in Fig. 16.3. Top level constraints, such as *amount source* and *amount object type*, are considered to be independent of each other. They represent orthogonal features for the purpose of classification, and they correspond to the notion of facets in [Prieto-Díaz *et al.*, 1987]. Their descendent constraints represent specializations and are mutually exclusive from their siblings and their siblings' descendants. They may be considered to comprise the range of feature values. For example, *income* and *sales* are specializations of *amount source*, and it is not possible for a data object to have both *sales* and *income* as values of the *amount source* feature at the same time. We say that the *sales* and *income* constraints are *incompatible*. Another way to view constraints is as unary predicates. Thus the following statements are true: $sales(X) \Rightarrow amount\_source(X)$, $income(X) \Rightarrow amount\_source(X)$, and $sales(X) \not\Rightarrow income(X)$. To express these relationships in the constraint framework, we introduce the $\sqsubseteq$ ordering relation, with $sales \sqsubseteq amount\_source$ and $income \sqsubseteq amount\_source$.

The use of constraints extends the vocabulary with which users may describe data objects, since it permits their specification in terms of abstract and related data objects plus additional constraints. This increases the flexibility of the data object selection process and the subsequent reusability of the associated components.

Data Types as Sets of Constraints. In the faceted classification scheme, data objects are classified according to the various values of their facets. This notion is extended in IDeA to include a definition of data typing where an object's data type is defined to be the object's set of *type constraints* [Lubars, 1986b]. For example, using the constraint abstraction hierarchy in Fig. 16.3, we might define the following data types: $tax = \{revenue\_domain, taxation, dependent\_amount\}$; $commission = \{revenue\_domain, commission\_type, dependent\_amount\}$; $income\_tax = \{revenue\_domain, taxation, dependent\_amount, income\}$; and $revenue = \{revenue\_domain, primary\_amount\}$.

The constraint abstraction hierarchy ordering ($\sqsubseteq$) can be extended to data types, resulting in the construction of a type lattice. To better understand this, we introduce the following definitions.

FIGURE 16.3
PORTION OF A CONSTRAINT ABSTRACTION HIERARCHY FOR
REVENUE-RELATED PROBLEMS

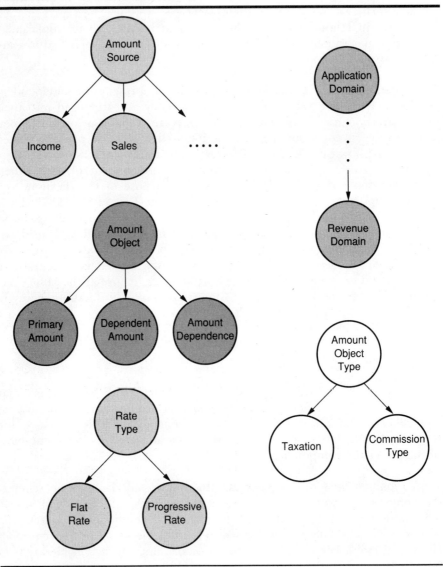

Definition 1. The *maximal chain* of a constraint c, denoted $[c] \uparrow$, is defined as:

$$[c] \uparrow = \{c_i | c \sqsubseteq c_i\}$$

Thus, we have $[sales] \uparrow = \{sales, amount\_source\}$ and $[income] \uparrow = \{income, amount\_source\}$.

Definition 2. The *maximal chain* of a set of constraints C, denoted $C \uparrow$, is defined as:

$$C \uparrow = \bigcup_{c_i \in C} [c_i] \uparrow$$

According to definition 2, $\{sales, income, taxation\} \uparrow = \{sales, income, amount\_source, taxation, amount\_object\_type\}$.

Definition 3. The data type ordering ($\sqsubseteq^*$) is defined on data types as follows:

$$T' \sqsubseteq^* T, \; iff \; T \uparrow \subseteq T' \uparrow$$

The top element of the type lattice is the totally unconstrained type, $\{ \; \}$. The bottom element is the set consisting of all the constraints. Since this set contains sibling (incompatible) constraints, it describes an impossible data object. In fact, any data type that contains incompatible constraints is considered to be equivalent to the bottom type. The following examples and relations are typical of the type lattice constructed from the constraint abstraction hierarchy of Figure 16.3.

$\{sales, taxation, revenue\_domain, dependent\_amount\}$
$\qquad\qquad \sqsubseteq^* \{taxation, revenue\_domain, dependent\_amount\}$

$\{sales, commission\_T, revenue\_domain, dependent\_amount$
$\qquad\qquad \sqsubseteq^* \{commission\_T, revenue\_domain, dependent\_amount\}$

$\{sales, taxation, revenue\_domain, dependent\_amount\}$
$\qquad\qquad\qquad \sqsubseteq^* \{amount\_source, revenue\_domain\}$

$\{sales, commission\_T, revenue\_domain, dependent\_amount\}$
$\qquad\qquad\qquad \sqsubseteq^* \{amount\_source, revenue\_domain\}$

$\{income, taxation, revenue\_domain, dependent\_amount\}$
$\qquad\qquad\qquad \sqsubseteq^* \{amount\_source, revenue\_domain\}$

Data types that are commonly referenced can be associated with *data type names*. In addition, synonyms for data type names and constraints can be defined to further extend the domain vocabulary for describing data objects. In order to interpret user descriptions of data objects, IDeA maps all the terms in a user's description to sets of constraints. The union of these sets is then reduced to a canonical form in order to identify a particular data type in the type lattice. That data type is then used as an initial interpretation of the user's data object specification.

16.3.2 Design Schemas and Type Constraint Variables

Design schemas represent the reusable functional design components, which correspond to data flow transformations in IDeA. Schemas are constructed as abstractly as possible to increase their reuse potential. This is achieved by assigning abstract data types to the input and output data flows of the schema. Figure 16.4 shows the skeleton of the *Compute Dependent Revenue* schema, which can be applied to various revenue-related problems such as tax and commission computations.

Design schemas may be considered to be *polymorphic* in the sense that they can be applied to a variety of specific data types. Polymorphism has been used in the area of functional programming to achieve higher degrees of functional reuse [Milner, 1978]. In addition, polymorphic functions use *type variables*, which can be assigned particular type values, to represent relationships between different instances of polymorphic data types. This permits type checking and type inference to be applied with the individual applications of the polymorphic functions. These same capabilities are important for improving the reusability of design schemas. In particular, type checking makes it possible to check the applicability of a design schema during the schema selection process to ensure that it is indeed a viable candidate for the particular design situation. Type inference makes it possible to propagate design information from a context that is established by the user specifications. This reduces the burden on the user of supplying complete specifications, since the missing details can be filled in from the design context.

FIGURE 16.4
SKELETON OF THE *COMPUTE DEPENDENT REVENUE* SCHEMA

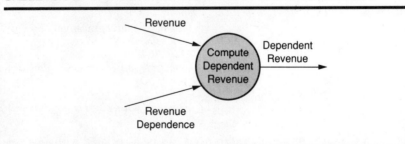

In order to accomplish type checking and type inference in design schemas, constraint variables must be associated with the various facets of the schemas' data flows. These constraint variables are shared between data flows so that when a constraint variable on a particular data flow is assigned a particular value (a constraint), that constraint propagates to the other affected data flows (those sharing the same constraint variable). To continue the analogy with polymorphic functions, we can consider the type variables of polymorphic functions to be constraint variables restricted to a single facet (basic data type). A polymorphic approach has been used in constructing software algorithm templates [Volpano *et al.*, 1985]; this approach defines two separately constrainable facets, basic data type and representation, which extends the level of algorithm reusability. The design schema approach, however, permits the definition and use of an arbitrary number of independent facets and associated constraint variables. This is a necessary feature for capturing the various domain-oriented facets in software specification and high level design.

Figure 16.5 illustrates the extended *Compute Dependent Revenue* schema, with constraints and constraint variables. As can be seen, all three data flows are constrained to be of a type having the same *amount_source* (*AS* variable). In addition, the *revenue_dependence* and *dependent_revenue* data flows are constrained to be of the same *amount_object_type* (*AOT* variable). Thus it is possible for the *Compute Dependent Revenue* schema to be applied to the problems, *sales_revenue* $\times$ *sales_commission_rate* $\rightarrow$ *sales_ commission* (*AS* = *Sales*; *AOT* = *Commission-type*) and *income_revenue* $\times$ *income_tax_rate* $\rightarrow$ *income_tax* (*AS* = *Income*; *AOT* = *Taxation*), but not to *sales_ revenue* $\times$ *income_tax_rate* $\rightarrow$ *sales_ tax* (*AS* = *Sales, Income*; *AOT* = *Taxation*). In fact, the schema can be used with partial user specifications to infer omitted type information.

FIGURE 16.5
THE *COMPUTE DEPENDENT REVENUE* SCHEMA WITH CONSTRAINTS AND CONSTRAINT VARIABLES

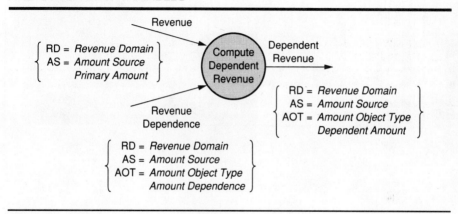

FIGURE 16.6

SELECTION AND APPLICATION OF THE *COMPUTE DEPENDENT REVENUE* SCHEMA IN IDeA

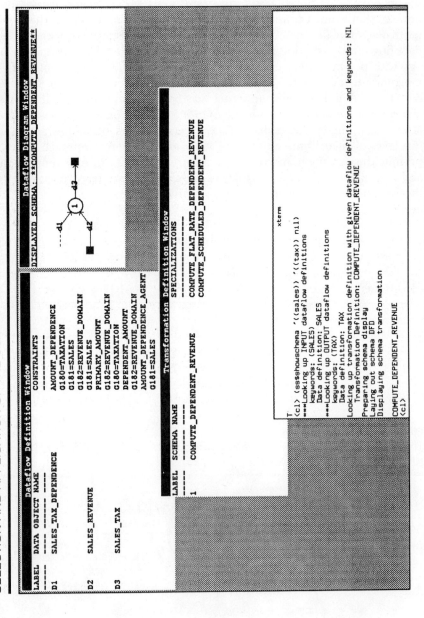

Figure 16.6 shows IDeA applying the schema to the user specification of *sales* → *tax*. IDeA infers the complete types of the specified data flows, *Sales_revenue (d2)* and *Sales_tax (d3)*, as well as suggesting the unspecified data flow, *Sales_ tax_dependence (d1*, denoted with a dotted line in the data flow diagram).

16.3.3 Design Families, Subfamilies, and Specialization Rules

Abstract design schemas represent large design families and often cover a number of related application domains. Constraining information frequently takes the form of committing to a restricted class of design decisions and thus reduces the family of possible design solutions to a particular subfamily. These design family relationships are represented in the design schema abstraction hierarchy through the use of *specialization rules*, which are used to select the most appropriate design subfamilies. A specialization rule may be viewed as saying IF (*design family is X*) and (*Y* ∈ *available constraints*) THEN (*design subfamily is X'*). Another view of the situation is that the abstract design family is *overloaded* in the sense that the design subfamilies (specializations) correspond to the various unique forms of the operations. This is similar to the way in which the arithmetic operations are overloaded in high-level programming languages. For example, the *multiplication* operator in Pascal corresponds to both integer and real multiplication, and a particular instance of multiplication depends on the types of its operands.

The *Compute Dependent Revenue* design schema represents an abstract design family that is independent of the particular type of the *revenue dependence* input. As shown in Fig. 16.7, the schema can be specialized to either the *Compute Flat Rate Dependent Revenue* or the *Compute Scheduled Dependent Revenue* schema depending on whether the *Revenue Dependence* input is constrained to be *flat_rate* (input is *revenue_percentage*) or *progressive_rate* (input is *revenue_schedule*). Thus *Compute Dependent Revenue* is considered to be overloaded with two applicable specialization rules.

The abstraction hierarchy of design schemas enhances design reusability because incomplete and ambiguous user specifications may still adequately specify a design schema. The information in the schema and the applicable specialization rules can then be used to guide the user to his intended design solution.

16.3.4 Refinement Rules and Generic Design Solutions

Refinement rules are used to decompose design components into more detailed designs. In the design schema approach, these refinements represent generic design solutions for their associated schemas. In other words, a schema's refinement is applicable to all the members of its abstract design family. Typically, the components of the refinement are instances of other abstract design schemas that can themselves be later refined and specialized

FIGURE 16.7

SPECIALIZATION RULES FOR THE *COMPUTE DEPENDENT REVENUE* SCHEMA

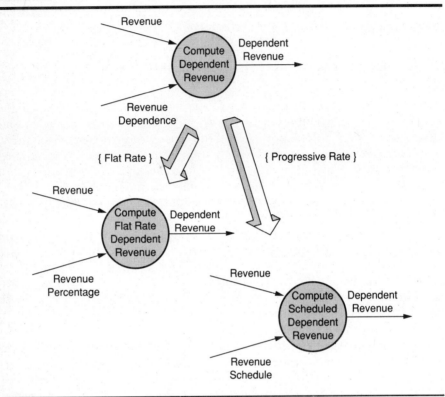

in the design process. In IDeA the refinements are represented as more detailed data flow diagrams, and the application of the refinement rules is used to produce additional leveling in the data flow design. Figure 16.8 shows the refinement rule for the *Compute Flat Rate Dependent Revenue* schema. The decomposition involves the conversion of the *revenue_percentage* to a *revenue_fraction*, which is then multiplied by the *revenue* input to produce the *dependent_revenue*. Constraints and constraint variables are associated with the data flows in the refinement in order to infer the appropriate data types and to propagate the constraints from the input and output data flows to the intermediate data flows (see Fig. 16.8b). These constraints are then used by IDeA in the subsequent specialization of the refined components.

The use of generic refinements increases the reusability of the refinement rules by making them applicable to the entire design family. Commitments to particular implementations are deferred until enough constraint information is available to permit the selection of the appropriate specialization rules. Only then can the correct design subfamily be chosen. For example, the

FIGURE 16.8a

REFINEMENT RULE FOR THE *COMPUTE DEPENDENT REVENUE* SCHEMA—
SKELETON OF THE RULE

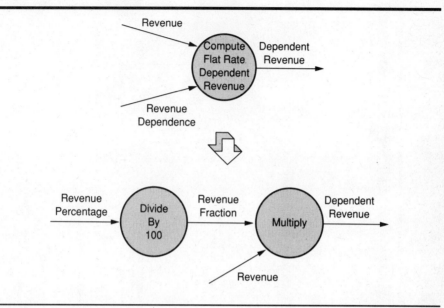

real constraint on the *Revenue_fraction* data flow (*D1*) in Fig. 16.8b can be
used to specialize the *multiply* operation to *Real_multiplication*. Similarly, the
Divide_by_100 operation can later be refined to use *real division*. Frequently,
it is desirable for a design schema to contain several alternative refinement
rules. In order to represent this, each of the refinements must be associated with different design subfamilies through the use of subschemas and
specialization rules. One or more constraints are then used to distinguish
between the different specializations that characterize the nature of the refinements.

16.3.5 Reusable Code, Templates, and Prototyping

The most detailed and refined design schemas correspond to components that
contain readily available code, are themselves easily codable, or can be better expressed with some other form of representation. In the first case, the
design schema contains information for locating the available code and linking it with other design components. When the schemas correspond to abstract
algorithms, reusable templates of those software algorithms [Volpano *et al.*,
1985] are better suited for expressing the nature of the solutions. Constraint
information in the data flows can then be used to produce implementations
from the templates. Other representations [Rich, 1981] are often more appropriate for expressing the lower level design qualities of program pieces and are

FIGURE 16.8b

REFINEMENT RULE FOR THE *COMPUTE DEPENDENT REVENUE* SCHEMA—
THE REFINEMENT AS DISPLAYED IN IDeA

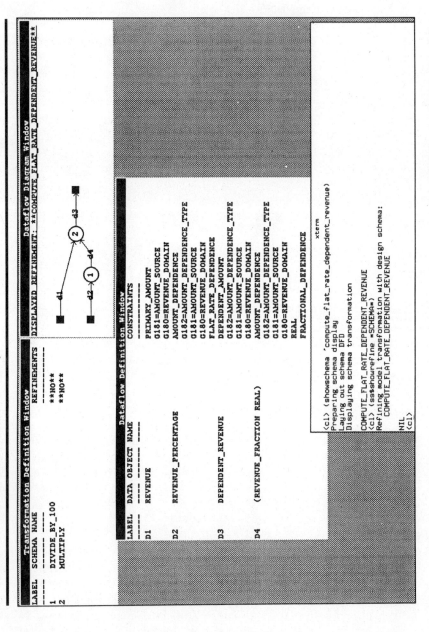

especially well suited for the reuse of common programming clichés. Pointers to these can also be included in the schemas. In each of these cases, the use of design schemas provides significant leverage for addressing code and algorithm reusability.

IDeA's detailed data flow designs can easily be interpreted as process graphs. With an appropriate module interconnection language and supportive message passing architecture, the process graph structure can be extended with reusable code to construct a prototype of the designed system. IDeA has been interfaced with the Polylith system [Purtilo, 1985] to provide this capability (see example in Appendix A). To accomplish this, the design schemas contain Polylith port-binding information as well as pointers to the executable code. Other possibilities for generating prototypes and programs from IDeA designs include the conversion of data flow graphs to functional [Backus, 1978] and data flow programs [Acherman, 1982] and the transformation of data flow designs to structured designs using techniques such as transform and transaction analysis [DeMarco, 1978; Yourdon *et al.*, 1979].

16.4 SELECTION AND CUSTOMIZATION OF DESIGN COMPONENTS

The two key reuse problems are finding the appropriate reusable components and fitting them into the particular situation. IDeA provides considerable assistance with both of these problems through the design schema representation, constraint-based data typing, and the application of specialization and refinement rules.

16.4.1 Schema Selection

The use of constraints and data type names provides a domain-oriented vocabulary with which the user can describe the data objects comprising the input and output data flows. IDeA can interpret these descriptions to identify particular data types in the type lattice. Since the data types are abstractions of domain-oriented objects, they are generally processible by just the relatively small number of design schemas that apply to those related application domains. Thus the data flow descriptions can be used to suggest a set of candidate schemas. Furthermore, users may sometimes find it easier to describe domain objects than to describe particular functions in standard domain terminology. For example, when referring to the components of an airline reservation system, it is relatively easy to identify the data objects *airline reservations*, *airline tickets*, and *boarding passes*. In contrast, it may be somewhat more difficult to uniquely describe operations such as *making airline reservations* and *checking in for a flight*, the latter corresponding to the transformation of *airline tickets* into *boarding passes*. In some situations, the user may feel that he knows what the function operates on but not what the function is.

Design schema selection is therefore oriented toward finding design schemas that satisfy the requirements of the input and output data objects. The user's description of function is used as additional information to distinguish between good candidate schemas, or as an alternative strategy when data objects are not suitably specified. The schema selection strategy consists of the following major steps:

1. Finding data types for the specified data objects.
2. Finding candidate schemas that account for one or more of the specified data objects and function.
3. Verifying that the specified data objects are generally consistent with the constraints of the design schema by performing a *modified type check* of the schema against the specifications. In this type-checking variation, a certain degree of mismatching is permitted in order to cope with some incompleteness and inconsistency in the user's specification. A result of this modified type check is a heuristic measure of the degree of matching between the schema and the specification.
4. Selecting the best matching schema.

A certain degree of flexibility is required in the schema selection strategy to account for problems with the user specifications:

1. The user may specify some data objects that cannot be handled by a single schema. This may occur if the specifications require the composition of several schemas to account for all the data objects. Alternatively, some of the data objects may have been incorrectly specified by the user.
2. The user may only specify a subset of the data objects that are components of the candidate schemas. This implies that either the user specification is incomplete or the schema operates on more data objects than the user desires.

IDeA's schema selection strategy is flexible enough to handle a certain amount of incompleteness, incorrectness, and ambiguity in the user's specifications. As an overall heuristic, schemas that provide the highest degree of matching with the most user-specified data objects are considered the best candidates.

As described earlier, the user's description of a data object can be interpreted by mapping the description to a set of constraints, and then locating that set in the data type lattice. An initial set of candidate schemas is then constructed by considering all schemas that account for the specified data types or any of their abstractions in the type lattice. Since the data objects and schemas are domain-oriented, this usually results in a manageable-sized set of schemas. For example, when considering schemas that operate on revenue-related data objects, it is unnecessary to examine schemas outside the revenue domain (or appropriate abstractions).

The next step is to match the candidate schemas with the user specifications to determine which schemas best satisfy the user-imposed constraints. This is very similar to type-checking the schema with the user specifications, but it is extended to permit a certain amount of mismatching to account for specifications that are incorrect or incomplete. The matching phase includes the unification of user-imposed constraints with schema-supplied constraint variables. As a consequence, some candidate schemas may be quickly rejected due to a failure of constraints to unify. Unification also results in the inference of the complete type information (at the appropriate level of abstraction for the schema).

As an example, let us consider the following incomplete user functional specification, *sales* → *tax*. *Sales* is a subconstraint of *amount_source*, and *tax* is a data type that is defined to be {*revenue_domain*, *dependent_amount*, *taxation*}. One of the abstractions of *tax* is *dependent_revenue*, which is defined as {*revenue_domain*, *dependent_amount*}. Since *dependent_revenue* is an output data flow from the *Compute Dependent Revenue* schema (see Fig. 16.5), that schema is added to the list of candidates. The result of matching the schema with the user specifications merges the *sales* constraint with the *revenue* data type, resulting in *sales_revenue*. Similarly, the *tax* data type definition is merged with *dependent_revenue*. Together with the shared *sales* constraint, the match results in an output type of *sales_tax*.

IDeA contains heuristics for evaluating the quality of the match. These are largely based on the specificity of the least upper bounds of the supplied data types (schema supplied and user specified) in the type lattice. In our example, *tax* is determined to be a good match with *dependent_revenue* so IDeA finally selects the *Compute Dependent Revenue* schema as the best alternative. The result of this schema selection process is shown in Fig. 16.6. In situations where IDeA finds several schemas that match equally well, IDeA shows the user the schemas with the matched pairs of data flows, and it requests that the user pick the best one. Generally, there are few remaining candidate schemas at this point, and it is easy for the user to make a final selection. If none of the candidate schemas seem appropriate, then either the user has failed to adequately specify the desired solution, or IDeA does not contain the appropriate schema in its library. The user may either provide new specifications or she may design that component herself, with IDeA's assistance.

16.4.2 Schema Instantiation and Refinement

The schema selection process generates an instance of the schema with the complete types inferred for the component data flows. The constraints in the user's specification are unified with the constraints and constraint variables of the schema. These constraints are then used by IDeA to choose appropriate specialization and refinement rules to apply to the schema in order to introduce additional detail. In this way, the initially selected design schema is customized to the user's specifications.

Additional information that is required for further specialization and refinement can be determined by IDeA. If the user fails to provide this information, IDeA can prompt the user for it at a later time. Thus IDeA can direct the user to provide complete and unambiguous specifications. For instance, in our *sales_tax* example, the user has provided enough information to select and instantiate the *Compute Dependent Revenue* schema but has not indicated whether the *sales_tax_dependence* is *flat_rate* (a *sales_tax_rate*) or *progressive_rate* (a *sales_tax_schedule*). IDeA can prompt for this information in order to select either the *Compute Flat Rate Dependent Revenue* or the *Compute Scheduled Dependent Revenue* schema specialization.

A larger design example is included in Appendix A, showing the application of IDeA's schema selection and refinement techniques.

16.5 CONSTRAINT PROPAGATION

Constraint propagation is an important feature for directing the customization of design components to new situations and for reducing the required amount of user specifications. We can view the propagation of constraints as facilitating the reuse of design decisions. Once a particular design decision has been committed to, the associated constraint propagates to all the affected components of the design. That decision does not have to be restated when the other affected components are later refined. As a result, constraint propagation helps to reduce the amount of user interaction required.

We have already seen how constraints are propagated within a schema instance through the use of shared constraint variables. We have also seen how constraints propagate in schema refinements through constraint variables that are shared between the components of the refinement. When new components are added to a partial design, they are connected to existing design components that also contain certain constraints. Those constraints then become available to the newly connected component and the components of their refinements. Furthermore, these newly available constraints may be unified with existing constraints and constraint variables and consequently propagate to additional components that also share the same constraint variables. Thus the addition and connection of design components can cause the propagation of constraints across the connection and subsequently to other far-reaching parts of the design. As an example, consider the connection of a *Compute Dependent Revenue* schema instance to another transformation with an output data flow of *sales_revenue*. That connection provides the *sales* constraint that is unified with the *amount_source* constraint variable, which is shared by the other components of the schema.

The propagation of constraints models the effect of committing to a design decision at a particular point in a design and its impact on other design components. The consequence is that the availability of these propagated constraints can then be used to enable the selection of specialization and refinement rules for all the affected components.

16.6 USE OF PLANNING TECHNIQUES IN DESIGN CONSTRUCTION

In many cases, the design reuse library will not contain a single schema that is capable of satisfying all of the user's specifications. To accomplish the complete design, it becomes necessary to compose several schema instances together. Planning techniques provide assistance in discovering such compositions from the user specifications and thus further improve the reusability of the library schemas.

Means-end analysis [Newell *et al.*, 1959] is used in IDeA to find simple compositions of schemas. Since we expect design knowledge bases to include schemas that are useful at various abstract design levels, small combinations of schemas will generally be sufficient to achieve the desired functions. Thus even weak methods such as means-end analysis should provide adequate planning capability.

Means-end analysis requires a distance function to determine the distance between the current state and the goal state of the problem. As a coarse approximation, this distance is measured in data flow diagrams as the number of data flows that have not yet been accounted for as the output of transformations or through user specifications. IDeA uses a finer distance function that approximates the degree of matching between the schema and the unaccounted-for data flows. This function is similar to the one used in the schema selection process. In fact, one may view IDeA's planning component as resembling successive application of schema selection. Once a design plan has been generated, IDeA instantiates and composes the selected schemas to ensure that the plan satisfies the constraints of the specifications and schemas. If the constraints are not satisfied, IDeA continues the planning process to find a consistent solution.

As an example, let us consider the computation of a combined *sales* and *use tax* from inputs of *sales_revenue* and *use_revenue*. The *Compute Dependent Revenue* schema is capable of computing *sales_tax* from *sales_revenue*, and *use_tax* from *use_revenue*. However, additional information is required to generate a *combined_tax* from the two separate taxes. To provide this, IDeA contains a *Compute Combined Tax* schema that converts input data flows of *sales_tax* and *use_tax* into an output data flow of *combined_tax*. The result of simply having IDeA select a design schema to account for the specifications ($sales\_revenue \times use\_revenue$) $\rightarrow$ *combined_tax* is shown in Fig. 16.9. The *Compute Combined Tax* schema accounts for the specified output data flow but fails

FIGURE 16.9
IDeA SELECTING A SCHEMA THAT ONLY PARTIALLY SOLVES A SPECIFIED PROBLEM

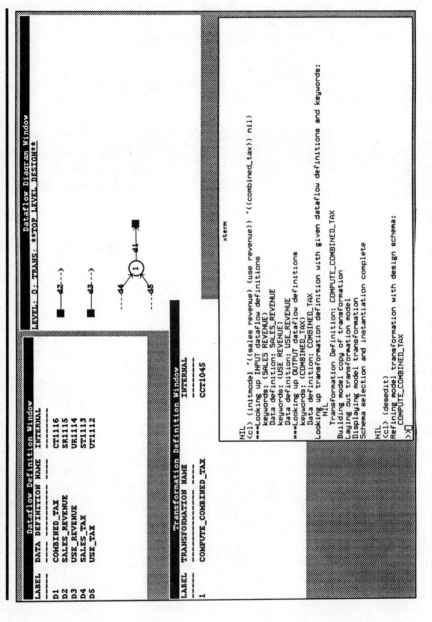

FIGURE 16.10

A DESIGN SOLUTION GENERATED THROUGH PLANNING IN IDeA

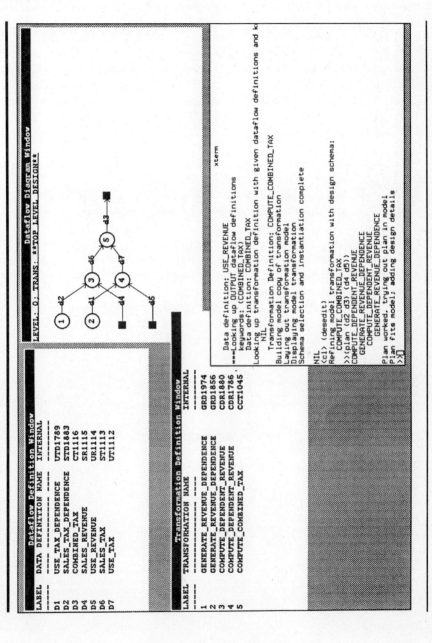

Dataflow Diagram Window

LEVEL: 0: TRANS: **TOP LEVEL DESIGN**

LABEL	Dataflow Definition Window DATA DEFINITION NAME	INTERNAL
D1	USE_TAX_DEPENDENCE	UTD1789
D2	SALES_TAX_DEPENDENCE	STD1883
D3	COMBINED_TAX	CT1116
D4	SALES_REVENUE	SR1115
D5	USE_REVENUE	UR1114
D6	SALES_TAX	ST1113
D7	USE_TAX	UT1112

LABEL	Transformation Definition Window TRANSFORMATION NAME	INTERNAL
1	GENERATE_REVENUE_DEPENDENCE	GRD1974
2	GENERATE_REVENUE_DEPENDENCE	GRD1856
3	COMPUTE_DEPENDENT_REVENUE	CDR1880
4	COMPUTE_DEPENDENT_REVENUE	CDR1786
5	COMPUTE_COMBINED_TAX	CCT1045

```
                                                           xterm

    Data definition: USE_REVENUE
****Looking up OUTPUT dataflow definitions
    keywords: (COMBINED_TAX)
    Data definition: COMBINED_TAX
Looking up transformation definition with given dataflow definitions and k
     NIL
    Transformation Definition: COMPUTE_COMBINED_TAX
Building model copy of transformation
Laying out transformation model
Displaying model transformation
Schema selection and instantiation complete

NIL
<cl> (desedit)
Refining model transformation with design schema:
        COMPUTE_COMBINED_TAX
>>(plan (d2 d3) (d4 d5))
COMPUTE_DEPENDENT_REVENUE
        GENERATE_REVENUE_DEPENDENCE
        COMPUTE_DEPENDENT_REVENUE
           GENERATE_REVENUE_DEPENDENCE
Plan worked, trying out plan in model
Plan fits model; adding design details
>>
```

to account for the input data flows. Furthermore, it requires two additional input data flows, *sales_tax* and *use_tax*, these now unaccounted for as well.

Planning can be used to account for the four unaccounted-for data flows. In Fig. 16.10, IDeA has completed a successful plan to account for those data flows. Two instances of the *Compute Dependent Revenue* schema have been incorporated, one each for computing *sales_tax* and *use_tax*. These new transformations require additional inputs of *sales_tax_dependence* and *use_tax_dependence*, which are also accounted for through further planning. The abstract schema *Generate Revenue Dependence* generates an output data flow of *revenue_dependence*, which is an abstraction of the two desired data flows. Since this schema does not require any new input data flows, two instances of *Generate Revenue Dependence* complete the plan. After planning, IDeA checks the consistency of the various constraints. Since there are no inconsistencies, IDeA expands the plan into the design shown in Fig. 16.10. IDeA can now refine the components of this design in the usual top-down way by applying specialization and refinement rules.

One important view of the planning process is as an application of bottom-up design strategy. Reusable components are located and combined to accomplish the user's desired function. This is in contrast with the refinement-based top-down methodology where single reusable schemas are located and then specialized and refined to the desired design solution. The combination of these methods enables IDeA to support users in both of these modes of design reuse.

16.7 MANAGEMENT OF DESIGN GOALS

IDeA maintains a goal agenda to track the various design goals for the user. These permit IDeA to monitor the state of the design and, if necessary, to take the active role and prompt the user for additional required information. In this way, specification and design can occur as parallel processes through a constructive dialogue between IDeA and the user.

IDeA tracks two major classes of goals:

Unaccounted-for Data Flows.   These come primarily from two sources—user specifications that have not yet been incorporated into the design and schema-suggested data flows that have not yet been specified by the user. Figure 16.9 shows examples of both of these types of data flows before they are resolved by planning (indicated as data flows with dotted lines). At a more pragmatic level, these types of unaccounted-for data flows may be a symptom of a partial design, of incorrect user specifications, or of incomplete user specifications. These problems must be resolved before IDeA will recognize that the goals are satisfied. The solution involves accounting for both the origin and termination of the data flows.

Refinement Goals. Each design component must be refined to the maximum level of detail and specificity for which IDeA contains rules in its knowledge base. IDeA maintains a refinement goal for each component that can be further refined. These unrefined components include data flow transformations that are instances of schemas with pending specialization, refinement, or prototype-binding rules. Only when a transformation is an instance of a schema with no applicable rules will it be considered completely refined. The user can direct IDeA to pursue all outstanding refinement goals for the current design. IDeA will then examine available constraint information in order to select the appropriate specialization and refinement rules. If there is not enough information available to satisfy any of the pending goals, IDeA will choose one of the goals and determine what additional information is required to satisfy that goal. IDeA will then prompt the user for that information and continue trying to satisfy the remaining goals. As a consequence of constraint propagation, the satisfaction of other goals may also become possible.

16.8 CONCLUSION

IDeA has been presented as a knowledge-based environment for supporting the reuse of design components and other early software process concepts. Design knowledge is captured in the form of abstract reusable design schemas and refinement rules that can be applied to solve classes of related design problems. Domain-oriented data object definitions are organized into a type lattice based on the definition of data types as sets of constraints. The constraint-based organization provides a faceted approach to the data type categorization that can be easily extended to support an object-oriented representation of data objects. Furthermore, the use of constraints and data type names provides a reusable domain vocabulary with which users can describe the appropriate data objects.

Two major problems in addressing software reuse are finding the reusable components and customizing them to the particular situation. IDeA includes a schema selection strategy based on the notion that it is frequently easier to describe a function's data objects than to describe the actual function itself. The type lattice provides a means for identifying user-specified data objects. A modified type-checking algorithm is used to identify suitable schemas that satisfy the constraints of the user's specifications. The selected schema is then instantiated with the properly inferred types and incorporated into the design. Constraints in the schema instance are used by IDeA to select and apply the appropriate specialization and refinement rules. Furthermore, newly incorporated design components may have their constraints unified with the constraints of existing components. This causes additional constraint propagation within designs and further enables the selection and application of rules. Such constraint propagation models the way in which particular design decisions impact a number of design components.

IDeA selects schemas and applies specialization and refinement rules as users provide specifications. Thus IDeA supports a refinement paradigm of software development in which specification and design occur in parallel. This permits the design process to be used as a means of checking the completeness and consistency of the specifications. In fact, IDeA may guide the user through the process by requesting additional information as it becomes necessary for the refinement of the design. This reduces the burden on the user of initially supplying complete specifications.

By addressing reuse early in the software development process, leverage is gained for the later portions. For example, the most refined and detailed design schemas may contain pointers to reusable code, software templates, or program designs that can be used to construct executable code or prototypes of the generated plans. IDeA has been interfaced with Polylith, which provides a module interconnection language and supporting software architecture, in order to demonstrate such a prototyping capability. The availability of such prototypes is important because it quickly provides the users feedback about the quality of their specifications and designs.

In addition to the top-down assistance that IDeA provides through its specialization and refinement rules, IDeA provides planning support to assist with bottom-up design methods. A goal agenda is also incorporated so that IDeA can track design goals and take the design initiative, if desired by the user. IDeA has been implemented on a graphics workstation running 4.2BSD UNIX and is implemented in a graphic-enhanced version of Franz Lisp.

Appendix A: A Larger Design Example

This section carries through a slightly larger design example to demonstrate how IDeA uses schema selection and refinement to complete the design and prototype of a small system from reusable components. The topic of this example is a system for updating a data flow of student records with class grades, producing a list of updated student records. In addition, the system is intended to determine which students are failing and which students should be placed on probation, and to prepare notification letters to send to them.

IDeA contains a schema, *Update And Notify Achiever Records*, that is an abstract solution to the described problem, where *students* are interpreted to be *achievers* in the context of *scholastic_achievement*. Thus IDeA contains definitions for the types *achiever* and *student*, with *student* defined as *achiever* ∪ {*scholastic_achievement*}. In addition, other types such as *student_record*, *class_grade_record*, and *failure_letter* are defined in terms of the appropriate constraints.

In Fig. 16.A1, the user initially specifies the desired system as ((*list student record*) → ((*list failing letter*) × (*list borderline letter*)). The input description is interpreted to be a data flow of *student_records* and the outputs are understood to be data flows of *failure_letters* and *warning_letters*. The understood data types are used in the schema selection process to locate and instantiate the *Update And Notify Achiever Records* schema. Furthermore, the *achievement_domain* constraint (variable) is unified with the *scholastic_achievement* constraint from the *student_record* type, so that each of the resulting data flow types is also specialized in the context of *scholastic_achievement*.

One of the ways of having IDeA apply design refinements is by entering its design editor. IDeA's editor always refines the design one level ahead of the displayed level so that it can make design adjustments to keep the design levels consistent with user modifications. In Fig. 16.A2, the user has caused IDeA to display the first level design refinement. This refinement was generated through IDeA's application of the generic design refinement rule associated with the *Update And Notify Achiever Records* schema. In order to display this refinement, IDeA has also applied available refinement rules for the components of that design level.

Each of the data flows of the refinement has been specialized due to propagated constraints from the original user specifications, the top level schema, and the refinement rule. These constraints are similarly used to refine the additional design components. For example, Fig. 16.A2 includes two separate instances of the abstract *Prepare Assessment Letters* schema. One of those is applied to the problem of generating *warning_letters* and the other to the problem of generating *failure_letters*. The particular way in which each of these is refined depends on the particular propagated constraints, such as the type of *assessment_domain* (*borderline* or *failing*) and the particular type of *achievement_domain* (*scholastic_achievement*). Figure 16.A3 shows the refinement of the *Prepare Assessment Letters* transformation for generating *warning_letters*. It consists of an instance of the abstract *Prepare Form Letters* schema, plus components that generate information on the sender and recipients of the letter and the letter body. The generation of the letter body is differentially specialized depending on the available constraint information (*borderline* and *scholastic_achievement*).

The remaining design components are similarly refined until the design has been completely generated. As can be seen in the lower right window of Fig. 16.A3, a number of IDeA's applied rules prepare the design for eventual execution as a prototype by setting Polylith port bindings. These bindings establish communication links in the Polylith module interconnection language so that the Polylith system can execute the design as a process graph. Pointers to executable code are also established to enable the Polylith system to link the code together in constructing the prototype. An example of the final top level design and some of the associated Polylith code is shown in Fig. 16.A4.

FIGURE 16.A1

IDeA's SELECTION OF THE *UPDATE AND NOTIFY ACHIEVER RECORDS* SCHEMA

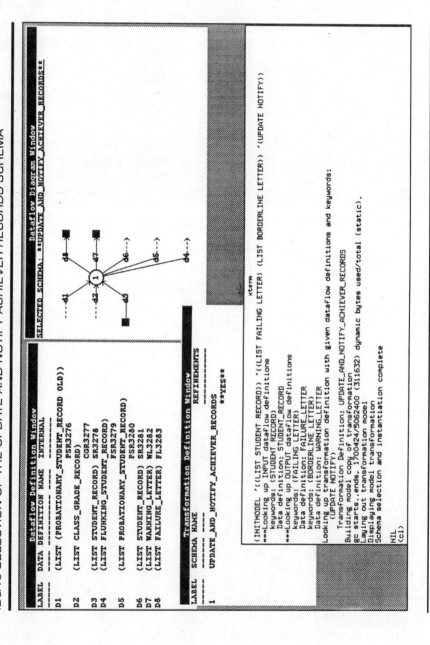

```
         Dataflow Definition Window              Dataflow Diagram Window
                                    SELECTED SCHEMA: **UPDATE AND NOTIFY_ACHIEVER_RECORDS***
LABEL   DATA DEFINITION NAME   INTERNAL
-----   --------------------   --------
D1      (LIST (PROBATIONARY_STUDENT_RECORD OLD))
                               PSR3276
D2      (LIST CLASS_GRADE_RECORD)
                               CGR3277
D3      (LIST STUDENT_RECORD)  SR3278
D4      (LIST FLUNKING_STUDENT_RECORD)
                               FSR3279
D5      (LIST PROBATIONARY_STUDENT_RECORD)
                               PSR3280
D6      (LIST STUDENT_RECORD)  SR3281
D7      (LIST WARNING_LETTER)  WL3282
D8      (LIST FAILURE_LETTER)  FL3283


         Transformation Definition Window
LABEL   SCHEMA NAME              REFINEMENTS
-----   -----------              -----------
1       UPDATE_AND_NOTIFY_ACHIEVER_RECORDS
                                 **YES**
```

```
                                                    xterm
(INITMODEL '((LIST STUDENT RECORD)) '((LIST FAILING LETTER) (LIST BORDERLINE LETTER) '(UPDATE NOTIFY))
***Looking up INPUT dataflow definitions
   keywords: (STUDENT RECORD)
   Data definition: STUDENT_RECORD
***Looking up OUTPUT dataflow definitions
   keywords: (FAILING LETTER)
   Data definition: FAILURE_LETTER
   keywords: (BORDERLINE LETTER)
   Data definition: WARNING_LETTER
Looking up transformation definition with given dataflow definitions and keywords:
   (UPDATE NOTIFY)
   Transformation Definition: UPDATE_AND_NOTIFY_ACHIEVER_RECORDS
Building model copy of transformation
gc starts..ends. 1700424/5062400 (311632) dynamic bytes used/total (static).
Laying out transformation model
Displaying model transformation
Schema selection and instantiation complete

NIL
<c1>
```

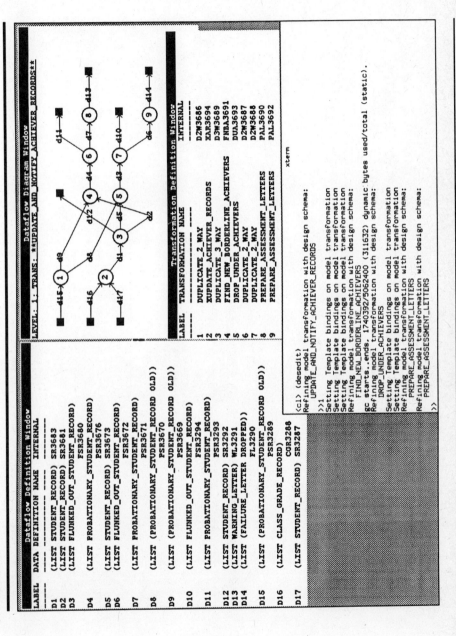

FIGURE 16.A3

IDeA's REFINEMENT OF THE *PREPARE ASSESSMENT LETTERS* SCHEMA FOR GENERATING
WARNING LETTERS

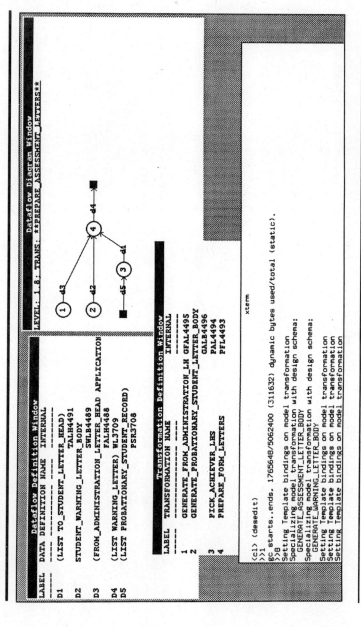

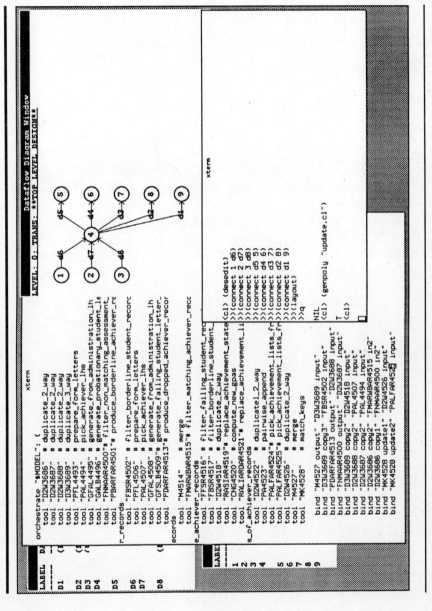

The generation of design prototypes is especially useful, because it provides the user with a means of evaluating the quality of her specifications and subsequent design. Other prototyping alternatives include the generation of functional and data flow programs from the detailed designs.

REFERENCES

Acherman, W. B. Data flow languages. *IEEE Computer* 15(2): 15–25, 1982.

Adelson, B., and Soloway, E. The role of domain experience in software design. *IEEE Trans. on Software Eng.* SE-11(11): 1351–1360, 1985.

Backus, J. Can programming be liberated from the von Neumann style? A functional style and its algebra of programs. *Comm. ACM* 21(8): 613–641, 1978.

Baker, F. T. Chief programmer team management of production programming. *IBM System Journal* 11(1), 1972.

Brooks, F. D. *The Mythical Man-Month.* Reading, Mass.: Addison-Wesley, 1978.

Curtis, B. Substantiating programmer variability. *Proceedings of the IEEE* 69(7): 846, 1981.

DeMarco, T. *Structured Analysis and System Specification.* New York: Yourdon, Inc., 1978.

Gane, C., and Sarson, T. *Structured Systems Analysis: Tools and Techniques.* New York: Improved System Technologies, Inc., 1977.

Harandi, M. T., and Lubars, M. D. Knowledge-based software development: A paradigm and a tool. In *Proceedings of the 1986 National Computer Conference,* pp. 43–50. AFIPS Press, June 1986.

Lubars, M. D. Affording higher reliability through software reusability. *ACM SIGSOFT Software Engineering Notes* 11(5): 39–42, 1986a.

———. A knowledge-based design aid for the construction of software systems. Ph.D. thesis, technical report no. UIUCDCS-R-86-1304, Department of Computer Science, University of Illinois, Urbana, Illinois, 1986b.

Milner, R. A. A theory of type polymorphism in programming. *Journal of Computer and System Sciences* 17: 348–375, 1978.

Newell, A.; Shaw, J. C.; and Simon, H. A. Report on a general problem-solving program. In *Proceedings of the International Conference on Information Processing,* pp. 256–264, June 1959.

Prieto-Díaz, R., and Freeman, P. Classifying software for reusability. *IEEE Software* 4(1): 6–16, 1987.

Purtilo, J. Polylith: An environment to support management of tool interfaces. In *Proceedings of the ACM SIGPLAN Symposium on Programming Issues in Programming Environments,* pp. 12–18, June 1985.

Rich, C. A formal representation for plans in the programmer's apprentice. In *Proceedings of the Seventh International Joint Conference on Artificial Intelligence,* August 1981.

Sackman, H.; Erikson, W. J.; and Grant, E. E. Exploratory experimental studies comparing online and offline programmer performance. *Comm. ACM* 11(1): 3–11, 1968.

Volpano, D. D., and Kieburtz, R. B. Software templates. In *Proceedings of the Eighth International Conference on Software Engineering*, pp. 55–60. August 1985.

Yourdon, E., and Constantine, L. L. *Structured Design: Fundamentals of a Discipline of Computer and Systems Design*. Englewood Cliffs, N. J.: Prentice-Hall, 1979.

INDEX

Abstract data types, 8–11, 22, 25, 48, 49–50, 354
Abstraction; *See* Levels of abstraction
Abstraction hierarchies, 350, 357
    constraint, 351, 352
Accounting system, MODEL, 106–14
    incorporating FAS 33 into the, 118–20
Accounts payable applications, 209
Action equations, 44
Activity modules, AXE, 145, 147
Ada, 5, 6, 7, 9, 21, 42, 50, 69, 158, 278, 322, 332, 333–34
ADABAS, 106
Advanced programmers, 246, 251
    fill in the blank study and, 238, 251, 254–59
    recall study and, 241, 262–64
Algol 68, 6
Algorithmic formalisms, 321, 322
Alphard, 69, 322
Analysis-of-variance model, 217, 218, 219, 229
Analyzer module, 332
Annotations, 304, 305–6, 307
AP3, 292, 305, 306, 307, 308
AP5, 305, 306, 307, 308
Application program generators, 73, 106
APPLY method, 44, 47
Array, 14
Array graph, MODEL, 120–21, 122
Asset valuation, MODEL, 106
Assignment statement, 246
Attribute evaluation algorithm, Reps's incremental, 48
Attribute grammars, 37, 44
Attributes, 10
Audit report logic structure, 134
Automatic compilation, 304–6, 307
Automatic programming, 289–90
    automatic compilation, 304–6
    extended, 291–92
    formalized system development, 306–309
    specification acquisition, 292–304
Automatic reasoning systems, 327–30
Auxiliary equations, 48

AVERAGE program type, 246
AXE system, 144–45
    activity modules, 147
    data modules, 146
    interface modules, 146–47
    module concept in, 145
    module identities as data, 147–49

Banking applications, 198, 205
Behavior, 296–98
    Smalltalk-80, 65–66
BNF, 37
Bootstrapping approach, 26
Bottom-up design strategy, 26, 77, 78, 291, 368
Box-and-arrows graphics interface, 99
Browser, Smalltalk-80, 64–65
B-tree, 27
Burroughs Program Product Library, 198
Business programming, 187, 197–211

C + +, 29, 214
C language, 29, 31, 59, 79, 120
Caching, 92, 100, 304
CAKE, 327–30, 341
Calculate functions, 201, 202, 204–11
California, University of, at Irvine, 212
California, University of Southern, Information Sciences Institute, 289
Call-by-reference parameter, 144
Calling modules, 147, 148
CASE statements, 79
Cedar Mesa, 69
Ceyx, 29, 214
Chain-enumeration component, KBEmacs, 334, 335, 338
Chain structure, AXE, 149–50
Chunking, 271
Class, object-oriented extension to Lisp, 74, 79
Classes, 10, 26
Classification scheme, Prieto-Díaz's, 280–81, 283